W9-BCK-414

CASE STUDIES OF INTERNATIONAL CONFLICTS

THE SAAR CONFLICT
1945–1955

FORTHCOMING BOOKS IN THIS SERIES

The Franco-Moroccan Conflict, by Stéphane Bernard, Institut de Sociologie Solvay, Brussels.

The Trieste Conflict, by Jean-Baptiste Duroselle, professor at the Institut d'Etudes Politiques in Paris.

The Cyprus Conflict, by François Crouzet, professor at the University of Lille.

The Anglo-Iranian Conflict, by Sven Henningsen, professor at the University of Copenhagen and Institutet for Samtidshistorie og Statskunskab in Copenhagen.

Concluding Analysis and Summary, by John Goormaghtigh, Director of the European Centre of the Carnegie Endowment for International Peace.

THE SAAR CONFLICT
1945–1955

By

JACQUES FREYMOND

With a Foreword by

JOHN GOORMAGHTIGH

Published under the auspices of
THE CARNEGIE ENDOWMENT FOR INTERNATIONAL PEACE
EUROPEAN CENTRE

LONDON
STEVENS & SONS LIMITED

NEW YORK
FREDERICK A. PRAEGER, INC.

ENGLISH LANGUAGE EDITION

*First published in 1960
by Stevens & Sons Limited
of 11 New Fetter Lane
in the City of London
and printed in Great Britain
by The Eastern Press Ltd.
of London and Reading*

*Published in the U.S.A. by
Frederick A. Praeger, Inc.
64 University Place
New York 3, N.Y., U.S.A.*

All Rights Reserved

Library of Congress Catalog Card No. 60–8716

FRENCH LANGUAGE EDITION

*Editions de l'Institut de sociologie Solvay
Brussels*

GERMAN LANGUAGE EDITION

*Forschungsinstitut der Deutschen Gesellschaft
für Auswärtige Politik e.V.
Frankfurt/Main
R. Oldenbourg, Publisher, Munich*

CONTENTS

PART ONE

HISTORICAL STUDY

France and the Saar

France and Germany

PART TWO

ANALYTICAL STUDY

v

14024

FOREWORD

WAR, as might be expected of such a constant and devastating phenomenon, has been the object of countless studies. The origin and causes of many great international conflicts have been dealt with extensively. But, until recently, these studies were carried out almost exclusively by historians and jurists. The former, by the very nature of their discipline, have been more concerned with the particular character of each event than with the possibility of common denominators among various conflicts. The latter, basing themselves on juridical norms, have sought to assign responsibility. Only recently has an effort been made, using the tools of other social sciences, not only to analyse the sequence of events in time but to understand the structure of international tensions and the interaction of basic forces, and to bring out constants and analogies —one can hardly speak of " laws," which at best would have to be qualified as imperfect. It is within the framework of such concerns that the series of studies on international conflicts was undertaken by the Carnegie Endowment for International Peace.

This research implies as a prerequisite the adoption of a premise. " Science," Henri Poincaré has said, " is determinist, it is *a priori*; it postulates determinism, because without it it could not exist." [1] If this postulate is as indispensable for the social sciences as it is for the so-called exact sciences, it does not necessitate—as is too often believed—adoption of any particular philosophical dogma. In the sense in which we use it, determinism is the basis of human knowledge. Man cannot even conceive the idea of an undetermined universe which would appear a senseless chaos. [2] We will come back to these considerations in the synthesis which will conclude the present series.

This study of the conflict between France and Germany over the Saar territory is the first of five monographs. The others will deal with disputes between France and Morocco, between Great Britain and Iran, and with the Trieste and Cyprus conflicts. In

[1] Henri Poincaré, *Dernières Pensées* (Paris: Flammarion, 1913), p. 244.
[2] *Cf.* Ludwig von Mises, *Theory and History* (New Haven: Yale University Press, 1957), p. 74.

order to eliminate at least one of the many variables—the general international situation—all the studies cover the same period, roughly the first decade after the Second World War.

In his Preface, Professor Jacques Freymond explains what determined the choice of subjects. The reader might well be surprised that disputes of secondary importance were selected at a time when far more dangerous ones were rending the world asunder. The reason is simple. It was necessary to limit ourselves to cases that lent themselves to analysis, in other words, in which there was a reasonable chance of determining the essential elements. It might perhaps also be asked, why, if the object was to attempt certain generalizations, we did not limit ourselves to a group of more homogeneous cases. Theoretically, this would have been justified, but the field is still so new that no generally accepted typology exists. It thus became necessary to explore, and that is what explains the selection. In the present state of our research, it looks as if the study of the Franco-Moroccan conflict will make it possible to develop a model that can be used as the basis for a new series of studies, selected this time within the same category—disputes between colonial Powers and overseas territories.

The purpose of this project, as has been said, is not primarily to describe a phase in the relations between the countries concerned. But the analysis we have sought to make could not be arrived at without establishing the succession of events. Thus each study contains a detailed description of the various stages of the crisis. Some will question whether history can be written so soon after the event. But while we are perfectly aware of the inevitable shortcomings, it should be noted that, although it has not been possible to have access to all the official documents, a certain number of other sources, such as private notes and private documents, have been used to great profit. In the Preface to the present volume, Professor Freymond explains the use made of the press and of interviews. Above all, the opportunity for discussing events with the principal protagonists has been of inestimable value for the authors of the different monographs—though it goes without saying that this kind of source must be handled with caution.

Everything has been done to make the inquiries as objective as possible. Each study has been entrusted to a scholar who is not a national of any of the states party to the conflict, while research assistants from these countries have collected the documentary material. An advisory committee composed of eminent individuals from the countries concerned has closely followed the work.

To make the " case method " fruitful, studies must be comparable. To this end, we asked the authors to follow—at least in general—the method proposed by Professor Freymond. Each study director, nevertheless, has had his own contribution to make, and it is principally by frequent meetings that they have been able to ensure the indispensable minimum of homogeneity.

Unquestionably, a different approach could have been envisaged. The Preface to this volume suggests a few. The one we chose has at least the merit of coming to grips with the realities and of being feasible, given the means and personnel at our disposal.

Will we be reproached for basing the whole project on overoptimistic premises and for placing excessive confidence in science? Undoubtedly it would be dangerous to believe that the day is near when norms of conduct could be derived from a study, even one in depth, that would make it possible to avoid international conflicts. Those responsible for this series have never been so ambitious! If they were inspired by methods appropriate to the natural sciences, they nevertheless recognized the limits of the application of such methods to the social sciences. However, the dangers which may stem from conflicts between states are so appalling and our ignorance on the subject is so great that the enterprise was worth trying. Even if no generalization emerges from it, the effort will not be vitiated, because the studies inevitably will have contributed to our comprehension of the problems of war and peace. On the practical plane, we may hope to provide statesmen with food for thought, to call their attention to the dangerous turning points in the evolution of international disputes, and perhaps to suggest certain lines of action.

It remains for us to extend our warm appreciation to Professor Jacques Freymond, Director of the Institut Universitaire de Hautes Etudes Internationales in Geneva, for accepting the thankless task of directing this first study in the series. Not only did he have to devise a technique for tackling the problem, elaborate a method that would serve in other cases, organize a basis for collaboration with the research assistants, and critically sift an abundant mass of documentation, but he also had to write a study which largely oversteps the boundaries of history as a discipline. In effect, what we asked him to do was to venture into a domain, that of political science, which was not really his own. This he did not only graciously but with great competence. However, by so doing he has exposed himself to a double criticism, that of being at the same time too historical for the political scientists and too " political-science " for the historians. Such is the price for exceeding the limits of one discipline; it is also a condition of progress in the social sciences. The author himself would be ready to acknowledge that his work suffers from being the first. But those who follow will profit from his experience, and his merit is all the greater for having run this risk in order to act as a pioneer.

Finally, we would like to thank the members of the advisory committee: Mr. Stéphane Bernard, of the Institut de Sociologie Solvay in Brussels; Mr. Jean-Baptiste Duroselle, of the Institut d'Etudes Politiques in Paris; Mr. Alfred Grosser, also of the Institut d'Etudes Politiques in Paris; Dr. Fritz Hellwig, member of the Bundestag; Professor Eberhard Menzel, Director of the Institut für Internationales Recht of the University of Kiel; Mrs. Dorothy Pickles, of London, author of a number of works on international affairs; Mr. Mario Toscano, Professor at the University of Rome; and Professor Arnold Wolfers, Director of the Washington Center of Foreign Policy Research—all of whom, throughout the period of the study, gave freely of their counsel.

JOHN GOORMAGHTIGH
Director of the European Centre
of the Carnegie Endowment

PREFACE

THIS study of the conflict between France and Germany over the Saar is only one component of a much wider undertaking, the aims of which have been set out in the Foreword.

Why choose the Saar? Why, when one is nursing the ambitious hope of making a contribution to the establishment of peace, devote time to a matter of secondary importance and not to one of those major conflicts that oppress the world today with their war potential? Since 1944 the Saar question has played only a sporadic role in international relations. It scarcely affected the Great Powers. Though it complicated Franco-German relations for some years, it never assumed a very serious character. Neither the Saarlanders, the French, nor the Germans thought at any time of recourse to arms. This being so, can one indeed talk of a " conflict " over the Saar? Was it not rather a " difference of opinion " which gave rise to " tension "? This is what some people maintain.

But war, or the risk of war, is not the only criterion of a " conflict " situation. The renunciation of violence—explicitly or not— and the rejection of recourse to armed force do not abolish either the social contradictions or the political opposition that can persist in a so-called period of peace and create serious obstacles to collaboration between states. Certain international conflicts threaten peace by the simple fact that they prevent its consolidation and encourage an atmosphere of mistrust, tension, and uneasiness conducive to other incidents. Such conflicts have a certain breadth, that is, they affect interests and principles which, rightly or wrongly, are considered essential, or even vital, to the members of the particular national entities in question.

The selection of cases of international conflict worth studying, therefore, rests as much on an appreciation of their degree of intensity and their influence on co-operation between states as on the threat of war implicit in them. This threat, moreover, diminishes proportionally as the development of the destructive power of modern armaments raises the cost of war and tends to discourage governments from embarking on it.

Such is the rationale for including the Saar question in this series of studies. It was not a question of a difference of opinion affecting a few kilometres of frontier or a small area of territory, but of a conflict in which interests, principles, and feelings were inextricably mixed and which at times aroused passions far exceeding the problem at issue. It was not only the mines and industrial equipment of the Saar that were in question but the problem of the balance of relative strength and of the principle of self-determination of peoples. There were also questions of prestige. The governments concerned entered the conflict in such a way as to make retreat difficult. Finally, the long period of mistrust between the two peoples complicated and thus delayed a settlement of the Saar question and this, in turn, had repercussions on Franco-German relations: Insistence that the Saar problem be solved as a prerequisite to action on other questions, an insistence born of an instinctive French reaction of self-defence against a recrudescence of German nationalism, was to constitute a barrier to the European Defence Community (E.D.C.).[1]

The French and Germans were not the only ones to be affected by the fate of the E.D.C. The Benelux countries and Italy were also involved. The United States considered the E.D.C. a factor in the unification of the West, a stage on the road to European union. None of these could remain aloof from a matter that indirectly affected their own interests. For all that the Saar conflict might seem local, it was not one which could be localized. It found its way into the contemporary international scheme of things, undergoing influences and occupying a place that tended to become more important as time went on. For the uncertainty it produced became an embarrassment, not only to the states directly concerned, but to their friends, thus calling for outside intervention.

The choice of the Saar conflict is justified for still further reasons. It will be readily observed that this is a problem which can be easily circumscribed. We are dealing here with the last phase of the conflict which opened at the end of the Second World War and finished, after the decisive referendum of October 23, 1955, with the agreements of October 27, 1956. The issue was simple: it was a question of whether the Saar territory would be politically detached from Germany and economically united with

---

[1] In the same way, the rejection of the E.D.C. led to the failure of the effort to europeanize the Saar.

France, whether it would revert to Germany, or, as an intermediate solution, whether it would be transformed into a European territory. The number of protagonists was limited: France, the Federal Republic of Germany—and the Saar. Around this nucleus were the Allies—Britain and the United States—and, a little later, the Council of Europe. In the farther distance stood the U.S.S.R.

There is another measurable advantage in making this study; ample information is available. We shall return later to the problem of sources. For the moment, we shall limit ourselves to emphasizing the fact that the Saar territory was accessible, that a preliminary sounding had revealed the existence of an abundant literature on the subject, and that we had a reasonable hope of being able to consult some of the chief protagonists.

Finally, sharp though the struggle had been at times, passions were a little stilled. We felt we could probably approach this hearth in which the fire had just died out without too much risk of burning our fingers.

Problems of Method

How were we to set about this study? We were immediately faced with certain problems of method, in terms of the general aims of the investigation.

The individual responsible for the study of the Saar, which was considered, at least in the beginning, as a pilot study, owed it to himself to think of the final goal of the whole enterprise—that of drawing observations and conclusions of general application from the comparative analysis of various particular international conflicts, of identifying, if possible, through the examination of phenomena of a political, social, and economic nature, of individual and collective action, and of emotional reactions, certain kinds of interaction and chains of events.

To this end, was it better to formulate a few hypotheses first, and concentrate on verifying them, to the exclusion of other research? Or was it better to ask a few rather general questions that could also be raised in the subsequent studies? Hypotheses or questions would then have constituted a common infra-structure of the various studies, making comparability possible, or at least less difficult. This solution appeared to have advantages; it would have saved time and enabled the research to be adapted to the final aim.

Furthermore, it would have made it possible to avoid what some people called an escape into history.

But there were obvious disadvantages in this method. By limiting the inquiry to verifying hypotheses, we were in danger of anticipating the conclusion by underestimating the importance of factors specifically applicable to the case under consideration. Moreover, how was it possible not to recognize that, as every conflict occurs within a span of time, it was imperative to reconstruct the curve of its development and to discern its rhythm?

It might also have been possible to concentrate attention on the " turning points " of the conflict, on periods of crisis and of major decisions, making a cross-section that would enable us to study side by side the various elements of the crisis and the factors entering into the decision.

But how were we to choose the " turning points," or how establish a hierarchy among the decisions, or how explain the origins of these crises if we did not have beforehand an over-all view of the succession of events? And how were we to know whether the decision might not have preceded the crisis? History, in which everything follows from what has gone before, cannot be thus broken up and questioned at the whim of need, and he who tries to use history as an arsenal of facts, though he has a good chance of finding in it the elements of the proof he has in mind, is not thereby any surer of the value of his conclusions.

It thus seemed to us necessary to begin by reconstructing the history of the struggle over the Saar which, from 1945 to 1955, divided France and Germany. We say the history of the struggle intentionally. For it was not a question of writing or re-writing the history of the Saar people but of studying and revealing the process of the conflict. We have thus selected certain material, eliminating among the mass of accumulated information everything that did not seem directly relevant to an understanding of the problem we were examining. What was important was to bring out the sequence of events and the combination of factors that explain the decisions—the changes that transpired in the international atmosphere and in the relationship between the powers, the modification in the relative strength of Germany and France, the effect of internal policy considerations, the action of men and of groups, the influence of economic factors or emotional reactions, or, again, the influence of propaganda.

From this there stems a rather dry account in which facts and arguments are sometimes only outlined so as not to overload the study and divert attention from the main objective, namely, the reconstruction of the flow of history.

Some of the actors in the drama will doubtless find that their parts have been unduly cut. Perhaps they will be so good as to remember that everything could not be put in and will try to accept their sometimes rather modest place in the history of the conflict.

Other objections might be raised, and we have raised them ourselves. For example, there is no historical introduction covering the previous phase of the Franco-German conflict over the Saar during 1919–1935; and there is only brief mention of the treaties, agreements, and conventions concluded between the governments of Paris and Saarbrücken. We have also passed very briefly over the campaign for the referendum of 1955 and summed up in a few pages the numerous negotiations that prepared the way for the agreements of October, 1956.

Cuts and summaries seemed to us justified by the need to pull the story together and keep it within the bounds laid down for this study. An historical introduction would have led us into new and fairly extensive research. We have assumed that the reader knows enough to grasp the essentials of the Saar problem in 1945, or that he could find supplementary information in existing literature. This same reasoning prevailed when it was a question of deciding on the usefulness of including long analyses of agreements and conventions. We decided that the reader could find the information that he might want in texts and in other studies. As for the electoral campaign of the autumn of 1955, interesting and rich in vicissitudes as it was, it did not seem to us that a study would be very rewarding. In fact, positions had already been taken before the campaign opened; by then there was a large majority that was scarcely affected at all by the arguments of those in favour of the proposed Statute.

In trying to reveal the process of the conflict, the diplomatic struggle is laid bare. Is it thereby given too much importance? We think not. If the development of the conflict was influenced by many and varied forces, if it depended upon the actions of individuals, of pressure groups, of changes that took place in relative strength, and of changes in the political atmosphere, it was nevertheless articulated in a series of decisions emanating from the governments concerned. That they were prompted to their decisions by very different considerations, that they were driven by pressures from without and led by circumstances more or less clearly understood, is quite certain. But the whole responsibility did fall on them, and it was into their hands that all the threads were gathered and all the various forces converged. The historian is thus naturally led to concentrate his attention on the conditions and modalities of their action, especially in those phases of a crisis preceding or following a decision.

The historical analysis is followed by an analytical study in which the various elements of the final decision, which we first sought to locate in time and in the unfolding of the action, are the subject of a new examination that endeavours to evaluate more precisely their importance.

Various ways were open to us. We could, considering the outcome of the conflict and the victory of Germany over France, have assumed that the most decisive factor was the change in relative strength between the two states and concentrated research on the explanation of this change. Attention would then have been directed to the internal development of France, to an analysis of the reasons for her weakening, and, alongside this, to the study of the conditions of Germany's revival, in order to demonstrate the effects of this on the Saar and the consequences for the settlement of the Saar question.

It might have been felt, too, that since the conflict involved not only the governments of the two states but the population of the contested territory and the people in France and Germany who had interests in the Saar, it would be more useful to concentrate research on the action of groups which, for different reasons, sought to influence government policy.

Both solutions had their advantages, but they had the major disadvantage of being too exclusively focused on only one aspect of the conflict, on one element of its development, thus making only a partial contribution to an explanation of how it worked. They relegated to the background individual actions or the analysis of the constantly changing mood in which the controversy developed.[2]

---

[2] The mood, or to use another word, the atmosphere, is just as much the expression of a state of mind, of a way of tackling problems and throwing light on them, as it is of a clearly formulated opinion.

We could, equally, have envisaged the adoption of one of the formulations advanced by certain specialists in political science. Quincy Wright,[3] for example, had proposed a study of international conflicts from four different angles: the relations between the opposing parties, which implies particularly an examination of the " distance " separating them, from the technological, strategic, legal, ideological, social, cultural, and psychological points of view and from the point of view of their attitudes towards recourse to war [4]; the internal structure and policy of the states under consideration; procedures available and used for the adjustment of opposing interests; and the state of international relations during the period under consideration.

As for Edgar S. Furniss, Jr.,[5] he considered that the study of conflicts should be concentrated on the international environment and be based on observable facts such as government declarations or decisions, and on an evaluation of various categories of " distances " (geographic, economic, cultural, political, ideological, military) which go to make up what he calls " strategic distance." And he proposed a certain number of model cases of interaction as a basis for analysis.

Karl W. Deutsch,[6] for whom a study of decision-making is the important thing, submitted a long list, although he considered it incomplete, of the questions which would make it possible to comprehend not only the men who make decisions, but the influences of background, opinion, and circumstances, with particular attention to a reconstruction of the subject-matter and the flow of information on the basis of which images of the situation are created that determine the decision.

These various suggestions are definitely interesting. However, we discarded them for a variety of reasons. The first was a fear that the extent of the research required would go far beyond the scope of the enterprise we had in mind: the mass of necessary facts and information could only be gathered by engaging a team of research workers for a long period of time. Furthermore, and this

---

[3] *Cf. Memorandum on Interstate Conflicts* (New York, Carnegie Endowment for International Peace, December, 1955). (Mimeographed.)

[4] " War expectancy distance."

[5] *Cf. Memorandum on Interstate Conflicts* (New York, Carnegie Endowment for International Peace, December, 1955). (Mimeographed.)

[6] " Mass Communications and the Loss of Freedom in National Decision Making: A Possible Research Approach to Interstate Conflicts," *Journal of Conflict Resolution*, Vol. I, No. 2 (June, 1957), pp. 200–212.

was our second reservation, it was not certain that the results would justify the efforts and the expense undertaken. The division of the history of societies into tiny sections, as is done in detailed questionnaires, is not in itself a guarantee of a more valid reconstruction. On the contrary, faced with certain questions, we felt that extreme danger lies in the over-rigorous schematization inspired by an abstract view of man, which confuses the juxtaposition of facts of unequal importance with the differing shades of reality. Furthermore, where were we to find some of the replies we needed, and how? The methods envisaged could only give very approximate results and lead to conclusions just as subjective and open to question as those reached without the help of an impressive-looking scientific research organization. Finally, however interesting some of the studies undertaken on tensions and conflicts by specialists in political science, their contribution to an explanation of international relations is often limited by the form in which evidence and conclusions are presented.

These are the various considerations that led us on the one hand to concentrate our systematic study on an explanation of the evolution of the decision and a search for the factors governing it, and on the other hand to eliminate questionnaires, suggestive but overly detailed, in order to adhere to a broader and more flexible plan. After an initial summary of the basic decisions, we defined insofar as possible the attitude of the principal actors—those responsible for government decisions—towards the problem under consideration. Then, widening the circle, we sought behind the explicit motives the direct and indirect influences at work on them. These included the immediate entourage, the little group from which the decision emanated, the political and social *milieu*; the groups, more or less well organized, formed more or less adventitiously, more or less conscious of being groups, groups expressing opinions, sharing prejudices, representing the interests of a region, of an economic sector, of a party or a religious faith.

Beyond this we tried to take into account the mood or atmosphere in which the action unfolded and decisions were taken. Hence we attempted to analyse public opinion in France, Germany, and the Saar, partly in order to ascertain the extent of interest in the Saar question and partly in order to isolate trends and evaluate their influence. In addition, there was an examination of the international context within which we considered the effects of modifications in the system of alliances, of the attitude of the United Kingdom and United States, of the intervention of the Council of Europe, and of the evolution of the relationship between the material and moral strength of France and Germany.

This in brief is the subject-matter of the *Analytical Study*, in which the reader will find, or so we hope, elements useful in the explanation of the evolution of the conflict. Some will perhaps wish to know more about the actors' intentions, their motivations, the interplay of influences. We simply remind them that the desired information was not always forthcoming; furthermore, in probing too far into detail there is a danger of increasing the possibility of error and of losing sight of the essentials, namely the reconstruction of a process.

Now it is precisely on this point that history can make a decisive contribution. For its mission is not so much to range facts in chronological order—which is what people try to reduce it to at times—as to restore in their actuality the flow of related events, which mutually interact. That is why we felt it necessary to stress, in conclusion, the importance of resituating in time the elements of the decision and to emphasize the dynamics of the struggle. The farther we progressed with this study, the clearer it became that it was impossible to explain the evolution of the conflict by any one predominating element (economic influence, pressure of a dominant group, reversal of the relative strength of France and Germany) and, by the same token, that it was necessary to reconstruct the interaction of forces.

We tried in our conclusion to show how, from a given moment, a combination of forces was formed whose cumulative thrusts brought about the crisis from which the decision sprang. The study of this decision in isolation does indeed indicate somewhat schematically the various elements from which it stems. But such a study cannot tell us how and when these elements found themselves, as it were, related. This is precisely what we must know if we wish to grasp the moment when the situation becomes one of crisis.

SOURCES

It is always something of an adventure to launch into research on the recent past. Where, indeed, is accurate and verifiable information to be found? The fifty-year rule which obtains for archives, at least in Europe, is usually strictly applied. Administrative correspondence is in principle inaccessible. Men who have taken on responsibility are discreet. So the contemporary historian frequently remains starved for material. In addition to inaccessibility of sources, there is also the problem of the accumulation of so much material that the investigator runs the danger of being submerged.

We tried to overcome both these problems; we succeeded only partially. Though we feel we have managed to place men in context and reconstruct events, though the elaboration of the development of the conflict seems to us based on valid sources, we are nevertheless conscious of the gaps that still exist. Undoubtedly, research undertaken when the German and French archives become available will make it possible to round out certain aspects of the observations we have made and bring us nearer to the truth.

Printed Sources

After this reminder of a few necessary reservations, let us look briefly at the various categories of sources.

Official declarations, expressions of a policy already worked out and submitted to public opinion are fairly numerous. If we add parliamentary debates, available verbatim reports of diplomatic negotiations, and the texts of various agreements, conventions, and treaties, we are in a position to establish what might be called the infra-structure of the conflict.

Periodicals and newspapers enabled us to round out this basic source of information. The most useful were the Saar periodicals and, more especially, the newspapers of the Saar trade unions and of professional organizations, which often furnished precise and detailed information on conditions of life in the Saar, economic difficulties, and political tensions. In contrast, for France and Germany there was little to be gleaned in the professional press which, except for a few papers in Alsace and Lorraine, was only spasmodically concerned with the Saar question.

As for the big dailies, the use that an historian or specialist in political science can make of them is fairly obvious. It is not through them that events can be reconstructed as they really happened. Yet the information they supply, however inexact it may often be, is nonetheless useful. If it is not possible to draw upon them without checking the facts, it is still helpful to take note of them and to use them to further research. Often certain items of secondary importance or certain commentaries have put us on the track of a development we had missed until then. But, although daily papers can serve only as contributory sources of very doubtful value for those who attempt to establish facts, their value is quite different when it is a question of analysing a mood and following the various currents of public opinion. For this particular aspect of research, the newspapers are still, at the present time, the richest and most useful source of information. This certainly does not mean that they must be considered representative of public opinion, and we shall discuss in the chapter on public opinion [7] certain of the principal reservations we think should be made.

It was obviously not possible to go through the whole daily press of France and Germany. We therefore made a selection, choosing the newspapers we thought were the most influential or especially representative of one section of opinion, particularly the section that most closely follows politics and foreign affairs and therefore has most influence on governmental decisions. Furthermore, bearing in mind both the time needed to go through complete collections and our own time limits, we concentrated our research on certain periods of varying length during which the Saar question was under discussion. Sometimes this revolved around a date. We combed the newspapers for comment during the weeks or days preceding an important decision. Under other circumstances our reading covered a period of some months.

It would clearly be possible to have reservations on the value of conclusions drawn from such a selection. But the cross-checking that we did was thorough enough for us to believe that the picture thus obtained of French, German, and Saar opinion is sufficiently representative, and that we have not missed any position taken that was of interest to this study. The papers were tackled in different ways by various individuals, some devoting their attention to the opinion of the paper, others attempting—not very conclusively—to make a quantitative analysis of the contents, while the individual responsible for the establishment of a file on the protagonists looked for evidence of their activity. Finally, we ourselves felt it necessary to consult repeatedly the back numbers of certain papers over fairly long periods.

---

[7] Cf. *Analytical Study*, pp. 270 *et seq.*

Among the printed sources we should also mention pamphlets and tracts of all kinds. The conflict over the Saar gave rise to polemical publications that were very useful to us as, for example, the publications of Comel Verlag in which the opponents of the régime in the Saar expressed their views.

Considered as a whole, the printed sources are rich in useful information. The actors in the drama, however discreet they meant to be, said more than they were aware of about their aims and motives. Parliamentary debates often drive people to more thorough explanations than they intended. There are many leakages which journalists know how to use and even how to provoke, and which the opposition exploits shamelessly.

Manuscript Sources

As we have already said, we did not have access to the archives. So we had to try to fill this gap in various ways, and we owe our thanks to the confidence various people were kind enough to place in us because of their interest in our study.

We were able to consult numerous mimeographed documents that constituted an intermediate form between manuscripts and printed sources. It is in this form that the reports of the *Deutscher Saarbund,* which were very useful to us, as well as the bulletins of the *Mission diplomatique française* are issued. The same is true for the texts of various conferences and reports coming from parties or groups that distributed documents for their members and others with whom they were in contact. As everyone knows, this form of publication has developed considerably. From the moment the number of people to be circularized is more than ten, organizations tend to use more rapid processes of reproduction and so multiply the risks of leakages, thus providing the historian with more opportunities of coming to grips with the activities of administrations or organized groups.

Certain private documents were very useful to us because of the part, often important, played by their owners in the discussions and negotiations relative to the Saar. But however valuable this source of information—valuable because of the constant interplay between action taken on personal grounds and action taken as a public servant—the use of it is fraught with difficulties. These private documents prepared by an individual through the accident of events in which he was involved are sometimes oddly slanted, and the historian runs the risk of magnifying the importance of one personality to the detriment of those who cannot furnish him with any documents, or of throwing some sections into exaggerated relief. Furthermore, the discretion required if people who are still alive are not to be compromised makes it impossible to identify the source, however essential it may be. Thus we must confess that we more than once found ourselves in an embarrassing situation: we would have liked to give the exact reference (we did this wherever we could), but we were not always authorized to do so by the people who had given us access to their documents. All that we can say is that, thanks to the assistance of numerous individuals in the Saar and in Germany, as well as in France, we were able to gain insights into government action, uncover the motives of some decisions, and interweave the information from printed sources with that drawn from valid manuscript sources.

Oral Evidence

Contemporary history offers the possibility of recourse to oral evidence. We made wide use of it, as is indicated by the list of names of men who, involved in various capacities in Saar affairs, were kind enough to grant interviews that were particularly useful to us. We express our gratitude to all of them. Among the French there were: Robert Baboin, Jacques Delarüe Caron de Beaumarchais, Jacques de Bourbon-Busset, Tanguy de Courson de la Villeneuve, Michel Debré, Michel Denis, Pierre Eude, Henri Gauthier, Gilbert Grandval, Robert Herly, Gonzague Lesort, Pierre Maillard, Frédéric Schlachter, Robert Schuman, Maurice Schumann, Charles de Vaulx. Among the Germans: Wilhelm Bodens, Walter Böx, Erwin Dittler, Fritz Hellwig, Hubert Hermans, Rolf Lahr, Heinrich Lietzmann, Karl Mommer, Paul Mühlbach, Rudolf Thierfelder, Alois Zimmer. Among the Saarlanders: Franz Bungarten, Kurt Conrad, Albert Dorscheid, Peter Hahn, Johannes Hoffmann, Theodor Jansen, Hans John, Paul Kutsch, Kurt Lenhard, Gotthard Lorscheider, Eduard Martin, Erwin Müller, Fritz Pfordt, Friedrich Regitz, Aloys Schmitt, Franz Schlehofer, Heinrich Schneider, Walter Sender, Paul Senf, Peter Zimmer.

Oral testimony is indisputably valuable, first because it offers an opportunity to be in contact not only with the witnesses but with the actors. This kind of relationship throws light on a character, a way of reasoning, an intellectual process. The accounts and replies also make it possible to reconstruct the mood in which events happened and the circumstances under which decisions were taken much better than can be done through documents. These personal encounters still hold a considerable interest for the organization and orientation of research. It happened more than once that an interview put us on the track of a very useful document, or led us to press our investigations further in a direction we had not thought of till then.

But this source of information has limitations that historians know well. A personal interview can be most deceptive, one might almost say misleading. Of course one prepares for interviews, because it is obvious that the answers will depend on the questions asked. But can one be sufficiently prepared? How can one be sufficiently well informed so that the informer does not escape into generalities but gives the supplementary information desired? Yet, if the questions are too precise and detailed, is there not a risk of inadvertently influencing the individual being questioned and thus leading him to give the hoped-for reply? For memory has its limits. Witnesses and actors forget not so much the event as the circumstances. Even if they manage by an effort of rather unusual modesty to avoid assigning themselves the main part, they are nonetheless led to distort, as they try to explain and reconstruct, by the simple fact that they cannot help trying to present events as logical that were not necessarily so. We made very useful experiments in the course of this study. How varied were the opinions on the importance of a decision or the influence of economic, political, or emotional factors! We can only conclude with a reminder that this kind of source must be used prudently, though, despite this caveat, it is not to be neglected.

THE COLLABORATORS

This study is the result of team work. This does not mean that no one takes the responsibility for it. Quite the contrary. The director of research, who is solely responsible for the text of this book, wishes to stress that he considers himself alone accountable for the analysis of the evolution of the Saar conflict, for the judgments on the men, the groups, and policies concerned, and for the interpretation of events.

Having said this, recognition must be given to the valuable assistance from many sources and in various fields he has had in making this study. It would indeed have been impossible to complete such a relatively onerous undertaking without a combined effort.

Mme Marlise Steinert, Doctor of Philosophy, of the University of Saarbrücken, was good enough to accept the post of research assistant. All those who have seen her at work in the last two and a half years have appreciated the value and importance of her contribution to the study of the Saar conflict. It is she who, within the framework of the plans laid down by the director of this study, carried all the weight of the real research and established the personal contacts in Germany, France, and the Saar that were indispensable. It is on her that the co-ordination of the work of our various collaborators depended and it is thanks to her that we were able to base the study on relatively solid sources and to operate within the time limits set for us. Therefore we would like to express to her our most grateful thanks.

We would like, also, to mention the names of collaborators who helped us in our research and to whom we here express our gratitude. We entrusted to Mlle Marina Cerne, doctor of political science, the file on the protagonists. The analysis of the French newspapers, and especially of the *Journal officiel*, was carried out by Mlle Janine Bourdin, *licenciée* in history; that of the German papers by Mme Elisabeth Hemmer, librarian. Henri Burgelin, *agrégé* in history, was kind enough to take on the study of the attitude of economic circles in the French frontier regions and also to make a preliminary examination of the policy of the Council of Europe. The study of French economic papers and reports of the Economic Council was made by Mlle Françoise Desmasures, *diplômée* of the Institut d'Etudes Politiques in Paris, who also attempted a quantitative analysis of the contents of various French newspapers. A similar study of the German press was undertaken by Hans Reiner Limbach. Lazlo Nagy, doctor of political science and *licencié* in social science, carried out a systematic analysis of the minutes of the National Assembly and the Bundestag. The study of German political parties was made by Georg Droege, doctor of philosophy, and that of French parties by Mlle Ugné Karavélis, *diplômée* of the Institut d'Etudes Politiques. Professor Helmut Hirsch, Director of the Auslandsinstitut in Dortmund and one of the best specialists on the Saar problem, kindly analysed for us the attitude of the United States Government and of American public opinion towards the Saar question. The maps, which are published in the appendix, were drawn by Erwin Fell of the Bundesanstalt für Landeskunde at Remagen. Some of them were kindly lent by Klaus Altmeyer, *diplômé* of the Institut d'Etudes Politiques and Press Attaché of the Staatskanzlei in Saarbrücken. Mr. Altmeyer, who is preparing, among other things, a monograph on the electoral geography of the Saar, was good enough to follow our research and more than once was able to furnish useful information.

We would also like to thank Mlle Maryvonne Stéphan, head of press and information services at the French Ministry of Foreign Affairs, and the librarians of the Fondation Nationale des Sciences Politiques in Paris, of the library and archives of the city of Saarbrücken, of the United Nations library at Geneva, and of the Institut Universitaire de Hautes Etudes Internationales in Geneva for all the help they have generously given. The thankless and difficult task of preparing the final text was handled by Mlle Christiane Trény with the help of Mlle Violette Fayod and Pierre Pagneux. For the English translation we are indebted to Mrs. Jozy Townley.

We would not like to end without expressing to the Consultative Committee, to the Directors of the series of studies on conflicts, and most particularly to John Goormaghtigh, Director of the European Centre of the Carnegie Endowment, our very real gratitude for the interest they never failed to take in this study. It is not enough to remember how useful were their many suggestions and criticisms. All those who took part in the discussions which went on in Geneva for nearly three years, under the chairmanship of Mr. Goormaghtigh, know that those discussions were not just a source of information but a stimulus to the mind and a constant encouragement to research. This is by no means the least of all the services the Carnegie Endowment has rendered in recent years.

JACQUES FREYMOND,

Professor of International History and Director of the Graduate Institute of International Studies, Geneva.

GENEVA,
April, 1958

ABBREVIATIONS

AZW	*Allgemeiner Zeitungsdienst West*
B.P.	Bayernpartei (Bavarian Party)
C.A.T.S.	Commission d'administration du Territoire de la Sarre (Administrative Commission for the Saar Territory)
C.C.F.A.	Commandement en chef des forces Françaises en Allemagne
C.D.U.	Christlich-Demokratische Union (Christian Democratic Union)
C.D.U./Saar	Christlich-Demokratische Union (Saar Christian Democratic Union)
C.G.T.	Confédération générale du travail
C.G.S.	Christliche Gewerkschaften des Saarlandes (Syndicats chrétiens)
COMISCO	Comité international socialiste consultatif (Committee of the International Socialist Conference)
C.S.U.	Christlich-Soziale Union (German Christian Social Union)
C.S.U./Saar	Christlich-Soziale Union (Saar Christian Social Union)
C.V.P.	Christliche Volkspartei des Saarlandes (Saar Christian People's Party)
D.P.	Deutsche Partei (German Party)
D.P.S.	Demokratische Partei Saar (Saar Democratic Party)
D.S.P.	Deutsche Sozialdemokratische Partei (German Social Democratic Party in the Saar) (after the plebiscite became S.P.D./Saar)
D.V.P.	Demokratische Volkspartei Saar (Saar Democratic People's Party) (since 1952)
E.C.S.C.	European Coal and Steel Community
E.G.	Einheitsgewerkschaft der Arbeiter, Angestellten und Beamten (Syndicat unitaire)
Emnid-Institute	Institute für Erforschung der öffentlichen Meinung, Marktforschung, Nachrichten über Wirtschaftslage, Informations-Dienst
E.D.C.	European Defence Community
E.R.P.	European Recovery Programme
e.V.	Eingetragener Verein (incorporated)
F.D.P.	Freie Demokratische Partei (Free Democratic Party)
G.C.B.	Gewerkschaft Christlicher Bergleute (Syndicat chrétien des mineurs)
G.m.b.H.	Gesellschaft mit beschränkter Haftung (limited liability company)
I.C.F.T.U.	International Confederation of Free Trade Unions
I.F.O.P.	Institut français d'opinion publique (French Institute of Public Opinion)
I.P.S.A.	International Political Science Association
I.V. Bergbau	Industrie Verband Bergbau der Einheitsgewerkschaft (Syndicat unitaire des mineurs)
J.O.	Journal officiel de la République française
K.P.	Kommunistische Partei (Saar Communist Party)
K.P.D.	Kommunistische Partei Deutschlands
M.L.S.	Mouvement pour la libération de la Sarre (later M.R.S.)
M.R.P.	Mouvement républicain populaire
M.R.S.	Mouvement pour le rattachement de la Sarre à la France
NATO	North Atlantic Treaty Organization
N. p. or d.	No place or date
N.S.D.A.P.	Nationalsozialistische Deutsche Arbeiterpartei (National Socialist [Nazi] Party)
O.E.E.C.	Organization for European Economic Co-operation
R.P.F.	Rassemblement du peuple français

Abbreviations

S.F.I.O. . . Section française de l'Internationale ouvrière
S.N.C.F. . . Société nationale des chemins de fer français
SND . . . *Saarländischer Nachrichtendienst*
S.P.D. . . . Sozialdemokratische Partei Deutschlands (German Social Democratic Party)
S.P.D./Saar . . Sozialdemokratische Partei Deutschlands (German Social Democratic Party, Saar branch)
S.P.S. . . . Sozialdemokratische Partei des Saarlandes (Saar Socialist Party)
Syndicats . . (see C.G.S., E.G., G.C.B., and I.V. Bergbau)
SVZ . . . *Saarländische Volkszeitung*
W.E.U. . . Western European Union
W.A.V. . . Wirtschaftliche Aufbau-Vereinigung
Z. . . . Zentrum (centre)

PART ONE

HISTORICAL STUDY

France and the Saar

1

DEVELOPMENT OF A POLICY,
1945–1947

IN 1945, the downfall of Hitler's Germany awoke in Europe a feeling of relief and yet of anxiety. A threat had disappeared but in so doing had created a gap which would have to be filled. How? No one quite knew. The collapse was so abrupt, the failure so complete that any plan seemed possible, as though history were no longer of any consequence either in the present or in the future. The very diversity of the possibilities, which acted as a stimulant to the imagination, was a source of uneasiness. Confusion reigned everywhere, the unavoidable consequence of a total war whose nature was revolutionary. This confusion, complete among the vanquished, broke through among the victors who, despite their solemn proclamations of unity and despite their common struggle, approached the post-war period bearing the marks of the most varied historical experiences. The situation was further complicated by the contradictory claims of peoples freed from fear, all of them convinced of the rights they had earned through years of oppression and suffering. Here was the opportunity for a final reckoning and everyone was determined to seize it.

And yet there remained the awareness of certain limits which went to make up the premises of the German problem. The destruction of the National Socialist régime did not necessarily imply the destruction of the German people. These people had to live, to eat, and to organize themselves economically and politically within frontiers which would have to be established. Moreover, the very principles in whose name the victors had made war imposed upon their actions limits which must be respected. However much they might like to be free of moral obligations towards a country which itself had had scarcely any, they were nonetheless committed to themselves. Indeed, and however different the circumstances might seem, they found themselves facing a problem very similar to the one their predecessors had been obliged to face after the First World War. They were only too well aware of the

fact. The ghost of Versailles haunted them. They both thought
and proclaimed that those same errors which led to Hitler and the
1939 aggression must be avoided. But this reaction against the
past, while an indirect tribute to the influence of history, contained
in itself no solution. At the very most, it added to the confusion
and emphasized the opposition between the Western nations and
the Soviet Union, which lived by an entirely different concept of
history.

What, then, was the situation in France? France was trying to
recover her rank and her role as a Great Power. She would seem
to have achieved this because she took part in the final victory and
made her contribution to it. But she remained nonetheless branded
by her earlier defeat and by the years of occupation. The war had
broken her military power, disorganized her economy, and severely
damaged her industrial plant and equipment; she was thus placed,
relative to her Allies, in a position of dependence all the more
humiliating in its contrast to the position she had occupied as part
of the victorious coalition of 1918. Certainly the country had considerable resources, but it was rent by internal struggles. New
factional disputes had superimposed themselves on the old party
quarrels inherited from the nineteenth century, and these forces
ranged men of the Resistance against Collaborationists and those
who sat on the fence. Even in the heart of the Resistance itself,
the Communists were set against the other groups. Thus France
did not possess the means to implement the major policy to which
General de Gaulle was urging her. The outburst of patriotism
which greeted the liberation masked but inadequately a deep
weariness. Greatness implied too many risks for most people
to be tempted by it. The majority aspired only to security. They
wanted above all the guarantees and the compensations to which
they felt entitled as a result of the ravages of the war. Moreover,
the French had the feeling that they had had a more accurate
understanding of the situation in 1919 than the United Kingdom
and the United States, and they were indignant at having been left
out of the first discussions on the future organization of Germany.
At times, French policy was to take a carping tone towards the
Allies, indicative of weakness.

Such was the state of mind in which the French approached
solution of the German problem. Nothing was more significant

than the debates which took place on November 21 and 22, 1944, in the Provisional Consultative Assembly. Here the determination to make the voice of France heard in the settlement of German affairs asserted itself. The French demanded the right to participate in the occupation; they claimed a substantial share of the reparations; they recalled the necessity for a viable frontier— in short, for the Rhine territories they insisted on a régime that would give France a sufficient guarantee of security. Some speakers definitely rejected any idea of annexation, while others, such as Maurice Schumann, let it be understood that France should avoid discouraging peoples who, " in the dissolution of the German State, of the *corpus germanicum*, might again voluntarily feel the traditional attraction of France." [1]

Security, reparations, and, to obtain these guarantees, participation in the occupation of German territory—these were the French demands in the closing days of the war. Realization of them was to be achieved only with difficulty. It was not until the Yalta Conference, and then at the insistence of Winston Churchill, that the Allies decided to provide for a French Zone of Occupation in Germany and to grant France a seat on the Allied Control Council. Even so, these concessions did not imply the admission of France to the concert of Powers on an equal footing. In fact, certain fundamental decisions establishing the bases of the settlement of the German question were taken without France. When the French representative, René Massigli, was admitted to the European Advisory Commission on November 27, 1944, the conditions of German surrender had already been drawn up, as had the agreements on the zones and on the Allied Control Council. Moreover, France was not to be represented at Potsdam.

This struggle to assure her participation drained France's energy and monopolized her attention, but did not detract from the study of the German problem, especially the territorial status of Germany. How could French security be achieved? By the dismemberment of Germany? By the application of a plan similar to that proposed by Henry Morgenthau, Jr., to President Roosevelt? By international control of the Ruhr? By a modification of the frontier that would push Germany back to the other side of the Rhine? Many possibilities were discussed in private and in public.

[1] *Cf. Journal officiel, Débats parlementaires, Assemblée consultative provisoire,* November 23, 1944, pp. 323–325.

General de Gaulle himself reacted immediately and bluntly. At his press conference on January 25, 1945, he said:

> The Rhine represents French security and I also believe it represents in large measure the security of the rest of the world. But it is France who is the party chiefly interested. It is France who has been invaded on each successive occasion, France who has been almost destroyed and therefore wishes to be solidly guaranteed behind the whole length of this natural frontier.[2]

Thus it was necessary to have a plan which would provide for special treatment of the Ruhr, the Rhineland, and the Saar. The argument used by the head of the Provisional Government, which found its inspiration in the reasoning of Marshal Foch and from the theory of natural frontiers, was to be taken up later by Georges Bidault and was to represent from then onwards the official policy of France. But, clearly formulated though the objectives might be, the methods of achieving them were not precisely defined. Furthermore, there was to be opposition among the Allies, and in France itself: amputation of German territory might well turn out to be the source of a new wave of German nationalism.

These considerations were more valid for the Ruhr and the Rhineland than for the Saar; the question of the Saar, originally approached as one factor in an over-all policy, was to be increasingly dissociated from the whole and treated as an individual problem. This was to be expected. The Saar, or at least part of it, had been French. It was true that this had been the case only for short periods, between 1681 and 1697 and again between 1792 and 1815, but that was a reservation of which public opinion, unresponsive to subtleties, was scarcely aware. Moreover, the Saar had already served as compensation in the years 1919 to 1935,[3] that is to say, recently enough for the fact to be remembered and to have conditioned certain attitudes of mind. Certainly, the Saarlanders had indicated vigorously their own wish to be German, but the plebiscite had belonged to the period of the Hitler régime; whatever its value might have been, it came under the general moral condemnation accorded to all the political operations of that government. In short, the links which had previously bound the Saar to France made an approach to the problem easier.

[2] *Cf. L'Année politique 1944–1945* (Paris: 1946), p. 101.
[3] See Appendix III, Map. No. 1.

Some people, those for whom the Saar was a living, concrete reality, were especially conscious of such ties. These included the militant adherents of the *Association française de la Sarre*. This Association, founded in 1928 [4] by Commandant Lanrezac and Robert Herly, an administrative official of the mines, had as its first president Jacques Bardoux, member of the Institut de France.[5] It had engaged in certain activities during the years preceding the plebiscite of 1935, when it had endeavoured to unite the Saarlanders living in France and fight for maintenance of the *status quo*. In 1945 the Association was re-formed. At the same time a group of expatriates from the Saar founded the *Mouvement pour la libération de la Sarre* (M.L.S.),[6] first in Toulouse, where some of them had taken refuge, then in Paris in March of 1945.

It is doubtful if these two groups had much influence, but they were nonetheless important by the mere fact of their existence, which guaranteed a " *présence sarroise* " in France. The *Association française de la Sarre* was limited, in principle, to cultural activities. This was, indeed, a condition laid down for the granting of a government subsidy. And yet the Association's " doctrine," as expounded on February 10, 1945, by one of its members, Edgar Hector, a Saarlander by birth, went far beyond " cultural " bonds. Mr. Hector was addressing a meeting of the *Comité d'étude pour les frontières orientales de la France* at which were present, among others, Maurice Schumann, Edmond Vermeil, and Wladimir d'Ormesson. He stressed first the economic importance of the Saar, its coal resources and its iron and steel industries. Then he went on to strategic considerations, and from these he drew the conclusion that the eastern frontiers of France would have to be modified in such a way as to imply inclusion of the Saar territory.

---

4 It succeeded the *Association des amis de la Sarre* founded in 1925. For a history of these two groups before 1935, see Helmut Hirsch, *Die Saar von Genf (Rheinisches Archiv)* (Bonn: 1954), and in Robert Herly, " Le mouvement francophile en Sarre," *ibid.*, Appendix, pp. 92–96.

5 From 1945 its President was General Joseph Andlauer, Commander of the French troops in the Saar after the First World War. With him were Robert Herly as Vice-President and Mlle. Boucly as Secretary-General. After their deaths General Andlauer and Mlle. Boucly were replaced, respectively, by General de Grancey and Commandant Bouret. Mr. Herly published numerous articles on the Saar problem under the pseudonym of Jean Revire. See Bibliography.

6 The Executive Committee of the M.L.S. was made up of: Walter Sender, lawyer; Alfred Levy, jurist and later President of the Senate; Thomas Blanc; Father Molitor; and Pastor Schmidt. *Cf. Bulletin du Mouvement pour la libération de la Sarre* (Paris: 1945), one issue only.

What, then, should be the status of the Saar?   Mr. Hector's views
on the point deserve to be quoted.

> If this status requires enactment of special legislation in order to take
> into account the particular character of the people, it should always be
> considered as an essentially practical measure, a means of assimilation.
> . . . One principle is fundamental and must always be kept in mind:
> this territory, re-united with us, becomes an integral part of France, who
> establishes herself there on a permanent basis and who alone exercises
> sovereign rights.   Indecision would be harmful, not only to the people
> of the Saar but also to the peace of Europe.[7]

As for the administration, this " must be placed in the hands of a
responsible leader answerable only to the office of the President;
legislative changes would be made by decree."   A consultative
commission would assist him and would also be responsible for
screening the population, since French nationality and all the civil
rights it confers would be accorded only gradually, after careful
examination of the " background " and the " record of behaviour "
of each citizen.   Mr. Hector ended by emphasizing the need for a
" firm and determined " policy on the part of France.

This statement seems to have made some impression, for the
Comité d'étude decided to adopt as its own the conclusions of the
Association française de la Sarre.   But the significance of the statement lay much more in the personality of its author, who was also
a founding member of the M.L.S.[8] and was subsequently to play
an important part in the government of his country.   His statement
on this occasion marked the first public attempt to define clearly a
future régime for the Saar.   It should be noted in passing that
during this same winter of 1944–1945, a *Comité de la rive gauche
du Rhin* called for a modification of the frontier which by implication would bring the Saar within the boundaries of France.[9]

Thus from the outset organizations made up of both Frenchmen
and Saarlander *émigrés* declared themselves for annexation.   Obviously, they were committing no one but themselves, but they
represented, nonetheless, a clearly defined current of opinion.   The
Foreign Affairs Committee of the Provisional Consultative
Assembly, at the close of its meetings of May 3, 4, and 5, 1945,

---

[7] Quoted in *Le Rhin*, No. 2 (Paris: February, 1945), pp. 3–4.
[8] The case of Mr. Hector is not an isolated one.   There were in fact fairly close relations
between the *Association française de la Sarre* and the M.L.S.
[9] In a statement of December 9, 1944, this Committee declared itself in favour of the
annexation of the left bank of the Rhine and the dismemberment of Germany.

voiced the same views in its unanimous decision to ask that, as reparations, the Government open negotiations to make the Saar mines immediately and definitively French, and that the necessary manpower be assigned for this purpose. The majority of the Committee felt that this transfer of ownership and the employment of labour should bring in its wake political annexation of the territory, although the population should retain the right of ultimately expressing its views both on the régime and on the incorporation of the territory into France.[10]

The government itself appeared in no hurry to spell out its plans. It had presented its claims to Prime Minister Churchill during his visit to Paris on November 11, 1944. It had repeatedly affirmed its rights and the need to establish a régime for the Saar within the framework of a general settlement of the problem of the western frontiers of Germany. The fate of the Saar was still, for the government, a subordinate part of the whole settlement. " The particular form of government set up in the Saar will depend on what we do in Germany," declared Mr. Bidault at a press conference in San Francisco on May 2, 1945.

This caution on the part of the French Government was perhaps imposed by circumstances, for the Saar was still in the hands of the United States military administration, which was vigorously suppressing any form of political agitation.[11] This did not mean, however, that no economic measures were taken. France was able to work with the United States military command, which from December, 1944, had concentrated on putting the Saar collieries back into working order and had requested that French engineers be sent to help. A mission was immediately set up, first at Merlebach, then, after a withdrawal to Nancy following the Rundstedt offensive, at Sulzbach at the beginning of May. The dominating sentiment at this period, both in official circles and among the

---

[10] *Cf. Le Monde*, May 8, 1945.

[11] The Allied Military Tribunal at Saarbrücken condemned to ten years' imprisonment a member of the M.L.S. who had tried to distribute pamphlets advocating the union of the Saar and France. It must be pointed out, however, that the United States officer in charge of military administration in the Saar, Colonel Louis G. Kelly, had taken it upon himself to appoint, on May 4, a Saarlander lawyer, Hans Neureuther, as *Regierungspräsident* for the Saar. This decision, taken, it would seem, without previous consultation with the military authorities in Neustadt, occasioned a rather sharp reaction from the man responsible for the *Oberpräsidium Rheinland-Pfalz-Süd-Hessen*, Hermann Heimerich, who saw it as a separatist move. *Cf*. Georg Kratz, *Mittelrhein-Saar* (Stuttgart: 1954), pp. 30–31.

general public, was that it was imperative to resume the mining of coal; the interest taken in the Saar problem was essentially economic. The few articles which appeared in the French press on the Saar at this time were devoted primarily to an inventory of coal resources and of industries, in an attempt to evaluate the immediate and future worth of this territory as a security.[12]

As soon as French troops arrived in the Saar on July 10, intentions became clearer. Three days before, when the news of the dismissal of Hermann Heimerich from his post as *Oberregierungspräsident* of Mittelrhein-Saar was received, Hans Neureuther, President of the " Government " of the Saar,[13] had sent a circular letter to all councillors and mayors. In it he announced that henceforth he would assume full responsibility for public administration.[14] Then, on July 25, a letter to Mr. Neureuther by General Morlière, aide to the Military Government, informed him that the organization of the French Military Government required that in future the Saar territory be constituted as an administrative unit, independent of all the agencies to which it had hitherto been attached. Thus the President of the Saar " Government " found himself endowed with all the prerogatives which had formerly been accorded to the *Oberregierungspräsident* of Mittelrhein-Saar. He was given the authority to take measures necessary for the sound administration of the Saar territory, but he was reminded that it was important to maintain certain contacts with neighbouring countries, in particular those contacts which would guarantee the maintenance of food supplies.[15]

This letter from General Morlière gave the impression that a decision in principle had been taken as to the place to be given the Saar in the ensemble of French Military Government in Germany. But a policy still had to be defined. Apparently for this purpose a mission of some twenty members was established, under conditions that were not too clear, to go to Saarbrücken to study the facts of the Saar problem. At the head of the mission was Abel Verdier, then *Directeur des chancelleries* in the Ministry for Foreign Affairs.

[12] *Cf.*, especially, the articles published in *Le Monde*, April 8, 9, 14, and May 15, 1945.
[13] *Regierungspräsident.*
[14] This decision gave rise to a protest from Hans Hoffmann, Mr. Heimerich's successor as *Oberregierungspräsident* of Mittelrhein-Saar. In reply he was told that the circular had been previously submitted to the heads of both the United States and the French Military Administrations, and moreover that it was not motivated by any separatist notions. *Cf.* Kratz, *op. cit.*, pp. 65–66.
[15] Kratz., *loc. cit.*, pp. 66–67.

He was considered to be well acquainted with the Saar and he had spent his pre-war years as French Consul-General in Saarbrücken. However, his mission was not able to arrive in the Saar until after the entry of the French troops in July. Moreover, it played only a secondary role, for there was but a short interval between its arrival and that of the man who was to dominate Saar politics for some years—Colonel Gilbert Grandval.

If the Verdier mission merits attention here, it is for its report, the essential passages of which, published in *Le Monde* of May 7 and 8, 1946, may still be remembered.[16] The primary objective of the report was to legitimize French claims. It drew first upon the historical arguments: "For almost three hundred years the Saar has been disputed territory, and except for the years 1815–1919 and 1935–1944, France has always had a place there." Then followed the strategic considerations (omitted in the articles in *Le Monde*): the heights overlooking the Saar provided a good line of defence, valid even in a century preparing to exploit atomic energy; in addition, there was the important contribution to be made by the iron and steel and the metallurgical industries of the Saar to France's war potential. "The Saar presents, therefore, a real interest for France from the military point of view, since it would provide her with an excellent natural line of defence on her exposed north-east frontier and would considerably increase her war potential." Given these conditions, the solution was the "unhampered, smooth integration of the economic entity of the Saar into the economic life of France, the gradual familiarization of the people to frequent contacts with our country, our way of life, our political ideal. Let the people of the Saar come under the spell of France's cultural influence and of her inherent qualities so that they may grow really close to us and become sincere and disinterested members of that great political entity, the *Union française*." An "integrated" Saar should have its own status: an "autonomous, administrative entity," linked with France by a customs and monetary union responsible to the Ministry for Foreign Affairs, with France represented in the Saar by a High Commissioner.

The Verdier solution, as may be seen, was very close to the one that had been envisaged by the *Association française de la Sarre* and the *Mouvement pour la libération de la Sarre*.

[16] Except for the purely strategic considerations, the text has been reproduced in *La Documentation française, Notes documentaires et Etudes*, No. 326, June 15, 1946.

So far all of this activity consisted only of studies and plans. But with the administration of Mr. Grandval, French policy embarked upon the practical road of action and achievement.

Here was a man who commanded immediate attention. He had had a career in industry. When the war came, he joined the resistance movement and assumed ever-increasing responsibilities. Appointed to the command of the Twentieth Military District, he found himself offered the choice between the posts of Deputy to General Koenig in Germany and that of Governor of the Saar. Mr. Grandval chose the Saar, and he ruled it as a proconsul. He possessed a strong sense of the greatness of his country, a taste for authority, and a full realization of the obligations that power imposes on the one who wields it. He arrived in the Saar with no precise instructions, and by his actions he developed a policy to be followed. Some of his decisions were dictated by necessity, some by his instinct for leadership that led him quite naturally to be constantly on the watch for the best interests of those for whom he was responsible. Circumstances and the mood of the post-war period were equally favourable to a man of his mettle, trained in conflict. Carried along by the flush of victory, free, by the very nature of the occupation régime, of legal restrictions and political commitments, he was, for some time at least, able to shape and remodel to his own liking.

The situation Mr. Grandval found on his arrival,[17] difficult though it might be on the practical level, was not unfavourable to the implementation of French policy. The Saar had suffered heavily from the war.[18] Out of a population of less than a million, 30,000–35,000 were dead, more than 100,000 were prisoners, and, in addition, there was a high percentage of wounded and missing. Aerial bombardments and land battles had destroyed or damaged almost half the houses; schools, hospitals, and factories had been hard hit, bridges destroyed; economic life was virtually paralysed. All political activity had been cut short by the arrival of the Americans, who had been content to set up a government with purely administrative functions in which they found positions for men who had been suggested to them by *émigré* organizations.[19]

[17] The appointment of Colonel Grandval was made on August 30, 1945. The new Governor took up his post on September 7, 1945.
[18] For the estimates of damage, cf. *Saarbuch 1955* (Saarbrücken: 1955), p. 21.
[19] Kratz., *op. cit.*, pp. 30–31.

It was essential to feed the people and, in France's own interest, to re-establish communications and to resume and encourage the mining of coal. These were the tasks that were to occupy most of the administration's attention, and, if certain reports may be believed, they were carried out with some success.

This effort towards reconstruction, comparable to that taking place all over Europe, did not preclude discussion of plans for the future of the Saar. There were various possible solutions to the problem: permanent acquisition of the Saar mines, economic union of the Saar and France, or complete annexation.

Very early on, the Governor found spokesmen, for the most part *émigrés*, among former adversaries of the National Socialist régime. In the forefront of their ranks was Johannes Hoffmann, who returned at the age of fifty-five to the land of his birth. A controversial figure, he had been too closely implicated in the struggles and disputes that had stirred his native country between the two wars not to have made serious enemies. His way of life and his skill in intrigue had often aroused either uneasiness or derision, and his opponents did not fail to draw upon his past record for proof of an adaptability which they found somewhat exaggerated. They were all the more successful because Mr. Hoffmann's years as a journalist had inevitably left traces. But this past, which was to be dug up later, was not remembered when Mr. Hoffmann came back from Brazil with the glory of the *émigré* about him. War and unconditional surrender had created a gap. Potential leaders were few. Mr. Hoffmann, who had a liking for combat and a revenge to take, was a political force.

Another figure stands out among the *émigrés* who in 1935 had opposed the return of the Saar to Germany—Edgar Hector, a naturalized Frenchman and captain in the army.[20] Mr. Hector was bound to France by family tradition, so that, when he proposed the union of France and the Saar, he was only following his father's example.

In this same group of men who in 1945 again took up the policy for which they had fought in 1935—a policy advocating a status that would ensure the political separation of the Saar from Germany—there were also Heinrich Wacker, who was to become President of the *Syndicat unitaire*, some Socialists, such as Richard

[20] Mr. Hector was not a captain in the regular army; he belonged to the category of those specially commissioned for the occupation forces.

Kirn, Heinz Braun,[21] and Georg Schulte, and a former Communist, Fritz Pfordt.[22] Among the returned *émigrés* were also men who in 1935 had stood for the return of the Saar to Germany, but because of the persecutions of the National Socialist régime, and particularly its anti-Semitism, had reversed their stand. These men, such as Walter Sender and Emile Straus, now came back with a determination perhaps even firmer than that of many others to fight for liberation of the Saar from the German nationalism of which they had been the first victims.

Finally, there were possible supporters of the Military Governor among Saarlanders who had not been forced by circumstances to emigrate. A certain Peter Zimmer, a miner and subsequently an official of the League of Nations Government Commission of the Saar Basin, editor of a Socialist newspaper at Bochum, survived after a fashion the period of National Socialist domination, although he had been closely watched by the Gestapo. Franz Singer, a Catholic of rather more fluid political views, did the same. The lawyer Erwin Müller, like Johannes Hoffmann a member of the *Zentrum*, had been legal adviser to the French Consul-General in Saarbrücken before the war. Freed from a prisoner-of-war camp in 1945, he was known to the French and could work with them to achieve mutual understanding.

The number of those with whom the Military Governor could deal was necessarily small, and their action was very limited. Until June 22, 1946, there was only one newspaper, the *Neue Saarbrücker Zeitung*, and this came out only twice a week under close scrutiny of the French authorities.

These few Saarlanders at least held their own opinions, inspired by the conditions under which they had lived and the experiences they had undergone. Very soon, two attitudes towards France became apparent. One group, led by Johannes Hoffmann, came out in favour of an economic union with France that would entail no political attachment; the other, which included such individuals as Mr. Hector, Mr. Sender, and the members of the M.L.S., opted for complete integration. As for public opinion, it had little or no opportunity to express itself even if it wished to. The Saarlanders had much more pressing concerns than politics; they had to build

---

[21] Heinz Braun is the brother of Max Braun, the Socialist leader who led the group in favour of the *status quo* before 1935.
[22] In contrast, Communist leaders such as Karl Hoppe, Fritz Nikolay, and Friedrich Bäsel opposed separation from Germany.

anew, to work, to feed themselves. They were completely alone. Germany had ceased to exist, and no one knew if she would be resuscitated or under what conditions. France, for her part, was there in association with the victors, and had the strength to command respect. By her mere presence, she exercised an inevitable attraction. The Saarlanders had nothing to lose and everything to gain by a *rapprochement* with France. "The Saarlanders are turning to the strongest power," declared one of the editors of *Le Figaro* in an article in May, 1946, "and what is remarkable after so many hardships is that it is we who are once again that power." [23]

So it was that everything combined to make France's role in the Saar easier. The French had the advantage of strength. In support of their claims they could invoke their right to reparations and the necessity, universally recognized, of ensuring their own safety. Even in the Saar itself there were opinions favourable to France, asking for unification with her.

What action was the French Government going to take? Was it to follow the advice of the *Association française de la Sarre* and of the Saarlanders of the M.L.S. who were calling for annexation? No doubt more than one French politician was toying with the idea of annexation. This found expression, for instance, in the discussions that took place in December, 1945, at the M.R.P. Congress. Jean Letourneau, who submitted the report on foreign affairs, stated that the problem of the Saar "is a problem for the French economy" and concluded by placing his confidence "in the legal experts to find a formula which, without jeopardizing the political position of the territory, would place its economic wealth at the disposal of France." Some of his colleagues spoke in favour of annexation pure and simple, and Mr. Letourneau called for a definite pronouncement on this point. The reply came in the final motion adopted by the Congress: "[The Congress], conscious of France's need for coal . . . requests integration of the Saar territory into France in accordance with a statute to be drawn up." [24]

"In accordance with a statute to be drawn up"—the formula revealed rather clearly the hesitancy in French policy. General de Gaulle himself was also noncommittal and restricted himself to addressing encouraging words to the Saarlanders. "We are with

[23] May 21, 1946.
[24] *Cf. Compte rendu du Congrès*, Archives of the M.R.P.

you," he told them in his Saarbrücken speech on October 3. " The French Government stands ready to help you. As Western Europeans, despite what may have come between us, we should work together and understand each other." [25]

The first decisions of the occupying Power were of an essentially economic nature. On December 28, 1945, the Saar mines were sequestrated and, on January 2, 1946, placed under French administrative authority. On January 17, at the end of a long debate on foreign policy, Georges Bidault announced, amid the applause of the Assembly:

> The Saar mines, ownership of which was given to France by the Treaty of Versailles, are to become French property once again and, as a corollary to this, the territory is to be included in the French customs and monetary system, the two economies being complementary. French troops will be permanently stationed in the Saar to guarantee the future of such an arrangement. As for the eventual status of the territory, it will be the subject of a decision to be taken with our great Allies at a later date.[26]

This declaration by Mr. Bidault, in which, for the first time, the French Government outlined its concept of the settlement of the Saar question, was the prelude to other negotiations. Indeed, on February 12, a note was handed to the Allies. The French Government, it stated, considered that the time was ripe for an agreement on the future of the Saar. It did not seem possible to take any decisions on the setting up of certain central bodies in Germany, or on the establishment of levels of industry, " especially the productive capacity in steel to be left to her," or on the amount to be levied as reparations, so long as there was no agreement on whether the Saar would, or would not, be incorporated into the French customs area.

The note then stated the reasons underlying the solution proposed by France. " The régime envisaged rests above all on a basis of economic principles: to deprive Germany of some of her war potential and to incorporate the Saar into the economic and monetary entity of France." The French Government asked in conclusion the recognition of French rights of ownership of the mines and the inclusion of the Saar territory in the customs and

---

[25] *Cf. Renaissance de la Sarre* (Saarbrücken: 1947), p. 45.
[26] *Cf. Journal officiel, Débats parlementaires, Assemblée nationale*, January 18, 1946, p. 80.

monetary system of France, the latter implying an immediate substitution of the franc for the mark. As for the political status, the note admitted that this could not be finally established until the peace settlement. But it nevertheless laid down the French conditions: " The Saar must be removed, as of now and in perpetuity, from a central German administration. France will have the right to maintain troops there permanently and to supervise the Saar administration." Furthermore, the note announced the French Government's intention of immediately taking all the necessary steps to separate the public utilities, such as the railways and the postal services, from those of the Reich and to guarantee the protection of Saar nationals and of Saar interests abroad. As for the status of the inhabitants, their nationality, their right to be consulted—these were questions to be determined later.[27]

Then began a long battle to persuade the British, American, and Soviet Governments to accept the French proposals. Resistance was strong. The United States and United Kingdom, trying to set up the central administration provided for in the Potsdam agreements, were primarily concerned with the effects that a separation of the Saar would have on their own problems as well as on decisions relating to the levels of industry and to reparations. Little by little, however, a compromise began to emerge. Secretary of State James F. Byrnes and Foreign Minister Ernest Bevin declared that they were prepared to allow the Saar to be placed under French administration until the final settlement of the western frontiers, on condition that the French Government give its support to the decisions taken at Potsdam on the creation of a central German administration. Mr. Bidault, for his part, said he was ready to accept the establishment of a central administration on condition that the Saar became part of the French sphere of influence and that an international government be envisaged for the Ruhr.[28]

[27] *Cf. Documents relatifs à l'Allemagne, août 1945–février 1947* (Paris: 1947), pp. 7–12.
[28] Mr. Byrnes, in fact, stated at the time of the meeting of Foreign Ministers on May 11, 1946, that the United States was willing for the Saar to be placed outside the competence of the Central Administration and to remain under the authority of the French Administration until the western frontiers were finally delimited. On July 12, after Mr. Bidault had given his consent to the creation of inter-allied administrative offices on condition that the Saar become part of the French economic area and that the coal question be solved by the integration of the Saar and by the internationalization of the Ruhr, Secretary Byrnes proposed the formation of certain central administrative bodies. Then he stated that representatives of the Four Powers might be instructed to carry out the Potsdam proposals with the following amendment: the Saar should be

Mr. Molotov, on the other hand, remained adamant and this Soviet opposition prevented any formal decision. But the French position improved as a result of the deterioration in relations between the Soviet Union and the United States and United Kingdom. In the struggle which began over Germany, the Americans and English needed allies and showed themselves more inclined to make concessions.

The French Government did not wait for a formal decision from the Council of Foreign Ministers before moving ahead. On the contrary, the resistance it had encountered only served to strengthen its determination to translate its resolve into deeds. While the Military Governor was working to win over the greatest possible number of Saarlanders to the French cause, the *Commissariat général* for German and Austrian affairs undertook to examine the various economic and financial measures involved in an economic union with the Saar. At the end of May, René Mayer, *Commissaire général*, instructed one of his colleagues to embark on the necessary studies.

This was not an easy task. Before the Saar territory could be included in the French customs system, it was vital to know the extent to which France was capable of taking on the material responsibility. Could France assure the feeding of the Saar? Might she not be risking an unfavourable reaction from the Allies that might take the form of an unwarranted cut in the value of the industrial plant to which she was entitled as reparations? There was keen competition between the iron and steel industries of the Saar and those of Lorraine. A means must be found to reconcile their opposing interests and above all to overcome the resistance that had grown up in the Moselle to the policy of union.

The task was all the more difficult because of the delicate question of determining the monetary rate of exchange. At the beginning of 1946, the purchasing power of the mark was valued by French experts at thirty to thirty-five francs. But for the people

excluded from the Central Administration; it should be administered within the framework of the French economic system. He added, however, that this arrangement did not commit any member of the Council regarding the ultimate fate of the Saar territory. He returned to this problem in the broadcast report he made on the Paris Conference on July 15, 1946. *Cf.* "The Paris Conference of Foreign Ministers, June 15–July 12, Report of the Secretary of State," Department of State *Bulletin*, Vol. XV, No. 359 (July 28, 1946), p. 171.

Mr. Byrnes confirmed this position publicly in a speech at Stuttgart on September 9. Ernest Bevin, for his part, declared himself in favour of the French demands in two statements in the House of Commons on June 4 and October 22.

of Alsace and Lorraine the exchange was at the rate of fifteen francs. It was agreed that, for obvious political reasons, it was not possible to show favouritism to the Saarlanders, in spite of the devaluation of the franc which occurred after the exchange of marks for francs in Alsace and Lorraine. But if the rate of exchange were fixed too low, was there not a danger that this would provoke considerable opposition in the Saar to economic union?

These questions demanded the immediate attention of the French authorities and there were others concerning the harmonization of legislation on which the various ministries would have to be consulted. The necessary adjustments would take time.

True enough, agreement was reached fairly quickly on the aims of the economic union and on the principles that should govern their application. Parallel with the inclusion of the Saar in the French customs area and the introduction of the franc, there was also envisaged the development of commercial exchanges between the Saar and France, the entry of the Saar into the French industrial system, French participation in the Saar economy, and even modifications in the structure of Saar industries to the greater benefit of the French economy.

The operation was conceived entirely in terms of French interests. There was nothing surprising in that. A major war had only just ended and the men whose responsibility it was to manage the affairs of their ravaged country were concentrating all their efforts on economic recovery. They did not hesitate to think in terms of a real distraint by France upon the Saar economy by substituting French interests for German interests or by using, to the profit of France, the readjustments which would necessarily follow the change of currency and the re-evaluation of assets and liabilities. This did not mean, however, that the French were deliberately sacrificing Saar interests. They knew, as is proved by some of their statements, that economic union with the Saar implied a contribution from France towards putting Saar industry in working order again.[29]

The agreement on principles, which may be deemed to have been reached at the end of June, did not prevent the expression of

[29] "The immediate problem with which we will be faced when union comes," remarked one of them, "is to guarantee the continuity of Saar industrial activity. This will demand, on the one hand, credits from French banks to lessen the danger of financial crisis after the monetary change-over; and, on the other hand, France must guarantee uninterrupted supplies of essential raw materials."

certain disagreements subsequently. A slight tension became apparent between the Military Governor and the departments to which he was answerable. Mr. Grandval was giving himself wholeheartedly to his task. He grew impatient with the dilatoriness of the ministries producing the studies required before economic union could be put into effect. The delays created vacillation in the Saar and this he was in a better position than anyone to sense. Had he not prepared public opinion for the announcement of economic union? Was it not he who had encouraged the political parties and the trade unions to appeal directly to the Council of Foreign Ministers, as they did in their telegram of April 27? [30] There could be nothing more dangerous than this prolonged period of waiting. The Saarlanders, ready to accept a decision but not seeing it materialize, might assume that the French were wavering. Might they not then look about for another solution?

In Paris, however, Mr. Grandval was taken to task for his independence. His insistence in urging that the Saar have its own currency, which he believed would shield the Saarlanders from the effects of the fluctuation of the franc, was interpreted by his critics as the latest example of a personal policy. A high official of the *Direction des finances* of the Military Government of the French Zone even went so far as to refer to " a principality in embryo." [31]

The final step was at last taken. When the deputies met at the beginning of December, 1946, Maurice Couve de Murville informed the Allies that circumstances might lead the French Government to take new measures in the Saar. He said that it was becoming imperative to stop exporting foodstuffs to Germany. It was not without difficulty that they had been sent from France. Moreover, an end must be put to the influx of marks occasioned by the approaching economic union of the Saar with France. On December 22, the French customs barrier was extended to the eastern frontier of the Saar.

Thus, at the beginning of 1946 the Government in Paris took a decision and formulated a policy. Its choice was not complete annexation but economic union, subject to certain political conditions that were to guarantee the separation of the Saar from Germany and the *présence française* in the Saar.

Immediate economic concerns did indeed influence the decision. France needed coal. The conditions laid down by the Allies for the distribution of coal left her a very limited quantity; moreover, she was compelled to pay for it in dollars.[32]

Economic union with the Saar had the effect of easing this double burden. Moreover, if the Saar remained within the political framework of Germany, it would be included in the scheme envisaged for reparations and dismantling. As a result, the returns it would bring and its value as a security would be lessened.

Mr. Grandval, whose first concern was to be reconstruction and the development of production, could not fail to be struck by the contradiction between a policy of *présence française* in the Saar aimed at a *rapprochement*—indeed even a complete union—and the demands the victors were making on the Germans. Quite obviously there was a choice to make, and that as quickly as possible. Moreover, the Saarlanders shared the French interests here. By not being subject to the treatment accorded to the vanquished, they avoided reparations and dismantling. On March 17, 1946, the Military Governor told them so in no uncertain terms in his speech inaugurating Radio Saarbrücken: "Every crime must be punished and that is the meaning of dismantling and reparations. But there is hope for the Saar. Will it be able to understand better than in 1935 that its prosperity and happiness are bound up with the establishment of good relations with neighbouring provinces?"[33] To this Johannes Hoffmann replied that the Saarlanders accepted the opportunity offered them. He was not the only one to express this opinion. One of the first declarations of the Christian People's Party (C.V.P.) and the Socialist Party was

[32] These conditions provided for the holding of German coal in an inter-Allied pool to be allocated by the European Coal Organization, first among the different zones of occupation and then among the Allies. The result of this was that France received only 100,000 tons of Saar coal a month out of a total production of 900,000 tons, that is to say, one ton in every nine of Saar coal mined. Thus, from August 1, 1945, to May 31, 1946, France only drew 16 per cent. of the total of Saar coal, 60 per cent. having been allocated to the zones of occupation and 24 per cent. to the other Allies. Furthermore, all the German exports that were not in the nature of reparations—and this was true of coal—had to be paid for in dollars. For more details, see Robert Müller, *Le rattachement économique de la Sarre à la France* (Paris: 1950), p. 113.
[33] Cf. *Neue Saarbrücker Zeitung*, March 19, 1946.

an approval of the Bidault proposals.[34]   On April 27, jointly with the *Syndicat unitaire*, they sent a telegram to the Council of Foreign Ministers to request the economic union of the Saar with France.[35]

Another motive for the decision to propose economic union was to be found in the anxiety not to compromise the French position in Germany.   Here again, the Saar was only one aspect of the French Government's German policy.   Might not a policy of complete annexation weaken the French argument concerning the Ruhr and the Rhineland?   Might it not compromise French rights to reparations?   As Mr. Sender accurately pointed out in his article of August 14, 1947:

> If France had completely annexed or taken over the Saar, she would have run the risk of seeing the value of the Saar deducted from her reparations and thus had her other claims refused; on the other hand, by giving the Saar self-government, this pitfall was avoided because the resources of the Saar territory remained under the direct administration of the Saar people and so could not be credited to France.[36]

These economic concerns, urgent though they were, were nevertheless subordinate to essentially political ends.   The men at the *Commissariat général* for German and Austrian affairs who were responsible for developing French policy towards the Saar saw the economic union not so much as an end in itself but as a means to weaken the bonds between Germany and the Saar and to break up, in some measure, their " politico-economic " bloc.   " The realization of these fundamental aims of French policy," wrote one of them at the time, " must take precedence over all other considerations and should lead to economic union with the Saar even if there be no economic advantages in addition to political interests." The over-riding force of political pre-occupations could not be more sharply emphasized.

But clearly it was much easier to obtain agreement on economic union with the Saar than on full-scale annexation.   The firmly established belief that both victors and liberated countries were entitled to reparations, the existence of a precedent in the years 1919–1935, predisposed people's minds to a solution of this kind. The establishment of French rights of ownership in the Saar

---

[34] The Socialist Party made a declaration on April 10, the C.V.P. on April 16, and the *Syndicat unitaire* on May 1.
[35] *Cf. Renaissance de la Sarre, op. cit.*, p. 50.   [36] *Die Neue Saar*, August 14, 1947.

seemed, in France, a completely natural and even an absolutely essential measure. In the Assembly and in the press, the importance of the economic bond linking the Saar and Lorraine since 1871—not completely broken by the brief period of Hitler's domination from 1935 to 1944—was constantly stressed.

The argument was a good one. Everyone well knew the part played in the Saar iron and steel industry by iron ore from Lorraine and in Lorraine's industry by Saar coal. Between the Saar and Lorraine, moreover, the geographic links are plain to see. While the carboniferous anticline running from Saarbrücken-Völklingen to the region of Ottweiler Neunkirchen is separated from Germany by the schistous massif of the Rhine basin, it is turned in the direction of Lorraine because of the Saar River which is navigable from Merzig to its upper reaches. There it joins up with the Coal Canal opened in 1866.

These observations, fairly widespread in the French press in 1945 and 1946, were not in fact the full story. The experiment in economic integration tried out between 1919 and 1935 did not, as Laurent Champier has noted, succeed in " completely breaking up solidarity between the Saar and Germany. Economic co-operation was only reached on certain levels. The basic industries did not find sufficient outlets on the French market—always a small steel consumer and never an expanding market." [37] But these reservations, however valid, had in fact little importance because, at the time when the decision was taken, what counted was not so much the actual situation itself but the idea people had of the situation. And in 1945–1946, what dominated opinion in the Saar, as in France, was the theme of the economic unity of the Saar-Lorraine basin.

There was, however, a current of opinion favourable to the political integration of the Saar. It was even fairly strong in the Saar itself. The *Mouvement pour le rattachement de la Sarre* (M.R.S.),[38] founded in February, 1946, by the men who had founded and directed the M.L.S., was the moving force behind this

[37] *Cf.* Laurent Champier, " La Sarre, essai d'interprétation géopolitique," *Arbeiten aus dem Geographischen Institut* (Saarbrücken: Universität des Saarlandes, Philosophische Fakultät, 1956), Vol. I, p. 42.

[38] This movement was directed by a committee of three members: Louis Arend, President of the *Chambre des métiers de la Sarre*, Walter Sender, lawyer, former Socialist Deputy in the Saar *Landesrat*, and Mr. Diwo, *Landrat* of the district of Saarlouis, member of the C.V.P. The administrative director was Fritz Pfordt, former Communist. *Cf. Le Fait du jour*, No. 21 (October 1, 1946).

current. The movement did not hesitate to announce its aims and, on May 18 and 19, organized a big rally, the *Französische Festtage an der Saar*, to unveil a memorial to Marshal Ney. This gave Mr. Bloch, Mayor of Saarlouis, the opportunity of demanding, in the presence of General Koenig, the re-establishment of the 1814 frontiers.[39] This demonstration focused attention on the issue and was widely commented upon in the French press.

There was no doubt that the M.R.S. had support in France. However, resistance to political union was strong. It came in the first place from the Allies, but it was also apparent in France. From 1945, certain members of the Socialist Party[40] had expressed very clearly their opposition to any policy of annexation, and this feeling was shared by many Frenchmen who were aware of the contradiction between such a policy and the principles they had always upheld.

The strongest opposition came from the Saarlanders' nearest neighbours, the people of Lorraine. One might have thought that the proximity of these two regions and their recognized need for economic exchanges would have contributed to the creation of a community of interests and would have made them the natural spokesmen for the principle of the unity of the Saar-Lorraine basin. One might rather have expected that it would be in Lorraine that one would find the most ardent supporters of annexation, since it offered both economic advantages and military guarantees. Such was not the case. Indeed, the attitude of the Lorrainers seemed on the contrary characterized by reservations and even mistrust. In 1945 they had paid scarcely any attention to what was going on in the Saar or to discussions about the Saar. The reconstruction of their own country and of their own industry occupied their full attention. But when in 1946 the French plans for the Saar took shape, they became uneasy. This was because they saw in the Saarlanders competitors whom they blamed for having skilfully turned to account their position as intermediary between France and Germany, to the detriment of Lorraine's industry. Certain Lorrainers had very unhappy recollections of the part played by the Saarlanders during the German occupation. A statement by the Chamber of Commerce of Saarbrücken on May 7, asking for close

---

[39] *Cf. Neue Saarbrücker Zeitung*, May 21, 1946.
[40] Léon Blum and Salomon Grumbach spoke very bluntly on this point.

economic co-operation between France and the Saar, and a demonstration by the M.R.S. in Saarlouis in favour of political union aroused very lively reactions. The Chamber of Commerce of Metz announced that it was " disturbed by the propaganda in favour of annexation " and asked for consultation between all interested parties in the region before any decision of an economic nature was taken. *Le Républicain lorrain*, generally held to have friendly connections with the Chamber of Commerce, launched an inquiry into the whole question, " should the Saar, or should it not, become French? " and concluded with a number of requests: (1) no immediate annexation; (2) fifteen to twenty years of probation; (3) " economic utilization," with sequestration of the mines and of iron and steel, and " occupation "; (4) immediate adjustment of the frontier in the Saarlouis and Warndt forest areas.[41] *Le Courrier de Metz* declared that " the people of Lorraine are in favour of economic integration of the Saar into the French system," for, it said, " Lorraine is an agricultural region for which the Saar may be an outlet, and commercial relations with the Saar appear desirable." But it added:

> The people of Lorraine are of the opinion that it will never be possible to make a good Frenchman out of a Saarlander! For all we consider economic annexation as desirable, indeed even necessary and indispensable to the expansion of our own agriculture and commerce, we still consider it a grave error to baptize the Saarlanders French, even should they, at first, give themselves up willingly to this conversion.[42]

This was not opposition expressed under the stress of emotion aroused by demonstrations in favour of annexation. The Chamber of Commerce of Metz, which had devoted its meeting of May 11 to the discussion of the report on the Franco-Saar economic union, came back to this problem at its meeting on June 27 and discussed it in the light of the experiments tried out between 1919 and 1935. The first report stressed critically the privileged position accorded to Saar industry in the Franco-Saar customs union prior to 1935. The second report, which examined the position of the metallurgical industries of Lorraine relative to the union of France and the Saar, contained extremely interesting observations. It called attention to the fact that, from the point of view of the provision of fuel, the Saar basin, which could in theory furnish fifty per cent.

[41] May 21, 1946.
[42] May 14, 1946.

of the coal imported into France, was of scarcely any use. It was badly situated very near the coalfields of Lorraine, which were developing rapidly and which produced coal of the same quality. Saar coal could be converted into coke of only mediocre quality, of which merely thirty-five to forty per cent. was useful to Lorraine's iron and steel industries. Better coal had to be imported from the north of France, from Belgium, and from the Ruhr. If the imports of Saar coal did not result in a lowering of coal imports from the Ruhr, then France would be making a bad bargain. Furthermore, the effects of union on the French iron and steel market would not be favourable. France was tending to increase the volume of her steel exports. But the Saar, by robbing the French steel industry of some of its home markets, would not leave a sufficiently solid basis for French iron and steel.

The report noted, however, that some groups of French metallurgists had interests in the Saar which they had to protect. It concluded by declaring that the iron and steel industrialists might accept annexation for political or military reasons but that they should require in return that political and customs frontiers should coincide, that the Saar should be placed under French administration if there were an economic union, that Saar iron and steel should be subject to the same regulations and taxes as the French, and that, as a general principle, the Saar should have no special privileges in its trade relations with Germany. Thereupon the Chamber of Commerce drew up a resolution which, after recalling that " it cannot subscribe to the thesis that the Saar and Lorraine should form an economic whole " and that Saar coal " is not worth much," expressed the desire that " if the over-riding interest of the state necessitates economic and customs union with the Saar, this union should be carried out simultaneously in administrative, fiscal, financial, and social fields," on the understanding that the Saar was not to benefit from any special treatment in her relations with Germany.[43]

No doubt all reactions were not so negative as this one. The Chamber of Commerce of Metz was much more outspoken than that of Nancy, in which were represented the ironworks of Pont-à-Mousson and the *Forges et Aciéries de la Marine et de Homé-court*. These two enterprises had had interests in the Saar, while

[43] *Cf.*, for the full account of this debate, *Chambre de commerce et d'industrie de la Moselle, Compte rendu des travaux, 1945–1946*, pp. 47–69.

none of the large enterprises of the Moselle appeared to have any direct interest in Saar undertakings. The most general feeling, however, seems to have been one of uneasiness towards a rather-too-active neighbour which had not done too badly for itself out of the political events of recent years.

The opposition in Lorraine did not become apparent until after the decision to proceed to economic union had already been taken in principle. It therefore had little or no influence, although it was known to the *Commissariat général* for German and Austrian affairs. The officials who were responsible for dealing with the problem were fully aware that in certain areas the economies of the Saar and the Moselle were competing and that some arbitration would be necessary; but they were nevertheless determined that the general interests of France should prevail over any local interests. And they did not intend to be diverted from the path they had chosen. The most striking feature of French policy in 1946 and during the year following was its continuity. The plan outlined by Mr. Bidault in January, 1946, and then developed in his notes to the Allies was to be implemented point by point, though, it is true, not without considerable effort.

These proposals inevitably met with Mr. Molotov's opposition in 1947 in Moscow, as at previous conferences. But acceptance by the British and the Americans was confirmed,[44] and that was what counted in the long run, because the United States and the United Kingdom had by now come to realize the impossibility of reaching an understanding with the Soviet Union on a common policy for Germany. The proclamation at the opening of the Moscow Conference, which at once became known as the Truman Doctrine, emphasized in a spectacular way the change that had taken place in the situation. The hopes that had been entertained in 1945 of co-operation between the various conquerors of Germany had by now disappeared. A new war was beginning which, although it

[44] It was on April 10 that Mr. Bevin again summed up the British Government's position on the Saar question. He repeated his willingness to agree to detachment of the Saar from Germany, with the reservation that the frontiers should be defined and reparations adjusted accordingly. He was supported by General George C. Marshall, who was also in favour of incorporating the Saar into the French economic system. The political autonomy of the territory and the rights of its people to govern their own local affairs should be carefully safeguarded; this ruling necessitated certain modifications in the measures dealing with the amount of industry to be permitted in Germany. It also called for adjustments in the handing over of reparations and the retention of certain factories in the Saar that were due to be dismantled. *Cf.* " Moscow Meeting of the Council of Foreign Ministers, Statements by the Secretary of State," Department of State *Bulletin*, Vol. XVI, No. 407 (April 20, 1947), pp. 695–696.

was not openly declared, was nonetheless bitter and was to set the former Allies against one another all round the world.

The break between the U.S.S.R. and the United States and United Kingdom freed France from the obligation of winning Soviet approval, and at the same time made for a more relaxed attitude on the part of the Americans and the British. The French Government therefore felt free to develop its policy in the Saar. The re-organization of the public services, begun in 1945, was continued in 1946. After the local elections,[45] the Military Governor instituted, on October 8, an Administrative Commission for the Saar territory which represented, to his mind, the first step towards a Saar government.[46] At the same time, certain modifications in the frontier, which had been suggested by Mr. Bidault, were carried out.

These adjustments followed very closely those suggested by Abel Verdier and Edgar Hector and occasioned reactions from the Allies that compelled the French Government to make further alterations. The modifications in frontiers were designed, as Mr. Bidault explained at the Moscow Conference, partly " to complete the system of communications in the coalfields by including one of the main northern railway lines which provides transport for the workmen." They would also serve to " establish a connection between the Saar and Luxembourg so as to avoid the difficulties of customs supervision and of communications." [47]

From the beginning of 1947, arrangements were made in Paris to facilitate the drawing up of measures by which the economic union should be carried out. On January 4 the *Mission de coordination des études pour le rattachement économique de la Sarre*

---

[45] Held on September 15, 1946.

[46] This Commission (C.A.T.S.) was made up as follows: Presidency and Justice, Erwin Müller (C.V.P.); Interior, Georg Schulte (S.P.S.); Labour and Social Security, Richard Kirn (S.P.S.); Economy, Heinrich Danzebrink (C.V.P.); Finance, Christian Grommes; Food, Robert Neufang (K.P.); and Education, Emile Straus (C.V.P.).

[47] *Déclarations de M. Georges Bidault, président de la délégation française au Conseil des ministres des affaires étrangères, Session de Moscou, mars–avril 1947* (Paris: 1947), p. 41.

These alterations in the frontier brought into the Saar territory the districts of Saarburg and Wadern and some of the communes of the Trier-Land district, including the town of Konz, at the junction of the Saar and the Moselle. On June 8, 1947, the communes of the Trier-Land district and of the greater part of the district of Saarburg, including the town of Saarburg itself, were withdrawn from the Saar, and thirteen communes of Ostertal, detached from the districts of Birkenfeld and Kusel, were embodied in it. In 1945, therefore, the area of the Saar was 1,924 square kilometres; on August 23, 1946, it was 2,866 square kilometres; and on June 8, 1947, it was 2,544 square kilometres. *Cf.* Appendix III, Map No. 2.

was created. This answered two purposes: it satisfied the Military Governor's desire to see drawn up in Paris a clear-cut policy for the Saar on which he could base his own actions, and it granted those responsible for German affairs their wish for greater control over this independent man.

The appointment of Michel Debré as head of the " Co-ordination Mission " also contributed to re-establishing the necessary hierarchies. This man was indeed a match for Mr. Grandval. He had the same sense of government. Like Mr. Grandval, he was fully aware of his responsibilities to his country, whose interests demanded the most extreme vigilance. Uncompromising, almost merciless when it came to defending the authority of the state, he was not deaf to the arguments of his colleagues; he knew how to temper his severity and unbend on occasion and how to adapt himself to political realities. The Military Governor therefore had in Paris a worthy equal on whom he could rely and who was a man to be reckoned with.

The intervention of the Co-ordination Mission soon made itself felt. If matters were ever to move out of the provisional stage, it was vital to be clear about the consequences of economic union between France and the Saar. It was upon this that Mr. Debré concentrated in the early months of 1947.

One basic fact emerged immediately: the economic union of the Saar with France implied political separation from Germany. As France had no wish to annex the Saar, the only logical solution was a formula providing for autonomy. The régime should be based on the principle of an independent government under the supervision of a High Commissioner. A constitution therefore had to be prepared as quickly as possible. To this end a constitutional commission was set up in the Saar on February 13. It was necessary to provide for the simultaneous organization of the administrative services in such a way that the relationship between France and an autonomous Saar was clearly defined, the degree of autonomy granted to the Saar being in proportion to the nature of the administrative control which France intended to retain for herself.

There was a basic question to be answered in the matter of the economic union proper. Under what conditions could the Saar economy be embodied in the plans for modernization? Equally, how far could France benefit from what the Saar had to give without harming those French industries that would be meeting competition? In the course of the investigation immediately undertaken by a *Commission du Plan de la Sarre*,[48] the fundamental opposition of certain interests again became very clear. The representatives of the iron and steel industries, the potteries, and the tube manufacturers expressed considerable anxiety. In their view, the opportunity now offered to eliminate dangerous competitors must be taken. If this were not possible, then steps should be taken at least to limit the effects of the competition.

In opposition to these ideas, dictated by selfish considerations of immediate gain, a coalition formed in the heart of the Commission. In this coalition were men who, like Gilbert Grandval, made it their duty to assure the Saarlanders normal living conditions and thus prevent the union from symbolizing to those whom France sought to win over merely a cessation of economic development and a general impoverishment.

The representatives of the French Government services were, for their part, opposed to a short-sighted economic Malthusianism. All of them, whether members of the Commission or of the Saar Military Government, agreed to lay down as a first principle of French economic policy in the Saar that the legitimate pre-occupation with French interests should not lead to any measures detrimental to the Saarlanders. For, if the two countries were to be considered as a whole, with identical interests, then their development and their prosperity would inevitably be intertwined.[49] If the Saar economy was to bear the same burdens as those weighing down the French economy, it had an equal right to share in the effort being made to modernize and re-equip. Besides, the Saar could play a very useful part for France in so far as she could keep up and even expand her sales on the south German market. Such an operation, even in the long run, had the double advantage of providing currency and preventing or slowing down the revival of competition from similar industries in Germany. These were

---

[48] This Commission was set up within the framework of the *Commissariat général du Plan de modernisation et d'équipement*. It held its first meeting on February 3, 1947, with Mr. Debré presiding.

[49] The discussions were particularly animated on the subject of the Saar iron and steel industries. They closed with the recommendation that Saar and French iron and steel should be merged into one and placed under the control of the same administrative body, that is to say the *Direction de la sidérurgie* in Paris. The control was to be exercised for the Saar by the future High Commissariat.

the arguments that finally prevailed, and a decision was taken to forbid any move that might systematically restrict Saar activities.

These discussions lasted throughout 1947.[50] Meanwhile the development of plans for a French administration had progressed. The powers of the High Commissioner were defined and the foundations of the organization of the High Commissioner's office laid. There were to be three chief colleagues of the High Commissioner—an economic counsellor, a financial counsellor, and a legal counsellor. To these it was felt necessary to add a cultural adviser and, naturally, an officer responsible for police matters.

As for the constitutional commission,[51] it worked with equally commendable zeal. Created by an *ordonnance* of May 23, it began its work on May 27 and finished on September 16; on September 25 it published its draft Constitution. Ten days later, on October 5, after a brief electoral campaign, the elections to the Landtag took place and these elections returned a large majority for the C.V.P., whose leader was Johannes Hoffmann.[52] The first task of this Landtag was to examine the Constitution, which it approved on November 8. But France's approval was slower to come. It was given only after the Landtag had already voted two fiscal and legal measures. Finally, on December 15, the new Constitution was officially proclaimed. Five days later Mr. Hoffmann formed the first Saar Government in which he brought together under his own leadership the C.V.P. and the Socialists. A month before the proclamation of the Constitution, the *Régie des mines* was established and the French franc introduced into the Saar as well as various economic and financial measures.[53] On December 31, Governor Grandval was appointed High Commissioner.

[50] It was only in the spring of 1948 that the principles of the economic policy for the Saar were adopted.

[51] *Cf.* Robert Stöber, *Die saarländische Verfassung vom 15. Dezember 1947 und ihre Entstehung* (Cologne: 1952). The author of this book, which is a collection of texts, is none other than Heinrich Schneider. Robert Stöber is but a pseudonym; see Bibliography.

[52] The C.V.P. obtained 51·2 per cent. of the votes; the balance went to the S.P.S. (32·8 per cent.), the K.P. (8·4 per cent.), and the D.P.S. (7·6 per cent.). *Cf. Amtsblatt der Verwaltungskommission des Saarlandes*, No. 51, October 29, 1947, pp. 514–516.

[53] Law No. 47-2158, of November 15, 1947 (*Journal officiel, Lois et Décrets*, p. 11294), was supplemented by a sheaf of other measures taken by France with a view to putting the economic union into effect. The most important of these had to do with the introduction of French prices and wages into the Saar, with the traffic of goods between the Saar territory and neighbouring countries, and with the extension to the Saar of French regulations governing foreign exchange and French organization of credit. By this same law of November 15, a re-discount bank, acting as correspondent to the *Banque de France*, was set up at Saarbrücken. Its Statute was defined by an order from the Military Governor and it took over the capital, rights, and obligations of the

So, at the end of 1947, France seemed to have achieved the aims she had set for herself. The economic union of the Saar with France was, if not quite complete, at least within reach. The break with Germany was accomplished with the agreement of the United States and the United Kingdom, thanks to the re-organization of the administration of the Saar and to the election to the Landtag of a majority, favourable to self-government, that could count on the backing not only of a Constitution but of France, watchful and protective.

In the Saar, opinion seemed favourably disposed. The Governor progressively eased the bonds that had fettered political life without loosening them completely. As early as the autumn of 1945 he had authorized the rebirth of the trade unions. At the end of the same year he permitted the re-establishment of political parties,[54] and in the course of the summer of 1946 he allowed the publication of additional newspapers. There was no opposition to the policy of economic union with France except from the Communists. On the contrary, demonstrations in favour of the decision became more numerous during the second half of 1946 and all through 1947. The extension of the French customs barrier to the frontier gave rise to no adverse comment, again with the sole exception of the Communist Party.

The only political argument of any significance was that which set the M.R.S., that is to say the partisans of political union, against the partisans of economic union within the framework of political autonomy. The M.R.S. stated its case forcefully on various occasions. It had influential leaders, a newspaper, *Die Neue Saar*, and supporters in all parties. At least, this is what it claimed in a

Landeszentralbank Saar which was none other than the successor to the *Reichsbank*, liquidated by Decree No. 200 of February 18, 1947, by the French *commandement* in Germany.

As for the other banks, which had been sequestrated (the Roechling bank on July 30, 1945, and the others on September 29, 1947), their holdings, converted into French francs, were taken over by the *Crédit sarrois*, founded for this purpose with French capital, and by the *Banque nationale pour le commerce et l'industrie*. Very similar treatment was reserved for the insurance companies for which autonomous control was set up in the Saar on October 21 and 28. Order No. 34 of November 13, 1947, transferred the life insurance policies and the assets of certain German insurance companies in the Saar to six French insurance groups, three of them nationalized. *Cf. Amtsblatt der Verwaltungskommission des Saarlandes*, No. 58, 1947, p. 575.

[54] The trade unions were authorized by Decree No. 6 of September 10, 1945. *Cf. Amtsblatt des Regierungspräsidiums Saar*, No. 9, October 18, 1945, p. 27. The political parties were created in January, 1946; their formation had been authorized by General Koenig, by Decrees Nos. 22 and 23 of December 12, 13, 1945. *Cf. Journal officiel du Commandement en chef français, Gouvernement militaire de la zone française d'occupation*, December 21, 1945, pp. 53–54.

memorandum presented at the beginning of 1947 in which it emphasized its own strength—60,000 subscribers to its paper and 150,000 requests for party membership in the first year of its existence. What the M.R.S. wanted, and said in no uncertain terms, was " full-scale union of the Saar with France " and, to achieve this end, the formation of a current of opinion strong enough to make itself heard. The party did not envisage immediate annexation, but rather the total integration of the Saar into France after a transition period in which the Saar would be governed by a High Commissioner, who would appoint the members of the administration, and during which a " gradual rapprochement, both cultural and political " would take place. The policy they had in mind seemed to them the only one calculated to put an end to doubts and uncertainties. The memorandum maintained that there were too many interpretations of economic union and, among those who declared themselves in favour of autonomy, a mental reservation that this might leave the way open for reconciliation with Germany. " Self-government in the Saar would give the idea of a Federated Rhine State and, in the end, would lead to the re-establishment of a Greater Germany. Autonomy also means, in fact, the preservation of the right to dispose of an industrial region with a considerable war potential. It is an interim measure only, inopportune and uncertain." [55]

The supporters of economic union inevitably rallied vigorously against these attacks. Even in 1946 the C.V.P. and the Saar Socialist Party had kept their distance from one another. In a report presented to the first Socialist Party Congress on June 30, 1946, Ernst Roth stressed the complete independence of the party from the M.R.S. Some time later, Johannes Hoffmann, in a circular of September 18, 1946,[56] instructed responsible members of the C.V.P. to declare themselves in favour only of economic union so as to frustrate the schemes of those who wished to use the first meeting of the newly elected communal councils to demand political union. During the following year, these parties continued their struggle against the M.R.S. but without coming to any open breach. Apparently they were anxious not to antagonize those members who supported the M.R.S. In the Socialist Party it was Mr. Sender himself who became the spokesman of the M.R.S. in

[55] The M.R.S. memorandum was presented to Mr. Bidault in February, 1947.
[56] " Johannes Hoffmann und das M.R.S.," *SVZ*, February 3, 1956.

order to prevent denunciation followed by an open break. But the party leaders, while reacting against the attacks of the M.R.S. and maintaining their stand against political union, did not seem inclined to define their own position. Mr. Hoffmann avoided the subject of autonomy, although this was the main object of the M.R.S. attacks. Nor did the C.V.P. speak of it during the campaign for elections to the Landtag. No doubt the topic seemed to it too dangerous.

What was the position of the French Government as between the M.R.S. and its opponents who favoured economic union with self-government?

At first sight it seemed perfectly clear. France had in mind self-government for the Saar. The French note presented to the Moscow Conference in 1947 stated: " The Saar will constitute a territory whose inhabitants will have their own rights as citizens, but whose external relations will be assumed by France, as will the protection of its nationals and that of Saar interests abroad." The paragraph which followed provided that a Saar Constitution should determine the organization of all public powers. " The legislative power and the executive power will be founded on the principle of universal suffrage by direct secret ballot." It was further explained that these powers would be restricted only by provisions creating a French High Commissioner in the Saar who would be " charged with the task of ensuring on the legislative and administrative level the proper respect by the Saar authorities of the principle of economic and monetary union." [57]

The Preamble to the Saar Constitution was just as clear in stating the double principle of economic union with France and of political detachment from Germany.[58]

[57] For complete text in French, see *La Documentation française: Notes documentaires et Etudes*, No. 620, May 12, 1947, p. 38.
[58] Here is the essential of the Preamble: " Le peuple sarrois, appelé après l'effondrement du Reich allemand, à rénover les principes de sa vie culturelle, politique, économique et sociale,
    " pénétré de la conviction que son existence et son développement peuvent être assurés par l'intégration organique de la Sarre dans la sphère économique de la République française,
    " confiant en un statut international qui fixera la base obligatoire garantissant sa vie propre et son relèvement, fonde son avenir sur le rattachement économique et sur l'union monétaire et douanière de la Sarre à la République française, d'où découlent:
    " l'indépendance politique de la Sarre vis-à-vis du Reich allemand,
    " l'exercice par la République française de la défense du territoire et des relations

As mentioned earlier, it was in this spirit that the *Mission de coordination des études pour le rattachement économique de la Sarre* worked and drew up its recommendations. In its opinion, the system envisaged would resemble very closely the classic protectorate. The Saar State, or the Saar territory, would have its international personality. It would have autonomy in legal, administrative, and political matters, but a certain amount of its internal and external business would be handled by France.

It thus seemed fairly certain that the French Government had in fact opted for autonomy and wanted no part of the political integration proposed by the M.R.S. And yet the M.R.S. retained considerable freedom of action. Leaders of the opposition that developed later even claimed that the Military Government had imposed a decision that half of the members of the constitutional commission should be members of the M.R.S.[59] They wanted to know why such an important place was reserved for the M.R.S. when the latter publicly proposed an aim which was not that of the French Government, and proposed it, moreover, in a commission that was supposed to take as its terms of reference the principles laid down by France. The Military Governor indignantly denied these accusations, declaring them unfounded. It should be noted, however, that the wish to give as much support as possible to members of the M.R.S. was in evidence at the time of the preparations for the elections to the Landtag.[60]

The attitude of the French authorities to the M.R.S. thus left some doubt as to their real conception of Saar autonomy. Perhaps they had merely wished to avoid antagonizing those Saarlanders who were particularly well-disposed towards France and whose support was needed to establish the régime firmly. Perhaps they were not displeased to be able to show the Allies that they could count on a vast number of warm supporters, thus emphasizing by

extérieures du territoire avec les Etats étrangers, l'application en Sarre des lois françaises relatives au statut monétaire et douanier,

" l'attribution à un représentant du gouvernement de la République française d'un pouvoir de réglementation pour assurer l'unité douanière et monétaire, ainsi que d'un droit de contrôle destiné à garantir le respect du statut,

" une organisation judiciaire, établie de manière à assurer l'unité de jurisprudence nécessaire dans le cadre du statut." *Cf. Amtsblatt des Saarlandes*, No. 67, December 17, 1947, p. 1077.

59 *Cf.* Robert Stöber, *op. cit.*, p. 13, and Ludwig Pistorius, *Der Hohe Kommissar und die D.P.S.* (Cologne : 1952).

60 The M.R.S. did not present lists of its own but sought to introduce as many as possible of its members into the lists of officially authorized parties.

contrast the moderate nature of French political aims. Finally,
perhaps they felt, as did the leaders of the M.R.S., that the solution
to which they were committed was temporary and that they must
look ahead. It is true that this was not the view of the Military
Governor, if his firm statement of October 31, 1948, may be taken
as evidence. This statement was made at the annual Congress of
the M.R.S. at Saarlouis. He told his listeners that he had wished to
revisit " faithful friends " but that French political aims " remained
unchanged." Entrusted by the French Government with the
responsibility of guaranteeing respect for the Constitution, he would
not fail in his mission. And he added these significant words:
" Do not pursue ends that are more or less distant or fanciful, but
rather give all your attention to developing the particularism of the
Saar, the most solid insurance against destructive nationalism." [61]

This lack of firmness towards the M.R.S. was probably only a
secondary manifestation of the uncertainty that remained concerning the scope and limitations of Saar autonomy. True, it was not
a question of annexing but rather of watching over the preservation
of the territory's independence from Germany and of developing
its political liberties. It was true that France must—as one of the
men very close to the problem said—guide, counsel, and control,
but not direct. But however desirable it was to limit intervention
and control so as to avoid arousing hostile opinions, it was inevitable that precautions would be increased against the return to
power of a neighbour whom one had good reason to mistrust. So,
the measures taken were not directed solely to defending French
interests but to promoting them. The legal counsellor was to
orient Saar legislation gradually towards an adapted form of
French legislation in order to create a gulf between the law of the
Saar and that of Germany.[62] Similarly, an effort was made to
spread French culture, to give it a preponderant influence on the
radio and in the most important newspaper, and, through education, to bring about an inter-penetration of cultures in the hope that
this would attach the Saarlanders closely to France and, at the same
time, would help to extend French civilization towards the German
Rhineland.

[61] *Speeches by Gilbert Grandval.* See Bibliography.
[62] This made it unnecessary for Saar tribunals to follow closely the development of
German law.

Those responsible for French policy were probably not unaware of the contradiction between this ever-present anxiety to pervade the Saar with French influence and the declarations concerning Saar autonomy. " French policy in the Saar," wrote one of them, " must take its inspiration from two kinds of considerations which may seem contradictory: on the one hand, the consolidation of the French position, on the other, the free development of Saar autonomy." And he added, " Keeping the balance between these two tendencies must be our constant concern."

Could such a balance be kept, even supposing that it existed to begin with?

There was the further question of how the population of the Saar would react. Until now, apart from the Communists, the inhabitants had not shown any real opposition to French policy. The only important public exchanges, as has been seen, had been between supporters and opponents of political union.

It is true that censorship remained vigilant and that the Governor exercised his authority with a firm hand. During these two and a half years, he had guided the Saarlanders towards the régime adopted by France and to the principles of which he had largely contributed. The elections to the Landtag took place before the population really had the time to familiarize themselves with the Constitution, published only ten days before. In the Landtag itself, the discussion took place without apparent complications. Was this because of opportunism, indifference, or approval of the proposed status? It is very hard to know after the event, for men give different reasons for their attitudes with the passing years. The few objections raised, particularly by the Socialist Party, dealt mostly with the conditions under which the Constitution had been submitted for general approval and were directed particularly against the Preamble.[63] The objections were over-ruled by a majority of votes so compact and so well-disciplined that it was impossible not to feel that there had been some pressure.[64]

[63] Cf. *Mémoire de Parti social-démocrate allemand concernant la question sarroise*, drafted by Representatives Gerhard Lütkens and Ernst Roth. (Mimeographed brochure, n.p. or d., translated from *Die Sozialdemokratie und das Saarproblem*, containing the memorandum of the S.P.D. for the Hastings Conference, March 15, 1950.)

[64] These elections to the Landtag were the source of many subsequent controversies. *Cf.*, especially, the first *Mémoire du Parti social-démocrate allemand* and the *Denkschrift der Bundesregierung*, March, 1950.

It might therefore be asked to what use the Saarlanders would put the relative liberty accorded to them with the proclamation of the new Constitution. No one knew. Germany at the end of 1947 was still very weak, and France, ever present, was sufficiently strong to inspire respect from a tiny neighbour despite increasingly obvious internal difficulties.

2

THE START OF THE CONFLICT, 1948–MARCH, 1950

THE proclamation of the Truman Doctrine on March 12, 1947, had meant the end of post-war illusions. Thenceforth the struggle between Communists and non-Communists was to dominate international relationships and to give to the years which followed their particular "mood," the mood of the Cold War, of the Marshall Plan, of the Prague *coup d'état*, of the Berlin blockade. Hence, on both sides there was a re-grouping of forces. Through the succession of pacts and agreements could be seen an attempt to weld Europe into a political corpus, and to this ideal the Western nations pinned their hopes for a time. Fear of the U.S.S.R., aroused as much by the fact that the East European countries had been forced into line as by the activities of the Western Communist parties, pushed nationalism into the background, led to the North Atlantic Pact, and, finally, to the shift in alliances.

So it was that, four years after the end of the war, Germany took her place again in Europe—a truncated Germany, it is true, but one whose vital energy was unimpaired. Monetary reform marked the beginning of an economic recovery attributable not only to an economic policy backed by Marshall Aid, but also to the will to live and to the political stability of that part of the country which, in 1949, became the Federal Republic of Germany.

This rapid recovery of Germany inevitably had its political repercussions, all the greater because it coincided with the weakening of France. The departure of General de Gaulle was the prelude to an internal crisis that became more and more serious and threatened the hard-won achievements on the economic front. General de Gaulle was the symbol of the apparent unity that had been forged in the Resistance. His retirement, motivated by the opposition of political parties to the policies he believed he was carrying out in their name, dealt a decisive blow to the legend of the Resistance. The three-party system that survived for more than a year could not hold out after the breach between the Soviet Union and the Western Powers. From then on the Communists, out of office, were to oppress the country with the heavy burden of a parliamentary opposition representing a quarter of the electoral body, a party organized as a state within a state, supported both by legal and illegal means. The formation of the R.P.F., which, in the view of its founders, was designed to make possible a re-grouping of all political forces, found itself up against party opposi-tion, and its only achievement was to aggravate further the divisions and confusion. As for the members of the government coalition, they were themselves incapable of formulating a coherent policy, divided as they were by the implacable opposition between *dirigistes* and liberals, to which was added the old anti-clerical quarrel.

Under these circumstances, it is hardly surprising that govern-ment crisis followed government crisis. No majority emerged on which to found a policy, and the lack of authority that resulted could not fail to have repercussions on France's position in Europe and in the world at large. Eroded by these internal divisions, France was in no state to play her part as a Great Power. By placing an even heavier material and moral burden upon the life of the nation, the war in Indo-China, which was just beginning, laid bare the contrast, sharpening to contradiction, between the ends and means of her foreign policy. It is true that, to all appear-ances, the continuity of French foreign policy seemed assured in spite of government crises by the continued presence at the Quai d'Orsay of members of the M.R.P., but Robert Schuman, who suc-ceeded Georges Bidault, had to work under increasingly difficult conditions.

There was thus added to the shift in alliances a progressive alteration in the relative strength of France and Germany that had a decisive influence on the Saar question. Properly speaking, there was no Saar conflict until the end of 1947 because of the pre-dominance of France. But from 1948 the situation changed. Opposition arose which became more pronounced as Germany recovered.

The change-over in the Saar from occupation to autonomy took place, as has been indicated, with a speed that limited if it did not altogether eliminate public debate.

The economic union of the Saar and France raised technical problems for relations with the Allied Zones of Occupation which still had to be worked out with the Allies. This was done by the agreements of January 27 and February 20, 1948, which settled questions relating to coal, to reparations, and to trade between the Saar and the Bizone.[1] Plans were made for the gradual withdrawal of Saar coal from the German pool before April 1, 1949. In regard to reparations, an estimate was made of the sum to be withheld from the French share of plant and equipment.[2] As for trade with the Bizone, it was agreed that from April 1, 1948, dealings between the Saar and Germany should be treated as " foreign trade operations."

The Agreement of February 20 settled these delicate questions in accordance with the objectives of French diplomacy. Did this mean the final consent of the Allies to France's Saar policy? That was another matter. The United States memorandum on the Ruhr and the Saar, prepared for the Six Power Conference in May–June, 1948, in London, but not submitted because of French opposition, revealed the reservations in some circles in the United States with regard to the French policy. Did not this memorandum in fact envisage as a solution to the problem of control of the Ruhr the kind of solution that would be incorporated later in the Schuman Plan, one that inevitably called into question the principle of the economic union of the Saar and France? Over and above this, in October, 1948, the State Department published, in its periodical, *Documents and State Papers*, a study on the Saar by its research division, in which some of the weaknesses of the French

---

[1] *Cf.* "Accords franco-anglo-americains sur le charbon de l'Allemagne occidentale," *La Documentation française : Notes documentaires et Etudes*, No. 855, March 19, 1948.

[2] Robert Müller in his thesis, *La rattachement économique de la Sarre à la France, op. cit.*, pp. 276–277, gives precise details on this : "On February 20, 1948, France, the United States and Great Britain agreed in Berlin that the economic union of France and the Saar should result in the deduction from France's share in German reparations of a corresponding amount made up in the following way :

    (a) residual value of the Saar factories which would have been handed over as reparations if the Saar had remained an integral part of Germany;

    (b) residual value of the factories held back as surplus in Germany with a view to maintaining German industry at the level fixed by previous agreements, regardless of the separation of the Saar.

" The Berlin Protocol signed by the three interested powers fixed France's total debit at 70 million RM 1938. This sum was calculated in such a way that its relationship to the total volume of reparations in the western zones (valued at approximately 1,500 RM 1938) would be equal to the relationship between the economic potential of the Saar and that of Western Germany (about 2 per cent.). Beyond this, though this discrimination did not appear in the protocol, the negotiators were agreed that France, with the Saar debited to her share of reparations, could transfer to her own profit the ownership of the Saar factories to a value of 46 million RM, the transfer entailing no actual dismantling of plant, as was provided for in the Potsdam agreement."

position were emphasized, as well as the provisional nature of the régime set up in 1947. Concluding, the study maintained that only an international status could give the French and the Saarlanders a real sense of security.[3] But this had to await the signing of the final peace treaty. The period of waiting was to be one of constant anxiety for those responsible for French policy because the provisional nature of the régime in the Saar stimulated discussion that threw doubt on all the basic decisions.

There was scarcely any real resistance in the beginning; serious opposition was slow to appear. As has been seen, the French authorities in the Saar had the situation well in hand. But French policy could not escape the contradiction inherent in the position of a liberating conqueror. No matter how one might try to disguise it, the new Saar régime was unmistakably the consequence of a defeat with which the Saarlanders, as Germans, had been associated. It was hard to make the change from the position of conquered Germans to that of Saarlanders associated with France. The severity of the occupation itself must have made it clear to them that, as far as the French were concerned, they remained Germans.

The head of the *Mission de coordination des études pour le rattachement économique de la Sarre*, Mr. Debré, did not fail to draw the attention of the Military Government to these problems. He insisted on the need to mark very definitely the transition from occupation to autonomy in all spheres—political, legal, economic. After what might, at least theoretically, be considered a special régime, meaning that the French authorities had retained, as it were, quasi-discretionary powers, the Saar should feel indebted to France for the exercise of its democratic freedoms and individual rights. So there should be no direct intervention in the administration of the Saar territory, because constant intervention by the French administrative authorities would be counter to the interests of France. On the cultural plane, too, it was important, in the view of the head of the Co-ordination Mission, that the French avail themselves of every means " to avoid any danger of extreme positions taken by France awakening a nationalism which might later find in a resurgence of Germanism the encouragement it lacks at the moment."

[3] U.S. Department of State, "The Present Status of the Saar," *Documents and State Papers*, Vol. I, No. 7 (October, 1948), pp. 435–450.

However, complications did arise. They were inevitable. Diplomatic adaptability, discretion, tact—effective though they might be—could not mask the real fact of the *présence française*. This became obvious in the very early stages, as is borne out by remarks made at the beginning of February by one of the men responsible for Saar affairs. Paris was aware that there was a crisis in the Saar. The factors precipitating the crisis were varied. One of them was undoubtedly the introduction of the franc and the effects of this on wages and prices; but it was even more a psychological crisis, the origins of which were to be found in the disappointment some of the people of the Saar felt over the policy of economic union. They had had a very different idea of it, and had imagined that there would be a much more noticeable difference between occupation and autonomy. The question was, what could be done under these circumstances? One solution was to follow the lead of Gilbert Grandval, who sought to give more importance to the Saarlanders. Were they, then, to be granted ownership of the mines? Or might they be given more freedom in certain aspects of economic life? Impossible. Such a solution ran the risk of endangering French interests. It was rather in the *form* of the relationships that a remedy, or at least an easing of the situation, must be sought. The change of régime had not been sufficiently marked. The Military Government " took over office from itself: same men, same methods." Thus changes would have to be made: officials dismissed, the buildings that had housed the Military Government abandoned, the administration eliminated or completely transformed. " In short, the official life of the Saar should be completely changed and everyone should not have the right to give instructions to a Saar Minister." All this must be done in such a way as to destroy the atmosphere and way of life of the occupation to which the civilians, as well as the military, had become accustomed. Furthermore, the proposals continued, the Saar parliamentarians should be given work and kept occupied. " The *Mission juridique* must keep feeding them projects." Finally, it would be a good thing to encourage the increasing participation of the Saarlanders in such enterprises as were not exclusively reserved to the French.[4]

---

[4] It should be noted that, on January 1, 1948, an administrative re-organization took place in conformity with the modification of the status of the Saar and the Saar's

A firm stand on the substance, concessions on the form. The fundamental interests of France should not be lost sight of, but once these were assured, the Saarlanders should be given the greatest possible freedom of action, the framework being as discreet as possible. If the policy was easy to define, it was much more difficult to carry out. There was no doubt that Mr. Grandval shared the opinions expressed—he may even have been responsible for them—as to what should be the attitude of French officials towards the people of the Saar, and most particularly towards those having responsibility for the administration. Had he not drawn up, as far back as the end of December, 1945, a departmental memorandum, a genuine reprimand to those of his colleagues who, without any sense of the respect due to a high Saar official, had taken upon themselves to instruct the *Regierungspräsident*? The High Commissioner was equally in agreement on the necessity of cutting down the French administrative services [5] and of appointing more Saarlanders to senior posts.

On this latter point, however, he came up against a serious obstacle which he was not the only one to notice, namely, the shortage of qualified Saar personnel,[6] a real shortage which had the further disadvantage of giving a number of French civil servants who happened to find themselves in the Saar because of the occupation an excuse to cling to their posts.

But the major obstacle to the application of the method envisaged in Paris was to be found in the character of Mr. Grandval himself and stemmed from his very virtues. A statesman before he was a diplomat, he could not fail, even as High Commissioner, either to make the presence of France felt in the Saar or to make that of the Saar felt in France.

A process of identification took place between the man and the place that was in his charge, and this led him to give the Saarlanders the means of reinforcing their position both materially and

relationship with France. A new Department—a special branch—for the Saar was created within the European office of the Foreign Ministry; Mr. de Bourbon-Busset was appointed Deputy Director.

[5] Some of the Departments created by the Military Government had already been abolished or reduced by 1948. This policy was continued in the following year. The total personnel attached to the High Commissariat or under its jurisdiction (including teaching staff) was 712 in June, 1948. Of these, 500 remained in April, 1950.

[6] The same observation was to be made later by the Germans when they sought to establish more sustained contacts with the Saar. It was not only technical personnel that was lacking. In political circles there was a shortage of men of real worth.

politically,[7] risking certain sacrifices at the expense of what Paris felt to be France's basic interests while allowing his influence on the political life of the Saar to be much too apparent.

This attitude aroused a double reaction: inside the occupied region the inhabitants tried increasingly to escape from French influence; in France itself, and particularly in Lorraine, the French feared that the advantages demanded by Mr. Grandval for the Saar might harm their own interests.[8]

Finally, was Mr. Grandval the right man to carry out the policy that the Foreign Ministry had in mind? Was he not already too branded by his role of Military Governor to succeed himself in office by becoming High Commissioner?

Analysis of the psychological causes of uneasiness in the Saar should not, however, distract attention from the economic causes.

The measures the French Government took to complete the economic union—the introduction of the franc at the end of 1947—did, as might have been expected, produce a shock. It was not only in the establishment of the rate of exchange (one mark to twenty francs) that the explanation lay, but equally in the lack of uniformity in its application. Thus the schedules established by the Treasury in regard to wages or rents resulted in significant modifications of the original rate. The discrepancy between the latter and the purchasing power of the mark was further aggravated by the rise in prices that immediately followed introduction of the franc. The people of the Saar found themselves suddenly freed from the very strict regulations which, under the Allied occupation, had governed the distribution of goods and prices, and at the same time provided with a valid currency. They therefore sought to

[7] Thus Mr. Grandval was a supporter of the nationalization of the Saar mines. He felt that it was a mistake to take from the control of the Saar Government the country's one source of income when it was vital to put that Government in a position to resist Germany's attraction. It was in the same spirit that in the spring of 1948 the High Commissioner formulated his reservations on the setting up of a management group for the Roechling factories at Völklingen with a controlling interest in French hands. In his view, the establishment of a management group before it was known to whom the factories would be allocated as reparations and during the Roechling litigation would amount to plundering. It would be better to wait until it was possible to create a development group in which the Saar Government could participate. The kind of solution he preferred—and he was to come back to the Roechling problem in the course of 1948—was to cede ownership of the factories to the Saar State, retaining for France a controlling share in their operation.

[8] He was accused of following a policy too favourable to Saar interests and above all of not taking sufficiently into account the legitimate demands which the people in eastern France might make on the Saarlanders (*i.e.*, indemnity for sequestration of Moselle businesses or for the despoliation during the war).

satisfy immediately their need to buy, so long repressed, and pounced upon all available non-rationed goods. Quite soon, once the buying urge was exhausted, they became aware of the devaluation that had taken place.[9]

There was keen disappointment. Instead of an improvement in the material situation, economic union had only brought fresh difficulties. Bread and staples were more expensive, supplies short. Savings were used up as fast as accounts were unblocked. Under such conditions there could be no question of holding anything in reserve; hence a tightening of credit. So everyone was affected in one way or another: the investor, the official, the white-collar worker, the labourer, and even the business man and the industrialist, all of whom needed medium- or long-term credits even more urgently because they had to re-orient their sales and purchases almost completely while at the same time trying to meet the difficulties resulting from the administrative control of their country's economy after the war.

The general disappointment found expression in numerous protests. The Communists, enemies of economic union, emphasized the results of the mistake. There was discontent in the trade unions. The miners' spokesmen complained not only about the repercussions of the change in currency, which they felt they had particular reasons to object to, but they also demanded a 30 per cent. wage increase and, equally forcefully, the nationalization of the mines. They maintained, in fact, that they had been promised this before the economic union as a means of gaining their support. Their demand, formulated in mid-January, 1948, was renewed again and again; it became in some measure the battle-cry of the *Syndicat unitaire des mineurs*.[10]

Criticism became more widespread during the months that followed, albeit coming from quarters favourable to economic union and collaboration with France. There were complaints

[9] The Saar newspapers reflected this disillusion. *Cf.*, for example, in the *Volksstimme* of December 10, an article entitled " Währungswechsel-Wirtschaftssorgen ": " There are today many Saarlanders who feel that we were in a better position before our currency was changed than we are now."

[10] *Cf. Volksstimme*, January 17, 1948. Two articles give details of the miners' demands. In one the writer, Aloys Schmitt, stressed that the miners who received their wages after the twentieth of the month were paid in November in French francs, but this had to cover expenses incurred in marks. The article protested against the fact that prices in the Saar were higher than in France, but that the salaries of the Saar miners were lower than those of the miners in Lorraine. As for nationalization, the writer stated specifically that he considered it " an economic basis indispensable to the political autonomy of the Saar."

about the state of dependency in which the Saar found itself. Who was actually ruling the Saar? What was the Saar Parliament doing? Where were the laws governing the country? The influence of the Central Administration was assessed. The Saar was not merely attached to France through the intermediary of a High Commissioner answerable to a *Sous-Direction de la Sarre* of the Foreign Ministry. In its daily life it was directly under the authority of the office of the Ministry of Finance or of the Ministry of National Economy, which did not see why the Saar should be considered as a special case. As a result autonomy was only an illusion, and the Saar newspapers, whether Socialist or C.V.P., said so in no uncertain fashion,[11] emphasizing not only the particular situation of the Saar, but also its right to participate in the economic union on an equal footing in all questions—fiscal matters, equality of access to raw materials, and equality of treatment in the matter of imports, exports, and credit. The Saar should also be a partner in decisions instead of their being imposed by the central authority as had been the case with the banks and the Saar insurance companies.

The Saar Government upheld these demands made in the press, and this gave rise to rather sharp skirmishes with the High Commissioner. He was caught between two fires. He was the representative of France, and he was obliged to uphold the Saar Government's efforts to make autonomy a reality and resist the French Government's tendency to centralize. He had already foreseen the crisis he had to resolve. As early as 1946, and again in 1947, he had pointed out the unfortunate consequences of the introduction of the franc in a region where prices and wages had benefited from a long period of stability, and where a break with this stability would take the people unawares, since they were not used to the monetary " gymnastics " to which the French had become accustomed. This pessimistic outlook was confirmed, not only by what might be considered a temporary crisis, but by the uncertainty caused by the weakening of the franc in the course of the year.[12]

---

[11] *Cf. Volksstimme*, April 10, 1948; *SVZ* of April 13, 20, 1948.

[12] The titles of some articles published in the course of the second half of 1948 are significant: " Preissteigerung beunruhigt die Bevölkerung " (" Rising Prices Worry the People "), *Volksstimme*, September 18; " Mahnung zur Ruhe und Besonnenheit " (" A Warning to Keep Calm and Collected "), *SVZ*, September 25; " Im Strudel des Preissteigerung " (" In the Maelstrom of Rising Prices "), *Volksstimme*, September 28; " In der Lohn und Preiszange " (" In the Wage and Price Squeeze "), *Volksstimme*, October 7.

It was this very prolongation of the economic difficulties that in September, at the Congress of the Saar Socialist Party, precipitated the crisis which had been brewing for many long months. Ernst Roth, editor-in-chief of the *Volksstimme*, rose in rebellion against even the principle of economic union. All the current difficulties, he asserted, stemmed from the policy of separating Germany from a Saar inhabited by eight or nine hundred thousand Germans who were economically and politically bound up with the fate of Germany.[13]

These views were not approved by the majority who upheld Heinz Braun and Richard Kirn, defenders of an economic union which they were convinced was compatible with a policy of autonomy. Mr. Roth had to resign as editor-in-chief, and this was the first step in his gradual alienation from the Socialist Party of the Saar.

The economic situation of the Saar improved in the course of the following year. A report from Adolf Blind, Director of the Statistical Office of Saarbrücken, on April 10, 1949, notes in this connection that at the end of 1948 wages in the Saar had reached the levels of those in France. A report of January 10, 1950, states that in 1949 the general state of the Saar economy was satisfactory. In fact, a very remarkable recovery had taken place attributable to French policy. In the mines the labour force grew in three years from 27,000 to 60,000 and the amount of coal extracted daily from 15,000 to almost 42,000 tons.[14] During this same period the number of employees in the coal and steel industry rose from 6,000 to nearly 23,000, while smelting production increased from 11,000 to 86,000 tons, steel from 9,000 to 99,000, and rolled iron from 9,000 to 67,000.[15]

This economic recovery was coupled with a considerable reconstruction effort from which the population benefited directly, since over 50 per cent. of the allocation of building materials between 1946 and 1947 was for dwellings.[16]

The 1948 crisis, however, did not weigh less heavily on Franco-Saar relations. Close on the heels of economic integration, the

[13] *Volksstimme*, September 14, 1948.
[14] From September, 1945, to June, 1948. *Cf.* " Trois ans de présence française en Sarre," *La Documentation française: Notes documentaires et Études*, No. 991, September 13, 1948, pp. 37–38.
[15] *Ibid.*, p. 40. The study cited contains other revealing data on the recovery that had taken place in the various branches of industry.
[16] *Ibid.*, p. 72.

crisis gave rise to criticisms which until then had not been publicly voiced. These criticisms, the result of the disappointment and irritation caused by economic difficulties, were directed more or less openly not only to the practical application but also to the principle of economic union. Further, they brought out the contradiction inherent in the formula of autonomy and, even more strongly, certain contradictions of French policy in the Saar. In a fairly short space of time most of the arguments were formulated that would be taken up again in the years to come by the opponents of the policy France had adopted for the Saar. The completion, in the autumn of 1948, of the Franco-Saar Cultural Convention created further tension. The Saar Government, endeavouring to bypass Mr. Grandval by appealing directly to the Minister for Foreign Affairs, succeeded only in setting the High Commissioner against both the Saar Government and the minister.[17]

This first crisis in the Saar did not go unnoticed in Germany. It was reported in certain newspapers, although this was no new departure: from 1946 onwards, the German press had carried criticism of French policy in the Saar. Some of the papers protested on the ground of the need to maintain the political unity of Germany. Others stressed the apparent contradiction between a policy of indirect annexation and the great ideal of internationalism. There was scepticism and regret over a decision that weighed heavily upon Franco-German relations. At the end of 1947 and the beginning of 1948, there appeared more vigorous comments on the " protectorate " set up in the guise of autonomy, while at the end of the year attention was called with much satisfaction to the opposition that was growing up inside the Saar itself.[18]

[17] It appeared that Mr. Grandval, under pressure from the Saarlanders, had refused to allow certain concessions which Robert Schuman had permitted over his head. But the difficulty of his position was even more clearly shown by an incident which occurred concerning the inclusion of the Saar football team in the French football league. This was provided for in an article of the Cultural Convention. Mr. Grandval, who attached great political importance to the establishment of close ties between Saar and French sportsmen, met with resistance from sporting circles in Alsace and Lorraine. He made numerous representations to the Minister for Foreign Affairs. Mr. Schuman ended by giving way to Alsatian pressures, which angered Colonel Grandval, and a certain tension resulted. This matter was of rather secondary importance, but it has been quoted here to give an example of the influence sport can have on international relations. It is sufficient to note Heinrich Schneider's shouts of joy when he learnt of the setback to the negotiations regarding the admission of the Saar footballers into the French league.

[18] *Cf.*, among others, *Frankfurter Neue Presse*, November 3, 1948; *Christ und Welt*, end of 1948.

As to the political parties, they had already decided on their attitude. On September 23, 1946, Kurt Schumacher had declared that he could not approve the statement of Secretary of State James F. Byrnes concerning the Saar. At the beginning of 1947 (on January 4), the German Socialist Party had sent a telegram to the *Section française de l'internationale ouvrière* (S.F.I.O.) to remind it that the Saar problem must be settled in some way which took into account the need to preserve German unity just as much as the legitimate requirements of France. From then on there were periodic statements from the Socialists expressing open opposition to all attempts to separate the Saar from Germany. The Christian Democratic Union expressed the same views.

The position in which Germany found herself, and the limitations imposed by censorship, forbade, it is true, the expression of any sustained opposition. Moreover, the problem of the Saar was not the most urgent one for Germany.

However, responsible circles were preparing for the eventual negotiation of a peace treaty. It was with this goal in mind that the Friedensbüro was set up in Stuttgart. To this Friedensbüro was added a " Saar office " under the control of Gustav Strohm who, before 1935, had been the deputy to the head of the Saar Office of the German Foreign Office.

It was around this nucleus that a Saar policy was to develop. It was inspired by one man in particular, Fritz Hellwig, a Saarlander by birth. Before 1935, Mr. Hellwig had already had an opportunity to show his attachment to Germany. Returning from prisoner-of-war camp in the summer of 1947, he took up the struggle again and contacted the Friedensbüro, which entrusted him with a study of the economic ties between the Saar basin and its neighbours.[19] Mr. Hellwig acquitted himself of this task with a competence that quickly made him one of the greatest specialists not only on the economy of the Saar but on the whole Saar problem. This intellectual to whom different types of people turned was also a man of action who was to fight for some years with remarkable zeal for the return of his country to the German Fatherland.

---

19 The mission entrusted to Mr. Hellwig was defined as follows: " The investigation will be directed to the political consequences in order to ensure that, in the interests of the Saar, the Saar economy, Franco-German economic relations, and a new order for Europe as a whole, any unilateral solution in the Saar is avoided since the transitory advantages anticipated by one side would place a burden on the other partner in the interdependent economy of the Saar."

From 1947 onwards he was to be found wherever an effort could be made or action taken towards ensuring a German Saar. It was through him in particular that, in the summer of 1948, contact was established between Mr. Strohm and Heinrich Schneider of Saarbrücken. Before 1935 Mr. Schneider had fought passionately in the struggle for the return of the Saar to Germany. A member of the National Socialist Party since 1930, he seemed to lose some of his enthusiasm after Hitler's victory.[20] Nonetheless, he was branded by his political past and, although he returned to the Saar in April, 1946, he had to wait until the beginning of 1950 before obtaining authorization to re-open his legal practice. Unable to take an active part in politics, Mr. Schneider followed events as an onlooker preparing to take up the struggle again at the first available opportunity. When in July, 1948, the *Stuttgarter Rundschau* publicly raised the question of whether Germany had lost the Saar, Mr. Schneider, using a *nom-de-plume*, at once replied in the negative. Contact was established. MM. Hellwig, Strohm, and Schneider worked together from then on with the support of another Saarlander, Richard Becker. They were not alone in their struggle. The Friedensbüro was in fact in close contact with Karl Arnold, the President of the Council of Ministers of North Rhine-Westphalia, and his collaborator on foreign affairs, Theo Kordt. Mr. Arnold, responsible for the policy of the *Land* most directly concerned with the problem of the western frontiers of Germany, made it his main concern to find a solution for the Ruhr that would do justice to German interests and at the same time be acceptable to the Allies.

Now, while Mr. Arnold was working out his own plan, he became aware of an American plan, published in December, 1948, by Stephen Raushenbush in the series of publications of the Public Affairs Institute. Two months earlier, the State Department had made public the memorandum on the Saar that has already been mentioned. Mr. Arnold took advantage of the opportunity offered him to give favourable publicity to his own ideas by using these American texts, reproduction of which was officially authorized. The United States memorandum on the Saar was translated into German with the aid of the *Friedensbüro*; it appeared in June, 1949, with an introduction by President Arnold and an appendix—

[20] He was even expelled from the Party in 1937.

a summary of the American plan for control of the Ruhr and the Saar.

There was also another centre in Germany where growing opposition to French policy was crystallizing and finding expression, and this was the *Land* of Rheinland-Pfalz. This *Land* indeed was the only region that had a common frontier with the Saar. So it was very directly affected by the modifications made in the frontier between 1946 and 1949.[21] Many lines of communication from north to south as well as from east to west had been cut. Men and goods had to make long detours which meant delays and extra costs. Moreover, industries had been cut off from their sources of raw materials or from their Rheinland-Pfalz factories. This was the case, for example, with the metallurgical industry of Rheinland-Pfalz, which relied on Saar coal and on iron ore from Lorraine. After 1946 this industry had to turn to the Ruhr for supplies, which involved substantial additional costs because of the greater distance involved. As for continued trade with the Saar, that was possible only at the expense of heavy taxes and customs duties. The same applied to many other industries, for between Rheinland-Pfalz and the Saar very close economic and political links had been forged in the past.[22] Their economic co-operation had involved an interchange of persons and especially of workmen between the poor areas of the Palatinate and the over-industrialized areas of the Saar. To these ties must be added those of blood and of friendship, which were many. The presiding minister, Peter Altmeier, was himself a Saarlander by birth. Another example is that of Alois Zimmer, one of the first if not the first, apparently, to oppose the policy of Johannes Hoffmann. He was born in the Saar as was his wife; both grew up in the Saar, and it was there that most of their relatives still lived.[23]

Thus, on both the material and the personal planes, Rheinland-Pfalz had many contacts and many ties with the Saar. It is not surprising that it felt the need to safeguard the interests of Germany in that region, over and above its own interests. But only slowly

[21] Between the years 1946 and 1949, Rheinland-Pfalz was bereft of 102 communes or parts of communes, covering an area of 662 square kilometres and with 65,698 inhabitants, not counting the former Saar basin as defined between 1920 and 1935. *Cf.* Paul H. Kaps, *Rheinland-Pfalz und Frankreichs Saarpolitik nach 1945* (Kaiserslautern : 1955), p. 54.

[22] The two provinces had been placed under the political responsibility of one *Gauleiter* after 1935, though remaining two separate administrative units.

[23] Mr. Zimmer was President of a section of the C.D.U. in the Landtag of Rheinland-Pfalz from 1947 to 1951.

did those in charge of the conduct of affairs come to express their opposition to the policy of Mr. Hoffmann in the Saar. They still had points of agreement with him in 1946–1947. His refusal to take part in the conference of the *Länder* at Munich, on June 6, 1947, foreshadowed a break in relations that was not to take place finally until the autumn of 1948, a break that was due in no small measure to the pressure brought to bear by Mr. Zimmer. At the beginning of 1949 Mr. Altmeier intervened personally with the French Foreign Minister. He took advantage of the opportunity offered by an interview with Mr. Schuman to raise the question of the frontier between the Saar and Rheinland-Pfalz.[24] Mr. Schuman replied that the question would be settled when the peace treaty was drafted, and that in any case France had no wish to annex German territory. Mr. Altmeier was not, however, satisfied. Remembering that the first adjustments of the frontiers in 1946 had been presented as mere administrative changes, Mr. Altmeier's scepticism was not surprising, nor was the close attention with which those in charge of the state of Rheinland-Pfalz followed all matters relating to the Saar. Their sense of responsibility was to continue even after the creation of the Federal Republic.

There remained one further hub of resistance, which was to be found in the ecclesiastical circles. At a very early date the Bishop of Trier, whose See included four-fifths of the Saar,[25] proclaimed his opposition to any policy tending to separate the Saar from Germany. In his pastoral letter of March 15, 1947,[26] he declared that devotion to duty strengthens when one's country is in danger. Those who abandon their country for selfish motives are acting against true Christian principle. The Bishop of Speyer, whose authority also extended over part of the Saar, adopted a similar attitude, albeit in a less categorical fashion.

Faced with this hostility, the French Government reacted. It forbade the Vicar General of the bishopric of Trier access to Saar territory, while negotiating through diplomatic channels to obtain from the Holy See the separation of the Saar from the dioceses of Trier and of Speyer and the setting up of a bishopric at Saarbrücken. The Vatican, basing itself upon established tradition,

[24] *Cf.* Kaps, *op. cit.*, pp. 22 *et seq.*
[25] The area concerned was the former Prussian section of the Saar which constituted the wealthiest part of the diocese of Trier. *Cf.* Appendix III, Map No. 6.
[26] *Cf.* Maxime Mourin, " Le Saint-Siège et la Sarre," *Politique étrangère*, Vol. 21, No. 4 (July–August, 1956), p. 419.

deemed that it would not be possible to re-organize the dioceses until the status of the Saar had been determined by a peace treaty. So, in January, 1948, the Vatican contented itself with appointing Father Michel Schulien, a Saarlander by birth, who was Director of Museums at the Lateran, as religious inspector in the Saar. A little later, on May 8, he was named Apostolic Visitor. Thus, the Holy See acceded in part to France's request while taking into account the opposition of the German clergy. It was an adroit solution but one that nevertheless served to emphasize the provisional status of the Saar.[27] It was inevitable that the Saar clergy should take sides in this struggle for or against Germany, and from its midst some of the most determined adversaries of French policy were recruited, as, for example, the priests Franz Bungarten and Landolf Wisskirchen.

In the beginning, resistance to French policy seemed to come from isolated individuals motivated by varying considerations: some saw their livelihood threatened, others were inspired by their feelings as patriotic Germans. These individual protests expressed a point of view fairly widely held in Germany, as far as can be judged by articles published in the press or statements issued by political groups, but they did not have support in economic circles until late in 1949. Neither industrial groups nor German trade unions participated collectively in any activities indicating an awareness that their interests were at stake and that they intended to defend them. As for the political parties, even if they manifested hostility to French policy, they did not actually take up the cudgels for the Saar. Manifestations of resistance therefore continued to be rather scattered.

Those in favour of active resistance to the Hoffmann Government had, at times, the feeling that they had undertaken a hopeless struggle, so great did the indifference of German opinion seem to them. The difficulty they experienced in obtaining a hearing was clearly revealed in a protracted exchange of letters between Mr. Hellwig and Mr. Strohm.

As a matter of fact, this was not surprising. In 1948 and during the winter of 1948–1949, the Germans had more urgent concerns: monetary reform, the Berlin blockade, the preparation of their

---

27 The French Government had hoped to obtain the nomination of an Apostolic Administrator, but the Vatican pointed out that this decision could only be taken at a later stage when the way for it had been prepared by an Apostolic Visit.

future constitution on which must be founded the state whose reconstruction was an essential condition of German revival. The Saar represented merely a peripheral problem that would be solved automatically once Germany was economically and politically on her feet again. " The Saar policy of the Quai d'Orsay and of the German politicians who are today at the head of the Saar Government is both harmful and short-sighted," wrote the *Echo der Woche* on July 24, 1948, on the occasion of the introduction of Saar citizenship. " It is harmful and short-sighted because the German population of the Saar will do a right about face as soon as the economic situation in Western Europe, and therefore in Germany, is stabilized." Events were to confirm the accuracy of this prediction.

From the summer of 1949, indeed, German pressure increased noticeably. The newspapers were more violent, and the articles more numerous in which it was recalled that the Saar question could not finally be settled until a peace treaty had been negotiated. Kurt Schumacher returned frequently to this theme with all the passion for which he was noted. On July 16 Mr. Altmeier, President of the Council of Ministers of Rheinland-Pfalz, stressed the German character of the Saar and recalled that it was the special task of the people of the Rhine and of the Palatinate to preserve for Germany what rightfully belonged to her. Some days later, Theodor Heuss, President of the F.D.P., and Jakob Kaiser reminded the public in a restrained but firm manner that the Saar question was not finally resolved,[28] and this was reaffirmed by Konrad Adenauer on October 5.[29]

Meanwhile, Mr. Strohm, his friends, and the German Friedens-büro redoubled their efforts to organize resistance among all those opposed to French policy. They had in mind an association of Saar interests to be supported and financed by firms having interests in the Saar, or a *Saar-Verein* in which Germans expelled from the Saar would unite. In so far as political aims were concerned, these

[28] July 22, 30, 1949.
[29] *Cf.* Gustav Strohm, *Skizze für ein deutsch-französisches Abkommen betreffend das Saarland* (1949). (Mimeographed.) The memorandum recalls the declarations made on January 7 and October 5, 1947, by the Chancellor in his capacity as President of the C.D.U., especially these: " This excludes any annexation. Moreover, the right of the Saar population to self-determination is undeniable. This is also true in regard to the so-called economic separation. This right of self-determination can only be exercised by a free and secret popular vote. If economic integration means—as I am afraid it does—that the Saar region will be completely separated from the German economy, then it is a unilateral and arbitrary decision."

were still rather fluid. On one point, however, everyone was agreed: a political break between the Saar and Germany must be prevented, and this meant a struggle against autonomy for the Saar. Economic ties with France were not to be excluded, and, in fact, were to be encouraged. A memorandum drawn up by Mr. Strohm, after an interview given by Guy Mollet in Strasbourg on August 23 in which he reaffirmed his party's opposition to annexation, contained the germs of a solution designed to reconcile the economic union of the Saar and France with preservation of the Saar's political links with Germany.[30] Mr. Strohm himself, however, did not seem to believe in this solution. For him it was to be only a means of starting the discussion of the problem and of bringing the French to give up their economic domination. But other voices were raised expressing the desire for compromise. The theme of European unity, which had taken political shape after the spring of 1948, served as a starting point for repeated calls in the German press for men to transcend nationalism and to make the solution of the Saar problem an example of this new spirit.

The German Government for its part remained cautious. There was no word about the Saar in the government's first official statement, and this was a bitter disappointment to Mr. Strohm and his friends. They then tried to make the new leaders in German politics understand the need to take a definite line. On November 5, 1949, a meeting took place in Heidelberg attended by Mr. Strohm, Mr. Kranzbühler (the lawyer for the Roechlings), Mr. von Gemmingen, Max Roechling, Fritz Hellwig, Theo Kordt, and a nephew of Hermann Roechling, Wilfried Sarrazin At the meeting it was decided to approach Minister Eberhard Wildermuth, with whom they were on good terms. Through him and other members of Parliament whom they approached at the same time they sought to draw the attention of the Federal Government to the situation in the Saar and to the danger that lay in an over-guarded attitude towards it. The French Government, it was felt, was trying, in its negotiations with the Saar Government, to make Saar autonomy a reality and thus present Germany with a *fait accompli*.

These steps were taken with a definite knowledge of the situation in the Saar and of the state of relations between the Saar and France. Since the first half of 1949, the Quai d'Orsay had sought

---

[30] Strohm, *op. cit.*

to consolidate its position in full realization of the frailty of the Saar status. In spite of all efforts to reach a clear-cut solution and to effect a permanent break in the Saar's political relations with Germany, it had proved legally impossible to emerge from a provisional state of affairs until the signing of a peace treaty. Certainly the Western Allies had bowed before the French decision to go ahead with economic union. They had ratified the measures taken, but nonetheless they reminded France that nothing was final until the peace treaty had been concluded. The Holy See had adopted a similar attitude, and the French Foreign Minister found himself compelled to act accordingly.

Now, this prolongation of a temporary régime not only kept the Saarlanders in suspense but, by the very fact that nothing was final, called into question all the decisions already taken. The changes in the political climate, in the relationships among the Allies on one hand and among the victors and vanquished on the other, together with the improvement in economic conditions, all made it more difficult to maintain a state of affairs built on a unilateral decision. Thus, there was to be an endeavour to substitute a contractual agreement for a régime based solely on the superior strength of victor over vanquished.

The High Commissioner, who had had a difficult year and who knew better than anyone the criticisms levelled against France, was anxious that a move be made to consolidate his country's position as much on the international level as within the Saar. Thus, in the spring of 1949 he formulated certain proposals addressed to his own government. If France wanted to remain in control of the operation of the Saar mines, the railways, and the iron and steel industry, if she wanted to retain authority over credits, insurance, currency, and customs and strengthen her position in the cultural sphere—in short, if she wished to preserve the existing status of the Saar—she must agree to make certain concessions. France would have to grant the Saarlanders more independence, widen the scope of their sovereignty to include the ownership of the mines, ease conditions of trade between the Saar and Germany, and change the High Commissioner's office into a French delegation headed by an Ambassador.

These suggestions were not the only ones the High Commissioner made. During this same period, he intervened several times with the government, and particularly with certain departments, to instil in them greater understanding of the special situation obtaining in the Saar. He felt that the Central Administration was paralysing his efforts. How could the Saarlanders be expected to maintain an economic union if France did not honour her own obligations and if she did not give the Saarlanders the Marshall Aid plant and equipment to which they were entitled?

The Minister for Foreign Affairs did not remain deaf to the arguments put forward by the High Commissioner in favour of a relaxation of French policy. He was particularly responsive to the proposal that the Saar be given ownership of its mines.

A legal study of the French claims to the Saar mines showed how flimsy they were. It would be difficult, it was believed, to substantiate French claims to ownership once the peace treaty with Germany was concluded. In these circumstances it seemed better to envisage a solution that would grant to the Saar the bulk of the assets of the former Reich in its territory. The Saar would be in a better position than France to achieve ownership of the mines during the peace treaty negotiations. If France opted for this solution, however, it was important to take advantage as soon as possible of something that could still appear as a concession, for it was well known that the better informed Saar circles became about the situation, the more aware they were of the legal weakness of the French position. In exchange for recognition of Saar rights to ownership of the mines, it was believed, there should be a long-term agreement entitling France to operate them. This agreement, in short, would permit continuance of the existing organization of the *Régie des mines*, and the Saarlanders would not have " any rights whatever in the management of the workings of the Saar basin."

The Minister for Foreign Affairs did not rely merely on this commentary regarding the question of ownership of the mines but considered the problem as a whole. Experience had demonstrated that the idea of economic union, insufficiently defined in the texts, lacked precision and thus gave rise to differing interpretations. He recognized that the Central Administration had imposed on the Saar an economic structure adapted to France. The result had been an expansion of the duties of the High Commissioner's office and a relegation of Saar administration to a purely nominal role. It was, therefore, high time to modify a policy that the improvement in material conditions had rendered invalid—an essential modification if the Saarlanders were not to be swayed by the increasing pressure put upon them by Germany. Indeed, it was noted that " as conditions of living improve in the three Western Zones, the Saarlanders lose sight of the considerable material advantages that economic union with France has brought them."

The fact that the status of their country had not yet been settled by international agreement, coupled with the reticence of the United States and the United Kingdom, made the Saarlanders suspicious. Thus, if the power of German attraction was to be attenuated, it was essential to make an effort to support the individualism of the Saar and to associate its inhabitants with the government of a territory whose sovereignty was expanding. This objective, moreover, could be strengthened by the admission of the Saar to the Council of Europe. Mr. Schuman discussed this possibility at a press conference before his departure for the Ten Power Conference in London.[31]

The change in policy envisaged by the Quai d'Orsay may seem, at first sight, rather modest, for it was indeed towards just such an autonomist solution that the French Government had directed its efforts since 1946. It might almost be said, in the words of Senator Debré, that it was a question of a new step " logically following the policy of the last four years." [32] However, if the interpretation of autonomy in actual practice is compared with new proposals put forward by the Quai d'Orsay, the distinction becomes clear. In fact, the French Central Administration, despite the advice of the *Sous-Direction de la Sarre* in the Ministry for Foreign Affairs, had treated the Saar as a part of metropolitan France, imposing upon it a sort of protectorate. Now real self-government was proposed.

Why this change? Was France subjected to Allied pressure? It did not appear so. To German pressure? The Federal Republic did not come into existence until the autumn of 1949; only the German press and the political parties had expressed opposition. Was France, then, subjected to pressure from within the Saar? Had not the recent communal elections given 49.7 per cent. of the vote to the C.V.P. and 31 per cent. to the Saar Socialist Party, both officially favourable to the régime set up by the 1947 Constitution? And, apart from a few outbursts of bad temper, there was

31 *Cf. L'Aube, Le Monde, Le Populaire*, May 3, 1949.
32 *Journal officiel, Documents parlementaires, Conseil de la République*, November 7, 1950, Appendix No. 723, p. 909.

no evidence of any real hostility. A clue may be found in the comments of the Frenchmen responsible for Saar affairs. They proposed that conventions be negotiated with the Saarlanders while France was still strong and before the Saarlanders became aware of the weakness of the French legal position.

It might be deduced that the new direction of French policy came from the realization by those Frenchmen directing Saar affairs of the difficulty of obtaining agreement to their formula at the peace table and from a desire to make use of the advantage victory had conferred upon them.

The time for exploiting that victory was now past. The complete change that had come about in relations with a Germany in process of becoming an ally even before the problems arising from her defeat had been resolved transformed the settlement of outstanding questions into negotiations. At a time when the Soviet threat was compelling the West to think in terms of a re-grouping of forces achieved by surmounting the barriers of old national quarrels, how could the theme of European unity be held compatible with the subordination of the Saar to French interests?

The decline in a policy based on strength gave new validity to the legal arguments. This was exactly what the Minister for Foreign Affairs realized. Hence his move to retreat. For it was indeed a question of retreat. The French Government passed to the defensive, even before being driven to it by a resistance in the Saar, which it had deemed difficult to overcome,[33] or by strong pressure from Germany. Its defensive position was not merely the result of giving in to its legal conscience; the French Government no longer had the strength to pursue its policy of 1945–1948. France now lacked the means to carry out a major policy. Her freedom of action was sharply restricted. She could not do without the support of the United Kingdom and the United States. The simple fact that the governments of London and Washington had left the question open obliged France to take precautions that would not have been necessary had she had at her disposal the means that the Soviet Union, for example, had. The latter had been and remained strong enough to disregard legal scruples.

---

[33] Mr. Grandval, considering the position of the Saar and the attitude of the Saarlanders towards France at the beginning of 1949, was fairly optimistic. He pointed out that if it were ever necessary to organize a plebiscite to consolidate French policy in the Saar and to please the Allies, it would be advisable to hold it without delay, though he was not, in fact, in favour of a plebiscite.

But it was not easy for France to withdraw. It was even less easy because she demanded substantial recompense for the concessions she was preparing to make. Was this surprising? The Frenchmen responsible for Saar affairs had, above all, their own national interests at heart. They could not forget that the Saar had been, and remained, a form of security given to them at the end of a war not of their making. Their consciousness of the weakness of their legal position did not stifle a conviction that they had a right to fair compensation, and that the resources of the Saar were essential to the maintenance of the balance of power between a reviving Germany and their own country.

There was an underlying contradiction in this argument that was to weigh heavily upon French policy: the French were trying to obtain compensation that they deemed rightfully theirs, but their claims were based on a situation that had been created by unilateral decisions. This situation was becoming increasingly unfavourable to France because of the progressive modification in relative strength. The consequences of this contradiction soon became clear when France entered into negotiations with the Government of the Saar.

The French aims can be defined as follows: (1) to give to the economic union between France and the Saar a contractual nature; (2) to hand back to the Saar Government certain prerogatives exercised till now by the economic bureau of the High Commissioner's office; (3) to reduce considerably the complement of the economic mission. But at the same time it was proposed to strengthen the French position in all fields, especially in the mining and the iron and steel industries. In regard to the mines, the convention to be negotiated had to imply, in exchange for recognition of the Saar's claims to ownership, France's right to work the seams over a long period without any interference from the Saar Government. It was at this point, December 2, 1949, that the Director-General of the *Régie des mines*, Robert Baboin, concluded an agreement with the Director of the *Houillères du Bassin de Lorraine* concerning the Warndt area.

With regard to the railways, the convention was likewise to acknowledge the Saar Government's ownership of the network on the one hand and, on the other, the leasing of the railways to the *Société nationale des chemins de fer français*.

The French proposals were drawn up during the autumn, but

actual negotiations took place from February 8 to March 3, 1950, in Paris. The proposals received the approval of the Hoffmann Government after difficult negotiations. Might not Mr. Hoffmann be, as his opponents maintained, merely a tool of French policy? The man, however flexible he might be, even perhaps " opportunist," had, nonetheless, a policy of his own. He knew how to put his views to Mr. Grandval when need arose and did not hesitate to tell him of the adverse reactions his policy sometimes aroused.

He considered autonomy feasible and even desirable. So the French proposals suited him, designed as they were to turn this autonomy into a reality and to give it a political foundation. Besides, he was far too deeply committed to the struggle to retreat now. He had burned his bridges. He therefore supported the French proposals because his views and his interests happened to coincide with those of the Government in Paris; and he found in his Parliament solid majority support.

Opposing views, however, did exist, so strong that they might even be considered as the beginnings of an active " resistance " to French policy. The reactions in 1948 had signified disappointment but had not meant that battle was joined. Until now, opposition had come from individuals and had been scattered. It came from a few men whose material interests or feelings were affected. Was not Heinrich Schneider perpetually complaining that he was alone in the struggle? Those who were too heavily branded by the past to be considered capable of being assimilated into a French Saar were sent away as a preventive measure [34]; other expulsions followed in the case of men who, like Father Bungarten, had openly expressed their sympathy with Germany. The Hoffmann Government did not hesitate to take strong measures to impose its authority. At all events, if certain pessimistic remarks of Mr. Strohm and his friend Mr. Hellwig are to be believed, those Saarlanders who complained of the régime when in Germany held their peace when they were at home again.

This time open hostility broke out. As soon as the news of the negotiations on the Conventions was reported in an article in *Die*

---

[34] These expulsions provoked violent discussions; they appear nevertheless to have been less numerous than was claimed on all sides. According to certain indications, between 1945 and 1949, 668 heads of families (2,171 persons) were expelled. From 1948 on, an amnesty was proclaimed. It was recorded that in the spring of 1951 there were only 193 heads of families still deprived of the legal right to re-enter the Saar. These figures are not very high, especially when the very sharp reactions to the National Socialist policy are recalled.

Saar-Wirtschaft, in May, 1949, there was unrest in the trade unions. On August 3, 1949, the *Syndicat unitaire* took its stand against the plan to surrender the mines and the railways on lease to France. On October 31 a committee of twenty-four of the *Syndicat unitaire des mineurs* complained of the presence of too many " non-Saarlanders " in the administration of the mines. On November 13 a resolution against the transfer of the mines was adopted by the miners of Sulzbach. In the early weeks of 1950, the protest movement became even stronger; on January 26 the *Syndicat unitaire*—and it was not the only one to do so—protested against the law on the security of the State. During the negotiations in Paris in February, the representatives of the *Syndicat unitaire des mineurs*, Paul Kutsch and Aloys Schmitt, obstinately opposed the surrender of the mines for psychological reasons.[35] The union wanted no part of a French group which would be a state within a state. The surrender of the mines on lease implied also the transfer of the miners, which could not fail to lead to conflicts with the workers and to a new wave of nationalism as evidenced by the experiences of 1920–1935. It objected to the French plans; its representative could not accept as a basis of discussion a counter-proposal which put off a decision concerning the rights of owner-ship until conclusion of the peace treaty. It proposed, therefore, that the mines be managed by a joint Franco-Saar company. The plan seemed to make some impression on the members of the Com-mission for the Saar Mines, but it was rejected by the Hoffmann Government. This led to a break in relations between the govern-ment and the leaders of the *Syndicat unitaire des mineurs*, who left Paris in protest.[36] The Conventions between France and the Saar were signed on March 3. A few days later, on March 12, the union declared its opposition to the Conventions and was supported in its action by the *Syndicat chrétien des mineurs*. The ratification of the Conventions by the Saar Parliament on April 4 did not prevent the Economic Council of the S.P.S. from asking, on April 18, 1950, that new Conventions be negotiated giving the Saar increased independence.

[35] Aloys Schmitt had been the first to claim the promised nationalization of the mines.
[36] It would appear that the miners were not aware of the agreement concluded between the *Régie des mines* and the *Houillères du Bassin de Lorraine* about the Warndt area. On the other hand, Mr. Hoffmann knew of it, as is evidenced by his confidential letter of March 3, 1950, to Robert Schuman, stating that the Saar Government had no objection to this agreement. *Cf. Die Deutsche Saar*, No. 34 (May 30, 1956).

The opposition movement was becoming organized; it was increasing in depth and in scope. French pressure to reach an agreed settlement of the status of the Saar ended by forcing the German Government to clarify its position.

Gustav Strohm, Fritz Hellwig, and Heinrich Schneider had, as has been seen, increased their efforts in the second half of 1949 to persuade the Adenauer Government to protest against French policy. Thus they followed with the closest attention the debate in the Saar on the French Government's action. From the Saar itself came questions on the subject of the transfer of the mines on lease to France. Both Mr. Hellwig and Mr. Strohm were quick not only to reply but to give their replies the widest possible publicity.[37]

Another diplomatic effort by the French, part of the whole trend of the policy agreed upon in the spring of 1949, raised a storm of criticism in Germany. At the beginning of May, Mr. Schuman had proposed the admission of the Saar to the Council of Europe. The German press replied with a chorus of protests. Particular stress was laid upon the sharp contradiction between the repeated declarations of the French Minister for Foreign Affairs, that the final status of the Saar would be determined only when the peace settlement was negotiated, and the steps being taken, which in effect prejudged the outcome. Did anyone really think, asked one journalist, that the Saar could ever be evicted from the Council of Europe? Another denied that the Saar fulfilled any of the conditions which international law deemed requisite for the recognition of a sovereign state. The German reaction was the more vigorous because of the encouragement afforded by Ernest Bevin's lack of enthusiasm, which was even commented upon by the French press. Why should German journalists hide their feelings when they saw their French colleagues urging their own Government to act with moderation? "To make membership of the Saar in the Council of Europe a condition for the admission of Germany constituted both a political blunder and a legal absurdity," declared Henri Frenay in *Combat* on September 2, 1949.[38] Two months later, a meeting of French and German

---

[37] *Cf.* "Die Saargruben," *Materialien zur Saarfrage*, No. V (Stuttgart: Das Deutsche Büro für Friedensfragen, November, 1949). It was above all thanks to the representations made by the *Friedensbüro* that the question was discussed in Bonn at the Council of Ministers in November.

[38] Similar reflections appeared in *Le Populaire*, September 3, 1949.

groups in the European Movement [39] gave the Germans new proof of their French colleagues' desire to subordinate the Saar question to the issue of developing closer relations between the two great neighbours.

The good will evidenced in the French press, however, did not prevent the French Government from pursuing its efforts to obtain admission of the Saar to the Council of Europe. The Saar Government made an official move on its own behalf on October 31, 1949. But the Chancellor remained apparently unmoved. He was bound to be extremely prudent, as one of his colleagues explained at the beginning of November. For the present, the Saar was not one of his most pressing concerns. Most urgent was to settle the problem of dismantling German plants and to be admitted to the International Ruhr Authority. Only then would Germany be free to devote attention to her membership in the Council of Europe. [40] Moreover, because of Allied resistance, the Government in Bonn had not yet set up an Under-Secretary's Office for Foreign Affairs and so it was not yet possible to create a " Saar office " in the Chancellery. Thus the Friedensbüro had to continue its work. As for the Saar, the Federal Government had not renounced its objectives. It was fully aware of the fact that Germany had rights and that France had interests and that these two must be reconciled. It was unperturbed by the prospective entry of the Saar into the Council of Europe, feeling that this had no real bearing on the final settlement. In its opinion, this even contributed to a weakening of the French position, for the presence of the Saar in the Council of Europe limited the influence that France could exercise over Saar politics and, in addition, limited her right of diplomatic representation. Chancellor Adenauer's colleague maintained in conclusion that the study of the Saar problem must be pursued discreetly. The Chancellor was to be kept constantly informed. In the long run it would be possible to plan for a parliamentary group composed of representatives of various groups of opinion who would concentrate

[39] At this meeting which was held at Bernkastel on November 26, 27, 1959, the French were represented by René Courtin, Pierre de Felice, Henri Frenay, Léo Hamon, Claude Marcel Hytte, Fernand L'Huillier, and André Philip; the Germans by August Martin Euler, Ernst Friedländer, Günter Henle, Walter Hummelsheim, Paul Löbe, and Carlo Schmid.

[40] This reaction reflects very accurately the feelings in government circles at the time and not only those of the Chancellor. A member of the government wrote at that period: " The Government's task is to strengthen its position step by step in order to be accepted as an equal partner by the Western Alliance."

on the Saar problem. Here again, discretion was essential. The creation of a Saar association would also be useful. But it must bear a name as non-committal as possible, something like the " Association for Trade Relations Between Germany and the Saar," for instance.

Prudence as to the form, firmness as to the substance—such was the position adopted by the Government of the Federal Republic, which at the outset had too many other preoccupations to take sides openly. Nevertheless, a few months later, at the beginning of 1950, the Chancellor was to take a stand. This doubtless happened because in the meantime French manoeuvres had become more definite, and resistance had been growing in the Saar. By its very existence, the Federal Government exercised an attraction. It was towards Germany that all the opposition elements turned—towards a country that possessed the means to resist.

Thus, it was not surprising that the announcement of the Schuman-Adenauer meeting gave rise to a new outburst of activity. On January 13, 1950, shortly before the arrival of Mr. Schuman, a Saar delegation composed of Heinrich Schneider, Richard Becker,[41] and Eduard Martin of the former *Deutsche Bank* of Saarbrücken came to Bonn to hold talks with the officials of the Ministry for All-German Affairs, Mr. Strohm, Herbert Blankenhorn, and some members of Parliament.[42] The same day, Mr. Strohm prepared with Chancellor Adenauer the discussion to take place with Foreign Minister Schuman. The Chancellor seemed determined to raise the question of the Saar. He did it, moreover, to the great surprise of his opposite number from France, but he only won the promise of a definite settlement during the peace negotiations.

Although these talks were limited to declarations of principle, they nevertheless marked a stage of development: the German Government's stand was a reminder of Germany's rights.

Mr. Adenauer was quick, moreover, to indicate that Mr. Schuman's reply did not satisfy him. The negotiation of the

---

41 He had already met Dr. Adenauer in October, 1949, through friends of the Chancellor, the Sinn family in Cologne.

42 According to a note drawn up by one of those taking part, the three representatives of the pro-German opposition in the Saar had met the following individuals : (a) Mr. Blankenhorn and Mr. Mohr, during the interviews at the Federal Chancellery; (b) Dr. Strohm at the Friedensbüro; (c) Jakob Kaiser at the Bundestag and then, during the talks at the Hotel Königshof, Günter Henle, Heinrich Kemper, Robert Lehr, Franz-Joseph Würmeling, Bruno Dörpinghaus, Carl Otto Tewaag, Wolfgang Pohle, and Fritz Saenger, all Deputies or influential members of the C.D.U. In addition, there were representatives of the Administration and two journalists.

Franco-Saar Conventions, by furnishing proof of French determination to reduce the peace negotiations to a mere formality for the record, and the hostility this aroused, compelled Mr. Adenauer to make his attitude clear. On March 3 the signing of the Conventions gave him the opportunity.

Finally, on March 10, 1950, the German memorandum on the Saar appeared, a memorandum prepared, it seemed, in great haste and under the pressure of circumstances. But all the same it was skilfully drawn up to bring out the weakness of France's position in the Saar and the contradictions in her policy. The solution she had adopted was only a provisional one; everyone was agreed on this point. So said the brief historical survey at the beginning. The next chapter, devoted to the legal position of the Saar, refuted in passing the reasoning used by the French to justify economic union with the very arguments France had used in 1931 to oppose the customs union between Austria and Germany. The Saar, asserted this memorandum, was part of Germany as that country was defined by the Allied Declaration of June 5, 1945, that is to say, according to the frontiers of December 31, 1937. Consequently, the Federal Government was of the opinion that no alteration of the 1937 frontiers could be made except by the peace treaty in conformity with the Allied Declarations—the Potsdam agreement of June 5, the communiqué of June 7, 1948 (section IV), and the Six Power communiqué concerning the changes in the western frontiers of Germany.

After a section demonstrating that the Saar could maintain its economic existence only to the extent that it had access to the east as well as to the west, the memorandum proceeded to a more detailed and critical analysis of political conditions of existence in the Saar. Naturally, it challenged the interpretation that the results of the 1947 elections to the Saar Landtag indicated approval of the economic union with France and of political separation from Germany.[43] The Saarlanders had not been in a position to express themselves freely on these issues of principle any more than they had upon the Constitution, of which they had had only a fleeting glimpse before the elections. Under these conditions, why had the French Government not organized a plebiscite? It should also be

[43] " Die Entscheidung in der saarländischen Landtagswahl und bei der Verabschiedung der Saarverfassung kann nicht als demokratisch frei und unbeeinflusst angesehen werden."

noted that the circumstances in which the debate on the Constitution took place in the Landtag, and the way that certain objections were overcome clearly revealed that the Saarlanders had been led to accept a solution that did not necessarily reflect their preference and that was being upheld by compulsion. As for the Conventions of March 3 between France and the Saar, which were the subject of one section, they could not be considered, according to the Federal Government, as anything but an attempt to impose a permanent settlement of the Saar question without waiting for a peace treaty; Germany would thus be presented with a *fait accompli*. The Conventions were designed to consolidate the break with Germany while at the same time assuring France, both directly and indirectly, of a predominant position amounting to a disguised form of annexation. The Federal Government could under no circumstances accept this any more than it could admit the right of the Saar Government to agree to surrender on lease the mines which were the property of the Federal Republic. Germany's attitude in this matter was well known. Since 1946 she had made explicit reservations about any policy providing that France take over the Saar and Germany be excluded.

After this forthright condemnation of the French position in the Saar, the memorandum concluded on a more conciliatory note. It was possible to find a solution which would take into account both French interests and German rights. The creation of an " international authority " might be envisaged and account taken of the interdependence of the economic interests of the Saar, of Lorraine, and of southern Germany by means of a special customs arrangement. The Saar would thus find itself endowed with a relatively autonomous economic status which would not, however, involve political separation from Germany. Any solution must be arrived at in consultation with the inhabitants of the Saar.

The line now taken by the Federal Government might appear strange after the statements made in November by one of those close to the Chancellor. It would be an exaggeration to attribute the change in attitude solely to the influence of Mr. Strohm and his friends. Another consideration must have been at work. This was the need for the Federal Government to appear as the sole defender of the interests of the German people.

The Preamble to the Basic Law of May 23, 1949, reads as follows:

. . . the German people in the Länder Baden, Bavaria, Bremen, Hamburg, Hesse, Lower Saxony, North Rhine-Westphalia, Rhineland-Palatinate, Schleswig-Holstein, Württemberg-Baden, and Württemberg-Hohenzollern has, by virtue of its constituent power, enacted this Basic Law of the Federal Republic of Germany to give a new order to political life for a transitional period.

It acted also on behalf of those Germans to whom participation was denied.

The entire German people is called upon to accomplish, by free self-determination, the unity and freedom of Germany.[44]

Then Article 23 stipulated that the Basic Law was applicable first in the above-mentioned provinces. " It shall be put into force for other parts of Germany on their accession." This desire to be recognized as the only official representative of Germany was manifest in the text of the Constitution of the German Democratic Republic [45]; the first article defined " an indivisible democratic republic, the foundations of which are the German *Länder*." Moreover, the Constitution of the German Democratic Republic did not contain any limiting clause comparable to Article 23 of the Basic Law or to Article 146 which emphasized, as did the Preamble, its provisional nature. On the contrary, the authors of the Constitution definitely emphasized the permanent character of this Constitution.

Hence the Government of the Federal Republic could no longer ignore the challenge hurled at it. It felt bound to assert its duty to act in the name of the whole German people.[46]

Thus the French effort at disentanglement provoked a reaction from Western Germany forcing the Government in Bonn to take a stand even sooner than it had anticipated.

[44] For complete text, *cf. Constitutions of Nations*, Vol. II, ed. Amos J. Peaslee (2nd ed., The Hague: Martinus Nijhoff, 1956), pp. 30 *et seq.*
[45] For complete text, *cf. ibid.*, pp. 59 *et seq.*
[46] For this question of the *Gesamtdeutsche Legitimation* and that of the continuity of the German state, which became more and more acute, *cf.* " Die Rechtslage an der Saar," *Gutachten des Justiz ministeriums von Rheinland-Pfalz* (Mainz: May, 1954); Eberhard Menzel, " Die Diskussion über die gegenwärtige Rechtsstellung des Saarlandes," *Europa-Archiv*, No. 11 (June 5, 1954), pp. 6599–6616; Heinrich Schneider, " Die Diskussion über die gegenwärtige Rechtsstellung des Saarlandes, eine Stellungnahme zu den Ausführungen von Prof. Dr. Eberhard Menzel," *Europa-Archiv*, No. 21 (November 5, 1954), pp. 7003–7018; Klaus Vocke, " Politische Gefahren der Theorien über Deutschlands Rechtslage," *Europa-Archiv*, No. 19 (October 5, 1957), pp. 10199–10215.

France and Germany

3

THE FRENCH POSITION IS SHAKEN, MARCH, 1950–DECEMBER, 1951

WHEN Chancellor Konrad Adenauer publicly announced his government's position, a new phase of the Saar problem opened up. Until then, French policy had aroused the opposition only of isolated individuals and of various groups in the Saar and in Germany. As a result of the German decision, the conflict moved into the realm of inter-governmental relations involving, through the intermediary of the Saar, the Governments of Bonn and of Paris. The nature of the conflict changed; it widened and became more serious. Henceforth, two states faced one another in a struggle in which their prestige was at stake.

The change in the nature of the Saar conflict coincided with a new crisis in international relations. Scarcely was the Schuman Plan launched—the first attempt to put into practice a policy of European union—when war broke out in Korea. Now, the Korean conflict, while it seemed for the time being to have welded the non-Communist world together, was itself to become a cause of dissension. It divided the people in the United States who, during the winter of 1950–1951, argued passionately among themselves over the sending of troops to Europe and the recall of General Douglas MacArthur. It widened the gulf separating the United States from countries of Asia and, indeed, even the gap between the United States and her European allies. The force of American reaction was such as to arouse growing uneasiness in a Europe dominated by fear that the conflict would spread. Europe, while demanding United States protection and the presence of troops as a guarantee that she would not be abandoned, rebelled against a form of occupation that seemed oppressive. She was also afraid of being drawn in deeper than she wanted to be by an ally which was as powerful as it was enterprising. The military effort required by the situation soon became the source of further difficulties. Thus there grew up in the very heart of the Atlantic Alliance complications that weakened the Pact politically and morally at the very time it was gaining in military strength.

The reaction in France was particularly sharp. Paris had to face the possibility of German rearmament, an inevitable consequence of the threat of the conflict's spreading. Could one leave that area of Germany which was being forced to become part of Western Europe defenceless against an attack which the Korean conflict made a real possibility? If not, must France assume responsibility for her defence, thus adding to the heavy burden that the obligations of a Great Power had already imposed on her, and this at a time when the situation was becoming critical in Indo-China? Why not entrust to the Germans the responsibility for their own defence?

Faced with this conclusion, reached by the United States during the course of the summer of 1950, the French rebelled. The war and the Occupation were still too near and their memories too vivic to allow them to admit the possibility of co-operation with Germany. They did indeed try to get round the difficulty with a " European " solution by which they thought to control this ally whom they feared. But the European Defence Community (E.D.C.), conceived as a loophole to avoid inclusion of Germany ir. the Atlantic Pact, met with the increasing opposition of a public opinion stubbornly set against the idea of European integration. French mistrust of the Germans grew as the latter consolidated their strength, while France was progressively weakened by the political difficulties with which she was being overwhelmed both at home and abroad. This mistrust spread among all of France's allies, who sought to involve her in an unequal partnership. But opposition to German rearmament led perforce to a new assessment of Soviet policy. The very people who did not want an ally they feared were compelled in self-justification to minimize the danger of the Russian threat, and to stress the possibility of an agreement. They attached themselves to the formula of " peaceful co-existence ' because it satisfied their wishes rather than their expectations and offered them a means of escape from the alternative that confronted them.

Thus the European policy, born and formulated during the years dominated by fear of Russia, lost its efficacy because it no

longer seemed to answer a need at the very moment when its promoters were trying to give it institutional reality. The German
alliance implicit in such a policy crystallized resistance and banded
together a motley coalition—Communists, neutralists, nationalists
of the " classical " right, and some radicals. European integration
was to remain the focal point of discussion because the governments
which followed one another in and out of office considered it the
final aim of all their efforts. The creation of the European Coal
and Steel Community (E.C.S.C.) represented an encouraging success for the supporters of integration. But the wave of enthusiasm
was dashed. In the years after 1950 the European idea had less
and less hold on reality; it was in some measure cut off from public
opinion, which reacted to setbacks to French foreign policy with a
resurgence of national pride.

This change in climate weighed down those responsible for
French foreign affairs with a burden that grew heavier with each
passing year. The government embarked on a course of action,
but the people refused to follow, except at the price of concessions.
These concessions, adopted in the name of security or of French
interest, met with reservations in other countries; these reservations,
in turn, were interpreted in France as proof that she must surround
herself with new guarantees. Chancellor Adenauer, like Robert
Schuman, was meeting with nationalist opposition. The German
statesman was under attack, especially from the Socialists, and they
accused him of compromising the higher interests of Germany by
a collaboration from which only the French were deriving any
benefit.

Thus caught in the cogs of nationalism, the great European
project crumbled away, and the Saar found itself, by force of
circumstances, situated in the centre of the battle, a prize in the
competition. The Saar question, which until then had been discussed merely as an aspect of the Allies' German policy, now came
within the wider framework of the whole European policy of
Germany and of France. At the beginning of 1950, France still
held the advantage. Because of her presence in the Saar, the odds
were in her favour. Moreover, the signing of the Conventions put
Franco-Saar relations on the legal basis the French Government
had been so anxious to obtain; the alacrity with which the Saar
Landtag proceeded to ratify the Conventions strengthened the

feeling in France that a difficult hurdle had been cleared. Similarly, the admission of the Saar to the Council of Europe as an " associate member "[1] could be interpreted in France as indirect recognition by Germany and the other member states of the new status of the Saar.

However, the situation was not so clear as it seemed. The régime of the Saar had no definitive character. Did not the fourth Convention, for example, contain a formula stipulating that it was to regulate Franco-Saar relations " until said settlement is reached and under reservation of the ratification of said rights of the Saar Territory by the same settlement "?[2] This formula, as was indicated in the March 9 statement by the French High Commissioner, applied to the totality of the Franco-Saar Conventions that had just been concluded.[3]

In France, moreover, the few press commentaries emphasized the provisional nature of the agreement:

" This latest Convention, which maintains the present state of affairs," wrote *Le Monde* in its editorial of March 6, 1950, " will doubtless be considered satisfactory. We merely wonder whether the undertakings which it records have any permanent value, as Johannes Hoffmann announced yesterday. Are we to lose sight of the fact that his compatriots are going back on their decision of twelve years ago? "

The writer of the editorial in *Le Monde* went on to assert that it would not be easy for the Saarlanders to accept their political status as immutable:

> France has an apparently unlimited right to intervene in Saar affairs, but this right is in fact ill-defined and will have force only in its application: if it is interpreted broadly, the Saar will have quasi-autonomy; if it is interpreted narrowly, the Saar will be a kind of satellite state. Viewed even in the most favourable light, it is hard to believe that the Saarlanders will give up trying to achieve complete self-government some day.

The launching of the Schuman Plan further underlined the provisional nature of the settlement. Paul Ramadier noted this indirectly in his speech to the National Assembly on July 26, 1950,

---

[1] *Cf.* Letter No. D. 233/6, dated March 31, 1950, addressed by Camille Paris, Secretary-General of the Council of Europe, to Johannes Hoffmann.

[2] *Cf.*, in this connection, the statement of Mr. Adenauer to the Bundestag, March 10, 1950 (*Verhandlungen des Deutschen Bundestages*, I.46/1556B).

[3] *Cf.*, for English text of the Convention, Frank M. Russell, *The Saar : Battleground and Pawn* (Stanford : 1951), p. 180.

on the subject of the budget for the Saar High Commissioner's office. After praising the Schuman Plan, he said:

> The problem of the Saar, the problem of the Ruhr, these, it is true, you have not solved, and you have done well not to find a solution for them in these early days. The present regulations should remain in force, so that when the time comes to examine, this can be done in perspective and with the assistance of the new organization we have in mind.
>
> You are making this re-examination possible, and once economic frontiers become less rigid, it will take place under such conditions that the problems will change their appearance and their value, and there will be no further question of integration into the French economy or of integration into the German economy.[4]

Mr. Ramadier's speech placed in relief, perhaps inadvertently, the contrast, or rather the contradiction, between the policies that had led to the Franco-Saar Conventions and those that had led to the Schuman Plan: the Conventions had no other aim than to consolidate the French position in the Saar within the framework of the classical policy of the balance of power; the Schuman Plan was designed to lay the foundation for a united Europe.

So it was not surprising to find that the launching of the Schuman Plan heightened the uncertainty which hovered over relations between France and the Saar. The concern aroused in governmental circles in Saarbrücken by the announcement of the Plan was redoubled by fear of seeing France engage in direct conversations with Germany. The common administration of coal and steel seemed likely to call into question all over again the agreements reached between France and the Saar and, consequently, the issues both of Saar autonomy and of economic union. The opposition took pleasure in labouring this point. The COMISCO Conference at Copenhagen at the beginning of June emphasized in its resolutions on the Saar the provisional nature of the Conventions on the one hand, and, on the other, the necessity of entrusting control of Saar industry to a European inter-governmental organization.[5] This, it was claimed, was the only possible solution to the Saar problem. As for the government in Saarbrücken, it was reduced to asking itself questions about the intentions of its

---

[4] *Journal officiel, Débats parlementaires, Assemblée nationale,* July 27, 1950, p. 5978.
[5] *Cf. Volksstimme,* June 6, 1950; and *Die Verletzung Sozialdemokratischer Grundsätze durch die Sozialdemokratische Partei Saar, Denkschrift vorgelegt dem Büro der Sozialistischen Internationale von der Sozialdemokratischen Partei Deutschlands* (Bonn: February 23, 1953). (Mimeographed.)

powerful partner. The French Parliament's delay in ratifying the
March Conventions seemed to some people an indication of a new
direction in French policy. At various times the High Commissioner intervened to point out to the Quai d'Orsay the dangers of
the situation. He stressed the difficulty he was labouring under,
because the delay in ratifying the Conventions forced him to apply
the old legislation in force prior to the signing of the Conventions
and he had no power to rescind it. He emphasized the necessity of
bringing the Saar tactfully into negotiations on the Schuman Plan.
But reactions were slow in coming. Ratification of the Conventions by the National Assembly and the Council of the Republic
did not come through until October and November. As for its role
in the drafting of the Schuman Plan, the Saar Government had to
be content with sending to the Quai d'Orsay a liaison officer, in the
person of Erwin Müller.[6] This situation was doubtless forced on
the French Minister for Foreign Affairs by the desire to avoid any
German reaction which might complicate or delay negotiation of
the future plan, but nevertheless it revealed the subordination of
France's Saar policy to her efforts towards *rapprochement* with
Germany.

Robert Schuman, it is true, did not seem to see any incompati-
bility between his Saar policy and his Plan. If the régime of the
Saar had not yet achieved its final form, it was for two reasons
which he explained to the National Assembly on October 20,
during the debate on the ratification of the Saar Conventions:

> The first reason is beyond our control. The régime of the Saar
> cannot be final until there is a peace treaty.
> The second reason . . . is that . . . this régime is susceptible of evolu-
> tion in the direction of wider autonomy, especially in the matter of
> greater sovereignty over foreign relations.[7]

"Sovereignty over foreign relations"—this is a rather elliptical
formula. The Minister for Foreign Affairs defined his meaning
more clearly on November 15, during the debate on the ratification
of the Conventions in the Council of the Republic:

> Sovereignty over foreign affairs for the Saar involves certain rapid
> developments. It is to our interest to bring them about because we want

---

[6] *Cf.*, on this subject, the article of Heinz Braun in the *Volksstimme* of March 28, 1951,
which refers in particular to a letter from the Saar Government to Mr. Grandval on
November 8, 1950. It appears that the French Government did take the trouble to
inform Erwin Müller regularly of the progress of negotiations.

[7] *Journal officiel, Débats parlementaires, Assemblée nationale*, October 21, 1950, pp. 7081–
7082.

the international personality of this state to become increasingly clearly defined, and we also want the Saar's position, for example, in the Council of Europe, to be such as to enable its legitimate aspirations to be fulfilled.[8]

In fact, Mr. Schuman, in an effort to reconcile French policy in the Saar and French policy in Europe, sought to have the Saar admitted to the E.C.S.C. on the same terms as other states. Michel Debré and Léo Hamon made this clear in the course of the same debate.

The emphasis placed on the provisional nature of the Conventions, however, had several disadvantages. It made it easier for Germany to implement her policy. By declaring that the régime inaugurated in the Saar could be modified, the French Government was leaving the Saar question open and thus in fact was preventing the consolidation of its position.

This was what Mr. Debré pointed out in his report to the Council of the Republic:

> If there is one field in which French policy has been well conceived, it is the consistency of that policy towards the Saar. Indeed, we have no choice. In the months ahead, which will be decisive ones for Europe, the Government will either maintain and strengthen the policy of which these Conventions are evidence, or it will relax its efforts, and then it will not be a question of the restoration of the *status quo* but of abandoning five years of endeavour. In that case the authorization you are being asked for would be relatively meaningless. If the Government, for its part, does not consider the vote as a firm undertaking to continue its policy, this would be tantamount to asking you for a disavowal.
>
> In this context, only one phrase perturbs me in the texts that we have before us, namely, the statement that nothing final will be done until the peace treaty is signed. This poses a problem, for these words may have a double meaning; according to one interpretation, they might seem to suggest: nothing is final, everything is subject to change; in another sense, they might mean: this is only a formality, nothing will in fact be changed.[9]

Michel Debré had put his finger on the weak point in Robert Schuman's policy. By leaving the Saar out of the negotiation of the Coal and Steel Community, Mr. Schuman had merely delayed the outcome.

When the time came, he would have to be more precise about the position of the Saar in relation to the new Community. The

[8] *Journal officiel, Débats parlementaires, Conseil de la République,* November 16, 1950, p. 2939.   [9] *Ibid.,* p. 2933.

Saar Government, through the intermediary of the High Commissioner's office, pressed Mr. Schuman to make a statement and to allow the Saar to become the seventh member of the Coal and Steel Community. The Saar Government intervened several times [10] during the autumn of 1950 to obtain agreement to an interpretation of the Franco-Saar Conventions which, while open to discussion, revealed nonetheless the desire to establish and expand Saar autonomy. The High Commissioner, convinced though he was that France must retain control over Saar affairs for a little longer, nevertheless supported the efforts of the government in Saarbrücken to win recognition for the Saar at the international level. It seemed to him that the time was ripe for the new state to be accepted at a moment when the idea of sovereignty seemed to be weakening in the face of the effort to pool European resources. So he suggested certain modifications in the régime of the Saar. The Saar could thus assume its share of the military burdens imposed by defence of the European Community. There might be even more sweeping reforms looking towards installation of a chief of state and towards entrusting to the Saar responsibility for its own diplomatic representation in a certain number of capitals. [11] But most important to the High Commissioner, and to the Saar Government itself, was inclusion of the Saar among the signatories to the Treaty and, before signature, clarification of the Saar's position within the E.C.S.C. [12]

The Saar Government became insistent in pressing its demands. It was the more anxious because the long silence of the French Government added to its sense of isolation at the very moment when pressure from the Federal Republic and opposition at home became more active.

In Germany, the government memorandum gave strength to criticism of French policy in the Saar. There were many comments in the Bundestag—first during the debate following the Chancellor's statement of policy. Mr. Adenauer expressed himself

---

10 Letters from the Saar Government of November 8 and December 2.
11 Jacques Bardoux echoed these concerns during the debate on the ratification of the Conventions in the National Assembly. The same frame of mind was evident in some of Mr. Schuman's remarks during the debate in the Council of the Republic.
12 *Cf.*, in this connection, the motion adopted on December 2, 1950, by the Saar Parliament. The Saar Government would have liked to have the Saar signature constitute an undertaking quite separate from that of France, even though it were appended by a French plenipotentiary. It wanted to see Saar representatives in the Assembly but was prepared, in return, to send only an observer to the special Council of Ministers.

moderately but firmly on this occasion. He was obviously anxious
to avoid anything that would jeopardize co-operation with France
and bring about the failure of his European policy. But he refused
to accept a *fait accompli* and repudiated the Conventions. He
denied France's right to establish a régime for the Saar in agreement with a Saar Government he did not recognize, and he
protested forcefully against the procedures which, in his opinion,
the French Administration had used to ensure adherence of the
Saarlanders to its policy. He was supported by all parties. Kurt
Schumacher, as might have been expected, was even more incisive
while still stressing Franco-German understanding. He dismissed
the solution proposed by the government memorandum suggesting
an international authority for the Saar and he encouraged his
government to oppose admission of the Saar to the Council of
Europe.[13]

Between the points of view of the Socialists and the government there was only a difference of degree. While on the part of
Chancellor Adenauer, and even more in the very diplomatic speech
of Heinrich von Brentano,[14] there was a manifest desire not to
compromise the building up of Europe, Mr. Schumacher tended to
make the policy of European co-operation subordinate to the
settling of the Saar question in Germany's favour. For him the
main problem was the separation of the Saar from Germany. This
intransigence of Mr. Schumacher, who was supported by his party,
limited Chancellor Adenauer's freedom of action, especially as he
had only a very shaky majority. He was thus subjected to a pressure that was all the more difficult to resist because he himself had
publicly condemned France's Saar policy and the latest expression
of this policy—the Conventions.

Furthermore, the whole German press reiterated the declarations of the government and of the political parties. It gave its
support to the government and encouraged the government to

13 March 10, 1950. For Mr. Adenauer's speeches, *cf. Verhandlungen des Deutschen
Bundestages*, I.46/1555 *et seq.*; for those of Mr. Schumacher, *ibid.*, I.46/1562 *et seq.*;
and those of B.P. (Bayernpartei), D.P. (Deutsche Partei), Z. (Zentrum), W.A.V.
(Wirtschaftliche Aufbau-Vereinigung), *ibid.*, I.46/1574–1584.

14 "From the standpoint of German interests, and because I believe and want to believe
in the sincerity of this explanation of the French Government, I would like to advance
another interpretation, namely that these conventions have been included provisionally,
that is to say, that they will automatically cease in effect if express confirmation of
them is not embodied in the peace treaty. I believe that this interpretation is the
logical one because otherwise this explanation would be lacking not only in any
political but even in any true moral value." *Verhandlungen des Deutschen Bundestages*, I.46/1572CD.

remain firm in the position it had adopted towards France. This intervention of the press, which expressed or was intended to express public opinion, was by no means episodic in character. It was no short-lived campaign. It continued and developed throughout the year, evidence of the growing interest the Germans were taking in the Saar. The articles in the press frequently revealed a very precise knowledge of certain aspects of the situation. Naturally, they were for the most part critical and emphasized the difficulties of the Saar Government. They tended to exaggerate the importance of the opposition and to stress police interference and the pressures being exerted on the government. This was because their informants, generally members of the opposition groups in the Saar, inevitably underlined the shortcomings of the system, sometimes even dramatizing to the point of describing it as a " reign of terror." But, allowing for exaggerations, the picture they painted of the situation in the Saar was fairly accurate. German opinion could sense the hesitation that characterized Franco-Saar relations after the adoption of the March Conventions and the launching of the Schuman Plan,[15] and it became conscious of the existence of opposition within the Saar to the policy of the Hoffmann Government.

The Government of the Federal Republic derived a feeling of strength from the fact that popular pressure was urging it on rather than restraining it. The Socialist opposition pressed the government to go ahead. Neither the members of the government coalition, nor the small nucleus of Saar refugees living in frontier regions or provinces, nor the ordinary citizens with particularly strong national feelings wanted to see the Saar sacrificed to European reconciliation. Gustav Strohm, who had recently been elected to the *Bundeskanzleramt*, and Fritz Hellwig [16] had remained in touch with Heinrich Schneider and Richard Becker, who kept them informed about the progress of the struggle against the Hoffmann Government.

Through these men information was passed on to certain newspapers, to politicians, to business men—in short, to those people

---

[15] The stand taken by COMISCO also provoked a number of comments. Analyses were made of the repercussions in the Saar, the tensions created in the Saar Socialist Party and in relations between the Socialist Party and the Christian People's Party.

[16] It is known that Fritz Hellwig, founder of the *Volkswirtschaftliches Büro*, was often consulted by the industrialists and members of Parliament. He was thus in a position to give both groups information on the Saar.

who seemed to be in a position to work usefully for the common cause. From the beginning of 1950 there appeared to be a well-established liaison with the government, thanks to the position occupied by Mr. Strohm and also to regular contacts with Herbert Blankenhorn. Efforts to renew ties between German and Saar industry also began to show results. While in the spring matters had not progressed beyond an attempt to establish a centre for the exchange of information, by August the *Bundesverband der Deutschen Industrie* decided to establish, discreetly, direct contact with the *Saarländischer Industriellen-Verband*. But it did not meet with much success. No doubt the launching of the Schuman Plan had made them understand the importance of the Saar, thanks to which France could exert a counter-weight to the economic power of Germany. They became aware of the importance for Germany of strengthening the opposition in the Saar so as to limit French influence. An article in the *Industriekurier* of Düsseldorf, published on August 15, 1950, that is to say, during the very period when the Germans for their part were seeking to re-establish contact with the Saar, is very significant. It denounced the pressure brought to bear by the High Commissioner's office for the Saar on the *Saarländischer Industriellen-Verband*, whose President, moreover, was Georges Thédrel, a Frenchman, to make this organization " co-ordinate its policy with that of the High Commissioner's office."

Obviously, this was not the only channel through which the German Government and public opinion were kept informed of developments in the Saar. Mr. Schneider had other contacts in Germany, and he was not the only one. As the opposition developed, so the possibility of such contacts grew, either through the intermediary of the Socialists or of the trade unions, which did not recognize the Franco-Saar Conventions, or simply among those living along the frontiers. As for the Ministry for All-German Affairs, whose job was to protect the interests of those provinces lying outside the bounds of the Federal Republic, one can only suppose that it, too, was active, either seeking information or trying to encourage opposition to the policy of the Hoffmann Government.[17] Thanks to the support of this ministry, it was finally possible to set up an association for the protection of Saarlanders

---

[17] It is obviously impossible to provide concrete information useful to an historian on the work of this ministry.

who had taken refuge in Germany, a goal towards which Mr. Hellwig, Father Franz Bungarten, and others had been working for some years. Its intervention was to have a decisive impact on the steps already undertaken and was to pave the way, during the winter of 1950–1951, for the launching of the *Saarbund*.

The attitude of the German Government continued to be somewhat reserved. It was fully conscious of the limited means at its disposal. If it gave up its opposition to the admission of the Saar to the Council of Europe, if it was satisfied with the partial success represented by limiting the Saar to associate membership, it was because the government knew that it could not obtain more; moreover, obstinacy would only compromise fulfilment of a policy of European co-operation which was deemed to be the only means of saving Europe from the Soviet advance. The admission of the Federal Republic into the Council of Europe on an equal footing with the other member states afforded the opportunity of exerting an influence which was well worth the concession over the Saar. Furthermore, it was only a temporary concession because there would doubtless be an opportunity to draw the attention of the Council to the Saar question.[18]

And was not progress being made towards a formula of European economic co-operation which would permit solution of the Saar problem without further difficulty? Certain ministers, and by no means the least influential of them, were convinced of this prior to the Schuman Plan.[19] So no one was surprised to hear Chancellor Adenauer affirm, during the debate on the admission of Germany to the Council of Europe, that he felt that the Saar problem had lost much of its importance because the mines and

[18] One of the influential members of the C.D.U. made the following observations which are worth singling out: "If we were really determined to postpone participation until we could stipulate the terms, then we could strike the concept ' Europe ' forever from our vocabulary. There is only one political force that can assert that time is working for it. That, in my opinion, is Bolshevism, which would watch with the greatest pleasure while men in little Europe barricaded the borders and lulled themselves with dreams of national sovereignty until they suddenly awoke to find this sovereignty harshly exercised by a commissioner from Moscow.

"Nevertheless, I understand the concern of the Saar population, but I believe that we would have a unique opportunity in Strasbourg to throw the full light of publicity on the events in the Saar with no possibility of evasion.

"Whilst we are determined to co-operate at Strasbourg, that should by no means imply that we will be submissive partners."

[19] In a memorandum of January 12, 1950, Jakob Kaiser declared: "A solution to the Saar question should therefore be sought only within the framework of a united Europe: it will lose its significance once a unified Central European tariff and economic system comes into being in which it makes no difference whether the Saar exports to Germany or to France."

blast-furnaces of the Saar were included in the Schuman Plan. The Chancellor thought that the problem would resolve itself automatically when the forthcoming Saar elections were held. What, then, was the point of publishing this memorandum [20] demonstrating the degree to which the Saar was bound economically to France and to Germany respectively? However useful the study might be, it seemed to him inopportune. As far as the Chancellor was concerned, it was sufficient, for the time being, to forestall any French attempts to transform the provisional régime into a permanent one before the conclusion of a peace treaty.

This was clearly not the opinion either of Kurt Schumacher or of Heinrich Schneider who, on more than one occasion, protested bitterly against the passivity of the Chancellor and his colleagues. Mr. Schneider was amazed at the government's silence during the French debate on the ratification of the Franco-Saar Conventions. The Saar population could only draw one conclusion and that was that the Federal Government had crossed the Saar off its list of concerns.

During this period there were also Frenchmen who were levelling similar reproaches at their own government, but these revealed a very different concept of Germany's policy in the Saar from that of Heinrich Schneider. A passive attitude on the part of France might be justified, said one of them, if Germany were equally restrained. But this was not so. The effort being made by the Government of the Federal Republic to mould German public opinion was evident from the activities of Mr. Schumacher, the demand in the German press for inclusion of the Saar within the 1937 frontiers, the reservations of Walter Hallstein when the European Convention for the Protection of Human Rights and Fundamental Freedoms was signed, and the statements of certain German delegates at the Council of Europe.

This double criticism indicates fairly clearly the general attitude adopted by the two governments during 1950. Each had as its axis a European policy based on the importance of setting up the Coal and Steel Community and left the question of the Saar in the background. This did not mean, however, that they had abandoned their ultimate objectives.

[20] The document in question is the report prepared by Mr. Hellwig at the request of the *Friedensbüro*.

Opposition was growing in the Saar itself, particularly, as might be expected, in trade union circles. As soon as the Conventions were concluded, the *Syndicat unitaire des mineurs* publicly opposed them. Hostility also developed in other labour unions. Hans John, in charge of the *Syndicat unitaire des postiers*, could not bring himself to accept the Conventions and shortly after they were signed made contact with representatives of the German Social Democratic Party and with various Saar Socialists whose attitudes were hardening.

The *Syndicats chrétiens* were divided. Some of the members, such as Karl Walz and Karl Hillenbrand, who as Secretary-General held the most important post, were against the Conventions. Others, such as Hans Ruffing,[21] accepted them but at the same time attacked the French authorities and passed critical resolutions that revealed the nature, and even more the extent, of the disagreement.

All these protests had political implications. They appeared in trade union and professional newspapers in the Saar and at times were couched in fairly biting terms. Addressed to the government, they were, in fact, aimed at the High Commissioner's office, which, no matter what it did, was generally held responsible for Saar policy. Public opinion was not directed specifically and continuously against the Conventions. Criticism was levelled mostly against facts and problems directly affecting the conditions of the workers. The *Syndicat chrétien des mineurs*, for example, in a long letter requested certain guarantees of work and job opportunities on the following terms: " The production figure for the Saar mines shall be fixed at such a level that the present personnel can be kept on. France shall guarantee the disposal of the output. Hours of work shall not be less than those in the Lorraine mines." [22]

The letter went on to insist that Saar workers should be accorded the same treatment in regard to wages and conditions of work as that obtaining in France, especially with reference to their neighbours in Lorraine. Furthermore, it returned to the delicate matter of the distribution of key posts, stressing the importance to

---

[21] Hans Ruffing was, at that time, President of the union.
[22] Letter from Hans Ruffing to the Ministry of Foreign Affairs, March 11, 1950. This letter was referred to many times. In September, 1951, the *Gewerkschaftliche Rundschau* recalled its main points. *Cf.* also *Die Arbeit* and *Saar-Bergbau.*

the Saarlanders of a distribution that would give them a larger role. Why, for example, give the position of Secretary-General of the *Comité paritaire* of the mines to a Frenchman and not to a Saarlander, when the Director-General of the mines was already a Frenchman?

Questions and criticisms multiplied, social demands mingling inextricably with protests against the position assigned to the Saar. The rise in prices manifest by the end of the summer led to a demand for a rise in wages. In October a strike called by the miners spread and became a short general strike.

It was not only the unions that were active but also the Saar Socialist Party, which until then had followed a policy of co-operation with France. Naturally, it approved the Franco-Saar Conventions by a resounding majority. Naturally, it reacted vigorously, in a memorandum of March 14, 1950,[23] to the censorious note of the German Socialist Party,[24] setting itself up as the defender of Saar autonomy. But there existed in the heart of the Saar Socialist Party a small group of men who did not approve the government's policy and who were drawn increasingly towards Germany. At the Congress on April 2, Kurt Conrad, who had succeeded Ernst Roth as head of the opposition group, roundly attacked the Conventions and expressed his regret at seeing the party split from the *Syndicat unitaire des mineurs* under such crucial circumstances. Mr. Conrad thought the Saar Socialist Party should defer approval of the Conventions pending new negotiations to fill the gaps in them. Although this position was not accepted, the majority at the same Congress did make sweeping demands. It asked that sequestration of factories cease, that the special interests of the Saar as regards credit be respected, and that the Saar share directly in the benefits of the Marshall Plan.[25]

To these demands that directly affected the issues raised by the Conventions the Socialist Congress added others dealing with protection of democratic liberties, participation of workers in the management of industrial concerns, nationalization of key industries, and reforms in social security.

[23] *Cf. Denkschrift der Sozialdemokratischen Partei Saar zur Frage des Saarlandes, Eine Antwort an die Denkschrift der Sozialistischen Partei Deutschlands* (Saarbrücken: March 14, 1950). (Mimeographed.)

[24] *Cf. Die Sozialdemokratie und das Saarproblem, op. cit.*

[25] This protest against the inadequacy of the allocations of Marshall Aid was made with the greatest insistence and was repeated throughout the year.

These demands were not at all surprising. However, they took on a special character in the Saar because they were directed not only to the government but to the employer, and the employer was, in many cases, an official representative of France.

Demands for social benefits and the claims of nationalism therefore became associated in the minds of the Saarlanders; the temptation to believe that the achievement of social reform was conditional upon elimination of the foreign Power became increasingly strong. Widening the scope of Saar autonomy was thus logically the first objective of the Socialist Party. It was not surprising to see the labour or Socialist press rise more and more frequently against certain manifestations of the French *présence*, criticizing the intervention of young French engineers, or demanding that the management of the Saar railways be handed over to the Saarlanders.

As for the clergy, it joined in the chorus of protest. Its opposition was not new. It had already been expressed during the 1947 elections. The clergy's intransigence was fortified by the hardening of the German attitude and by the resistance in the Saar early in 1950. So it did not hesitate in March, 1950, to remind the government, in a declaration approved by all the deans, that ambiguity dominated the whole of Saar policy because the people had not been explicitly consulted on the question of economic union. This declaration was not intended for publication, said the author of a letter to Johannes Hoffmann.[26] This, however, did not prevent its contents from becoming widely known inside the country as well as in Germany.

Such an atmosphere explains the development of an even more adamant opposition to French policy, and this opposition, far from demanding wider autonomy within the framework of European collaboration, sought solely and simply the return to Germany of a Saar which was claimed to be wholly German. It was in the course of the summer of 1950 that the Saar Democratic Party, after a carefully prepared campaign, changed both its leaders and its policy. Heading the new team there were, alongside Richard Becker who took on the presidency, Heinrich Schneider, Karl Hillenbrand and, as legal counsellor, Franz Steegmann. Their eighteen-point programme left no doubt as to their final aim: the

---

[26] For text of the letter of March 26, 1950, by Dean Braun, *cf.* Martin Hoffmeister, *Wer regiert die Saar?* (Cologne: 1952).

Saar could only serve as a bridge between France and Germany when its inhabitants, who belonged to the German peoples (*Deutsches Volkstum*), could establish cultural and economic relations with Germany as well as with France. This was the substance of the first article in the programme; then followed an enumeration of the practical measures necessary for the realization of this freedom.[27]

The D.P.S. flung a direct challenge at the Hoffmann Government. It was therefore no wonder that it attracted to its ranks all those who, for one reason or another, did not approve of the government's policy, with which the High Commissioner's office was inevitably associated. Nevertheless, progress was rather slow. The Hoffmann Government had matters firmly in hand and was resolved to inject into the democratic régime the dose of governmental authoritarianism necessary to the preservation of its power.

The attack did, however, touch the government in a sensitive spot. If it is exaggerated to speak of a "reign of terror," it is nonetheless true that the High Commissioner's office exercised a careful vigilance and followed closely the behaviour of some of the most influential members of the opposition. An effort was made to carry out this surveillance unobtrusively, but it was widely known and provided ground for violent criticism.[28]

The government had been led by circumstances to limit freedom of contact between the Saar and Germany. Yielding to the injunctions of the leaders of the D.P.S. and the German press and opening the frontiers would play into the hands of those opposed to autonomy. Moreover, the Saar was bound by an agreement negotiated with France from which it could not free itself by unilateral action. But the defence measures, and the limitations on freedom they brought in their wake, had the disadvantage of legitimizing the protests of the D.P.S. and of all those who questioned the régime's right to consider itself democratic and fully representative of public opinion. These measures could only make the German reaction more unfavourable and place the Saar Government in an increasingly difficult position in the Council of Europe,

---

27 *Cf.*, among others, *Saarfrage in Dokumenten, die Beweise gegen das Verbot der D.P.S.* (Saarbrücken: 1952); also Ludwig Pistorius, *op. cit.*

28 *Cf.* Richard Kirn's protests in the *Volksstimme* of May 18, 1951, and the affair of the Schneider *Postrat* in 1955; *cf.* in this connection, "Postbeamte waren in Gewissensnot," *Der Öffentliche Dienst* No. 5 (May, 1955), which gives the list of the telephones tapped.

where its opponents would have a chance to accuse it of violating the European Convention for the Protection of Human Rights.

Thus it was that everything combined to prevent that consolidation of the Saar's position which was the aim of French policy. The signing of the Franco-Saar Conventions raised more problems than it solved. In the Saar and in Germany it aroused growing opposition without ending the debate in France, since it was generally agreed that the Conventions had only provisional value. The linking of social demands and the claims of nationalism, the attacks on curtailment of democratic liberties, the active intervention of a Germany now more sure of herself in European affairs put both France and the Saar Government on the defensive. The weight of the various opposition groups drawn together by circumstances imperceptibly influenced the general trend of public opinion. This change in climate complicated the execution of French policy. The Schuman Plan, while it temporarily gave France the initiative in developing European integration, did not save her from being cast in the role of guilty party by German and Saar criticism of the Conventions. If she really wanted European co-operation, they asked, why did she draw up and support Conventions prejudicial to the settlement that would be made when the peace treaty was negotiated? Why influence the final settlement by trying to gain recognition of Saar autonomy by such devious means as the admission of the Saar to the Council of Europe or to the E.C.S.C.?

Robert Schuman found himself beset on all sides. From the Saar came repeated calls for adoption of a firm position which would permit consolidation of the results so far achieved. However, the voice of Germany, that neighbour with whom co-operation was necessary in the common interest, was directed towards keeping the situation fluid so that the discussion could be re-opened. At the beginning of January, 1951, Mr. Schuman seemed to have taken a decision; he informed the government in Saarbrücken of his intention of asking the representative of the French Government in the future to append two signatures, one in the name of France and one in the name of the Saar. He also envisaged consultation with the Saar Landtag prior to publication of the treaty and reproduction of the text in the *Bulletin officiel* of the Saar. Furthermore, he supported Mr. Hoffmann's proposals for ensuring Saar representation in the organs of the E.C.S.C. as delegates to the

Common Assembly selected by the Saar Parliament and as observers at the Special Council of Ministers.

A few weeks later, in a statement made to the Council of the Republic on February 20, Robert Schuman seemed firmly determined not only to maintain but to consolidate the status of the Saar.

> In the realm of politics [he said] and especially in the field of foreign policy, we must recognize that there now exists an independent Saar Government, and if, in accordance with the Saar Constitution, France is empowered by subsequent Conventions to represent the Saar in dealings with a third power, each time this happens we must act not by virtue of an inherent right in the exercise of our own sovereignty but as agents carrying out a specific task expressly delegated to us by the Saar Government. Even when we act in the name of the Franco-Saar economic union, we act for two associated states which are distinct and independent. And this should be made clear by the signatures we are called upon to affix. This is the French Government's argument and I believe it is irrefutable.

Then Mr. Schuman announced the setting up of a Saar diplomatic mission in Paris and the forthcoming change in the form of French representation in Saarbrücken. He added this significant comment:

> In this connection, there is another problem which I mentioned the last time I talked to you. We must definitely achieve, and as quickly as possible—for this is a matter not within our control—recognition of the sovereignty of the Saar in regard to foreign affairs. We would like to see the Saar state acquire an individual entity which is fully recognized abroad, especially in political questions.

This control of foreign relations would be strengthened, as Mr. Schuman saw it, by another factor—the participation of the Saar in the newly conceived European Defence Community—" not by inclusion of Saar soldiers and contingents in the French army but by a direct contribution on the part of the Saar to the defence of Europe in the form of its own contingents. The Saar must be admitted and incorporated into the system of European defence by a decision of all the countries participating in this defence." [29]

This was the position of the Foreign Minister at the end of February and clearly it was very close to that of the High Commissioner. It provoked a heated reaction in Germany. The statements of Robert Schuman to the Council of the Republic,

---

[29] For text of Mr. Schuman's speech, *cf. Journal officiel, Débats parlementaires, Conseil de la République*, February 21, 1951, p. 532.

wrote Georg Schneider in the *Neuer Vorwärts* of March 2, 1951, were tantamount to a " declaration of war against the German Federal Republic on the subject of the Saar." Throughout the month of March and the early days of April, there were sharp attacks in Germany, denouncing the Franco Saar attempt to make use of the device of the double signature appended by France as a means of obtaining indirect recognition of the Saar State by the Federal Republic. All the newspapers were unanimous on this point : there could be no question of considering this double signature as a small " technical " problem, as a secondary matter of mere procedure. Germany would not sign the treaty setting up the E.C.S.C. if the French Government maintained its position. The attack, which was launched in an interview given by Mr. Hoffmann on March 8 to a journalist of the *Süddeutsche Zeitung*, spread into a wider criticism of the régime, its police methods, and its abuse of its powers, as demonstrated in the expulsion of citizens guilty of showing sympathy towards their German Fatherland. Inside the Saar the attack was supported by the D.P.S., which organized a vigorous campaign of meetings during this period. The news that on March 9 Chancellor Adenauer had received Richard Becker, President of the D.P.S., made the links between the Saar opposition and the Government of the Federal Republic more or less official and stressed, if indeed there was still any need to, the uncompromising nature of Germany's attitude.

In the Saar, meanwhile, differences of opinion within the government coalition became more acute. During the previous year,[30] the Socialist Party had already formulated certain demands and requested development of a joint programme. As it did not obtain satisfaction, it decided to break with the Christian People's Party; on April 9, the two Socialist representatives in the government, Mr. Kirn and Mr. Braun, resigned and the C.V.P. ministers followed suit. Thus at the very moment when the final negotiations were taking place to open the E.C.S.C. Treaty for signature, the Saar found itself without a government. Obviously Johannes

---

[30] This crisis, already perceptible in May, 1950, was aggravated by the COMISCO resolution. In the course of the year, the *SVZ* and the *Volksstimme* frequently engaged in polemics. On the Socialist side, it was particularly the editor-in-chief of the *SVZ*, who was also the head of the government information service, who was the subject of the attacks. An effort to put an end to the conflict made at the extraordinary Congress of the Socialist Party on October 14-15 met with no success. In fact, the tension that existed within the S.P.S. resulted in a constant barrage of criticism of the Christian People's Party.

Hoffmann was in a position to form another one fairly quickly; in fact, he presented his proposals to the Landtag as early as April 14. Nor was there any doubt that the ministerial crisis was due primarily to differing views within the Socialist Party on the subject of internal Saar politics.[31] But these events underlined at a critical moment the weakness of the Hoffmann Government.[32] The crises in internal affairs and in foreign relations may have moved along parallel lines. But this did not mean that they did not exert an influence one on the other.

When the Paris Conference of Foreign Ministers opened on April 11, 1951, Mr. Schuman was again in a difficult position. Facing him was Chancellor Adenauer, all the more unwilling to make concessions on the subject of the Saar because he knew that he was being closely watched by the Socialist opposition in his own country which, backed by a public opinion that the newspapers had worked hard to create, was determined to make capital of any weakness he might show. Mr. Adenauer and his colleagues could not fail to stress an argument they had already communicated to their opposite numbers in France: ratification of the E.C.S.C. Treaty depended in essence on the form in which inclusion of the Saar was presented.

In France, however, public opinion was but moderately interested in the Saar problem and the press only discussed it intermittently. From April 11 to 19, that is to say, from the arrival of Chancellor Adenauer in Paris to the signing of the Treaty, articles in the newspapers examined in the preparation of this study were confined either to Franco-German relations or to the Coal and Steel Community itself. Only *Le Monde*, on April 13 and 14 in an article and an editorial, went into the problems raised by the representation of the Saar in the E.C.S.C. and the signing of the Treaty. These were couched in a moderate tone; they presented French diplomacy as conciliatory, fully aware of the difficulties faced by Mr. Adenauer because of the opposition, and anxious to make things as easy for him as possible. Although an article published in *Combat* on April 16 dealt with the question, it did not come to grips with the main issue.

[31] According to certain rumours current at the time, the crisis had been occasioned by an intervention of the British Labour Party.

[32] The immediate reaction of the German Socialists to the news of the ministerial crisis was to increase their offensive in the Saar question.

The Saar itself, the focal point of the discussion, was the less able to defend its position because it had resigned itself to keeping out of the negotiation and because its political chief was busy re-forming his team of ministers.

The general mood did not favour French resistance to German claims. It would not be easy for people to understand why there should be a break just at the moment when the Treaty was about to be signed, a Treaty whose historical importance for Europe had been stressed for more than a year. It would appear that a great idea was being sacrificed to those very quarrels over petty interests which the Treaty was designed to overcome. The United Kingdom and the United States, although they had upheld the French claims in the Saar, did so with only moderate enthusiasm. In short, Mr. Schuman was not in a position to make conditions. Was he not rather the prisoner of his own plan? To push obstinacy to an open breach—and this at the last minute—would amount to political suicide.[33]

He therefore agreed to the concessions he was asked to make. It must be added that Chancellor Adenauer, who combined flexibility in carrying out his policy with firmness in holding to the objective, made retreat easier for Mr. Schuman by an apparently reassuring proposal: the signing of the Treaty should be accompanied by an exchange of letters in which the two governments would define their positions on the status of the Saar. More concretely, Germany should declare that the signing of the Treaty setting up the E.C.S.C. did not imply on her part any recognition of the present status of the Saar. The French Government should state clearly " that it does not take the Federal Government's signing of the Treaty as recognition by the Federal Government of the present status of the Saar." Robert Schuman was apparently not saying anything other than what he had always maintained, namely, that the final status of the Saar could not be established until the signing of a peace treaty. But his letter, following on the heels of his renunciation of the double signature, spelt failure for his efforts to consolidate the French position in the Saar.

It was a hard blow for Johannes Hoffmann and for the High Commissioner. Mr. Hoffmann, informed of what was happening in Paris, tried one last approach: abandonment of the position

---

[33] One should not forget that at this moment the M.R.P., like the other parties, felt menaced by the campaign of the R.P.F.

laid down in Mr. Schuman's letter of the beginning of January
would make the existence of a Saar Government and a Saar policy
impossible. Mr. Grandval, for his part, suggested at the last
minute various measures that would make it possible to call a halt
to the German diplomatic offensive and to find some formula by
which the continued existence of the Saar state could be assured.
The immediate application of the reforms already envisaged (suppression of the High Commissioner's office and of the inspection
services) and of certain others would amply demonstrate the French
desire to give the Saar full liberty. These two proposals, however,
had no effect whatsoever.

Then Mr. Grandval tendered his resignation. In his opinion,
the terms of the Treaty were such that the Saar appeared not as a
state but as a French dependency. The Germans had won this
round. Moreover, the conditions under which passages of the
Treaty relative to the Saar had been drawn up, the failure to keep
him informed about modifications in the French position, constituted, for the representative of France, such a betrayal that he could
only conclude he had lost the confidence of his government.
Henceforth, there was no other course open to him but to leave.
For him, as for the Saarlanders who had put their trust in France,
the situation had come to a dead end. Mr. Hoffmann was almost
of the same opinion. And yet both were to remain at their posts.
Mr. Grandval, impulsive though he might be, had too strong a
sense of the national interest and of his own duty not to retract his
decision to resign. The way in which he subsequently explained
the French Government's decision, in his speech of May 15, for
instance, showed his self-control. As for Johannes Hoffmann,
what could he do but remain? His fate was bound up with a
policy, and as long as there was any chance of its succeeding, he
had to remain at his post.

Mr. Schuman believed there were no grounds for pessimism.
His decision had been dictated solely by the conviction that it was
necessary to make a concession to his German colleague, Chancellor
Adenauer, in order to bring the principal issue under negotiation
to a successful conclusion.

On April 24, he declared to the Council of the Republic: " The
French Government has not changed its policy. The Saar will
retain its full autonomy in the execution of the Treaty. It will be
the Saar Government and the Saar Parliament which will be

responsible for putting the Treaty into effect once it has been ratified." The French Government holds to its intention of widening the Saar's sovereignty in foreign relations. But this must be recognized by other countries. " Not one of the signatories of the recent Treaty has recognized the present status of the Saar or considered sending diplomatic representatives to the Saar! We could not therefore on this occasion try to obtain this recognition from the signatories." [34]

However, neither then nor later did Robert Schuman contrive to convince his chief critic, who was none other than Michel Debré:

> In agreeing that your signature would, by implication, include the Saar Government—which was not your original intention—you have played into the hands of Germany who wanted nothing better than to show that the Saar had no individual personality, even as concerns an economic question.
>
> As far as the Saar is concerned, you do not say that you are abandoning your position, but neither do you contradict that of the German Government. [35]

Mr. Debré and Mr. Grandval were not the only ones who thought that the concession made by Mr. Schuman compromised French policy in the Saar. The reaction of public opinion, as far as it can be gauged from commentaries in the press, showed that in France and in the Saar, as well as in Germany, a significance was attributed to this decision which Robert Schuman had doubtless not envisaged. In vain did Maurice Schumann fly to the defence of his colleague by minimizing the event; he had few supporters. Without going as far as *L'Observateur* of May 3, which carried the headline, " France Abandons the Saar," *Le Figaro* of April 19, while accepting as reasonable the solution arrived at, noted that " it is not, however, possible to hide the fact that the Saar episode marks the return to the front rank of a question which our friends across the Rhine have always kept in the back of their minds." As for *Le Monde*, which followed the Saar question more closely than did the others, it stressed repeatedly, both in articles from its special correspondent in Saarbrücken and in its interviews, the growing difficulties the French Government would have to face to keep its

[34] *Journal officiel, Débats parlementaires, Conseil de la République*, April 25, 1951, p. 1287.
[35] *Ibid.*, p. 1288.

position. " There is an element of uncertainty as regards the future of the Saar." [36]

The discreet commentaries in *Le Monde* gave only a very imperfect account of the situation in the Saar. In fact, the vacillations of French policy, the disorganization in the Hoffmann Government which had been obvious for several days, the satisfaction of the German press, all served to strengthen opposition in the Saar.

At the Congress of the Socialist Party, held at Sulzbach on April 21 and 22, 1951, Kurt Conrad, who had not yet lost hope of modifying the policy of the Saar Socialists, attempted to take advantage of the party's shift to the opposition to get himself elected President. He gained but a little more than 30 per cent. of the total votes; this nevertheless represented a victory, because it proved the existence inside the party of a strong opposition minority. The delegates to the Congress also had the opportunity of listening to a contest in eloquence between a representative of the German Socialist Party, Willi Eichler, who declared that the Saar was German, and Salomon Grumbach, who spoke in the name of the S.F.I.O. and of COMISCO. By an overwhelming majority, resolutions were adopted confirming the party's policy, especially the decision in favour of economic union with France. But war was nonetheless declared on the Hoffmann Government and on the reactionary forces it represented. Above all, the Congress demanded revision of the Convention on the operation of the mines and the right to share in the management of the mines. The Socialist Party did not confine itself to these demands. Now that it had joined the opposition, it played its part conscientiously. As the weeks passed, the tone of the *Volksstimme* hardened. Socialist and union newspapers alike gave the government a hard time.

Soon there came a new attack. On May 3 the D.P.S. issued a manifesto containing proposals for a provisional solution to the Saar problem. It demanded first of all equal rights for Germans living in the Saar, an end to expulsions, and the return of those exiled. It demanded that the authorities observe fundamental freedoms and the rights of man, and that police control over public life and over correspondence and telephonic communications cease. The party also proposed that the Saar question cease to be treated as a political issue : two observers, one French and the other German,

[36] April 26, 1951.

should have the task of supervising the administration and, in case of disagreement, should submit themselves to a decision by a tribunal nominated by the Council of Europe.[37] Constitutional reforms would, in their turn, restrict the role of the government in the administration of routine matters. The manifesto then went on to deal with economic and social questions: it demanded economic independence for the Saar so that the Saar might become " the precursor of the economic community of European States "; it requested the opening of German markets to the Saar, the modernization of industrial equipment with the help of Saar capital at present diverted to France, and allocation of the share of Marshall Plan credits that would normally come to the Saar. The manifesto further asked for fiscal sovereignty, which would make possible adaptation of the tax system to the particular conditions prevailing in the Saar, for the reform of the social insurance system, for the revision of the mining Convention, and for the right to joint management in the mines.[38]

The attack was skilfully planned. Moderate in tone, it avoided criticisms of France and declarations of principle in favour of a return to Germany and considered the problem solely in the light of Saar interests and European co-operation. Moreover, this manifesto, by including all the social and economic demands as well as all the political ones emanating from various quarters, was designed to draw together all the forces opposing the Hoffmann Government. From then on, the D.P.S. was not just the party that stood for return to Germany. It embodied in itself all the various opposition groups and constituted a central, national rallying point. At the same time, by the simple fact of calling into question again the foundations of the régime of the Saar, it dealt a new blow at the government and compelled it to take a position.

The response came quickly. On the very day the manifesto was published, the government refused permission for three deputies of the Bundestag to enter Saar territory to attend a public meeting of the D.P.S. On May 9 Mr. Schuman asked Mr. Hoffmann to take the necessary steps to end the activities of a party that was a threat to Franco-Saar relations and that was calling into

[37] Elements of the C.S.U., the F.D.P., and the *Zentrum* in the Bundestag had drawn up a similar proposal in a call to account on April 5. This was developed by Franz Josef Strauss in the debates of May 30, 1951, in the Bundestag. *Cf. Verhandlungen das Deutschen Bundestages*, I.114/5672A.
[38] *Cf.* Pistorius, *op. cit.*, pp. 81–85.

question the economic union. On May 21 the *Minister-Präsident* ordered the dissolution of the party and the seizure of its assets.

This action naturally brought the Saar question again to the forefront and unleashed a new wave of widespread resentment. The German press [39] seized upon this and redoubled its attack against a régime that remained in power only by virtue of extra-ordinary measures. Chancellor Adenauer protested. The whole problem was raised in the Bundestag in a big debate on May 30, in the course of which the head of the German Government, supported by representatives of all the parties, rose once more against the arbitrary methods of the Saar Government and expressed surprise at the letter in which Robert Schuman had felt it necessary to urge Mr. Hoffmann to take such measures. Nor did Chancellor Adenauer stop at this. He took the opportunity to review the whole problem in order to re-state the German position. It was an extremely interesting speech, which revealed not only an accurate knowledge of the facts but a penetrating analysis of the situation. He noted the irresolution of French policy and the uncertainty that resulted from it in the Saar. He observed the inner contradiction of French policy and exploited it by bringing out the inevitable subordination of a policy dictated by a defence reflex to the great European scheme designed to abolish national frontiers. He stressed, in passing, the importance of the diplomatic victory represented by the exchange of letters of April 18.[40] When it had already admitted that the status of the Saar could not be determined until the conclusion of the peace treaty, how could the French Government oppose discussion of the provisional régime? How could a government claiming to be democratic prohibit, without self-contradiction, a debate that merely sought a constitutional revision? And the Chancellor ended by emphasizing that it was essential in this affair not to lose one's nerve and to avoid being

[39] Cf. *Frankfurter Neue Presse*, May 22, 1951; *Frankfurter Allgemeine Zeitung*, May 23, 25, 1951; *Kölnische Rundschau*, May 23, 1951; *Rhein-Neckar Zeitung*, May 23, 1951; *Neue Ruhr-Zeitung*, May 23, 1951; *Die Welt*, May 23, 24, 1951; *Industriekurier*, May 24, 1951; *Neuer Vorwärts*, May 25, 1951; and *Deutsche Zeitung und Wirtschafts-Zeitung*, May 26, 1951.

[40] " In the exchange of letters with which you are familiar between the French Foreign Minister and myself on the 18th of April, which forms an integral part of the agreement about the mining union, the German and French Governments, while maintaining their own positions, agreed that the final settlement of the Saar question could be achieved only by means of a peace treaty or similar agreement." Then he stressed the following: " I want to emphasize that until now there has been no such understanding between the German and French Governments." *Bundesanzeiger, 1951*, No. 102, May 31, 1951, p. 6.

side-tracked from the main objective, which was still European co-operation.

This did not prevent him from making very firm representations to the Allied High Commission of which he informed the Bundestag. He addressed himself to the High Commission because this was the body responsible for the protection of its democratic liberties. The Federal Republic could not be indifferent to events in the Saar because she had not accepted the thesis that economic union with France implied political separation from Germany. Furthermore, it had been agreed with the French Government that no decision concerning the status of the Saar should be taken before there was a peace treaty. Nor could the Federal Government accept the measures taken by the Saar Government to muzzle opposition. She therefore asked the Allies to intervene to establish liberty of thought and action on those questions which could not definitely be settled until the peace was signed.

French opinion reacted rather apathetically.[41] The press was concerned with other problems. An article by Salomon Grumbach in *Le Populaire* of June 4 pointed out the difficulties inherent in the Saar problem. *Le Monde* in its editorial of June 1 made a frontal attack on the questions raised by the disbanding of the D.P.S.:

> During the transition period, the Saar has a Government and a French High Commissioner who lay down a certain policy. It is not surprising that this policy is designed to consolidate the present state of affairs. But need it go so far as to stifle all attempts to achieve divergent goals? This seems to be the objective in some circles and it is against this that the Germans and some of the Saarlanders are rising. Must the Constitution voted by the Parliament of 1947 be considered sacrosanct? Is it not even open to discussion? This appears to be the position of Mr. Hoffmann. But is not constitutional reform openly talked about in France? If, therefore, the Saar Government tried to make a decision irrevocable, it would offer far too easy grounds for criticism from outside —and not only from Germany.

It is clear that *Le Monde* was as much aware as the German Government of the ambiguity created by refusal to discuss a provisional régime and the shadow this cast on French policy in the

[41] And yet the Chancellor's speech had been based on a fairly sound argument. After summing up the exchange of letters, he added: " Such an agreement implies that up to that final settlement neither side may undertake activities or create conditions that make a final settlement by means of a peace treaty illusory." *Ibid*. Consequently, the agreement precluded the Germans from interfering in the Saar just as much as it precluded the French from trying to achieve a *fait accompli*.

Saar. High Commissioner Grandval replied in a speech at Völk-lingen on June 2, 1951, recalling France's rights and pointing out to Germany that democratic liberties were "better observed and more respected" in the Saar than in the German Republic. The latter freely criticized the Saar policy but avoided any presentation of the point of view of the Saar Government. The Saar press never hesitated to publish Chancellor Adenauer's speeches.[42]

The Germans for their part endeavoured to be temperate. They were aware that Germany had no more to gain than France from outbursts which would compromise the position she had lately won back in the international sphere. The memory of the war was still too close for an upsurge of German nationalism not to risk reper-cussions. In France, the government coalition which supported a European policy was engaged during the weeks of May and June in an electoral campaign in which it was defending itself at the same time against Gaullist and Communist offensives. Robert Schuman was attacked especially in Lorraine, where he had to face the hostility of groups which accepted neither his Plan nor his Saar policy and men who, for personal ends, used as a weapon against him the suspicious attitude of the inhabitants of Lorraine toward their Saar neighbour.

To defend himself, he was obliged to stress the measures he had taken or the efforts he had made to protect French interests, and his words were inevitably taken up by the nationalists in the Saar and in Germany.[43]

The moderate tone of the debate even at the height of the crisis was due to the desire to avoid a rupture.[44] In his speech of May 30, Chancellor Adenauer showed himself firm towards Mr. Schuman, but he did not engage in arguments. On June 8, 1951, an article appeared in the *Rheinischer Merkur* which was later said to have

[42] Mr. Grandval mentioned one or two examples: although the Saar press gave the main points of the speech made by the German delegate, Mr. Eichler, at the Socialist Con-gress at Sulzbach, the German press which reported it took good care not to quote the speech made by Salomon Grumbach or by the Netherlands delegate to the same con-gress. *Cf. Speeches of Gilbert Grandval, op. cit.*

[43] In the brochure published by the Saar opposition, Hoffmeister, *op. cit.*, there is a translation of a clarification by Robert Schuman originally published in *Le Courrier de Metz* on June 16, 1951.

[44] One of the best-informed men on the Saar question said: "It is regrettable that the prestige of Schuman's foreign policy has to be maintained for the present at the expense of the Saar question. Hence a way will be found for the expression of German criticism and the advancement of German interests without loss of prestige to the present French Government. What matters is to act according to the formula: *Fortiter in re, suaviter in modo!* . . . A possible way to implement such a German position should be a device to enable the French Government to pull out of the Saar adventure with dignity."

been inspired by Chancellor Adenauer and which revealed a genuine desire to find a positive solution in the spirit of the Schuman Plan. The author was not merely content to formulate a wish; he actually made a proposal: the Saar could be made the first European territory, freed from Franco-German "dualism" and administered by the Council of Europe until the evolution thus initiated came to fruition in a European confederation. There would be advantages for everyone in this. The reconciliation of French and German interests would take place at the European level without loss of prestige for either side. The Saar population would once again find itself in an atmosphere both German and European. In short, Germany would be the one to offer the first European territory and the gesture would not represent an undue sacrifice; if the European idea came to nothing, Germany's rights over the Saar would still be valid and her chances of exercising these rights would be more solidly established.

This theme was taken up again some time later (August 3 and 6) in the course of an informal exchange between Armand Bérard, acting French High Commissioner in Germany, and Ambassador Herbert Blankenhorn bearing on various subjects including the Saar. On the German side, the Chancellor's keen interest in finding a friendly solution to the question was emphasized. What the Chancellor wanted to avoid, in fact, was the creation of a second Luxembourg, that is to say, the establishment of a Saar state, which would imply the official abandonment by Germany of a German territory. In the solution outlined in the article in the *Rheinischer Merkur*, however, the status of the Saar appeared as a first step towards European confederation, which lessened the chance of strong nationalist reactions.

The German overture, which could be interpreted as the first official suggestion of a europeanization of the Saar, was sufficiently in line with the pre-occupations manifest in government circles to be more than a bait to draw the French into a discussion of a régime to which they had clung doggedly up till now. Moreover, there were circumstances that could explain the attempt to open such a discussion at this time. The German Government had just received the Allied reply to its note of May 29. This reply of August 3, 1951,[45] drawn up jointly by the High Commissioners of

[45] *Cf.* Ludwig Dischler, *Das Saarland 1945-1957* (Hamburg: 1957), Nos. 24 and 25, pp. 66-68. (Mimeographed.)

the United States, the United Kingdom, and France in order to stress their solidarity, was both negative and curt. It referred the German Government to the declarations made on various occasions on the status of the Saar and reminded Germany that the régime was " not in any way contradictory with the Allied statements of June 5, 1945." [46] In this connection, the reply made it clear that " the jurisdiction of the Federal Republic does not extend beyond its own territorial limits." After stating that the three governments were in favour of the development in the Saar of " democratic institutions and respect for individual liberties," it concluded with the hope that measures would be taken to prevent the Saar question from becoming a barrier to the progress of European collaboration.

This note acted like a dash of cold water on German opinion. Had not the Germans been buoyed up by the hope that the United States, and perhaps the United Kingdom, would seize the opportunity offered by the measures taken in the Saar to dissociate themselves partially from French policy? Thus direct negotiation seemed the only way out of the impasse, and the occasion for it was all the more propitious because the German opposition had just had proof of the limitations of the Federal Republic's possibilities of action.

On the French side, opinion was reserved. This was probably because greater importance was attached to frequent and public evidence of Germany's desire to reintegrate a " European " Saar in the *Deutschtum* than to the necessarily discreet suggestions of the Federal Government that the problem be settled in a manner satisfactory to all concerned.[47] As soon as there was agreement on any discussion with Germany, the status would, by implication, once again be brought into question. Moreover, the reasons underlying the German attempt to negotiate were the very ones that spurred the French to resist. As for the latter, the Allied note represented

---

[46] In which the reference to "Germany within her frontiers as they were on 31st December, 1937," had as its sole aim the determination of the territory which had to be divided for purposes of occupation. For text of the Statement, *cf. Documents on American Foreign Relations, 1944–1945*, ed. Leland M. Goodrich and Marie J. Carroll (London: Oxford University Press, 1947), p. 222.

[47] The French Government and the High Commissioner had been struck by the reservations of Mr. Hallstein in a letter of August 16 to François Poncet on the question of the interpretation given by the French Government to the Conventions governing reparations from certain Saar factories. It was the first time that the German Government had tackled this problem officially and by a formal overture had shown that it was fully conscious of the weakness of the French legal position.

a success which they must take full advantage of to consolidate their position. It was within the framework of the existing status that a European solution must be found. Thus, if need be, it might be possible to consider entrusting responsibility for the foreign relations and defence of the Saar to a European institution. Such, at least for the time being, were the feelings of the High Commissioner.

And there the matter rested.

The Saar question seemed to pass into the background. Attention moved to more pressing problems—the rearmament of Germany, the setting up of the European Defence Community—but those in Germany and in the Saar who were the most closely concerned did not give up the struggle.

On June 12, the *Deutscher Saarbund* was officially formed at Wiesbaden.[48] Its goal was to assure that the interests of its members, Saarlanders expelled from their country or friends of the Saar, were represented *vis-à-vis* the Federal Government, the Bundestag, and the German administration. Moreover, it intended to keep public opinion, both in Germany and abroad, informed of the true state of affairs in the Saar. Although preparations had been made a long time before, thanks to the unwearying efforts of Father Franz Bungarten, Gustav Strohm, Fritz Hellwig, and Prince Hubertus of Löwenstein,[49] and although at first it enjoyed a good deal of sympathy and the moral support of the authorities of Rheinland-Pfalz and of the Federal administration and deputies to the Bundestag, it experienced difficulties in its early days. Funds

---

[48] " The Executive Committee of the *Saarbund* is composed as follows: President: Franz Bungarten, priest, Bad Neuenahr; Vice-Presidents: Dr. Fritz Hellwig, Düsseldorf-Oberkassel; Dr. Heinrich Lietzmann, lawyer, Essen; First Secretary: Hubertus, Prince of Löwenstein, doctor of law, professor of history, Amorbach/Main; Second Secretary: Josef Hall, editor, Augsburg; Treasurer: Carl Arnold Becker, business man, Frankfurt; Assessors: Dr. Anneliese Dittmann, Heidelberg; *Pater* Landolf Wisskirchen, Bonn; Hans Treinen, student, Namborn (Saar); Dr. Volkmar von Zühlsdorff, Amorbach/Main; Alfred Daum, journalist, Cologne; Director: Heinz Voigt, Frankfurt; Press Officer: Georg Schneider, Bendorf." *Aufruf zur Gründung des Deutschen Saarbundes*.

[49] Hubertus, Prince of Löwenstein, had already drawn attention to himself by several daring actions, especially by his raid on Heligoland on December 31, 1949. His *Deutsche Aktion*, organized at the end of 1948 and officially inaugurated at the end of March, 1950, took every opportunity of demonstrating in favour of a return to Germany of the territory that had been taken from her. It was for these reasons that Prince Hubertus joined the *Saarbund* while still continuing a parallel action. He placed himself in the limelight on other occasions, as when on July 15, 1951, at Saint-Wendel (Saar) he organized a demonstration in which he suddenly appeared with a group of students who were carrying the flags of the Federal Republic, the United Nations, and even of United Europe.

merely dribbled in. The Ministry for All-German Affairs gave
only modest financial support; the industrialists had to be coaxed.
The number of supporters grew very slowly, with only ninety
individual and group memberships at the end of October, not
counting those in Rheinland-Pfalz, which were perceptibly more
numerous (about 300). But the organization took shape. The
existence of a secretariat facilitated the co-ordination of effort and
made possible the necessary continuity. Thanks to this *Geschäfts-
stelle*, more regular contacts were established with the Federal
administration, with the government of Rheinland-Pfalz, and with
the leaders of the opposition in the Saar. After a few months, new
branches were set up. The organizers began to think in terms of
founding a newspaper, the *Deutsche Saarzeitung*,[50] which could
be launched with funds advanced by the Ministry for All-German
Affairs. So, at the end of 1951, the *Saarbund* seemed to be in a
position to exercise a real influence on German and Saar opinion.[51]

Its activities were made easier by the evolution of opinion in the
Saar. The banning of the D.P.S. had not crippled the opposition
as the government had hoped. Neither had the efforts to undermine the prestige of its leaders met with success. Quite the
contrary, as often happens with repressive measures, they had
rather enabled those at whom they were aimed to increase their
importance in the eyes of a public more likely to be swayed by
sentiment than by reason. By their manifesto of May 3, Richard
Becker and Georg Schneider had become national leaders. They
now enjoyed the halo of martyrdom and their influence grew in
proportion as, in the heart of the trade union movement, the
defence of professional interests and nationalist opposition to the
French administration were welded ever more closely together. As
time passed, the trade union papers became increasingly violent in

[50] The first edition of the *Deutsche Saarzeitung* appeared on December 1, 1951. From
then on the publication of the newspaper continued until the day after the referendum.
The printing was undertaken by the Harrach Company, owners of the presses of the
Mainzer Allgemeine Zeitung. The editing was in the hands of Hermann Kresse, under
the pseudonym of Karl Heinz Francke. This same Mr. Kresse had a press service
(*AZW*). For some time Georg Schneider, who had been editor of the *Saarlandischer
Nachrichtendienst* (*SND*), collaborated with him. But the two men soon separated.
Georg Schneider went into the Saar Government service. It should be noted that the
Saarbund drew further and further apart from the *Deutsche Saarzeitung* whose policy
it did not approve. By December 29, 1952, the paper no longer carried the sub-title
Mitteilungsblatt des Deutschen Saarbundes. It became known more and more as the
mouthpiece of the German opposition in the Saar, particularly that of Heinrich
Schneider.

[51] Certain publications of the *Deutscher Saarbund* were even sent abroad in the hope of
attracting European and American attention.

their criticism of an administration too exclusively subjected to French control.

The *Saar-Bergbau* led the offensive. One day it protested against the fact that there was as yet only a single Saarlander occupying a key post; another day it attacked the High Commissioner because he had vetoed the proposal to lower the retirement age for miners from sixty-five to sixty and to raise the ceiling on sickness insurance benefits to 39,000 French francs. Several days later, when the High Commissioner had modified his attitude, the *Saar-Bergbau* loudly proclaimed its victory. But a much more serious matter arose, that of the Warndt mines. The news of the agreement between the *Régie des mines* of the Saar and the *Houillères de Lorraine,* which had been kept secret for some time, finally leaked out. Mr. Strohm discussed it with Paul Kutsch at their first meeting. Shortly afterwards, the *Syndicat unitaire des mineurs* got hold of it. On November 8 the *Saar-Bergbau* [52] began an attack that was followed, on November 22, by a protest from the directors of the thirteen industrial groups of the *Syndicat unitaire* during a conference at Saarbrücken. The Socialist Party [53] decided, for its part, to make representations to the Landtag for a speedy settlement of the problem.

This was only to be expected. The Warndt coalfield was indeed of great importance, not only for the depth of its seams and the quality of its coal, but also for the enormous reserve it represented.[54] This reserve was one the Saar had always counted on against the day when certain beds, such as those of St. Ingbert, Hirschbach, Mellien, Heinitz, and Dechen would give out. So the Saar miners resented the farming-out to France of the Warndt coalfields as a despoliation that threatened them with future unemployment. They were not the only ones to protest, for the disputes that had taken place between 1919 and 1935 had given the Warndt a symbolic significance. The Saarlanders, in their quasi-unanimity, tended to see in France's attitude over this affair an earnest of her intentions towards the Saar. Mr. Grandval sensed this and felt the need to draw his government's attention to the effect that would

[52] "Der Warndt—die Zukunft und Zuflucht des Saarbergbaus," No. 21; "Die Warndt-frage—Unsere Schicksalsfrage," No. 22 (November 20, 1951); "Vorständekonferenz der Einheitsgewerkschaft nimmt einstimmig Warndtentschliessung an," No. 23 (December 5, 1951); "Unsere zweite Stellungnahme zum Warndtproblem," No. 24 (December 15, 1951).
[53] *Volksstimme,* November 30, 1951.
[54] Approximately 800,000,000 tons.

certainly be produced in the Saar by the news of the agreement, which was also highly questionable from the legal point of view.

The *Syndicats chrétiens* did not lag behind the other trade unions. All of them, unions of railway workers or of employees of public utilities, accompanied their demands for social benefits with vigorous criticism of the High Commissioner and his activities, with protests against the limits imposed on the autonomy of the Saar. And so it was that social struggles became struggles for the freedom of the country.[55]

At the root of the social agitation was the marked rise in prices.[56] Economically attached to France, the Saar was feeling the effects of the growing inflation there. Tension was increased, not only by a sense of dependence emphasized by the presence in the Saar of senior French officials, by the interventions of the High Commissioner, and even more, by the consciousness of unequal treatment,[57] but also by the friction which arose from differences of concept or of custom.[58]

The Socialists could only sound the same note.[59] Their opposition to the Hoffmann Government became more and more an opposition to his whole policy, that is to say, to the High Commissioner's office. Furthermore, contacts with Germany had become more frequent. A regular link was established between

[55] " Wir kämpfen für die Freiheit der Saar, ' declared an article in *Der Öffentliche Dienst*, November, 1951.

[56] *Der Öffentliche Dienst* of October gave figures which made it clear that the price index had gone up by 14·9 points between January and August. On December 21, the *Volksstimme* noted that the index had gone up by 2·2 between mid-November and mid-December.

[57] The *Gewerkschaftliche Rundschau* of August, 1951, for example, made the following remark : " As we well know, there are two scales of wages for chauffeurs, based on nationality. Chauffeurs of French nationality are paid according to the established wage scale, while citizens of the Saar get paid only when on a job, which leads to a substantial difference in earnings for the same time spent at work." It is well known, however, that the seriousness of the conflicts which arose over salaries, especially in the *Régie des mines*, did not stem merely from the desire of the Saar workers to be given the same treatment as those in Lorraine, but also from the basic difference that existed in the methods employed in France and in Germany for determining salaries.

[58] In March, 1951, *Der Öffentliche Dienst* protested, for example, not only against the way in which, in the Convention concerning the railways, France had secured for herself the last word in the administration of Saar railways, but also against the attempt to impose regulations for the employees based on those of the S.N.C.F. In November the same paper made this remark : " The principle of employees' rights in the Central European area is different from that obtaining in the French democracy."

[59] *Cf.*, for example, the article by Richard Kirn in the *Volksstimme* of June 30, 1951, enumerating the problems still awaiting solution : when would the High Commissioner's office become an embassy ? When would Saarlanders have posts as customs officials ? When would the Saar have a share in the Marshall Plan ? It also demanded the employment of a larger number of Saarlanders at higher levels in the administration of the mines.

Kurt Schumacher and the group, still a minority one, led by Kurt Conrad and Friedrich Regitz. In the winter of 1951–1952, the German trade unions began to invite Saar union members to study-groups they were organizing.

So by the end of 1951, the opposition was firmly established. It had found its way into the most varied groups, into trade unions and political parties. The coalition of forces on which Johannes Hoffmann had sought to base his policy began to crumble.

One may well ask, What were the causes of this progressive change in the situation? One of the members of the Federal Government gave this reply: " Since the Chancellor has succeeded in making our voice heard once more in Europe," he wrote in early January, 1952, to one of his correspondents, " I no longer feel pessimistic. By the mere fact of our weight, even the Saar problem will find a solution in one form or another." The change in the relative strengths of France and of Germany did indeed play a vital role. France had lost the initiative. She lost it by the hesitancy of her diplomacy. Opting for a " European " policy, she did not dare assume all the risks involved when faced by a protagonist whose power she saw increasing. She tried to hold on to the position she had established, and while subordinating her Saar policy to her European aims—which weakened the position of the Hoffmann Government—she did not in return grant the Saar the self-government it demanded. In spite of the Conventions, France maintained a tutelage which was evident as much because Frenchmen occupied key posts as because of the presence and constant interventions of the High Commissioner, and could only lead the Saarlanders to condemn both their government and the régime it embodied.

France's tutelage was the more exasperating because in their everyday lives the Saarlanders were subjected to the effects of fluctuations in French internal policy, the slowness of her administrative machinery, her economic and financial difficulties. The most convincing proofs given to them of the advantages of economic union could not overcome the annoyance caused by the increasing cost of living and the feeling of being treated as second-class citizens. Germany, however, once more a rising Power, seemed as time went by to offer the Saarlanders prospects of a brighter future.

4

THE BATTLE OVER THE 1952 ELECTIONS

THAT the Saar opposition was determined on action became apparent in the early months of 1952. The new year brought the challenge of an approaching day of reckoning: the elections to the Landtag scheduled for the autumn.

Everyone was making preparations. As early as November, 1951, the *Saarbund* had underlined the importance of the campaign and the necessity of organizing well in advance. But it was also essential to present candidates, to have at one's disposal organizations and parties capable of leading the struggle. Since the banning of the D.P.S., however, the only opposition party was the Saar Socialist Party, whose chiefs accepted—even defended—the régime. So it was not surprising that opponents of the régime decided to take a further step and attempt to form new parties.

On February 2 a group consisting of Franz Steegmann and Karl Hillenbrand, together with the lawyers Hubert Ney and Egon Reinert and trade union secretary Karl Walz, agreed to form a Christian Democratic Union (C.D.U.) in the Saar [1] and asked the Saar Ministry of the Interior for a licence. A month later, a number of Socialists, represented by Richard Schultz-Tornau, a lawyer from Saarbrücken, but in fact led and inspired by Kurt Conrad and Friedrich Regitz, [2] made a similar request for the German Social Democratic Party which they had just created.

Thus began a struggle to undermine the Hoffmann Government which lasted throughout the year. Regarding both applications the Ministry of the Interior replied that it could reach no decision until the law governing the activities of political parties had been

---

[1] The first discussions on the creation of this party took place in September, 1951, at the house of Richard Becker. Chancellor Adenauer's advice was sought through other channels and Mr. Steegmann met him on October 11 and 12. He gave his approval, not without some hesitation, still recommending moderation and abstention from any action that might threaten the ratification of the treaties setting up the E.C.S.C.

[2] They sent their letters of resignation to the S.P.S., the former on April 26, and the latter on May 6, 1952. *Cf. Die Gründung der Deutschen Sozialdemokratischen Partei im Saargebiet* (n.p. or d.). (Mimeographed.)

voted and promulgated.[3] Then the ministry redoubled its questions and requests for clarification. Obviously, party leaders had to agree to respect the Saar Constitution and to give assurances that their party was not and did not intend to be part of any association with headquarters outside the Saar. They also had to promise that they would accept no outside financial assistance. Both groups naturally gave the necessary assurances.

But everyone was in fact playing with words; the real motivating force behind the struggle was the status of the Saar.[4] The leaders of the new organizations were well aware how much their ranks had been depleted. The founders of the C.D.U. had great difficulty in finding people willing to join. Consequently it was a question of getting organized early enough if there was to be any hope of victory in the elections or at least of winning key posts. As for the government, it was conscious of the split in public opinion and sought to foil the stratagems of the opposition and gain time. Its delaying tactics evoked the increasingly vigorous protests of its adversaries who called European opinion as witness to the incredibly autocratic methods of the government. Indignation[5] and confusion reached their height when, at the end of October, a Democratic People's Party of the Saar was launched.

However justified certain of the protests seemed, it is questionable whether the protesters were in fact justified in formulating their objections. Were they above reproach themselves? Was the support they were receiving from the German Social Democratic Party or the C.D.U. strictly ethical? Did they not have behind them the *Saarbund*, the *Deutsche Aktion* of the Prince of Löwenstein, and the Ministry for All-German Affairs, all indirectly and even directly promoting their efforts? One has only to refer to the report put out by the first two of these to the *Deutsche Saarzeitung* and to the many publications of the Comel Verlag in 1952 to measure the strength of the pressure exercised by the Federal Republic despite the fact that, according to the Allied note of August 3, 1951, its jurisdiction " does not extend beyond its territorial limits."

This playing for time on the part of the Hoffmann Government

---

3 The law was voted on March 17, 1952. *Cf. Amtsblatt des Saarlandes*, No. 16, April 4, 1952, pp. 369–371.

4 Proof of this may be found in the fact that the Saar Government did not use the Communist Party's non-acceptance of the 1947 Constitution and Preamble against it.

5 That this indignation was not as sincere as it appeared in public declarations was manifested in some of the polemics during the campaign preceding the Bundestag elections of 1957.

prevented the new parties from setting up their electoral machinery.
It could, however, only slow down the growing force of the opposition. The Church, or more precisely a part of the Saar clergy and
the Bishop of Trier, came out in favour of the new Christian Democratic Party. At the beginning of the summer, the Bishop,
Monsignor Mathias Wehr, decided on a course of action which was
to have considerable influence on the debate. On June 21 he sent
a letter to President Hoffmann in which, after emphasizing his
non-interference in political affairs unless they affected religious
questions, he expressed his regret that the political schism had
become an accomplished fact. However, since it was so, he felt
that authorization for the new C.D.U. could not be refused.
Prayers and meditation, *sine ira et studio*, had strengthened his
opinion that even greater detriment would ensue to the Catholic
cause if authorization were refused. The Bishop's intervention
threw the government ranks into confusion. He thought he was
acting in confidence, but the news of his intervention as well as the
purport if not the substance of his letter became known nonetheless
rapidly. The protest to the Vatican could do little to soften the
blow to the Christian People's Party.

The trade unions, and especially the *Syndicat des mineurs*,
which had the strongest influence on the *Syndicat unitaire*, were
to do for the new German Social Democratic Party in the Saar
what the Saar clergy did for the C.D.U. On March 29, Paul
Kutsch was elected the first President of the *Syndicat unitaire*,
while Kurt Conrad was put on the Committee. Mr. Kutsch, who
made contact on several occasions with Mr. Strohm and the
Ministry for All-German Affairs,[6] seized this opportunity to make
a statement at the conference of the *Deutscher Gewerkschaftsbund*,
held in July in Berlin, which was widely publicized: " The Saarlanders refuse to be handed over as reparations after each war, like
bees or ants, to some foreign state." He added: " As a solution of
the Saar question, we affirm our preference for Germany because
the language, the art, and culture of Germany are also ours."

In July, the significant election of Paul Kutsch to the presidency
of the *Syndicat des mineurs* made him not only the most powerful
union leader but the leader of the opposition in Socialist and union

[6] Cf. *Bericht des vom Landtag des Saarlandes durch Beschluss vom 7. Juli 1953 gemäss
Artikel 81 der Verfassung und gemäss Artikel 21 der Geschäftsordnung eingesetzten
Untersuchungsausschusses* (n.p. or d.); also, *Saar-Bergbau*, No. 22 (December 29, 1952).

circles. It emphasized, if emphasis was needed, that the protest was against the régime rather than against the government.

While this struggle was continuing inside the Saar and growing in intensity as the elections drew nearer, a new diplomatic battle opened between France and Germany. The French Government began it. On January 25, the High Commissioner's office in the Saar was abolished; French interests were represented by a Diplomatic Mission, at the head of which was Gilbert Grandval, now raised to the rank of Ambassador. This decision had been expected for some time and had been announced by Mr. Schuman himself; the necessary funds had been allotted in the 1952 budget. It was a decision that was inevitable in the logic of a French policy trying to give the Saar wider autonomy in order to consolidate the existing status.

In Germany there was no mistaking the true motive underlying France's action, and the decision aroused the anger of the opposition and protests from the press. People bristled at the attempt to present the Federal Government with a *fait accompli*. The appointment of Mr. Grandval, who was justly considered the French ringleader in the Saar, was not calculated to calm the mind of the public. The more subtle might perhaps realize that, in keeping Mr. Grandval in this post, the French Government was limiting the effect of its own action in the Saar. The man was too much an incarnation of the " *présence française* "; he had too much influence and too many means at his disposal for an illusion of autonomy to be created so long as he remained.

France's decision, even more than pressure from the opposition and from what might be called the Saar Party,[7] impelled the Federal Government to reply. On February 29, it sent a letter to the Council of Europe in which it announced its intention of informing the Committee of Ministers at its next session of the curtailment of democratic freedoms in the Saar. To this letter was attached a memorandum in which the Federal Government set out at length the facts which could be brought in evidence against the Saar Government.[8]

[7] *Cf.*, in this connection, the long article devoted to Heinrich Schneider in *Der Spiegel*, October 19, 1955. The author seems well informed, though biased.

[8] *Cf. Memorandum der Bundesregierung, Der Staatssekretär des Auswärtigen Amtes, No. 214–26, II. 799/52, vom 29 Februar 1952, an den Generalsekretär des Europarates, J. Camille Paris.*

But the Chancellor was circumspect. On February 5,[9] he made a rather significant correction to a previous day's statement in which he had subordinated Germany's adherence to the E.D.C. to the satisfaction of her expressed wishes concerning the Saar. Unknown to him, his carefully worded statement analysing the difficulties he had encountered had been transformed into what appeared to be an ultimatum. Later, at the Conference in London on February 18, at which were present the Foreign Ministers of the United States, the United Kingdom, and France, together with the Chancellor of the Federal Republic, Anthony Eden and Dean Acheson made repeated appeals to Chancellor Adenauer and Mr. Schuman to try to settle the Saar question amicably.

It seemed, too, as though the Chancellor and some of his colleagues, such as Walter Hallstein, were tired of the pressure exerted by the " Saar Party." Mr. Hallstein complained of certain publications which he considered inopportune. He suspected Gustav Strohm of being at the root of some of the difficulties that the opposition and public opinion were creating for the Federal Government. Was not Mr. Strohm politically linked with Karl Mommer, the Socialist expert on the Saar question? Thus it did not come as a complete surprise when, on March 17, 1952, Mr. Strohm was suspended from his post for having given information to a correspondent of the United Press.

The next day, in an interview with Mr. Schuman, Chancellor Adenauer again took up the discussion of the Saar problem which they had started in London on February 18. He repeated the proposals which he had made in the summer of 1951 and which the *Rheinischer Merkur* had re-stated in an article on February 1. Chancellor Adenauer and Mr. Schuman were in agreement that a settlement must be reached before the peace treaties were concluded, and that it would be submitted for the approval of the United States and United Kingdom Governments. Chancellor Adenauer sketched out the basic elements: an autonomous Saar to be placed under the supervision of the Council of Europe; Saarbrücken to be the seat of the organs of the E.C.S.C. Once its status had been determined, the Saar was to be completely independent in political, economic, and cultural matters. The Saar population would express its views through the medium of a new and freely

---

[9] *Cf. Documents on the Saar*, Vol. II (Bad Godesberg: Office of the U.S. High Commissioner for Germany, February, 1953), p. 99.

elected Landtag.[10] France and Germany would abstain from any actions that might influence the Saar's attitude. A part of the Saar territory, still to be determined, was to be incorporated into the Federal Republic.

This plan was to remain confidential. But Chancellor Adenauer intended to make a public statement that he would submit beforehand to Mr. Schuman. This announcement, made on March 20, stated that negotiations had been entered into between the French Government and the Federal Republic to settle the Saar question prior to the conclusion of a peace treaty.[11] Such a settlement would require the approval of the United States and United Kingdom Governments and of the population of the Saar as expressed through a freely elected Landtag. It was agreed that a commission should be set up composed of a representative each from France, from the Federal Republic, and from the Saar, and that its task should be to verify the validity of allegations that conditions prevailing in the Saar made free and democratic elections impossible.[12] Chancellor Adenauer added that since these negotiations gave promise of success, he would not make any further statements on the question of human rights in the Saar. In conclusion, he announced that in the light of the prospect of an approaching settlement he had not reiterated in Rome the reasons for the Federal Republic's opposition in 1950 to the Saar Government's signing the European Convention for the Protection of Human Rights.

Chancellor Adenauer's statement radiated optimism. In reading it, one had the impression that a solution of the disagreement was imminent and that everyone would be satisfied. Public opinion was all the more inclined to go along with the Chancellor because he spoke with the full agreement of Robert Schuman. Had not Mr. Schuman at a press conference in Lisbon, on February 26, 1952, let it be clearly understood that he was ready for Franco-German negotiations over the Saar? Everyone knew that the text

[10] This was an extremely controversial question in Germany and one upon which the Chancellor's own views had changed. Originally he was in favour of a plebiscite. But he met with the resistance of those who, like Peter Altmeier, thought that the plebiscite of 1935 had settled the question once and for all, and that the German Government would weaken its position if it so much as admitted the principle of a new plebiscite.
[11] Cf. *Documents on the Saar, op. cit.*, p. 118.
[12] Chancellor Adenauer had had something else in mind originally; he had proposed to Mr. Schuman the setting up of a commission composed of representatives of the United States, the United Kingdom, France, and the Federal Republic. This commission would not have been limited to inquiry but would have taken the necessary steps to create conditions indispensable to free elections. This formula was obviously unacceptable to Mr. Schuman.

read by the Chancellor was the result of his talks with Mr. Schuman. Moreover, Johannes Hoffmann had publicly given his approval. Present at the meeting in Paris, he spoke soon after Chancellor Adenauer and expressed his " earnest desire that direct negotiations take place in the near future on the question of whether conditions exist in the Saar for free and democratic elections to form a new Landtag." [13] He went on to approve in principle a European solution to the Saar question.

If Mr. Hoffmann showed himself so eager to accept a tripartite discussion implying a recognition of Germany's right to watch over Saar affairs, it was because he felt that he had just won a diplomatic victory. Did not the interview he had had with Chancellor Adenauer signify in the eyes of Germans and Saarlanders that the Chancellor recognized him as the official spokesman of the Saar people? Moreover could it not be said that the Chancellor's acceptance of a tripartite investigation of conditions in the Saar constituted the first gesture of recognition of the Saar Government, particularly as this government had been authorized to append its signature to the European Convention?

The hopes aroused by Chancellor Adenauer's statement and the brief negotiations that had preceded it were soon dashed. The ministers had gone too far. They had concentrated on finding a way out of the impasse in which they found themselves by delimiting those points on which agreement was possible and by deciding upon the procedure to be followed, but the reactions of those around them—of the press and of the opposition—forced them subsequently to re-emphasize the national aims they had purposely ignored in order to make negotiation possible. In Germany, on March 22, Erich Ollenhauer published a statement [14] in which he declared that the agreement reached in Paris " signifies abandonment of the German position and formal recognition of the Saar Government by Chancellor Adenauer." In the Saar there was abundant opposition to Germany along similar lines. The day before, *Combat* for its part declared that the Chancellor had obtained what he wanted, that the lesson of this " historic day " was that " henceforth Germany would have her say in Saar affairs." This was also the opinion of Ambassador Grandval and some of

[13] *Cf. La Chronique sarroise*, No. 1 (March 25, 1952).
[14] *Frankfurter Allgemeine Zeitung*, March 22, 1952.

Johannes Hoffmann's colleagues. As they saw it, Mr. Hoffmann had made a grave mistake in accepting the principle of tripartite examination of democratic freedoms in the Saar. French diplomacy, declared Mr. Grandval, had made a major effort in the summer of 1951 to ensure inclusion in the Allied note of the reminder that " the jurisdiction of the Federal Republic does not extend beyond its territorial limits." Moreover, France was bound by the Franco-Saar Conventions of March 3, 1950, to respect the autonomy of the Saar. Finally, it was clear that Chancellor Adenauer's statement did not imply any recognition on his part of the Saar Government. But was it possible to refuse to continue the negotiations? The French Ambassador at Saarbrücken did not think so. However, to escape from the predicament priority had to be given to negotiation of the European status of the Saar rather than to an inquiry into democratic freedoms. Only thus could Chancellor Adenauer's skilful move be foiled. Ambassador Grandval's pessimism was possibly excessive but it was compensated for by an acute sense of the need for action. He was not a man to allow himself to be put on the defensive.

But there was no action. Faced with the critical reactions to their policy, Chancellor Adenauer and Mr. Schuman allowed themselves to be gradually immobilized. The explanations they gave of their negotiations in the days following the Paris conversations were still temperate. But Mr. Schuman had to face an extremely violent attack in the Council of the Republic during the debate that opened on March 25 on the ratification of the Treaty establishing the E.C.S.C. Senator Michel Debré, who led the attack, spoke on April 1, 1952, and reproached Mr. Schuman for having, by a series of concessions, allowed the French position in the Saar to be called into question. What, he asked, was this formula of " europeanization "? Did it mean that henceforth the Saar would be answerable to the Council of Europe?

If so, it seems to me that it is very difficult to speak of political autonomy.

Does this mean that the Saar becomes a sort of *terra nullius*? If so, there is no more question of economic union or of retention of the Saar within the franc area.

In conclusion, you tell us we have established the basis of an agreement with the Federal Government. Agreement, perhaps, on this Control Commission, but not on the future at all. If it were otherwise, I

think you would not find it so difficult to define this word "europeanization," which sounds very vague to us and behind which we sense
nothing but surrender.[15]

In his reply, Mr. Schuman advanced the very argument that was
the keynote of the German opposition to Chancellor Adenauer's
policy: "What we want is the preservation of the *status quo*, with
the sole difference that the foreign relations of the Saar shall no
longer be the responsibility of France but of a European
organization." [16]

Preservation of the *status quo*, that is to say, maintenance of the
Saar's economic union with France and its separation from Germany, was exactly what the Federal Government did not want.
Mr. Schuman's reply was further thrown into relief by the motion
voted on April 1 by a large majority in the Council of the Republic
asking the government to " reject under any circumstances a status
for the Saar that did not include maintenance of the Franco-Saar
economic union along with the Conventions which are its foundation, as well as the internal political autonomy of the territory." [17]

Chancellor Adenauer tried nevertheless to continue the negotiations which had been announced. On April 12 he sent a letter to
Robert Schuman informing him that the German Government was
prepared to send three delegates to the Saar " to study with a
corresponding French delegation whether the requisite conditions
already exist for the organization of democratic elections in the
Saar." He wished to know whether the French Government was
prepared to do the same.

The fact that the letter made no reference to the discussion on
the status of the Saar seemed to confirm the observations made by
Mr. Grandval after the March 20 statement. The French Minister
for Foreign Affairs replied on April 21, reminding the Chancellor

[15] *Journal officiel, Débats parlementaires, Conseil de la République*, April 2, 1952, p. 817.
[16] In his historical survey of the Saar question in the Council of the Republic on April 1,
1952, the Foreign Minister gave a version of the discussion of the problem of the Saar's
signing the E.C.S.C. Treaty which was not quite correct: " It was not until 1951, in
March, on the eve of the signing of the Treaty, that a new wave of demands arose,
especially in France. . . . There was insistence that the Saar Government be permitted
to sign the Treaty itself. This meant, as you very well understand, creating at the last
minute a new problem that might result in re-opening the whole discussion; and,
legally, as I said at the time, the Saar Government could only have signed by virtue of
powers which we had given to it." *Ibid.*, p. 812. The fact was, however, that the
problem of the signing of the Treaty had already been raised in 1950 and had even
been the subject of a motion in the Landtag. Moreover, Mr. Schuman had formally
clarified his position.
[17] *Ibid.*, p. 825.

that the essential purpose of the March conversations had been to " seek a solution for the entire Saar problem." The investigation of conditions under which the elections would take place could only be made " within the framework of a forthcoming agreement on the final status of the Saar." The note added: " The French Government is ready to name its representatives but it is difficult to envisage their participation in the projected investigation before any serious attempt has been made to initiate such an agreement on the status." Robert Schuman did not close the door to negotiations; he was merely content to await a proposal from Germany.

The negotiations upon which they had embarked were thus interrupted. Chancellor Adenauer stated as much two days later to the Bundestag where he had to reply to a new attack from the Socialists, who reproached him with having accepted the annexation of the Saar by France under cover of the term " europeanization." [18]

" In Paris," he declared, " I believed, after my talks with Foreign Minister Schuman, that the ground was sufficiently prepared for a satisfactory settlement of the Saar question. The events that have occurred in the meantime have revealed that we had moved faster than actual developments warranted." He concluded that, unfortunately, the matter would have to be left in abeyance.

He, too, had been forced by opposition attacks to define his position in such a way as to furnish arguments to the opponents of Mr. Schuman both in France and the Saar. Never did he have in mind the recognition, even *de facto*, of the Saar Government. On the contrary, he was very careful not to refer to anything but the " representatives of the French Government and the representatives of the Federal Government." The Commission thus constituted would inevitably have had to meet with the Saar authorities. But never at any time was it suggested that these Saar representatives might have the right to vote in this Commission.[19]

[18] The attitude of Chancellor Adenauer showed, as Deputy Karl Mommer put it, " that the Chancellor was ready to depart from the earlier policy in the Saar and give up the Saar territory and that, under the attractive name of ' europeanization,' he was now prepared to give his consent to the unjust policy of the victor, the *de facto* annexation of the Saar territory by France." *Cf. Verhandlungen des Deutschen Bundestages*, I.205/8820, April 23, 1952.

[19] The formulation was in fact open to discussion and this immediately led to controversy. The wording used by the Chancellor in Paris was as follows: " Representatives of the French Government and of the Government of the Federal Republic should meet immediately to examine, with representatives of the Saar Government, whether the proper conditions for free, democratic elections exist in the Saar."

Thus the failure was obvious and its causes equally clear. The two men were caught between two opposition groups which, by the simple fact that they were pursuing contrary aims, actually strengthened each other's case. As though the better to emphasize the parallelism of the situations, the debate in the Bundestag ended in the same way as that in the Council of the Republic, by adoption of a resolution. Mr. Ollenhauer had conceived of a formula which would have made settlement of the Saar question a pre-condition to German participation in the E.D.C. He did not put this in the same form in the Socialist resolution which proposed the sub-mission of all decisions relating to the fate of a German territory to popular vote. The majority, however, made a counter-proposal in rather moderate terms, affirming that the Saar was part of German territory and that no German territory could be disposed of without the consent of the Germans.

Mr. Adenauer and Mr. Schuman would no doubt have liked to let the question rest until tension had eased.

But this was scarcely possible. In the Saar, feeling was rising as the date of the elections drew near. To the turmoil that per-vaded the trade unions was added the mounting tension resulting from the endeavours of the new Socialist and Christian Democratic parties to obtain formal recognition from the government. This struggle, supported in Germany by the pro-Saar opposition, rico-chetted and stimulated that same opposition which continued to harass the Chancellor. The day after the debate in the Bundestag,[20] the Social Democratic Party had asked the government to publish a White Paper on the Franco-German negotiations. On May 16 the Chancellor replied to the request in the negative. This did not prevent Mr. Mommer from interpolating a question on June 18 and charging the government yet again with irresponsibility. It had not taken advantage of the meeting of the Committee of Ministers on May 22 and had signed the Treaty setting up the E.D.C. without using the opportunity to raise the question of democratic freedoms in the Saar. Now, Mr. Mommer reminded his listeners, elections which might be of decisive importance for the future of the Saar were to take place in the autumn. It was vital, therefore, that the government plan to raise this question at the session of the Committee of Ministers in October.

[20] April 24, 1952.

On July 18,[21] there was a new intervention by the Socialists in the Bundestag, inspired by the difficulties that had been put in the path of the new parties in the Saar. What action was the government of the Federal Republic going to take in view of the renewed manifestations in France that she was determined to pursue her Saar policy? Was not the government going to ask for a discussion in the Council of Europe of its memorandum on democratic freedoms in the Saar? And to what extent did the rule of oppression to which Germans in the Saar were subjected affect the government's desire to ratify as soon as possible the Treaty setting up the E.D.C.?

The French Minister for Foreign Affairs and the Ambassador in Saarbrücken were conscious, as were certain sections of public opinion, that time was not necessarily on their side. Perhaps, it was suggested, it would be a good idea to take the initiative—or to arrange for it to be taken by a third party—in finding a European solution. Similarly, circumstances might require a revision of the Conventions in the direction of a widening of Saar autonomy. Revision of the Conventions and europeanization might, in the opinion of those who followed Saar internal affairs closely, constitute a fine electoral platform sufficiently positive to attract the elector and to resist the opposition's offensive.

The Allies, too, urged negotiations. The Saar conflict was becoming more and more of a drag on European collaboration. At each new step it rose again, more acrimonious than ever. On all sides the idea was already dawning that the settlement of the Saar question might be made a prerequisite to ratification of the Treaty establishing the E.D.C. The German Socialists had considered this publicly. In France it was discussed, but in rather cryptic terms.

This convergence of interests in favour of a resumption of conversations was expressed in the resolution adopted by the Council of Ministers of the six countries of the Schuman Plan on July 24, 1952. The resolution invited France and Germany " to seek, before September 15, a solution to the Saar question by direct negotiations designed to achieve the europeanization of the Saar." It added that, if an agreement were reached, Saarbrücken should become the headquarters of the E.C.S.C. Otherwise, the question would be taken up again.[22]

---

[21] Cf. *Die S.P.D. zur Saarfrage*, p. 203. (Mimeographed.)

[22] On the eve of the resolution, Robert Schuman had proposed Strasbourg as a provisional headquarters until the European status of the Saar had been defined.

On August 1, Franco-German conversations began in Paris, and Walter Hallstein and Robert Schuman took part. The exchange of views did not lead very far. The Germans were concentrating primarily on creating what Mr. Hallstein called a favourable atmosphere, by which he meant adoption of measures aimed at relieving tensions within the Saar. These were: permission to constitute new political parties, the end of sequestration, and the postponement of elections. It is clear that by these measures the government hoped to weaken French influence and to give those Saarlanders favourable to Germany a chance to increase their own influence. By this shift in relative strength within the Saar, the Federal Government hoped that its own position would be strengthened in the final diplomatic negotiations.[23]

But the French negotiator did not let himself be deflected by what he considered a diversion. As far as he was concerned, the discussion should concentrate on the conditions for europeanization of the Saar. Moreover, this europeanization had limits which he defined in the course of the discussion. He swept aside at once the suggestion tentatively advanced by his opposite number that France should make a contribution of some of its territory to the formation of this first European state.[24]

Furthermore, he observed, France intended to maintain Franco-Saar economic co-operation and the existing financial and customs union. What he envisaged was a modification of the Conventions linking France and the Saar and not their suppression. Whatever European organization was selected, and it might be the Council of Europe, it would be responsible for the Saar's foreign relations and for ensuring that the economic union with France did not mean a preponderance of French political influence.

Faced with these stipulations, Mr. Hallstein, who had not even outlined Germany's ideas on europeanization, gave little grounds for hope. Apparently disappointment was very keen, judging by the letters sent by Chancellor Adenauer, the first dated August 2, from the Bürgenstock to Robert Schuman. The Chancellor expressed his surprise at the hardening of his French colleague's position. Had the latter not stated, at the Conference of Foreign

---

23 *Cf.*, for these and later negotiations (in October), an article in the *Saarbrücker Zeitung* of November 17, 1952, entitled "Die Wahrheit über die Saarverhandlungen," which gives accurate information.

24 The suggestion of also europeanizing a part of Lorraine had been made publicly a few months earlier on February 1, 1952, by Carlo Schmid.

Ministers, that if the Saar were europeanized the Franco-Saar Conventions would cease to be in effect? Mr. Adenauer then let it be understood that a debate on the Saar in the Council of Europe would be inevitable. He feared such a debate, for the bitterness of the discussion could not fail to divide the two countries even further. Perhaps they could spare themselves this new crisis if France would see to it that the new parties were granted the authorization they desired and that the date of the elections was postponed. He closed with the suggestion that the two sides should put down their points of view in writing.

Mr. Schuman's reply, dated August 9, did not alter the French position in any way: questions relating to elections in the Saar could only be considered " in conjunction with the establishment of a new and adequately defined status for the Saar." The French Foreign Minister agreed, however, to set down his position in writing, but he declared that he was doing so in his own name and without committing his government.

Indeed, on August 13 he handed Mr. Hallstein an " outline of a political status for the Saar within the framework of a European organization " in which the French viewpoint was again set out. France agreed to give up all special prerogatives of a political nature. A European Commissioner " will be responsible for Saar interests abroad and in international organizations [and] will see to it that the status of the Saar is respected," and would have, for this purpose, a right of veto. In return, on the economic level, the existing customs union with France would be preserved, with the one reservation that European bodies would exercise general control over the functioning of the union. Finally, Mr. Schuman's memorandum proposed a special status for the European University of the Saar to guarantee its " European " spirit.

The German reply, submitted on August 19, accepted the bulk of the French proposals dealing with the political régime and with the Saar's cultural relations with other countries. But it expressed the objections which might have been expected to the proposed economic régime. The retention of the Franco-Saar economic union was incompatible with the European status being proposed at the same time.

Things were merely moving round in circles. However, on September 10, at the meeting of the Council of Ministers in Luxembourg, Mr. Adenauer and Mr. Schuman presented a rather optimistic report. According to their statements at press conferences, there had been progress in the negotiations. Face-to-face discussions had made it possible to come to grips more effectively with the problem of unauthorized political parties in the Saar. Mr. Schuman was disposed to intercede on behalf of their recognition on condition that Chancellor Adenauer for his part would persuade them to accept the principle of europeanization of the Saar. Dates were even fixed: Mr. Adenauer was to send a reply before September 22. But on September 19 the Chancellor asked for more time, and it was Mr. Schuman who, on the 24th, made the first move and proposed the text of a joint communiqué giving the broad outlines of an agreement on the Saar:

> It seemed to them [the two governments] that the Saar should be granted a European status which would respect her internal autonomy and which would be guaranteed by the interested states and that, furthermore, the economic, customs, and monetary union existing between France and the Saar should evolve with the progress of European integration.

The communiqué also provided for consultation with the population of the Saar " if necessary by a referendum."

The Chancellor's reply arrived on October 1 in the form of a new proposal. The discussions he had had, as anticipated, with the representatives of the unauthorized parties [25] had been encouraging. But the idea of europeanization still appeared hard to define. Because of this there had emerged a possible solution in the form of a five-year provisional status: an autonomous Saar would be placed under the supervision of a European organization; on the economic plane, a new set of regulations would replace the Conventions in order to realize a " balance between Saar, French, and German interests," and, in particular, to assure France " the purchase of Saar coal in French francs and the sale of agricultural produce from Lorraine in the Saar territory in exchange for French francs." The adoption of this solution would be facilitated by postponing the elections and granting the requested authorization to the unauthorized parties.

Thus the two spokesmen each tended towards a solution involving some sort of intermediary or provisional régime. Mr.

25 On September 17, 1952, Chancellor Adenauer had received in Bonn a representative of each of the three opposition parties, Richard Becker, Hubert Ney, and Kurt Conrad. *Cf.* the account of Heinrich Schneider in *Die Deutsche Saar*, December 29, 1956. A most colourful account appeared in *Der Spiegel*, October 19, 1956.

Schuman, in his letter of September 24, spoke of an "evolution" of the economic union "with the progress of European integration." Mr. Adenauer proposed a provisional five-year status and explicitly reserved certain of France's economic interests. They were not, therefore, so far apart in their views. And yet they made no progress. For Mr. Schuman, the Chancellor's suggestion marked a step backwards from his previous proposals. The interpretation which was given to it in France was that Mr. Adenauer was simply trying to gain the necessary time to win back the Saar to the German side. Naturally he denied this; he returned to the charge, but could not convince his opposite number.[26]

A last effort at agreement was undertaken between October 20 and 24 in a feverish atmosphere. Both sides felt that the matter could not be left to drag on any longer. In the Saar there was mounting tension; attention was concentrated on the battle being waged around the authorization requested by the new political parties and the date of the elections. On the German side, people were determined to obtain a postponement of the elections. In France there was a feeling that by forcing a solution one might still obtain a favourable decision and that any delay would weaken the French position. Among the Allies a certain impatience became evident because of anxiety aroused by the slowness of European rearmament. Thus they tried to obtain settlement of a matter that was poisoning the whole atmosphere and compromising ratification of the E.D.C. in which the United Kingdom and the United States, as well as Europe, had an interest. The Consultative Assembly of the Council of Europe, to which the Saar affair was now submitted, placed it on its agenda. On September 18 it entrusted to Marinus van der Goes van Naters the task of reporting on the question of the future of the Saar.[27]

So, as time passed the conflict tended to widen. The French Government was not ignorant of the fact that this development was

[26] This scepticism was not very surprising if one thinks of the interpretation of their interview given by the leaders of the pro-German opposition in the Saar. According to them the plan which the Chancellor presented to Robert Schuman was precisely that which they themselves would have suggested and which they had championed for a long time. Furthermore, the Chancellor had promised to consult them in good time whenever there was a decision on the Saar to be made and not to undertake anything against their will. *Cf. Der Spiegel*, October 19, 1956.

[27] An appeal was also launched by the Central Committee of the European Union of Federalists at its meeting on September 20–21, 1952, in Strasbourg. It invited the Governments of France and of the Federal Republic to agree on the organization of a plebiscite under international control to permit the Saarlanders to state their opinions on the principle of the europeanization of their country.

unfavourable to the French case. In 1952, even more than in the spring of 1951, the memory of the conditions from 1945 to 1947 that had justified the economic union of the Saar with France and the separation of the Saar from Germany had become blurred. The influence that Germany, a full partner, wielded in the Council of Europe continued to increase, while the position of the Saar Government and its French protector was seriously weakened by their repressive measures, which were widely publicized and vigorously denounced by the German press and public opinion.

The whole negotiation hinged on the text of the joint communiqué, and it is worthwhile comparing the successive versions to appraise precisely what divided the two governments and what drew them together. On October 21, Mr. Schuman received, through the intermediary of Mr. Eden, a plan drawn up by the Chancellor:

> Talks continue concerning the settlement of the Saar problem by some form of europeanization. A final settlement must await the peace treaty. Until this final settlement, the Saar must be given autonomy under the supervision of a European organization such as the Council of Ministers of the Coal and Steel Community, with a government and a freely elected parliament.
>
> We are convinced that the talks will lead to positive results in the foreseeable future. We therefore consider it desirable to extend the present session of the Saar Landtag to permit a successful outcome to the talks.

Mr. Schuman replied on October 22 with a counter-proposal:

> 1. Talks continue between France and the Federal Republic of Germany with the objective of conferring a European status on the Saar. Agreement has been reached on the following principles, on the understanding that their implementation is subject to the terms of a peace treaty.
>
> 2. The political autonomy of the Saar shall be guaranteed. The Saar Government will be responsible to a parliament freely elected under the provisions governing its status. The régime will be placed under the general supervision of a European organization such as the Council of Ministers of the Coal and Steel Community or the Committee of Ministers of the Council of Europe.
>
> 3. The existing economic union between France and the Saar will be adapted to this status and will evolve as European integration progresses.
>
> 4. The Saar population will be given an opportunity to express its views on this proposed status which will be guaranteed by all the interested states.

5. We are convinced that the negotiations will lead to positive results in the foreseeable future. In this spirit, we consider it desirable to extend the present session.

The next day—October 23—Chancellor Adenauer transmitted certain proposals for changes in the French text. In the second paragraph he wanted to delete the phrase " under the provisions governing its status."

In the third paragraph he proposed a different wording: " The form that the economic relationship between the Saar and France will take as European integration progresses will be the object of a joint study with a view to reaching a settlement in which France's interests will be respected."

For the fourth paragraph he also suggested another wording: " In any event, it is the population of the Saar which will have the final say on this status, which is to be guaranteed by all the interested states."

These changes, which plainly tended to disregard the existing status and deprived France of the security she had, were not accepted by Robert Schuman, who replied the same day with new proposals.

He suggested that " within the framework of the Statute " be replaced by " with due respect for the Statute." For the paragraph on economic union, a further step forward was made on the French side by the proposal that " the economic union existing between France and the Saar shall be adapted to the status of the latter. The future evolution of this union, as European integration progresses, will be the subject of a study by the interested states."

To this the Chancellor replied with yet another text for the second and third paragraphs:

> The political autonomy of the Saar will be guaranteed by a statute. This statute will be placed under the general supervision of a European organization. . . .
> The form that the existing economic relations between France and the Saar within the Franco-Saar economic union will take, as European integration progresses, will be the object of a study made by the interested states.

Obviously both sides had made an effort and it looked as though agreement was not impossible. This was probably the opinion of those who, like the two ministers concerned, bore in mind over and above any immediate interests in the Saar the vital role for

Europe of an agreement between France and Germany. But a spirit of inflexibility triumphed in the end, after long debates in which Roger Seydoux, Jacques Bourbon-Busset, Jacques de Beaumarchais, and Ambassador Grandval participated on the French side, and on behalf of the Saar a large delegation consisting of Johannes Hoffmann, Franz Singer, Josef Kurtz, Ludwig Geraldi, Peter Zimmer, Richard Kirn, Heinz Braun, Ernst Kunkel, Franz Schlehofer, and Emile Straus.[28]

It was finally decided to adhere to the French text submitted on October 23 and to ask the Chancellor for his reaction. His reply was negative. The two governments had no choice but to announce a temporary break-down in negotiations.

Why this set-back? *Le Monde*, in an article on October 8, had already given a reply:

> For two weeks, in France and in Germany, everything has been done by widely divergent groups to complicate these negotiations, if not to ensure their failure. To this end, all kinds of nationalists, people who hold Europe in contempt, opponents of Franco-German co-operation or merely of a European army, political enemies of the Chancellor and of Mr. Schuman have vied with one another. Unquestionably, the calculations of most of them are accurate: a failure of the negotiations over the Saar raises again the whole question of the policy of European integration.

The comment was right. During the period of the negotiations, the two Ministers for Foreign Affairs were subjected to pressure from French and German nationalists. But hostility to the policy of integration was not their only motive. Both sides were afraid of being duped in this deal. The Germans asked what kind of europeanization of the Saar it was that could still remain within the framework of the existing régime and preserve the economic union. Why, asked the French, abandon a régime, provisional though it might be, which was recognized by the Allies and had at least the virtue of existing, for another régime just as provisional, drawn up under conditions that robbed France of her last trump card?[29]

Mr. Grandval, who during this period of negotiation had no hesitation in giving his opinion publicly on several occasions, was absolutely categorical when he stated that France must adhere to

---

[28] *Cf. Volksstimme*, October 25, 1952.
[29] *Cf.* Mr. Grandval's speech to accredited United States newspaper correspondents in Paris, October 8, 1952.

the proposals she had made for the europeanization of the Saar which respected the existing régime and above all the economic union. Moreover, she must seek to obtain—and here there appeared again his old idea of the Saar settlement as a " prerequisite "—a settlement of the question " before the signing of contractual agreements."

> It is very clear [he added] that if we were not able to settle the Saar question when Germany was occupied, when the German economy was non-existent, when she had no army, how can we hope to do so now that German economy is again on a sound footing, when Germany's rights are again recognized and she will soon have twelve divisions in the field? I think that if we pass this point and the affair remains unsettled, it will be resolved entirely in favour of Germany to the greatest possible detriment of our joint Franco-Saar activity and of the balance of Europe.[30]

It is easy to guess what line the French Ambassador in Saarbrücken took in the decisive negotiations between October 20 and 24. One can assume that his intervention was not without influence on the negative stand taken by President Hoffmann and on the ultimately firm position of the French Minister for Foreign Affairs.

The break-down in negotiations was followed almost immediately by the official opening of the election campaign. On October 29 the Landtag adopted the electoral law and fixed the date of the elections for November 30. The battle raged fiercely. On all sides every possible weapon was used.

The government seemed to have the situation well in hand. The opposition parties had not been granted the authorization for which they had asked, so the struggle was restricted to the Saar Socialist Party and the Christian People's Party. The true issue was the régime itself. The leaders of the two parties knew that their influence would be measured by the number of people who voted in the elections. They thus redoubled their efforts to encourage the citizens to declare themselves, and for this they did not hesitate to make demands on France, which, to the outside observer, might seem in flagrant contradiction to their rejection of the German proposals for a new régime.[31] The French Government, which for

[30] Address by Mr. Grandval at a luncheon given by the *Association française de la Sarre* to the French regional press, October 8, 1952.

[31] Chancellor Adenauer raised this point in his speech to the Bundestag, November 18, 1952.

some months had planned a revision of the Franco-Saar Conventions of March 8, 1950, did not hesitate to promise satisfaction. Moreover, this was not the only support it gave. There was too much at stake for the French Government to remain passive. The opposition was very active. It could not express itself within the framework of an officially constituted party, so it demonstrated in many ways and co-ordinated in a very striking manner the action of the various groups. Paul Kutsch led the attack inside the trade unions. The government succeeded in robbing him of the presidency of the *Syndicat des mineurs* and then of that of the *Syndicat unitaire*, but this interference only heightened his prestige.

As for the clergy, it took an active part in the campaign. The Bishop of Trier set the example. Urged by President Hoffmann to address a pastoral letter to the Saar Catholics to encourage them to perform their duty as electors in favour of the Christian People's Party, he refused. He would have been willing to do this only if Johannes Hoffmann had officially declared that the elections of November 30 would not affect the final settlement of the Saar problem. This was obviously rather a lot to ask of the President of the Saar Government. Bishop Wehr was not content to abstain. On November 19 he announced publication of a letter in which he explicitly condemned the refusal to grant the pro-German parties the authorization they had requested and, recognizing that the elections could be interpreted as endorsing the separation of the Saar from Germany, he gave Catholics the choice either of voting for candidates upholding the interests of the Church or of abstaining entirely.[32] The French Government, warned by Johannes Hoffmann, immediately approached the Holy See, which gave instructions that this letter be modified. This, however, had only limited results. The Bishop did indeed order his letter to be withdrawn, but his instructions to this effect were only partially followed. True, the *Saarbrücker Zeitung* published an alleged interview with Vicar-General Weins, in which he recommended that people vote.[33] This electoral manoeuvre at the eleventh hour may have made some impression on the faithful, the more so as the denial was published very inconspicuously.[34] Its effect on the Saar

[32] *Cf.* Maxime Mourin, " Le Saint-Siège et la Sarre," *op. cit.*, p. 420.
[33] November 26, 1952.
[34] November 29, 1952.

clergy was, however, limited since the majority of them had already decided in favour of the German Fatherland.

Finally, the opposition was vigorously supported by the Federal Republic. The session of the Bundestag of November 18,[35] in which the Chancellor explained the negotiations and analysed the situation resulting from their failure, ended with an almost unanimous demonstration in favour of a German Saar and an appeal to the Saar electors to abstain from voting. The German press and radio, following the campaign closely, gave solid support to the opponents of the régime and, at the same time—through the intermediary of the *Saarbund,* the *Deutsche Aktion*, and numerous other agents—newspapers, tracts, and money crossed the frontier and penetrated into the Saar.

The opposition did not manage to win the day. The proportion of blank or invalid voting papers was not more than 24·5 per cent., while the pro-government parties gained approximately 64 per cent. of the votes.

It was a victory for the government, and one which was all the more resounding because the Government of the Federal Republic, the German political parties, and the press had openly taken sides. They had tried to show that Mr. Hoffmann's régime did not have any real support in the country and that it was only maintained by the backing and strength of France. There was now proof that it was more solidly established in power than had appeared and that a relatively high proportion of Saarlanders were in favour of the policy carried out since 1947. Mr. Hoffmann seized the opportunity of renewing his ties with the Saar Socialists by forming another coalition government.

Clearly, the opposition had not been able to get itself organized, and this had given the parties upholding the régime a monopoly of candidatures. Hence some doubt arose as to the reliability of this election. The result was nevertheless a fact and the conditions in which it had been achieved were less open to question than some people maintained. The violence of the attacks made by the pro-German opposition groups, and the dark accounts they had given of the régime did them a disservice by their very exaggeration. In fact, as many foreign journalists were able to note during the campaign, there was no " reign of terror " in the Saar. Though the

[35] *Verhandlungen des Deutschen Bundestages,* I.237/10922 *et seq.*

opportunities afforded the opposition to organize were restricted, it was nonetheless able to express itself freely and to campaign energetically, thanks in large part to the support it had received from Germany.[36]

[36] The elections of November 30, 1952, gave rise to an abundance of literature. The pressure brought to bear, the abuse of power, interference, and questionable electoral manoeuvres were brought out on all sides. *Cf.* the publications of the *Deutscher Saarbund*: Herbert Beckmann, *Wahlmanöver an der Saar*; Ludwig Brenner, *Freie Wahlen*; also *Die Saarwahlen, eine Untersuchung der Saarkorrespondenz* (Saarbrücken: Comel Verlag, 1952); Association Française de la Sarre, *Le verdict sarrois* (Paris: 1953); Hans Joachim Hagmann, *Die saarlandischen Landtagswahlen vom 30 November 1952* (Cologne: Deutsche Glocke, 1953).

5

THE SAAR SETTLEMENT AS A PREREQUISITE, JANUARY, 1953–SEPTEMBER, 1953

THE elections of November 30, 1952, gave the Hoffmann Government a brief respite. Would the government make use of it? Was it in a position to do so?

Conditions seemed favourable. The death of Stalin, following shortly after the election of President Eisenhower, heralded for the régime of dictatorship by the proletariat a period of uncertainty which coincided with the advent of a President of the United States who had considerable personal prestige. There were grounds for hope that international tension might be eased and that progress might be made in the attempts already begun towards the consolidation of Europe.

Nothing of the kind happened. The *détente* in relations between the U.S.S.R. and the West, superficial though it was—and it did not become apparent until the spring of 1955—had very different consequences from those that had been anticipated. The fear of war, which kept pace with the development of nuclear weapons and with the realization of the disaster that would result from their use, only made the Western world more sensitive to the slightest sign of decreasing antagonism. This sensitivity was quickly reflected in a relaxation of the efforts, which had been largely motivated by the external threat, to organize and integrate Europe. The opponents of German rearmament, for whom anything provided an excuse to justify their position, took advantage of every opportunity to bolster hopes of an agreement between the East and the West, and they played upon the theme of coexistence.

The link established by the European Defence Community between German rearmament and European integration boomeranged, turning opposition to the rebuilding of German military strength into rejection of European integration. This opposition, which had its centre in France, hardened and spread as a consequence of the progressive weakening of that country, a weakening that was itself the direct result of the instability of the authority of

129

the state. The governments which followed one another were, because of inadequate majorities, not in a position either to make political choices or to impose their decisions. It was all they could do to remain in power by means of uncertain coalitions, compromises, or contradictory promises. Thus they put off the debate on ratification of the E.D.C. But the more they delayed, the greater grew the opposition, nourished by the complications created both at home and abroad by the state's lack of authority. To the war in Indo-China, which from a military and financial, and above all, from a moral point of view was becoming an almost unbearable burden, was added the conflict with Morocco. The increasingly manifest inability of the government to resolve its problems, which reached its apogee under Mr. Laniel's leadership, gave rise to a renewed outbreak of nationalism, hostile to the United States but equally hostile to Germany and to the "Europeans" who maintained that France must sacrifice her sovereignty. So France remained rigidly on the defensive.

In the meantime, the Federal Republic pursued its spectacular recovery. The remarkable upward trend in the economy, as much the result of intelligent government policy as of the whole people's will to work, was further emphasized by the difficulties experienced in eastern Germany, of which the Berlin uprisings were only one manifestation. Chancellor Adenauer's Government, which had held the reins and enforced its policy despite the sometimes very obstinate opposition of the Socialists, reaped the benefit. The elections of September, 1953, gave it an absolute majority and the chance to assume full responsibility for another four years.

Thus the change in the relative strength of the two chief rivals in the Saar conflict, a change already perceptible in 1950, became more marked to the detriment of France, whose position was thereby weakened, while confidence in Germany grew. This change played a decisive part in the final settlement on the future of the Saar.

At the beginning of 1953, France seemed in a position to reassume the initiative. The victory of the Hoffmann Government was interpreted as a victory for French policy. But if France was to strengthen her position and that of the Saar Government, she would have to capitalize on this.

The new team of ministers succeeding that led by Antoine

Pinay apparently planned to do just that. The President of the Council, René Mayer, was reputed to be a man of action who, however much he favoured European integration, was nonetheless aware of the influence of the R.P.F. and of the growing surge of nationalism. So, too, was Georges Bidault, who returned to the Ministry for Foreign Affairs. Both declared themselves determined to pursue the European and Saar policies of their predecessors. For personal reasons, or because they had to take into account the particular atmosphere in which the government had been formed, they tended to show a more marked firmness towards Germany. A ministerial statement did, in fact, contain a formula that was to influence the future evolution of the discussion of the Saar problem. After underlining the fact that the recent elections had proved the desire of the Saar's population to preserve the autonomy of the territory and its union with France, the head of the government declared: " The time has now come to revise the Franco-Saar Conventions of 1950 and to re-open negotiations to draw up a European statute for the Saar. Elaboration of this statute is a prerequisite to ratification of the Bonn agreements or of the Treaty setting up the E.D.C."

Thus came into being the formula of a " Saar settlement as a prerequisite." It had been developing for some months, but Robert Schuman had not formulated it explicitly. It had been suggested in Germany, too, by the Social Democratic Party. During the debate of November 18, Erich Ollenhauer had again proposed recourse to it.[1] But the government had reserved its position. It had preferred another formula, that contained in the resolution carried by a majority vote in the Bundestag on December 5, which instructed the government, in the course of negotiations with the three Western Powers, to call attention to the fact that the terms of the Bonn Conventions did not in any way affect the solution of the economic and political problem posed by the Saar.[2]

Of these two methods—the one accepting European integration while reserving the case of the Saar, the other making this same integration subordinate to a favourable settlement of the Saar problem—which would have been the more effective? It is difficult to say. At the most, one can assert that the choice of " the Saar as

---

[1] " For the sake of Europe the Saar question must be settled before final action on the treaties." *Cf. Verhandlungen des Deutschen Bundestages,* I.237/10926B.
[2] *Ibid.,* I.242/11495.

a prerequisite" was more the expression of anxiety than of confidence. To those in France who had formulated the idea it appeared to be the last weapon left with which to compel the opponent to negotiate. Undoubtedly they gambled on the fact that the opponent had such a stake in the ratification of the Bonn Conventions—thanks to which he would find himself once again a partner with full rights in the Western community from which the war had expelled him—that he would be inclined to be more amenable.[3] This view underestimated the Chancellor's tenacity and overestimated that of the French Government. The "Europeans" who formulated this "prerequisite" were imprisoning themselves, perhaps unwittingly, in a formula that the adversaries of the E.D.C. would use against them, and they were not exacting in return the concessions they claimed they were going to obtain from the Federal Republic.[4]

The diplomatists noted that Mr. Mayer had used a carefully worded formula and that he spoke of drawing up a statute for the Saar, not of signing it, as a prerequisite to ratification of the E.D.C. The formula was nevertheless to be interpreted in its narrowest sense, that is to say, in the sense of a formulation precise enough to serve as an agreement to which a signature could be appended.

The prerequisite in the minds of those who formulated it, therefore, implied negotiation. Robert Schuman, before his departure from the Quai d'Orsay, had tried to resume negotiations. Georges Bidault, as soon as he arrived in office, proclaimed his

[3] For some months this had been Ambassador Grandval's opinion, and he publicly came out in favour of the "prerequisite" in his speech on January 21.

[4] The press comments were indicative of the climate in which the decision was taken. What chiefly preoccupied the papers was the fate of the government and the attitude the parties would take towards it. The "settlement of the Saar as a prerequisite" was only alluded to incidentally as it related to the principal goal that René Mayer had set himself: that of obtaining a majority. His desire to win the support of the R.P.F. was plain; Georges Altschuler, in an article published in *Combat* on January 7, even went as far as to suggest that, in fact, the R.P.F. Deputies saw in the "prerequisite" the manifestation of the new President's intention "to bury the project of a European Army or at least to postpone its ratification." In an intervention during the debates in the National Assembly on the government's European policy, between November 18 and 24, 1953, Robert Schuman emphasized the extent to which they were prisoners of a formula: "Such a stipulation," he said, "can only be understood when it is strictly interpreted, that is to say, when it means that ratification will not take place until there is a prior agreement between France and Germany on the basis of the constitutional status of the Saar. On this point there is no difficulty. . . . We note, however, a tendency to stretch this formula in such a way that no debate on the ratification can take place until this agreement is reached. It is this wide interpretation which I cannot accept. . . ."

desire to re-open conversations with the German Government. A month later, on February 26, in Rome, he discussed the question with Chancellor Adenauer, whom he met again on March 9 in Strasbourg. The official communiqué issued after this second meeting was worded with prudent optimism: the two ministers "have agreed on a method for re-opening negotiations." But weeks went by without any effort on either side to start the talks. Doubtless the two governments were busy with more urgent matters. Mr. Mayer left at the end of March for the United States. Chancellor Adenauer followed him at the beginning of April. They stressed at this time their interest in settling the Saar problem. But while the communiqué on the Franco-American talks spoke of the agreement reached on the need for a europeanization of the Saar, no allusion to this was made in the communiqué published after the visit of the Chancellor. The latter in a speech before the National Press Club merely asked for a plebiscite in the Saar.[5] The difference in wording was characteristic. Even more significant was the fact that the Saar question had been broached in the conversations in Washington, thus emphasizing the increasing attention with which the United States Government followed the progress of a problem that was delaying ratification of the Bonn agreements and of the E.D.C.[6] The German press naturally expressed considerable satisfaction.

It might have been thought that the Washington conversations had borne fruit when, on April 8, the very day on which the Chancellor addressed the National Press Club, the French Government took the step of proposing a date for the re-opening of negotiations. It suggested May 15. The occasion for the talks might be the Six Power Conference.

The talks took place a little before the proposed date, beginning on May 11. They were inconclusive. No one was prepared to compromise. On April 10, however, the Saar Government had itself launched a six-point plan for the europeanization of the Saar.

[5] April 8, 1953. The proposal for a plebiscite had already been made at the beginning of January by Gerhard Schroeder, Vice-President of the parliamentary group of the C.D.U., in an interview given to the *Frankfurter Allgemeine Zeitung*.

[6] At the beginning of April, the United States Embassy in Paris made representations on behalf of its government to place on record Washington's concern about the revision of the Franco-Saar Conventions of 1950. There was fear of the German reaction and the repercussions it might have on the solution of the conflict. The Ministry for Foreign Affairs replied that it was not France who was responsible for the delay.

This took up again some of the proposals made in the course of the previous year.[7]

The Saar was to become the first European territory and Saarbrücken the headquarters not only of the European Coal and Steel Community but of the administration of the E.D.C. and of other European organizations as yet in embryo.

The Saar would continue to govern itself, the conduct of its internal affairs being the responsibility of a freely elected Landtag.

France would hand over the external representation of the Saar to the High Authority which would also exercise general supervision until the formation of a European government.

The French Embassy in Saarbrücken would be replaced by a Consulate General having the same rights as the German Consulate General.

The Franco-Saar economic union would be retained until a European economic union came into being. Meanwhile, the Saarlanders would have greater liberty of action in economic matters and any differences of opinion that might arise with the French would be submitted to a European tribunal.

The final decision on the europeanization of the Saar would rest with the Saarlanders who would manifest their desires by means of a plebiscite supervised by neutral observers.[8]

This plan for the Saar, which revealed the Saar Government's desire for independence and which contained, in the paragraph relating to economic union, a proposal more satisfactory to Germany than to France, aroused scarcely any comment. There were a few encouraging remarks from Chancellor Adenauer in a speech at San Francisco, a fairly positive reaction in the *Rheinischer Merkur* of April 17, and that was all.

Neither of the two governments concerned seemed in any hurry to wind up the affair.

On Chancellor Adenauer, however, there was pressure to do so from the opposition which continued to reproach him for his passivity. At the beginning of March, Representative Karl Mommer had denounced the defeatism that had reigned since the elections of November 30 and against which the Chancellor had

---

[7] According to some sources, it would seem that this plan for the Saar was submitted without the knowledge of Johannes Hoffmann. He appears to have been angry but he published no disavowal of it. At the beginning of 1952, Richard Kirn had proposed a plan for europeanization. *Cf. Volksstimme*, February 1, 1952. As for Mr. Hoffmann, in an interview published by the *Rheinischer Merkur* of September 26, 1952, he had proposed a plebiscite to decide the status of the Saar.

[8] The plan was published in a propaganda leaflet, destined for the United States under the title, *The Saar, Key to European Unity*. The Saar press gave only a résumé of it. *Cf. Saarbrücker Zeitung*, April 13, 1953.

reacted not at all. The *Saarbund*, for its part, continued its offensive and lost no opportunity of reminding everyone that the Saar belonged to Germany. But Chancellor Adenauer was cautious, no doubt in order not to make matters worse; hence he had no hesitation in hurling at the heads of his critics the fact that it was not by continuing national indignation that a solution of the problem would be furthered.[9] For the moment, he had other things on his mind. The election campaign had virtually opened at the beginning of the year. It was to this that he had to devote most of his energies. Negotiations over the Saar would only involve loss of time and might even furnish his opponents with effective weapons against him. A renewed effort could give no very different results from previous attempts. He knew that the November 30 elections had not improved Germany's position. To settle the Saar question now at the beginning of the year, he would have to make concessions which he was little inclined to do and which would please his Socialist opponents even less. Whereas, all in good time. . . .

The idea that time was on Germany's side was not held by Mr. Adenauer alone. It was fairly widespread among his associates and it grew stronger as Germans became increasingly conscious of the extent of their country's economic and political recovery. Herein lay the explanation for Mr. Adenauer's delay, for the silence he preserved after receiving, on December 23, 1952, the letter from Mr. Schuman asking him to make concrete proposals on the subject of the economic europeanization of the Saar. It also explains why his offensive against the absence of democratic freedoms in the Saar was only half-hearted. Not until May 5 did the Federal Government send to the Council of Europe its second memorandum supplementing the information contained in the first one: it affirmed that the autumn elections of 1952 had not been free. However, it continued, it would not press for a discussion of this item at the next session.

The French were in no more of a hurry than the Germans. It was a thorny question and the government majority very slight. The government had other preoccupations: Georges Bidault was more sensitive to pressure from the R.P.F. than his predecessor.

---

[9] Broadcast interview of January 30. The tenor of the Chancellor's statement is interesting. He made it clear that the Saar was only one problem among many and drew the attention of his listeners to the progress being made in building up Europe. "In 1954 we will probably have direct elections to a European Parliament," he said. *Cf. Documents on the Saar, op. cit.*, Vol. II, p. 261.

Above all, there was a feeling that the victory of the Hoffmann Government had created the conditions necessary to put the régime of the Saar on a firm footing and this must be achieved before discussions were resumed. Priority should be given to revising the Conventions.

This had been in the air for a long time. Ever since the Conventions had been concluded in 1950, people had been aware that achievement of full autonomy for the Saar would necessitate their modification. Since then criticism in the Saar had been mounting steadily: the role assigned to France and to the French was much too large. These criticisms, as has been seen, fuelled the fire of an increasingly vigorous opposition. They corresponded to a feeling so widespread that even parties favourable to the régime adopted them,[10] and the French Government formally undertook to begin negotiations with a view to revising the Conventions.[11] It even defined the points to which the revision should particularly apply. These were as follows:

(*a*) creation of an arbitral authority to which should be submitted differences that the joint Franco-Saar Commissions could not settle; at the same time, the Presidents of these Commissions would be deprived of the right to cast the decisive vote—a rather important concession since the presidency was usually held by a Frenchman;

(*b*) suppression of the right of veto of the French representative in the Saar;

(*c*) a joint administration of the mines that would replace the *Régie française des mines*, and at the same time the application of the Saar law concerning collective labour agreements.

Furthermore, the French Government undertook to proceed to an examination of the problems created by the position of the Saar in regard to the external trade relations of the Franco-Saar economic union, its share in administrative and military expenditure, the re-organization of the iron and steel industries placed under sequestration, and the working of the Warndt coalfields.

Mr. Schuman ended the letter in which he informed the Saar Government of the decision of the Council of Ministers by expressing the hope that these proposals would be accepted. Did

10 *Cf.* the fifteen-point programme of the C.V.P. for revision of the Conventions, *SVZ*, November 14, 1952.

11 Decision taken in the Council of Ministers, November 26, 1952, submitted the same day to the President of the Saar Government. *Cf. La Documentation française, Bulletin quotidien, Textes du jour*, No. 2336, November 28, 1952.

they not fulfil almost exactly the hopes expressed by Mr. Hoffmann in recent months?

It appeared, therefore, that the negotiations which opened on February 9 might proceed fairly smoothly since those taking part seemed agreed on the fundamentals. But it was not so. Difficulties arose at various points. The negotiators from the Saar complained of the tone taken towards them. One of them was so out of patience that he withdrew from the negotiations.[12] In the end, the various Conventions that were to be signed on May 20 corresponded very closely to the original French proposal.[13] Unquestionably, they decreased the influence of France and gave the Saarlanders greater liberty. They did not give rise to a public outcry similar to that of 1950. The Saarlanders therefore had reason to be satisfied. But the conditions under which the Conventions had been negotiated neither eased Franco-Saar relations as much as had been hoped in Paris nor strengthened the cohesion of the team of ministers that Johannes Hoffmann had re-formed after the elections. Certain among his closest ministerial collaborators reproached him for allowing himself to be too easily pushed around by the French, who used him to overcome the resistance of the Saar negotiators.

If criticism in the Saar remained relatively muted, that in France did not. In Lorraine, that very Lorraine which was traditionally supposed to be a natural ally of the Saar, some of the old mistrust arose again. On March 16, a group of industrialists and business men representing small- and medium-sized concerns of the Moselle met at Metz. They voiced both the anxiety they felt at the prospect of Saar competition in France and their wish to be protected against it. They asked that the Chamber of Commerce of Metz and the *Conseil général* of the Moselle be represented in the negotiations on revision of the Conventions. According to them there were two possible solutions: either the introduction into the Saar of French legislation in fiscal, economic, and social affairs, or the re-establishment of a customs barrier. Tempers appeared to run rather high, and this was reflected in the tone of the meeting. Old complaints were dug up against the French Ambassador in

---

12 Erwin Müller reacted violently, according to some statements. He referred to these disagreements in an indirect and rather feeble manner in a speech to the Landtag on March 2, 1953.

13 *Cf. Amtsblatt des Saarlandes*, No. 53, December 15, 1953, pp. 770–800; *Journal officiel, Lois et Décrets*, December 31, 1953, pp. 11760–11787. See also Appendix I, Chart 4.

Saarbrücken, some of them accusing him of being a satrap who became a Saarlander to defend the interests of the Saar against France.[14]

At the end of June, in another meeting, this group formulated its complaints against the Conventions in more precise terms. It noted that the expansion of Saar autonomy and the privileges granted to the Saar for German imports made it much more difficult to defend the interests of Lorraine. French legislation was not applicable either to imports or to matters concerning the Warndt coalfields. Finally, Saarlanders selling goods in France were exempt from certain duties, such as taxes, and were thus in a more favoured position than the French.

This session, held in the presence of the deputies for the Moselle, ended with a unanimous motion of protest in spite of Mr. Schuman's intervention. A communiqué setting forth the point of view of the small- and medium-sized business undertakings of the Moselle was published on August 1 in *Le Lorrain* and *France-Journal*.[15] *La Chronique sarroise* pointed out that the Saarlanders could, on their side, complain of certain concessions to Lorraine, which they did not fail to do. It is interesting to note in this context that the little book in which Paul H. Kaps defended the interests of the state of Rheinland-Pfalz, which had been unfavourably affected by French policy in the Saar, contained a paragraph under the title " *Lothringen wird bevorzugt* " highlighting the favourable treatment he thought had been accorded to Lorraine.[16] But business circles in Lorraine did not see this side of the question and continued to make protests, either to the National Assembly, where Deputy Raymond Mondon spoke on the ratification of the Conventions, or through the Chamber of Commerce of Metz which, at the time of the reconstitution of the Commission for Alsace-Lorraine and the Saar, opposed the participation in this

[14] The Ambassador, publicly challenged, reacted with a vigour equal to that of his critics. He was able to point out by quoting figures that some of the enterprises in Lorraine had by no means lost through the opening of the Saar markets.

[15] These resolutions were analysed in a long article published in *La Chronique sarroise*, No. 26 (July 11, 1953), which, taking up point by point the objections formulated by the *Fédération patronale des petites et moyennes enterprises*, exposed various inaccuracies and exaggerations. This was its conclusion: there was no " perceptible disparity between the obligations imposed on the industries of Lorraine and on similar establishments in the Saar." The complaints of Lorraine only applied to extreme cases and overlooked the fact that, as far as food was concerned, the Saar represented a very important outlet for Lorraine.

[16] *Rheinland-Pfalz und Frankreichs Saarpolitik nach 1945, op. cit.*, pp. 45-47.

Commission of two representatives of the French Diplomatic Mission in the Saar.

The people of Lorraine were not the only ones to react. In Alsace, too, the progress of the Saar question had been closely followed. The Chamber of Commerce of Strasbourg returned repeatedly to the charge in an effort to limit the penetration of German goods into the Saar and through the Saar into the French market. They did not want a Saar commerce that would " set itself up as a privileged intermediary between German industrial production and French consumption." [17] So the Chamber of Commerce of Strasbourg joined the collective move of the chambers of commerce of eastern France to have the right to participate in drawing up the lists of German products affecting the Saar economy for which representatives of the Exchange Control Office of Saarbrücken would be entitled to issue import licences.

The signing of the Conventions also had repercussions in Germany, as was inevitable. In a statement to the press, Chancellor Adenauer did not mince words. The fact that these Conventions had been initialled twenty-four hours after he left Paris seemed to him " impolite " and " discourteous." A sharp exchange of letters with High Commissioner François-Poncet ensued, the latter replying that, at Mr. Adenauer's request, the initialling had been put off for several days in order not to take place while he was actually in Paris. For the rest, the failure of the negotiations might be more justifiably imputed to the Chancellor than to the French Government. Was it not he who had refused to commit himself in any way until after the elections to the Bundestag? The French Government was still waiting for the memorandum in which he was to set out his ideas on the economic aspects of the europeanization of the Saar.

After a few more skirmishes the argument died down, although in a letter of June 25 to the Allied High Commissioners the Chancellor renewed the protest he had already made on February 13.[18] Everyone was too busy to discuss the matter further. A new ministerial crisis had broken out in France immediately after the signing of the Conventions. René Mayer's government was replaced by that of Mr. Laniel, although Georges Bidault remained at the

---

[17] Cf. *Bulletin de la Chambre de commerce et d'industrie de Strasbourg*, No. 1 (1954).

[18] Statement of Secretary of State Hallstein in the debate in the Bundestag, July 2, 1953. Cf. *Verhandlungen des Deutschen Bundestages*, I.279/13933-13934.

Ministry for Foreign Affairs where he had to deal with the growing difficulties of the war in Indo-China. In Germany, the election campaign monopolized the Chancellor's attention, and the Saar passed into second place as one of his concerns.

This, however, did not improve the position of France. The signing of the Conventions had not brought with it the hoped-for consolidation of the position of the Saar. Criticism continued in Lorraine. In the Saar the opposition worked systematically to demonstrate that the Conventions only gave an illusion of auto-nomy and that in fact France retained the whip hand. Finally, in Germany there was indignation mingled with condescension. No French effort to consolidate the position of the Saar in the hope of achieving a *fait accompli* could change the essentially provisional state of affairs.

Moreover there was re-affirmation of German intransigence. In the Bundestag a unanimous resolution was passed on July 2 stressing first that the Saar was a part of Germany and then giving the government a mandate to obtain the re-establishment of demo-cratic freedoms and the return of the Saar to Germany.[19]

The discussion was resumed in the autumn under conditions favourable to Chancellor Adenauer. He had won a brilliant victory in the elections. The C.D.U.-C.S.U. group held the majority of seats in the Bundestag.

This meant that the head of the Government of the Federal Republic had considerable freedom of action both at home and abroad. Within his country, Socialist opposition might incon-venience or harass him; it could not gain a majority over him. Abroad, his prestige was the greater because he seemed to be the only person in Germany able to deal with the Allies and because the French were conscious of the growth of his influence. This freedom of action allowed the Chancellor to be generous (in other words, to accept a settlement involving concessions that the Social-Democrats were not in any position to forbid him to make) or to be uncompromising (in other words, to take advantage of the change in relative strength in order to exact from France the con-cessions she had refused up till now).

Actually, the Chancellor's freedom of action was more apparent than real. He was himself bound by the positions he had adopted

[19] *Ibid.,* I.279/13931 *et seq.*

previously and he could not abandon them without contradicting himself. It was not in his interest to antagonize the Socialist opposition—it was extremely important to maintain a certain degree of the national unity of which the Federal Republic stood so much in need—or to push intransigence towards France to the breaking point. He knew better than anyone how precarious was the majority by which his French colleagues held office. He knew, too, that an overthrow of the majority might compromise the realization of the European programme. So it was, paradoxically, the very weakness of the French Government that limited the Chancellor's diplomatic action. That he and his colleagues were conscious of it is very certain. On many occasions, in public debate or in less widely publicized exchanges, the anxiety to resolve the Saar problem " without offending France or losing sight of her interests " was apparent.[20] This seemed feasible because of Germany's recovery. The Germans were still convinced that time was on their side.[21]

From the Saar, moreover, came favourable news. After the first shock of the elections of November 30, the opposition again took heart. It was strengthened, thanks largely to lateral contacts with Germany—contacts that became more numerous and more sustained. The attempts of the Saar Government to break the trade-union opposition by dismissing its leader, Paul Kutsch, did not produce the hoped-for results. Mr. Kutsch was re-elected at the end of December, 1952, in an almost triumphal fashion, since out of 300 delegates 285 voted for him. All the government could do was to order, on February 5, 1953, the dissolution of the *Syndicat des mineurs* and work to set up a new and more tractable organization.[22] The most that was achieved by this was to widen the circle of opponents and to fray tempers. True, the Commission of

[20] Here, for example, is a comment made, in September, 1953, by one of the men in Germany who followed the Saar question very closely: " The goal must be the gradual reunion of the Saar with Germany while preserving French prestige and giving full consideration to French economic interests. It is incumbent upon the nation to act in this way, and we must avoid thoughts and acts which, abroad and also unfortunately sometimes at home, appear nationalistic."

[21] From the same pen we read also: " Discretion and moderation have often provoked criticism and mistrust, but little by little it has come to be realized that the policy of restraint, on the one hand, and the regaining of the respect of the world, on the other hand, will result in the return of the Saar."

[22] An attempt at mediation undertaken by the *Fédération internationale des mineurs* at the instigation of the International Confederation of Free Trade Unions (I.C.F.T.U.) was unsuccessful. *Cf. Saarbrücker Zeitung*, April 20, 1953; *Gewerkschaftliche Informationen*, No. 1 (February 1, 1954); *La Chronique sarroise*, September 4, 1953, April 8, 1954.

Inquiry created by the Landtag concluded by affirming that Mr. Kutsch and some of his collaborators had engaged in political activity contrary to the régime and to the law—that they had, in particular, accepted money from German industry for their propaganda against the régime.[23] But this finding justifying the government's decision to dissolve the *Syndicat des mineurs* did not prevent Mr. Kutsch from continuing the struggle and from tightening the bonds that linked him to the German unions. Moreover, he was sustained in his opposition to the government—which was supported by the Saar Socialist Party[24]—not only by his friends Kurt Conrad and Friedrich Regitz, but also by the German Socialist Party which multiplied its attacks on the Saar Socialists. On February 23, the German Socialists returned to the charge in a long memorandum[25] to the Socialist International; it denounced the wrongs done to socialist principles and the support the Saar Socialist Party was giving to an anti-democratic policy. In this memorandum the measures taken against Mr. Kutsch and the *Syndicat des mineurs* were singled out as a particularly serious attempt to undermine the freedom of the unions. This memorandum served as the basis of the campaign that ensued inside the Saar during the next few months. Elements of it were to be found in every issue of the *Freie Saarpresse,* an illegal paper of the German Socialist Party which began to appear in March, 1953.[26]

Encouragement to resist came also from the business world early in the autumn. According to information which reached the *Saarbund* from a reliable source, Saar industry seemed to be running into difficulties. The *Régie des mines* had ended the year 1952 with a deficit estimated at ten milliards of francs. There was even an increase in coal reserves, which seemed to suggest that French interest in the mines had slackened and that the government in

---

[23] Cf. *Bericht des vom Landtag des Saarlandes . . . , op. cit.*, especially the enumeration of the sums paid for publicity, *pro forma*, to the two newspapers, *Saar-Bergbau* and *Der Bergbau Angestellte, supra,* p. 108n.

[24] The Rapporteur of the Commission of Inquiry of the Landtag was none other than Deputy Ernst Kunkel, member of the Saar Socialist Party. *Cf.* verbatim report, meeting of the Saar Landtag, October 29, 1953.

[25] *Die Verletzung Sozialdemokratischer Grundsätze durch die Sozialdemokratische Partei Saar, op. cit.*

[26] The newspaper was first printed partly at Mannheim and partly at Merzig, the moulds being transported secretly to Merzig. But this arrangement was quickly discovered and the paper was then printed entirely at Mannheim and from there transported to the Saar. The editor-in-chief was Friedrich Regitz. The funds came largely from the Kaiser Ministry. Mr. Regitz was also associated with Aloys Schmitt in editing the illegal paper *Die Bergarbeiterzeitung.* In addition, he edited a third illegal paper, that of the *Fédération des ouvriers métallurgistes.*

Paris might be more amenable to a settlement. Furthermore, public opinion was the more conscious of the economic recovery of Germany because of the contrast with the instability of France, and this made all the more intolerable the obsolescent equipment in the iron and steel industry caused by lack of investment. A brief memorandum published by the *Saarbund* therefore recommended that nothing be done in a hurry and that for the present no agreement be concluded with France. The trend in Germany's favour could only strengthen in the days ahead.[27]

The observations made by the *Saarbund's* informer gave a rather gloomy picture of the state of Saar industry, but it was a fairly accurate one. It was a fact that Saar industrial production, the expansion of which in the post-war reconstruction period had been accelerated by the war in Korea, had since 1952 been going through a period of stagnation and had even been showing a decline.[28] It was equally true that exports of the French Union had decreased in 1953. There was no doubt either that Saar industry was suffering from inadequate investments, a source of serious criticism against France, who was blamed for not making on behalf of her partners an effort equal to that which she was making for herself.[29] But the chief thing that struck Saar public opinion was the difference that could be observed between the constant rise in German industrial production and the slower and more erratic progress in French production.[30]

[27] The memorandum concluded: "It is believed in economic circles that, at the latest within a few years, France will be prepared to content herself with the proposed economic concessions and to restore political and over-all administration of the Saar territory to German authority." *Cf. News from the Saarbund*, October, 1953.

[28] *Cf. Saarländische Bevölkerrungs- und Wirtschaftszahlen*, 6th Year, No. 1/4 (Saarbrücken: Statistisches Amt des Saarlandes, 1954), pp. 1–4; also, *Das Sozialprodukt des Saarlandes in den Jahren 1952 bis 1954*, Kurzbericht IV/13 (Saarbrücken: Statistisches Amt des Saarlandes, April 13, 1956).

[29] *Cf.*, on this subject, François Muller, *L'économie sarroise, ses problèmes, ses industries de base, sa position dans la C.E.C.A.* (thesis; Paris: April 7, 1956), pp. 334–351. (Typescript.) See also the author's remarks on debt liquidations, pp. 277–279. It should be remembered that in discussions on investments, France was always reproached for not giving the Saar its share of Marshall Plan credits. Attention should also be drawn to the fact that, according to all those who have made a study of this problem, the Saar suffered very heavily in the matter of credits from its dependence on France.

[30] Here are the comparative indices of industrial production in France and Germany, as given by Jacques Vernant, "L'économie française devant la C.E.D." in *La querelle de la C.E.D.*, published under the direction of Raymond Aron and Daniel Lerner: *Cahiers de la Fondation nationale des sciences politiques*, No. 80 (Paris: 1956), pp. 109–123:

			1951	1952	1953
France	..	..	109	108	109
Germany	..	..	119	128	139

Although the price index only rose by one point in 1953 (1·2), the effect of the sharp rise in 1951 and 1952 was still being felt and it was in contrast with the stability of prices in Germany.[31] People were more aware of the contrast because economic relations between the Saar and its neighbour Germany had been resumed and were expanding.

The *Saarbund's* memorandum was perhaps inspired by considerations of a tactical nature. In any case, its date coincided with certain representations on the part of leaders of the Saar opposition to the Chancellor[32] and to the German Social Democratic Party against the new negotiations that were being prepared. At the same time certain representatives of economic circles in the Saar submitted to the Bonn Government expressions of a desire to develop economic relations with Germany. Such relations would, of course, be directed so as to give favourable treatment to those individuals or firms whose sympathies with Germany were known. This must be carried out in a manner that would frustrate France's policy of distraint on the Saar economy. Among the proposals submitted to the Government of the Federal Republic was one that provided for the setting up in Bonn of a liaison office, responsible to the Chamber of Commerce of Saarbrücken.[33] The Chancellor, to whom these proposals were submitted, received some of the Saar business men at the end of November, and this enabled them to define their aims more clearly. It was on this occasion that the Chancellor announced the plan—which was never put into effect— of dividing the Saar into two regions, one industrial which would

---

[31] Here is the price index for the Saar and for the Federal Republic:

	1949	1950	1951	1952	1953	1954
Saar	100	105·8	128·7	144·1	145·3	147·1
Federal Republic	100	93·5	100·9	102·8	100·9	100·9

Cf. Die Entwicklung des Franken in der Nachkriegszeit, Kurzbericht IV/39 (Saarbrücken: Statistiches Amt des Saarlandes, October 16, 1957).

[32] *Cf.* letter from Richard Becker, Hubert Ney, and Kurt Conrad to Chancellor Adenauer, September 30, 1953, quoted in *Deutsche Saar*, September 29, 1956. It was not, however, the first time that opponents of the régime highlighted the economic difficulties they encountered. One has only to refer to the publications of the *Saarbund* and in particular to the *Materialien zur Saarfrage* which regularly carried an analysis of the economic situation, showing the unfavourable consequences for the Saar of the economic union and offering a dazzling picture of the advantages to be gained from Germany. The opposition continued to stress these difficulties in the months that followed. Each number of the *Freie Saarpresse* stressed the slowing down of production, the increase in surplus stocks of Saar coal in the iron and steel industrial centres of Lorraine, and the introduction of holidays at the end of the year to conceal partial unemployment.

[33] Opposition to the creation in Bonn of a branch of the Chamber of Commerce of Saarbrücken was so strong that the authors of the project had to yield to the opposition. There is no need to add that this came from economic circles in the Saar interested in preserving the economic union with France.

be " europeanized," the other agricultural which would be handed back to Germany.

Meanwhile, Chancellor Adenauer resumed contact with the French Government. On September 16, he sent Ambassador Herbert Blankenhorn to Paris with a letter in which he proposed to Mr. Bidault that there be discussions on the whole Franco-German problem.

This was a surprise move, coming so soon after the German elections and even before the formation of the new government. Questions were raised as to the motives behind this rather sudden decision. Some were tempted to explain it by the Chancellor's desire to get rid of the Saar problem in order to obtain ratification of the E.D.C. and of the Bonn Treaty. Other commentators, in France as in Germany, thought it had something to do with the visit to Bonn of Marinus van der Goes van Naters, Rapporteur of the plan for the europeanization of the Saar which was to be discussed by the Council of Europe.

6

EUROPE WINS AND LOSES,
SEPTEMBER, 1953–OCTOBER, 1954

THE presentation of what subsequently became known as the Van Naters Plan introduced a new personality into the conflict between France and Germany over the Saar: Europe. Her influence had already made itself felt, and since 1948 her name had been more and more frequently mentioned. It was to her that people turned as to a *deus ex machina* who could exorcise nationalism. It was under her auspices that the first supranational authority had its beginnings. It was partly through her that the Federal Republic was able to resume and enlarge its position in the Western community. Finally, it was in the name of Europe that French diplomacy, like that of Germany, had till now vainly sought solutions to the questions raised by the Saar. Those who represented Europe in any capacity whatever had even appealed several times to the two governments to put an end to a long, drawn-out struggle fraught with the possibility of more serious complications.

Now Europe herself appeared on the scene with a plan drawn up by men whose mission was not to consider national interests but those of the community as a whole. Intent on making this distinction clear, the explanation of the aims of the *Report on the Future Position of the Saar* cited a particularly felicitous passage published by R. Mangin:

> The basic reason for the failure of the plan for europeanization of the Saar as it was discussed (between M. Schuman and Dr. Adenauer, July–October, 1952) is to be found in the fact that the very concept of europeanization concealed an equivocation and that, under cover of this, both sides sought to pursue essentially nationalist aims [instead of realizing that] men in Europe do not belong only to national communities whose absolutism has been overtaken by evolution; and that our common European interests stretch beyond particular national interests. . . . In this sense alone can a solution of the Saar problem be found. A solution, not of compromise, but on a different level of understanding, which will have not gainers and losers, but only gainers; and which will imply, not

the abandonment of fundamental interests or aspirations by either side, but the satisfaction of the legitimate interests of all concerned.[1]

Some of the partners were themselves responsible for this intervention of Europe. At the beginning of March, 1952, Germany lodged her first complaint on the violation of democratic liberties in the Saar but withdrew it after the conversations that took place between Robert Schuman and Konrad Adenauer from March 18–20, 1952.[2] When the hopes raised by the agreement between the two men were dashed, the German delegation to the Council of Europe intervened, in its turn, on August 4, 1952, requesting that the Council examine the question of the violation of human rights in the Saar.[3] The German delegation further demanded that measures be taken to ensure that the forthcoming Saar elections should take place in full freedom.[4] In their opinion the Saar's membership in the Council of Europe gave the latter the right to demand that the obligations assumed in joining should be respected by a member state. The Saar delegation replied by requesting that there be no outside intervention in the Saar elections.[5] The first request of the German Government was deemed inadmissible as the Consultative Assembly did not think it could transform itself into a tribunal. However, on September 17, the very day on which it rejected the German request, the Consultative Assembly unanimously adopted a proposal submitted by Marinus van der Goes van Naters and twenty-nine Socialist representatives to place on the agenda the whole problem posed by the future status of the Saar in Europe.[6] The following day, at the second meeting of the General Affairs Committee, Mr. van der Goes van Naters was elected Rapporteur. On the same day, the second German request and that of the Saar representatives were referred to this Committee by the Assembly, which declared that the Saar question was " a matter of common interest for the peoples of Europe." Mr. van der Goes van Naters set to work zealously. By September 24 he was already

[1] *La solution du problème sarrois* (Paris: 1953), as quoted by Marinus van der Goes van Naters in "The Future Position of the Saar," Council of Europe, Consultative Assembly, 6th Ordinary Session, First Part, May, 1954, *Documents (Working Papers)*, Vol. II, Doc. 225, p. 3.
[2] "The government specialists had failed to solve the problem and in 1952 the parliamentarians took it into their own hands," wrote U. W. Kitzinger in the introduction to an excellent study entitled *The Economics of the Saar Question* (Oxford: 1958). (Mimeographed.)
[3] Council of Europe, Consultative Assembly, 4th Ordinary Session, Document 34.
[4] *Ibid.*, Document 53, September 17, 1952.
[5] *Ibid.*, Document 60, September 17, 1952.   [6] *Ibid.*, Document 54, September 17, 1952.

in a position to propose a plan of work in which his aim was clear. Of the three possibilities which he envisaged, his preference, not surprisingly, was for europeanization. His proposal was supported by the Socialist parliamentarians in the Council of Europe; the idea of a europeanization of the Saar had already taken shape in Socialist circles. Was it not at the Congress of the Socialist International in 1950 that a Commission for the Saar had a statement adopted declaring that " O.E.E.C. in Paris, and especially the Council of Europe in Strasbourg, are competent to reach a constructive solution"? [7] Mr. van der Goes van Naters kept his promise and worked so diligently that by the spring of 1953 he was able to present a preliminary report, but the General Affairs Committee did not feel that the time was ripe for a public discussion of the Saar problem in view of the approaching German elections; examination of the report was therefore postponed until autumn.[8]

The presentation of the report as well as the actual existence of a plan placed the interested governments in a delicate position. They found themselves faced with a project which, from the very spirit in which it had been drawn up, did not satisfy all their interests and in some ways went beyond their conception of the europeanization of the Saar. The political section of the report, which transformed the Saar into a European territory, robbed Germany of any hope that this lost province might be returned to the Fatherland. The economic section did, it is true, preserve the principle of the Franco-Saar economic union and only changed the status of the mines, ownership of which was vested in the Saar. But the spirit in which the europeanization was conceived nevertheless made it possible to foresee a modification of the union sooner or later.

The French and German Governments no longer were masters of the game. The bilateral negotiations, the pace of which they could adapt to suit their own convenience and of which they more or less knew the rules, gave place not merely to multilateral negotiations but to what Mr. van der Goes van Naters called a " supranational diplomacy." Had it been only a case of multilateral negotiations, the matter would not have been too complicated. The two governments had already tried on various occasions to

[7] Intervention of Heinz Braun, September 25, 1953, cited in *ibid.*, 5th Ordinary Session, summary record of debates, p. 676.
[8] The study of the report presented on August 26 was undertaken on September 11–12 by the General Affairs Committee.

out-manoeuvre their opponents by calling in Britain and the United
States. Remembering its success in the summer of 1951, the
French Government had in fact just tried, but in vain, to involve
Britain and the United States in a move designed to bring pressure
to bear on Chancellor Adenauer. But supranational diplomacy had
all the disadvantages of a public parliamentary debate—a debate
much more difficult to prepare for and to steer because of the
diversity of the participants. Their views could not but be different
from those of France and Germany. The Federal Republic might
fear isolation in a European assembly in which there was a majority
of representatives from countries with which she had recently been
at war. The French Government, for its part, might be afraid that
it would be asked to give up, in the name of Europe, the security
to which it clung.

Thus it was not entirely surprising to find that Chancellor
Adenauer showed a sudden enthusiasm for resuming Franco-
German negotiations and that Mr. Bidault agreed. The Consultative Assembly urged them to proceed. According to the author of
the report on the Saar, the Council should avoid putting itself in
the place of the interested states. Supranational diplomacy, according to Mr. van der Goes van Naters in his introductory speech,
did not exclude bilateral negotiation. Rather the objective should
be a combination of the two methods. If the bilateral negotiations
failed, " supranational diplomacy " offered a fresh starting point
and a new approach. If they succeeded, it would give the seal of
Europe's approval to the bilateral negotiations. In the more likely
event of partial success, " supranational diplomacy " would make
possible a broader frame of reference.

The Assembly followed in this path and on September 25 voted
a resolution recommending to the Committee of Ministers:

(1) that the states directly concerned be encouraged to enter into bilateral
negotiations without delay;

(2) that the President of the Committee of Ministers of the Council of
Europe convene, with the consent of France, Germany, and the Saar, a
special conference to meet at the beginning of 1954 to consider the according
of a guarantee to any agreements which might have been reached in the
course of the Franco-German negotiations and, if necessary, to find a solution
to any problem still outstanding.

Apart from the six countries which had agreed to form themselves into a European Community, the Saar, the United Kingdom

and the United States were to take part in this conference. It would take as the basis of its discussions the conclusions submitted to it as a result of the Franco-German negotiations and any proposals that might come from the Consultative Assembly.

Thus, just as they were preparing to resume discussions, the French and German Governments found themselves burdened with a new problem. They were not the only ones trying to find a solution to the Saar question, for the Assembly had instructed the General Affairs Committee to continue its studies. Parallel negotiations were under way by virtue of the fact that German, French, and Saar deputies shared in the work of the Committee, and possibly this did not facilitate solution of the problems as much as the author of the report to the Council of Europe thought it would. For the lessening of responsibility implicit in this duplication was further aggravated by the confusion arising from divided loyalties, national and European, and from the existence of two opposing points of view within the delegations.[9] The field was wide open for tactical errors, manoeuvres, and intrigues.

The dangers of these parallel negotiations and of the time-limit the Assembly sought to impose might, however, have acted as a stimulus and encouraged the bilateral negotiations. In fact, this was not the case. It was not until November 3 that André François-Poncet had his first interview with the Chancellor, followed by a second one on November 9, a third on the 19th, and a fourth on the 24th. They do not seem to have gone beyond preliminary exchanges of information.

The two points of view were no closer. On the contrary, press commentaries even reported a stiffening. The French Government held to the position it had always maintained:

(*a*) complete political autonomy for the Saar, which implied acceptance of a European status in the sense already outlined by Robert Schuman a year ago, approximating the formula envisaged in the Van Naters Plan;

(*b*) submission of the proposed status to a Saar plebiscite;

(*c*) supervision of the status by European authorities with Anglo-American guarantees;

(*d*) recognition of the definitive nature of the solution adopted;

9 The presence of Karl Mommer (S.P.D.) alongside Eugen Gerstenmaier (C.D.U.) and Karl Pfleiderer (F.D.P.) was not calculated to simplify the task either of the German delegation or of the Chancellor.

(*e*) maintenance of the Franco-Saar economic union with, however, the possibility of its progressive adaptation to the nature of a European status.

These views were those not only of the government, but of all the political parties with the exception of the Communists and their fellow-travellers, as was evident from the debates held in November in the National Assembly and in the Council of the Republic on the ratification of the Franco-Saar Conventions [10] and on the European policy.[11] Senator Auguste Pinton, Rapporteur of the Foreign Affairs Committee, said:

> Henceforth, for the Saar as for us, three terms are inseparable: political autonomy, Franco-Saar economic union, European status of the territory—these are the indissoluble elements of the Saar problem.
>
> The first two are clearly based and established on facts and received their final confirmation in the 1953 Conventions. Everyone should know, in France and, above all, outside France, that as far as we are concerned all discussions are pointless if these basic principles are not accepted. If the government shares this view, and I am sure it does, it will not fail to repeat this and, if need be, to instruct unequivocally those to whom it has entrusted the task if not of negotiating at least of speaking in its name.[12]

The Germans, for their part, no longer seemed disposed to make concessions to the Saar "prerequisite." They were more and more

[10] *Journal officiel, Débats parlementaires, Assemblée nationale*, November 7, 1953, pp. 4929–4943; *ibid., Conseil de la République*, November 20, 1953, pp. 1809–1814.

[11] *Ibid., Assemblée nationale*, November 18–25, 1953.

[12] *Cf. ibid., Conseil de la République*, November 20, 1953, p. 1871. Ambassador Grandval had taken it upon himself to state, unequivocally, in an interview with the *Süddeutsche Zeitung*: "Germany must realize that France cannot consent to any further lowering of customs barriers, and trade relations between the Saar and Germany must continue to be treated as foreign trade relations. . . . Europeanization must not, however, create another Tangier."

A few days earlier, Jacques Vendroux, reporting to the National Assembly on behalf of the Foreign Affairs Committee, recalled the reasons French negotiators, members of the government, and parliamentarians had continually given to justify the inviolability of the economic union: "If the Saar were to be united with Germany, France would not represent more than 24 per cent. of the whole [of the E.C.S.C.], while Germany would then reach 53 per cent. This requires no comment." And he continued: "The Franco-Saar economic union is also an essential element of our security. History has superabundantly proved that the expansionist dynamism of Germany has tended to increase with the development and strengthening of her industrial potential. To agree to give up the material contribution of the Saar and, *a fortiori*, to place it again at Germany's disposal, would be a real abdication on the part of France, with or without Europe." Thus, both France's interests and her security coincided with those of Europe and this made it possible for Mr. Vendroux to declare that any form of europeanization must be rejected if it did not respect the principle of Saar autonomy as "inviolable" and that of the Franco-Saar economic union as "definitive." These were the "prerequisites" to a settlement of the Saar question. *Cf. ibid., Assemblée nationale*, November 7, 1953, pp. 4930–4931.

tempted to reply with the opposite formula: No E.D.C., no
German concessions over the Saar; no Europe, no europeanization
of the Saar. Although the government was relatively guarded,
although a certain hesitation was apparent in the ranks of the
C.D.U., the opposition to any form of europeanization on the basis
of the existing régime was very strong. The Socialists remained
firm in their intransigence. But they were not alone. The small
parties that were members of the government coalition did not
want a political europeanization implying renunciation by Germany of a part of her territory. Deputy Thomas Dehler said so
in a debate in the Bundestag on October 28 with a directness that
more than matched that of the French parliamentarians.

> We are prepared to accept a europeanization of the economy of the
> Saar, to take into consideration certain economic interests of France, and
> to make some arrangements covering her participation in the Saar mines.
> We would even offer her the chance of importing Saar products without
> any problems of transfer or without any quantitative restrictions on
> imports for a transition period lasting until the economic integration of
> the Saar.
>   But we refuse to accept political europeanization of the Saar. We
> challenge the right of the Saar Parliament and the Saar people to decide
> on the political status of the Saar, that is to say, of a part of Germany.[13]

It is interesting to note that Mr. Dehler's opposition was based on
one of the points which had appeared to be leading to an agreement
the previous year. He expressed, however, a feeling that was
widely shared by the public and was reflected in the press: opposition to abandoning German territory.[14] Mr. Dehler did not carry
much weight. But the opposition of the small group he represented could make things difficult for the Chancellor in certain
decisions requiring a two-thirds majority.[15] This controversy had
implications for an even more delicate question. Any decision concerning the Saar that involved giving up German territory prior to
a peace treaty was bound to have some influence on the establishment of the eastern frontiers. For the Germans this was a factor
of prime importance and one of their main reasons for refusing the
definitive solution that France was demanding.[16] Nothing could

---

13 *Verhandlungen des Deutschen Bundestages*, II.4/55/C, October 28, 1953.
14 *Cf. Frankfurter Allgemeine Zeitung*, November 2, 1953.
15 For instance, the introduction of military service.
16 It will be remembered that as early as September 20, 1949, Kurt Schumacher had firmly
  emphasized the link which, he felt, existed between a settlement of the Saar problem
  and a determination of the eastern frontiers.

be more typical of the sensitivity to anything touching on the relationship of the two frontiers, on the east and on the west, than the sharp and almost unanimous hostility of all the parties to the attempt by Eugen Gerstenmaier in a speech in the Bundestag to make a legal distinction between the two situations that would make it possible to settle the Saar question without prejudicing the discussion of the Oder-Neisse question.[17]

The unwillingness to make concessions to France came equally from Chancellor Adenauer's own party. It had already been manifest on various occasions. Presentation of the Van Naters Plan served to strengthen it and especially to group around Peter Altmeier, *Minister-Präsident* of Rheinland-Pfalz, the C.D.U. Deputies opposed to europeanization of the Saar.[18]

All this explains the slow pace of the bilateral negotiations. On November 28, Mr. Adenauer and Mr. Bidault held a discussion on the Saar at The Hague, followed by another on December 12 in Paris. Although the communiqués spoke of some progress, apparently this had been limited to a statement of their differences of opinion on the Franco-Saar economic union and on the form that a settlement should take. Mr. Bidault insisted on the need for a permanent settlement while the Chancellor sought a more provisional formula. They parted on the best of terms.[19] Moreover, attention was beginning to focus on the Berlin Conference at which the French Government hoped, in spite of all previous disappointments, that a basis of agreement might be found that would contribute to a solution of the Saar problem.

Throughout the autumn the General Affairs Committee of the Council of Europe continued its work. Obviously the Plan met with various criticisms, especially from the Germans, who could not accept its economic clauses. So it was not surprising that the

[17] A similar reaction was evident in regard to the conciliatory interventions of Professor Adolf Süsterhenn, published in the *Bundesländerdienst*, November 3, 1953. *Cf.*, also, his article published in the *Rheinischer Merkur*, October 30, 1953.

[18] *Cf. La Chronique sarroise*, No. 38, April 8, 1954, which tried to give an over-all view of the attitudes of the various German parties towards the Saar question. The author of this study concludes very aptly: "If the Saar problem lends itself particularly well to such parliamentary manoeuvres, it is because it constitutes one of the mainsprings of the Chancellor's European policy. The Federal Republic is of the opinion that *the European community must inevitably bring with it as a consequence German unity* at some future date. It is in this spirit that it believes it can afford to sacrifice some of its claims to the Saar to facilitate adoption by France of the Bonn and Paris Treaties." Italics added.

[19] Moreover, the Chancellor made a statement to the press on his return from Paris which revealed how far they still were from agreement.

German delegation made an effort to obtain certain changes. In October, Eugen Gerstenmaier and Karl Pfleiderer tabled an amendment designed to facilitate access to the Saar markets for German goods.[20] The decision was then taken by the General Affairs Committee at a meeting in November to entrust the task of examining this section to a Sub-committee to meet in Brussels at the beginning of December. Mr. van der Goes van Naters himself made a proposal on December 3 which met the German requirement and established a certain balance between the French and German proposals. It was approved by the members of the Sub-committee. The entire report was then discussed by the Sub-committee, which approved it on February 6, 1954. However, a question remained concerning unauthorized political parties and this was to be considered by a Sub-committee on March 19 and 20. The whole report was not finally adopted until April 26 by seventeen votes to one, with one abstention.

The failure of the bilateral negotiations might yet have been made up for by the agreement reached within the General Affairs Committee on the plan for the europeanization of the Saar. What were the terms of this plan and what was the formula the members of the General Affairs Committee had hit upon?

The value of the proposed solution lay in the fact that they had allowed themselves to be guided by one ruling concept: Europe. A principle had been established from the outset: the Saar would become European territory just as soon as the European Political Community was instituted. It was in accordance with this that the details of the European Statute had been drawn up.[21] On the political plane, an interim solution had to be found until the formation of the European Political Community. Drawing upon earlier studies used in the negotiations between Mr. Schuman and Chancellor Adenauer, it was proposed that there be a European Commissioner (who could not be a Saarlander, a German, or a Frenchman) assisted by a Saarlander as Assistant-Commissioner, by an Advisory Board of five members of whom one should be French and one German, and by a small administrative staff " composed of European civil servants " with a Saarlander as Secretary-General.

[20] *Cf.* Kitzinger, *op. cit.*, pp. 26–27.
[21] *Cf.* " Proposals defining the European Statute of the Saar," Draft recommendation, Chap. I, paras. 1–11, in " The Future Position of the Saar," *op. cit.*, pp. 73–76. The project analysed here is, of course, that which was adopted by the General Affairs Committee on April 26, 1954.

The European Commissioner was to be nominated by the Committee of Ministers of the Council of Europe and be responsible to it. He would be in charge of defence and of the conduct of the foreign policy of the Saar; to this end, he would remain in close contact with the Saar Government which would exercise sole power in all matters " not expressly attributed to the European Commissioner by the European Statute."

On the economic plane,[22] the Statute provided for the preservation of " the common market between France and the Saar " in accordance with the provisions of a treaty to be concluded between the two countries to replace the Conventions. This provision, favourable to France, was counter-balanced by another proposing a tripartite agreement allowing for the gradual establishment of similar relations first for goods and services and then for capital between the Saar and the Federal Republic. Other clauses dealt with the methods of achieving this progressive transformation in the economic relations among the three countries, with the ownership and management of the mines that were to be attributed to the Saar, and with currency, which was to be the French franc, " until such time as a currency having a European character has been created."

On the cultural plane, the Committee proposed that an agreement be concluded among the three countries designed to preserve the German culture and language of the Saar people. The University of the Saar would become a European University.[23] As for the Franco-Saar Conventions, they would for the most part be abrogated.[24]

In the chapter on guarantees,[25] the Committee provided for an undertaking by the four governments—France, the Federal Republic, the United Kingdom, and the United States—to uphold and guarantee the Statute until the signing of a peace treaty. France, the United Kingdom, and the United States would undertake furthermore " to propose and support the acceptance of this solution as final," and the Government of the Federal Republic would " agree to this pledge." Thus the difficulty arising from the contradiction between the French demand for a definitive solution and the German opposition to any permanent settlement, before

22 *Ibid.*, paras. 12–15, pp. 76–77.
23 *Ibid.*, para. 17, p. 77.
24 *Ibid.*, para. 18, pp. 77–78.
25 *Ibid.*, Chap. II, para. 19, pp. 78–79.

Germany was re-united and the eastern frontiers fixed, could be overcome.

It was also recognized that it was essential to consult the population of the Saar.

There followed two chapters,[26] one of which established the procedure for drafting the Statute and having it approved (international conference, Saar referendum, election of a new Saar Parliament, assumption of office by the European Commissioner, ratification of the Statute), while the other clarified the position and representation of the Saar in the organizations of the European Political Community upon its establishment.

The second part of the plan for europeanization dealt with the controversial problem of the position of the political parties in the Saar.[27] Three phases were envisaged: the first, pending adoption of the European Statute, when the only requirement would be application of the European Convention for the Protection of Human Rights and Fundamental Freedoms; the second, before the entry into force of the European Statute, when political parties, associations, newspapers, and public meetings would no longer be subject to licensing, thus leaving them free for a fairly long period (twelve months) to bring their views before the people; the third stage, after the European Statute came into force, when the political parties would no longer be subject to licensing or be exposed to suspension or ban, on condition that they themselves respected democratic liberties and did not avail themselves of methods contrary to the preservation of the democratic foundations of the Statute.

The Committee tried to be fair, taking into account, as far as was possible, the interests of the parties concerned. Obviously, it could not give them both complete satisfaction, any more than it could overcome all the difficulties involved in drawing up the new Statute. It quite deliberately left to the proposed international conference the technical details of implementation. But the Rapporteur of the Committee felt that there were good grounds for optimism, given the moderate tone of the proposed solutions and the unswerving determination to transcend purely national considerations. Had they not, for instance, succeeded in " rendering permanent the dissociation of the Saar heavy industry from the

26 *Ibid*., Chap. III, paras. 20–26; Chap. IV, paras. 27–30, pp. 79–81.
27 *Ibid*., pp. 94–96.

national control of Germany" while seeking "to achieve progressively the equality of France and the German Federal Republic
as regards access to the Saar market"? [28]

Was this optimism shared? It would seem so, judging by the
decision of Mr. Bidault and Chancellor Adenauer at their meeting
in Paris on March 9 to adopt the Van Naters Plan as a basis for
future negotiations. The decision was not purely formal. Both
sides had good reason to be satisfied with the Committee's proposals. Moreover, it was clear that Chancellor Adenauer was
anxious to conclude this over-all agreement, as he was well aware
of the prospects it opened to Germany. He did not favour an
uncompromising policy, because he was convinced that the majority
of Saarlanders would vote for the existing status, not so much out
of preference for France rather than Germany but for pure convenience.[29] So he did not want to linger over this battle when the
future held so much for a Germany he knew to be rising rapidly.
Throughout the whole winter in Germany there had been signs of
the struggle going on between the man who, as head of German
diplomacy, was already looking beyond the Saar problem and those
who did not want to make any concessions on the Saar for fear of
compromising the future.[30]

Reactions soon revealed the persistence of certain major difficulties. The French were worried about what seemed to them to be
a too close, too apparent, link between recognition of the European
character of the Saar and establishment of the European Political
Community. It was also noted that the European Commissioner
had only an advisory role in the Committee of Ministers of the
Council of Europe, in the special Council of Ministers of the
E.C.S.C., and in the Committee of Ministers of the E.D.C. But it
was the economic provisions, less favourable than those in the
original plan, that were the primary target of attack. The extension
to Germany even on a gradual basis of the same relationship as
existed between France and the Saar could not be reconciled with

---

[28] *Ibid.*, p. 43.
[29] Statement to the Foreign Affairs Committee of the Bundestag, March 5, 1954.
[30] From various quarters attention was drawn to a new phase of tension between the
Ministry for Foreign Affairs and the Ministry for All-German Affairs. Moreover, Mr.
Gerstenmaier and Mr. Süsterhenn were especially watched and criticized for their
conciliatory attitude which was taken to reflect the point of view of the Chancellor.
A new division of responsibility for Saar affairs between the Ministry for All-German
Affairs and the Foreign Office brought protests from the opponents of Mr. Adenauer,
particularly from the S.P.D. and the F.D.P. who saw in this operation a victory for
the supporters of a compromise solution.

preservation of the Franco-Saar economic union; furthermore, the term "currency having a European character" sounded very vague.

These reservations on the part of the French were brought to the notice of Chancellor Adenauer and Walter Hallstein in the course of the talks held on March 8 and 9. At that time the French negotiator submitted a proposal for a protocol to include the principal points of the Van Naters Plan but with certain clarifications that he deemed necessary to safeguard his country's interests.

Thus, for Article 1, he proposed the terse formula: the Saar shall become a European territory. As for the Saar's participation in the organizations of the European Political Community, the Saar representative shall have the right to vote. The article concerning the Franco-Saar union provided that this union would evolve with the economic and monetary unification of Europe and the establishment of new common markets. While admitting the need for a new economic convention between France and the Saar and for provisions that took into account the needs of Germany and of the Saar, he made it clear that no alteration in the trade balance affecting the current balance of payments between France and Germany should result from those arrangements. Another article clearly recognized the Saar's rights of ownership of the mines, including the Warndt coalfields, but stipulated that the provisions governing the working of these Saar coalfields were to be determined in the economic convention to be drawn up between France and the Saar in the spirit of the Conventions of May 20, 1953.

Finally, the French text provided that the Statute could be adopted by a majority vote at the time of the referendum and that thereafter the question could not be reopened.

This French plan for a Franco-German protocol was clearly less complete than the Van Naters Plan. It did, however, contain two concessions the importance of which was stressed by the Paris Government: one, it is true, was made at the expense of the Saar Government, since the drawing up of a European Statute for the Saar was to be entrusted to a Franco-German conference at which the Saar representatives would take part only as experts. The other more significant concession involved abandonment of the requirement that political parties be licensed.

In the eyes of the German Government, however, the French concessions were not enough to compensate for the reservations. Its acceptance of the Van Naters Plan as a basis for discussion did not imply acceptance of the French proposals presented to Mr. Hallstein on March 8. Consequently, the negotiations between High Commissioner François-Poncet and Ambassador Blankenhorn, begun in Bonn in conformity with the decision in principle of March 9, were doomed from the outset. The German Government replied to the French formula making the Franco-Saar economic union one of the bases of the Statute by emphasizing its own desire to broaden this formula and to fix a relatively brief time-limit of two years for the progressive adjustment of economic relations between the Saar and Germany. Moreover, it maintained its opposition to any permanent agreement, for reasons already put forward on numerous occasions.

From the moment that bilateral negotiations were resumed, the apparent agreement reached on the " parliamentary " level, as Mr. van der Goes van Naters put it, gave rise to interpretations too divergent for reconciliation. These divergences were further emphasized and aggravated by newspaper comments and statements in Parliament. The discussions rapidly took a turn for the worse. In Germany, increasingly numerous statements from extremely varied sources indicated a determined resolve to oppose europeanization of the Saar. Mr. Gerstenmaier, albeit a moderate, who in the Sub-committee responsible for examining the status of the Saar parties voted against the text adopted for the first stage, took his stand categorically against the French demands. The *Minister-Präsident* of Rheinland-Pfalz submitted a veritable declaration of war against the Van Naters Plan in his Landtag.[31] He had a memorandum drawn up in which he formulated his numerous objections to the plan for europeanization.

As for the Bishop of Trier, he made the German Government very clearly aware of his opposition, for he feared lest the adoption of the Van Naters Plan might result in the creation of a Saar bishopric.[32]

[31] *Cf.* Rheinland-Pfalz Landtag, 55th Session, March 22, 1954, pp. 1861–1862. One of the reasons behind the opposition to the Van Naters Plan lay in the person of its author. In Germany, and especially in the governing circles in Rheinland-Pfalz, his sympathies for the Saar Government's views were held against him. Mr. van der Goes van Naters was bound by ties of friendship with Mr. Braun, and he got along very well with Mr. Grandval. He was also accused of neglecting to consult the Saar opposition.

[32] Monsignor Wehr did, in fact, approach the German Government to draw its attention to this aspect of the problem.

So it was not surprising that after a rather tense debate in the Bundestag, in the course of which Chancellor Adenauer pronounced himself in favour of the Van Naters Plan, a resolution was adopted on April 30 which, after restating the Bundestag's adherence to a European policy, recalled the resolutions taken by the previous legislature on July 2 and thus reaffirmed that the Saar was part of Germany.[33]

German diplomacy, influenced as always by public opinion, was about to gain the support of a rather unexpected ally: the Saar Government. In the Saar, at least in government circles, the Van Naters Plan had had a favourable reception. Together with the confirmation of European status so long hoped for, it brought a means of breaking free to some extent from French tutelage. So President Hoffmann was prepared to take certain risks. In a speech delivered on April 2, he said the Saar was tired of living in economic, political, and social insecurity and of being kept in tutelage. The Saar wanted autonomy within the framework of an integrated Europe. This integration, necessary to the Saar, implied not only that the French market should remain open to it but that the German market should also be accessible. Although it did not want to bring up again the question of Franco-Saar co-operation, it called for the establishment of a free market between France and Germany.[34]

During this period, the Chamber of Commerce and Industry at Saarbrücken publicly took a similar position in a study on the Saar economy and europeanization of the Saar that was bound to attract attention in Germany. The examination of the structure of Saar foreign trade and its development in the course of the last twenty-five years contained this significant phrase:

> The association with the partner who heretofore has been the dominant element in this union begins to have disadvantages; the capacity to absorb Saar industrial products is decreasing and, at the same time, the free exchange of goods between the countries of the Schuman Plan makes the position of the Saar even more precarious in relation to its competitors.[35]

---

[33] *Bulletin der Bundesregierung* (1954), pp. 725 *et seq.*
[34] This position taken by Mr. Hoffmann, influenced perhaps by new technical advisers, caused considerable tension between him and the French Ambassador. Furthermore, it was not approved by the leader of the S.P.S., Mr. Kirn. *Cf.* Council of Europe, Consultative Assembly, 5th Ordinary Session, *op. cit.*
[35] *Economie sarroise et européisation de la Sarre* (Saarbrücken: 1954), p. 15.

The study went on to criticize French economic policy and its effect on the Saar. It noted that imports from Germany suffered from the fact that France was in no position to liberalize her exchange arrangements or her payments. The inadequacy of means of communication, the need for modernization and for modification of transport tariffs, were pointed out. The study referred not without bitterness to the contraction of the natural outlets for Saar products. Eastern France was the market for Saar coal and south Germany for metallurgical products. The Saar, however, was cut off from south Germany while eastern France, whose heavy industry had been re-equipped, had become in turn a seller of coal and steel, thus competing with the Saar. The same problem in regard to outlets also existed for the transforming industries and for the consumer goods industry because France, which was for the time being absorbing the bulk of Saar production, did not offer a sufficiently large market, particularly since her own industries had been re-equipped and modernized. In short, the Saar—and herein lay the crux of the plea—needed a larger market. Frontiers must be opened both on the German side and on the French. The authors of the memorandum naturally refrained from questioning the Franco-Saar economic union. They were discreet, but the meaning of their statements was nonetheless clear; the Germans had no doubts about this.[36]

The Saar Government saw in the Van Naters Plan an opportunity from which to profit. But it still had to convince its partner and it did its best to do so. During the month of April, a memorandum was drawn up presenting the Saar concept of the application of the Van Naters Plan. It was handed to the French Government in Paris at the end of the month and served as a basis for the negotiations held at the beginning of May, in which the Saarlanders participating included Gotthard Lorscheider, Franz Schlehofer, and Eugen Huthmacher, assisted by Adolf Blind and Paul Senf.[37] The

[36] *Cf. Frankfurter Allgemeine Zeitung*, May 8, 1954. It is interesting to note that Fritz Hellwig's work appeared at the same time: *Die Saar zwischen Ost und West. Die wirtschaftliche Verflechtung des Saarindustriebezirks mit seinen Nachbargebieten* (Bonn: 1954). The work was an expansion of a study the author had made in 1947–1948 for the *Friedensbüro* and showed exactly the degree to which the Saar was bound up in a complex economic network which included Germany as well as France.

[37] *Cf. Saarbrücker Zeitung*, May 10, 1954. Mr. Blind and Mr. Senf had recently been called in by Mr. Hoffmann as technical advisers. Mr. Blind was also consulted by the Sub-committee charged by the General Affairs Committee of the Consultative Assembly with clarifying economic problems raised by the europeanization of the Saar. The President of the Saar Government was unaware that this individual was in contact with the opposition parties in the Saar.

negotiations were significant not so much for their results—for it was really only a question of an exchange of views—as for their mood and content. The Saarlanders left the meetings rather dissatisfied. Once more they accused their French colleagues of being somewhat off-hand. They alleged that the minutes of the conversations did not give sufficient weight to the Saar point of view. But the discussions themselves revealed that, in fact, the French were aware of the need to open the Saar frontiers with Germany and hence to modify the economic union fairly radically even if they were not able to comply with all the wishes expressed by the Saarlanders.

Were there indeed grounds for the Saar's complaints? Although it was true that Saar exports to Germany had grown steadily,[38] the volume of Franco-Saar exchanges remained nonetheless impressive. The French took care to remind the Saar of the remarkable upward trend of the country's economy after the Franco-Saar economic union came into operation [39] and of how important it was to the Saar to have access to a market which, including the French Union, amounted to a hundred million people. Further, special quotas had been allotted to the Saar for her imports from Germany; 250 million francs after the 1952 elections, 860 million, that is, 26 per cent. of the global imports, at the time of the Franco-German Agreement of January 14, 1954 (valid for the period October 1, 1953–March 31, 1954). The Franco-German Agreement of May 14, 1954 (valid for the period April 1–

---

[38] Saar exports to Germany in 1951 made up 15 per cent. of the total; in 1952, 18 per cent.; in 1953, 21 per cent.; and in 1954, 25 per cent. Exports to France, which had risen to 68 per cent. of total exports in 1952, fell to 61 per cent. in 1953, and to 60 per cent. in 1954. It was especially in the steel market that the changing trend was evidenced. *Cf. Saarländische Bevölkerungs- und Wirtschaftszahlen, op. cit.,* pp. 6–7.

[39] *Cf.,* among others, *Les données actuelles de la question sarroise* (n.p., January, 1952), especially pp. 5–7, in which are enumerated the advantages accruing to the Saar from the economic union: increase in the level of employment (270 per 1,000 inhabitants in 1936, 306 per 1,000 inhabitants in October, 1951); expansion of coal and steel production; development of the transforming industries; rapidity of re-construction (the building index was one of the highest in Europe); and raising of the standard of living for the Saar workers. It also stated that the Saar had benefited from the French decision not to dismantle the Saar industries; that there was an advantage in its financial autonomy—lack of long-term capital being explained as " a local manifestation of the general decline in propensity to save "; and that the Saar had, in fact, a balanced budget. It should be noted that this balance disappeared after 1953. *Cf.* Kitzinger, *op. cit.,* pp. 112–113. It should also be mentioned that the author of the study on *Les données actuelles de la question sarroise* pointed out the advantages to France of the Franco-Saar economic union. He mentioned in particular the fact that France still owed the Saar 800,000,000 francs which should have been paid to her as Marshall Aid for 1948.

September 30, 1954) provided for special quotas for the Saar of 1,241 million francs or 31 per cent. of the global imports.[40]

Negotiations continued between France and Germany despite the difficulties that had made their appearance from the first meetings between High Commissioner François-Poncet and Mr. Blankenhorn. Then from the beginning of April the locus of the discussions was moved to Paris, and Mr. Hallstein went there several times.[41] The atmosphere was not very favourable. The tension aroused in Germany by the pressure of the opposition against any concession on the very principle of europeanization of the Saar had its counterpart in France in the still more serious tension arising out of the war in Indo-China. On April 26, 1954, the Conference on Far Eastern problems opened in Geneva. On May 7 came the fall of Dien Bien Phu. The life of the Laniel Government hung by a thread. It survived only by refraining from any action whatever and thus allowing itself to be governed by circumstances. It remained on the defensive towards Germany.

However, on all sides, at least in those circles responsible for the conduct of foreign affairs in the two countries, there was a strong

[40] Cf. *Bulletin de la Chambre de commerce et d'industrie de Strasbourg*, No. 1 (1956), p. 38.

[41] Below is a summary, in chronological order, of the talks that took place between March 8 and May 20, if only to show how hard everyone tried during this period to reach a solution:

March 8. Van der Goes van Naters at Adenauer's.

March 9. Bidault-Adenauer agreement; acceptance of Van Naters Plan as basis of negotiations.

March 12–16. Talks between François-Poncet and Blankenhorn.

March 20. Meeting of the Sub-Committee of the General Affairs Committee in London to discuss authorization of Saar political parties; Jakobsen's proposal.

March 24–26. Exchange of letters between Bidault and Adenauer on the Saar.

April 3. Talks between Hallstein and Bérard.

April 5. Van der Goes van Naters in Paris.

April 6. Franco-Saar conversations in Paris (representing France: Bidault, Schumann, Seydoux, Grandval, Courson de la Villeneuve; representing the Saar: Hoffmann, Hector, Kirn, Müller, Braun, Kurtz, Lorscheider, Straus).

April 7. Van der Goes van Naters at Bonn.

April 9–11. Hallstein, Thierfelder, Ophuels and Lahr in Paris; talks with Schumann.

April 13. Van der Goes van Naters in Saarbrücken.

April 20. Hallstein-Bérard talks in Bonn.

April 26–27. Political Committee of the European Assembly in Paris.

April 29. Parliamentary debate in Bonn on the Saar.

May 3. Interview between Schumann and Hallstein in Paris; Hallstein submits German proposal; beginning of study by experts.

May 3–6. Saar Economic Commission meets in Paris.

May 11. Interviews between Schumann and Hallstein.

May 14. Interviews between Schumann and Hallstein.

May 18–20. Meeting of the Committee of Ministers of the Council of Europe in Strasbourg, presided over by Adenauer.

May 20. Interviews between Adenauer and Teitgen in the presence of Spaak, Monnet, van der Goes van Naters, Hallstein, Gerstenmaier, von Brentano.

desire to reach a conclusion. People were aware of the gravity of the crisis that threatened the policy of European integration and of the consequences of a break-down in negotiations.

But although efforts were made to find common ground, it was impossible to ignore the implacable opposition that existed in regard to certain basic points.

By mid-May Mr. Hallstein's position might be summed up as follows: he accepted the europeanization of the Saar as laid down in the Van Naters Plan and even sought to strengthen the authority of the European Commissioner in his relations with the Saar Government. On the other hand, he stressed the fact that europeanization must be economic as well as political, and that a definitive solution must entail establishment between the Saar and Germany of economic relations analogous to those existing between the Saar and France. Finally, he remained firmly opposed to any attempts to impose a definitive régime that would prejudice the final settlement when a peace treaty was signed.

The French negotiators became a little less inflexible on the question of economic relations between the Saar and Germany, on the freedom of action of political parties, and on the guaranteeing of the permanent nature of the Statute. But they insisted on maintaining the " principles of the economic, monetary, and customs union between France and the Saar." To obtain German acceptance of this union they were prepared to abandon the stipulation that German assent and Anglo-American guarantees be formally incorporated in the Statute (this could be settled by separate agreements). At the same time they were considering measures designed to establish closer links between the europeanization of the Saar and the European Political Community.

Meanwhile, a meeting of the Committee of Ministers of the Council of Europe was held in Strasbourg. It was the German representative's turn to take the chair and Chancellor Adenauer attended in person. He found as his opposite number Pierre-Henri Teitgen, Vice-President of the Council of Ministers and head of the French delegation. There were conversations outside the meetings in which Foreign Minister Paul-Henri Spaak, the Netherlands delegate, Marinus van der Goes van Naters, Jean Monnet and, representing Germany, Walter Hallstein, Heinrich von Brentano, and Eugen Gerstenmaier all participated. In this very European atmosphere, discussions developed favourably and resulted in an

agreement [42] according to which the German and French Governments undertook to settle the Saar question on the basis of the
proposals contained in the April 30, 1954, report of the General
Affairs Committee of the Consultative Assembly of the Council of
Europe, pending conclusion of a peace treaty or some equivalent
settlement.

This agreement also included the interpretation given by the
two governments to Articles 1, 12, and 19 of the Van Naters report.

Article 1 read: " The aim of the proposed solution is to make
the Saar a European territory." This aim was to be achieved in
three stages: in the first, pending election of a European Assembly
by universal and direct suffrage, a European Commissioner
appointed by the Committee of Ministers of the Council of Europe
would represent the interests of the Saar in matters relating to
foreign affairs and defence; in conformity with Germany's wishes,
he " will see that all clauses of the Statute are observed and put into
effect."

In the second stage, that is to say, from the time the European
Assembly was elected, this European Commissioner was to be
responsible to the Assembly. In the third stage, that of the creation
of the European Political Community, the Saar territory would be
European territory and the Commissioner or other authority carrying out his functions would be responsible to the Parliament of the
Community.

Article 12, in its first paragraph, upheld " the principles on
which the present Franco-Saar union is founded, principles which
will be incorporated in a convention dealing with economic
co-operation between France and the Saar." The second paragraph on economic relations between Germany and the Saar
acknowledged that the goal was the gradual development of relations similar to those existing between France and the Saar. This
paragraph, like the third one, was drawn up in such a way as to
give France the guarantees that would make it possible for her to
accept the loosening of the economic union foreshadowed in the
wording of the first paragraph.

Finally, Article 19 reduced the guarantee to the period up to the
peace treaty or some equivalent settlement; it reiterated that the
population of the Saar would be freely consulted.

---

[42] The text of this agreement was published in *Le Monde*, May 26, 1954, and may be
considered accurate. See also Kitzinger, *op. cit.*, pp. 74–80.

It seemed that an understanding had finally been reached; the news spread very quickly to Strasbourg that there had been an agreement on the Saar. All the papers reported it. But this agreement bound only the signatories; government approval still had to be obtained. Although the personality of the Chancellor and his authority over his government seemed a guarantee of success, this was not the case for Mr. Teitgen, Vice-President of a divided government, who moreover had negotiated without a mandate and had ceded on points which the Quai d'Orsay and above all the French Ambassador at Saarbrücken considered to be of cardinal importance: simultaneous political and economic europeanization, and the subordination of the question of economic relations between the Saar and Germany to the development of the economic unification of Europe. He was well aware that he had gone too far in a negotiation dominated by the influence of " Europeans," and the secrecy he observed towards officials of the Quai d'Orsay was proof of this. But if he hoped to achieve a kind of *fait accompli* he was to be disappointed. In fact, Foreign Minister Bidault, returning from Geneva, and his Secretary of State, Maurice Schumann, with whom Ambassador Grandval had intervened with great obstinacy, refused to give their approval. On the evening of May 21 a categorical communiqué from the Quai d'Orsay shattered all hope of an immediate settlement. Nothing could be decided at Strasbourg, said the document; it was only a question of an exchange of ideas permitting a closer survey of the Saar problem.

Wherein lay the explanation of this latest failure? Was it in the uncompromising attitude of the Quai d'Orsay and the French Ambassador at Saarbrücken? This in itself was not enough. The striking thing about this phase of the negotiations, from March 9 to May 20, was the acceleration in the steady weakening of the French position. At the head of the country there was a government without a majority led by a man without personality and hence without influence at home or abroad. The ineffectiveness of the government had repercussions in all spheres. Whether it was a question of economic or social policy, the government was no more capable of imposing discipline on the administration than of inspiring individuals with any sense of the authority of the state. Thus, it had neither the strength nor the prestige necessary to act in Europe and in the world at large, and it allowed its positions everywhere to erode—positions to which it clung all the more blindly because of its increasing uncertainty of maintaining them—issuing solemn declarations and making dramatic moves, always the refuge of the weak. The day of reckoning was indeed drawing near; in Indo-China and in Europe it was no longer possible to make the Allies, who were growing increasingly weary, exercise patience.

This French crisis was a public affair. The whole world could observe its ups and downs, see how it intensified, and gauge when matters would come to a head. The Federal Government knew just as much about it as everyone else. For more than two years it had been aware of the change in relative strength between France and Germany in its own favour; it knew that time was on its side. Germany was not the only country to realize this. The fact was so widely recognized that in London and in Washington, as in Saar-brücken and Strasbourg, it was taken into account.

In these circumstances, the task of the diplomatists who had to defend the French positions became more and more complicated as the contrast between ends and means became more apparent. The position of the Quai d'Orsay and of Ambassador Grandval on May 20 had consistency in its favour. But the policy was one which the government no longer had the means to implement. It was clinging to a position already lost when there was still time for a compromise that would allow it to salvage some of the advantages gained just after the war.

Negotiations had not completely broken off. Quite the contrary, Ambassador Grandval and responsible officials from the Foreign Ministry were already drafting new proposals. But contacts lessened and positions hardened. At the beginning of June, the French negotiators insisted again that the Saar should immediately be given a " permanent " European status, a demand they knew would meet with unrelenting opposition from the German Government, which was neither willing nor able to bind itself definitively to any agreement concerning frontiers.

The two parties were thus fairly far apart when Mr. Laniel' Government fell on June 10; the failure of this government opened the breach through which Pierre Mendès-France burst into office as Premier.

Did the advent of this dynamic and ambitious President of the Council of Ministers mean a complete break with past policy? Did it signify the end, not only of a policy aimed at European integration but of NATO, and finally of the overthrow of existing alliances? There was great uncertainty, and anxiety grew as decisions were made: the abandonment of Indo-China, the grant to Tunisia of the internal autonomy for which she was clamouring, rejection of the E.D.C.

Such an interpretation would be tantamount to forgetting that even the most powerful of nations have only a limited freedom of action. Mr. Mendès-France gave a rhythm to French policy and imposed on it choices of action dictated by necessity. He neither could nor would break the Atlantic Alliance and fling France into jeopardy. Freed from the encumbrance of the E.D.C., he resumed negotiations.

When he tackled the problem, his aims were no different from those his predecessors had set themselves. The current of nationalism which had led to the rejection of the E.D.C. might make him more intransigent. But, if he wished to succeed, he had to take into account Germany's desires and the relative strength of the two countries. The group of technical collaborators on the Saar remained the same. Contact had been immediately established with Ambassador Grandval on whom France's policy towards the Saar depended, thus assuring continuity of views. In addition to the Van Naters Plan and the Teitgen-Adenauer protocol, as well as the numerous proposals and exchanges of view that had taken place during the summer, there were basic documents which, if the negotiations remained within the framework already outlined, would simplify matters considerably.

Mr. Mendès-France was in a hurry. He did not intend to let this problem drag on longer than those he had already solved. He preferred to use what was already in existence rather than waste time and energy in a search for new approaches. His primary concern was to conclude the Saar question and go on to other matters. Circumstances helped him. The shock occasioned by the rejection of the E.D.C. had been so severe, fear for the Atlantic Alliance so acute, that everyone was anxious to resume negotiations. The French Premier found himself dealing with men who were the more favourably disposed towards him because they feared the worst. The discussion on the Saar question took place in more propitious circumstances than any that had obtained during recent months; inserted among a whole series of agreements to be concluded, this one was contingent on them and they on it. Thus, in a discussion bearing not only on Germany's relationship to France but on its position in the Western world, the negotiators could find means of agreeing to and obtaining agreement on concessions they sought in the settlement of the Saar question, outside the provisions dealing directly with the Saar. Mr. Mendès-France showed remarkable skill in taking advantage of this increase in the range of possibilities for bargaining. Was not the abandonment of supra-nationalism generously compensated for by the admission of Germany to NATO; were not the fairly small concessions on the Saar insignificant in view of the prospects of economic co-operation which would open the gates of Africa to Germany?

The negotiation appeared to have been carefully prepared, and there was less room for improvisation than seemed at first sight. By August, goals had already been established and the decision taken to work out with the Saar Government the essential pro-visions of the future treaty for Franco-Saar co-operation before signing the Franco-German protocol. It was essential to make sure of the support of the Saar itself, for its course was increasingly uncertain. After rejection of the E.D.C., the plan for the Franco-German protocol was modified to meet the new situation and to meet the appearance—or rather the re-appearance—on the scene of the Western European Union. Between the time of the London con-ference and that held in Paris, the Saar Government and the French Government not only agreed on the plan for a Franco-German protocol on the Saar but on the bases of future economic collabora-tion. Discussions were not easy because of the tensions that manifested themselves within the Saar delegation. The fluctuations in French policy in recent years, the alternation of authoritarianism with weakness that had earned for France the reputation of being an unreliable ally, served not only to encourage opposition in the Saar but to discourage those in favour of europeanization and collaboration with France. At the beginning of July, a new ministerial crisis broke up the Saar Government coalition. The immediate cause was attributed to the divergence of views between the two parties on the subject of the law concerning *conseils d'entreprise*. It may be, however, that a group of the Christian People's Party, that very group which for some months had been urging Johannes Hoffmann to show more independence towards France, seized this opportunity to split from the Saar Socialist Party because of its too firm adherence to the French point of view.

The new team of ministers was not any more homogeneous because of this. Some of the officials closest to Mr. Hoffmann could no longer be counted upon. As time passed and opportunities for contact with Germany increased, a growing number of people who had lost all hope of achieving their ends in collaboration with France sought to find reassurance from the Federal Republic.[43] The French Ambassador, on whom devolved the task of maintaining ties between the Saar and France and of keeping in hand a small ally who was compelled by the weakness of its protector to seek help elsewhere, had to intervene with a firmness all the less tolerable because it grew in proportion as French authority weakened.

Once again Mr. Grandval succeeded, despite violent arguments, in rallying his forces and obtaining from President Hoffmann the agreement that Mr. Mendès-France needed to enter into negotiations. On October 16, the heads of the French and Saar Governments exchanged notes in which they established the bases of Franco-Saar economic co-operation and clarified their interpretation of Article 12 of the plan for a Franco-German protocol defining the economic relations of the Saar with Germany.[44]

As for the decisive meeting between Premier Mendès-France and Chancellor Adenauer, it was carried on at the pace dictated by the French Premier, but this did not displease the Chancellor. The two men were facing the same problems, the same obstacles that their predecessors had faced before: one was determined to achieve a permanent status, while the other wanted to keep it fluid. Mr. Mendès-France sought to give a definitive character to the basic agreements, while Mr. Adenauer treated them as only provisional. The former sought to preserve the economic preponderance he had obtained, and the latter tried to take it from him. Finally, the French minister tried to reinforce the agreement he was about to conclude with his German colleague by means of a referendum in the Saar, while the Chancellor sought to preserve for the pro-German opposition parties the opportunity of expanding their influence. Hence the haste on the part of the French minister to

[43] Isolated contacts had already existed since the autumn of 1951 and had intensified after 1952, particularly since the elaboration of the Van Naters Plan.
[44] The *Allgemeiner Zeitungsdienst West* (*AZW*) on October 26, 1955, published the letter of the Saar Government of October 16, 1954, concerning the Saar mines. The letter on the Treaty of Economic Co-operation was also published on the same date, but not in the form of a letter. It contained a résumé of the letter of October 16 concerning trade relations between the Saar and the Federal Republic.

complete the negotiations, and the wariness of the Chancellor who, moreover, was restrained by protests from the Saar opposition which found a substantial echo in the majority party.[45] Mr. Mendès-France held one trump card, since he could deny the Federal Republic access not only to sovereignty but also to the Atlantic Alliance, and he did not hesitate to play it. He was both firm and flexible, and in the form of a second referendum he offered the Germans the way out they were seeking. He was dealing with a man who was no coward and who had always known how to keep the Saar problem within the modest dimensions it occupied in the ensemble of German foreign policy. Thus agreement was reached.

On October 23, after a last stiffening of positions, the two heads of government appended their signatures to a text, the essential provisions of which were relatively close to those proposed in previous protocols.[46]

The original objective was preserved: the Saar was to have a European status under the aegis of the Western European Union. It was therefore the Council of Ministers of this Union that would elect the European Commissioner and he would be responsible to it. He would be responsible for representing Saar interests in the field of foreign affairs and defence; he would also have the right to oversee observation of the Statute.[47]

The Agreement then went on to establish the conditions of Saar representation in the various European organizations in which the European Commissioner would participate in an advisory capacity. Provision was also made for Saar participation in European defence.

On the economic plane, with minor exceptions, the provisions previously agreed on were retained; the principles covering the Franco-Saar economic union were to be embodied in a treaty of

---

[45] Shortly before he left for Paris, Chancellor Adenauer had received representatives of the three Saar opposition parties. They once again emphasized the paramount need of ensuring freedom of action for their parties. A similar appeal came from the Socialist opposition. It is known, moreover, that on October 9, 1954, shortly before this meeting, Mr. Mommer presented in the *Stuttgarter Zeitung*, under the title of "Eine Saarlösung mit dem Risiko der Freiheit," a plan for the settlement of the Saar question in which he also stressed the granting of democratic freedoms in the Saar.

[46] Cf. *Journal officiel, Lois et Décrets*, April 8, 1955, p. 3544; *Bundesgesetzblatt*, II, No. 7 (March 25, 1955), p. 295. For the text in English, cf. *Agreement Between the Government of the Federal Republic of Germany and the Government of the French Republic on the Saar Statute, Paris, October 23, 1954* (London: H.M.S.O., 1954), Misc. No. 33, Cmd. 9306. Cf., on this subject, Kitzinger, *op. cit.*, pp. 81–106.

[47] The idea of a Saarlander as Assistant Commissioner and of a Consultative Committee had been abandoned.

co-operation to be concluded between the two governments. The evolution of economic relations between the Saar and Germany towards the ultimate establishment between the two countries of a relationship similar to that existing with France would take place gradually so as not to endanger trade within the economic union or relations with Germany. Moreover, in an exchange of letters with Chancellor Adenauer, Premier Mendès-France declared that the French Government was prepared to consider the question of the admission of branches of German banks and insurance companies into the Saar. In two other letters he undertook to end, before the referendum on the European status of the Saar, sequestration [48] and to take immediate steps to entrust to a Saarlander the direction of personnel and welfare services in the Saar mines as well as to increase the proportion of Saarlanders employed.

The provisions governing implementation of the Statute included, in return, innovations that were the result of the final tussle. The French negotiator, unable to obtain recognition of the definitive nature of the Statute, had made sure of certain guarantees he hoped were adequate: a referendum in the Saar; a guarantee that pending conclusion of the peace treaty the Statute that had been agreed upon could not be questioned; and an undertaking that there would be no outside interference in the Saar. He had allowed the introduction of a clause, however, that opened the way for constitutional revision during the interim period. He had agreed that licences would no longer be required for political parties, associations, newspapers, and public meetings. He had provided a relatively short delay (three months) between the entry into effect of the agreement and the Saar referendum. Thus he had limited, or so he hoped, the potential activities of the pro-German opposition parties.[49] But he had to accept the threat of a revision, a threat that was a very real possibility because of the concession as to a second referendum. The French representative, while staking everything on the trumps he held, counted on the Saar referendum to consolidate a position that was still favourable: the German negotiator sought comfort in the fact that he had

---

[48] He referred to the fact that Völkingen and Neunkirchen had been sequestrated in 1945, as well as the German share in the factories at Dillingen and Brebach. The sequestration of the last two had been ended in 1951.
[49] On the German side, and this was one of the points on which the Chancellor had reached agreement with the party leaders who convened in Paris during the conference, they wanted to leave the decision to a new Landtag which was to be freely elected after the new Statute had come into force.

nonetheless succeeded in opening the way for a revision and pinned his hopes on the second referendum.

As might be imagined, this Agreement was received with very mixed feelings. In France the first comments were both positive and restrained. The decisions which in effect consecrated the reversal of former alliances by including the Federal Republic in the Western security system were obviously more important. In fact, French opinion had taken very little interest in the Saar for itself. Its reactions had been dictated primarily by a defensive reflex against German efforts to win back the Saar. So France was fairly easily satisfied with an agreement which maintained the positions already won. She did not gloat over her victory, perhaps at the suggestion of the government which was well aware of the stiff fight that Chancellor Adenauer would have in Germany to force through ratification.[50]

In Saar Government circles, the immediate reaction was one of relief. Only one point was the subject of attention: the Agreement between the French and German Governments recognized the existence, if not the right to that existence, of an autonomous Saar. Doubtless, it was admitted, certain provisions of the Agreement could legally be considered as provisional. But, to repeat the expression of Mr. Grandval as did the Saar Government newspapers, on the political level a decision had nevertheless been reached. Optimism prevailed, reinforced by the conviction, shared by the French Ambassador, that the Statute would be accepted by a large majority.[51]

But these opinions were based on an evaluation of the current situation and the assumption that the referendum would be quick to follow.[52] That is indeed what the French negotiators had thought, for they saw a guarantee of success in the swift implementation of the Agreement. This optimistic reasoning was based on an error in reckoning how much time would elapse. They had allowed for three months between the entry into effect of the

---

[50] A bulletin of the *Saarbund*, noting the coolness of the French press as evidenced by the fact that news of the agreement on the Saar was relegated to the back pages, asked whether this was not an indication of government intervention. We have already noted this coolness on the part of the French newspapers. But some of the French who followed Saar affairs more closely were very critical. Michel Debré, for example, considered the introduction of a second referendum to be a major error.

[51] Figures mentioned varied from 70 to 80 per cent. in favour of the Statute.

[52] Thus, on October 26 Mr. Hoffmann declared that the referendum could be held in March or April 1955, for it would not be linked with the ratification of the Agreement on the Saar by the parliaments of Paris and of Bonn. *Cf. Le Monde*, October 27, 1954.

Statute and the date of the referendum. But they did not seem to have taken into account the time necessary for the ratification of the Agreement, an essential prerequisite for its entry into effect. In fact, ratification took even longer than had been anticipated because it gave rise to technical questions and met with impassioned resistance. Furthermore, the French and Saar Governments did not give sufficient attention to the delay in implementation, despite Mr. Grandval's reported warnings. The result was that the Council of the Republic did not ratify the Paris Agreement until March 26, 1955, and as the arrangements for the referendum took longer than anyone had anticipated, the date was finally fixed for October 23.

7

THE SAAR RETURNS TO GERMANY,
OCTOBER, 1954–OCTOBER, 1956

ONE year separated the referendum from the Agreement of October 23, a year in which there were profound changes in the situation.

For the Agreement of October 23 had met with lively criticism from the pro-German opposition in the Saar,[1] the German Socialists, and the small parties that were members of the government coalition. The Chancellor, and this is what was chiefly held against him, had not kept to the seven points on which agreement had been reached with the leaders of the German parties at the Paris conference.[2] Questions rained down. How could one speak of " europeanization " of the Saar after renouncing those supranational institutions which alone could embody Europe? How could anyone accept that mediocre substitute, the Western European Union? What was the meaning of the agreement not to re-open

---

[1] *Cf.* the brochure of the *Comel Verlag Die Saar deutsch oder europäisch ?* (Cologne: 1954). Text of a lecture by Heinrich Schneider on November 23, 1954, to the Rhein-Ruhr Klub at Düsseldorf.

[2] The seven points are as follows: (1) The final decision on the Saar will be made in a peace treaty or a similar settlement. Until then, interim measures will be taken, guaranteeing the economic interests of the Saar, ensuring the right of political freedom, and banning agitation on the French as well as on the German side. This will be obtained by means of a pact between Germany and France, approved by a new and freely elected Landtag. (2) To bring about peace in this interim period, France and Germany pledge themselves to abstain from any interference in the Saar's internal affairs. Any provisions in the present Constitution of the Saar which are contrary to this interim solution shall be modified. (3) Elections to the Landtag, which will act on the Saar's accession to the Franco-German pact, will take place one year after re-establishment of political freedom in the Saar. (4) A Commissioner or a committee appointed by the Council of Ministers of the Brussels Pact will have the following tasks: (a) representation of the Saar in foreign relations, (b) preservation of political freedoms. The Commissioner or committee shall report to the Council of Ministers of the Brussels Pact. (5) The customs and monetary union of the Saar with France will be preserved. Nevertheless, the Saar economy would be strangled if it were not able to renew the close economic relations it always used to have with Germany. (6) Mining installations in the Saar are obsolete. They require considerable investments, if the Saar population is not eventually to face complete ruin. The main source of the economy is the mines. The Saar, France, and Germany will share in these investments. (7) The pits will be the property of the Saar. Management will either become the responsibility of the Saar Government or be jointly exercised by the Saar, France, and Germany; the latter is preferable because Germany and France will participate in the investments.

the question of the Saar's status after the referendum? Why had there been agreement not only on the referendum, but on holding it so quickly that it was almost impossible for the opposition to organize itself?

The undertaking not to meddle in Saar affairs clearly favoured France, who already had people on the spot and held the reins. The economic concessions were much too great. Reference was also made to obscurities in the text. The very brevity of the Agreement was a source of ambiguity. What interpretation was to be given to paragraph (b) of Article 7, which provided for certain modifications in the Saar Constitution to meet the new situation? Would it be possible to undertake certain reforms in the régime without immediately coming up against the opposition of those who maintained that this would be tantamount to opening up the whole question again?

Furthermore, what was the significance of the second referendum? Would it enable Germany to re-affirm her intention of regaining the Saar? Would the pro-German parties be able to express their opinions freely? What would happen if, after some years, it became apparent that there was still no possibility of concluding a peace treaty? [3] In addition, there was an ever-present fear that this Agreement might have repercussions on the question of the settlement of the eastern frontiers. It is easy to imagine how acutely aware of this Jakob Kaiser and his colleagues were.

Attacked and questioned from all sides, the government tried to deal with the situation. As early as October 27, Ambassador Herbert Blankenhorn received the leaders of the Saar opposition, Richard Becker, Hubert Ney, Kurt Conrad, Heinrich Schneider, together with two deputies of the Bundestag, Karl Walz and Hermann Trittelvitz.[4]

He explained the articles of the Agreement of October 23 to them and tried to reply to the numerous questions they raised. Mr. Blankenhorn had a long interview in Paris with Jean Soutou on November 12 to clarify some of the problems of interpretation posed by the Agreement. The interview was satisfactory. The

---

[3] *Cf.*, on this subject, in addition to the press the publications of the *Deutscher Saarbund*, especially the *Informationen und Hinweise*; also Dischler, *Das Saarland, 1945–1957*, *op. cit.*, Vol. II, pp. 118–119. *Informationen und Hinweise*, published regularly by the *Saarbund*, is a most valuable source of information because its editor followed Saar affairs and discussions on the Saar very closely.

[4] *Cf. Deutscher Saarbund, Informationen und Hinweise* 1/106. Heinrich Lietzmann, President of the *Saarbund*, also went to see Mr. Blankenhorn.

only questions still not clear, and they were vital ones, related to freedom of discussion during the period between the two referendums.

The government's natural desire to appease public opinion led it to give the Agreement the interpretation most favourable to Germany and to reduce as much as possible the significance of the concessions it had made. This was of no importance as long as the exchanges of opinion were still confidential.

But when it came to public discussion, the matter became more complicated. On December 10 the government submitted to the Bundestag the Agreement on the Saar together with a summary of the underlying principles. In this *exposé* it stressed first and foremost the fact that the Agreement did not imply the Federal Republic's acceptance of the *de facto* situation created by France in the Saar. It was absolutely clear, the government insisted, that the Saar had not been designated " European territory." Its status was European only in this sense: arrangements for its administration were included within the framework of the Western European Union.

In the discussion of principles stress was again laid on the importance of the clause providing for revision of the Saar Constitution, particularly the Preamble, in order to adapt it to the new status. The government high-lighted the importance of the second referendum in which the Saar people would have the opportunity to determine their own destiny and the significance of the provisions concerning the freedom of action of political parties.

On the same day, the French Government gave its account of the principles, in the course of which it re-affirmed the European nature of the status of the Saar, on the one hand, and, on the other, the fact that the settlement really was final.

> We find ourselves faced with an international instrument conferring a European status on the Saar; it goes without saying that the French Government will demand confirmation of this instrument when it comes to negotiating the peace treaty which must ultimately determine the territorial limits of Germany and whose provisions concerning the Saar will be submitted to the inhabitants of the Saar for approval.[5]

[5] " On the economic plane, the Agreement categorically provides for maintenance of the monetary, customs, and economic union between France and the Saar." All the rest of the commentary is in the same vein.

The differences in interpretation of the Agreement in the debates
in the Bundestag on December 15 and 16, and in the National
Assembly beginning on December 20,[6] played into the hands of the
opponents. Once again opposition groups were in a position to
reinforce one another, each camp using the arguments put forward
in the other to force the partisans of conciliation to retreat. The
two heads of government did their best to avoid becoming engaged
in polemics. Mr. Mendès-France very aptly reminded the National
Assembly that it was to vote on the text of the Agreement and not
on the motives of the co-signatory. But each was led to appease
the opposition in his own country, and this was immediately made
use of by the opposition in the other country.[7]

These very difficult and even stormy debates, nevertheless,
ended favourably for the two governments. Chancellor Adenauer,
however hard pressed he might be by the Socialist opposition,
which was joined by the party leaders of the government coalition,
was able to impose party discipline.

Those deputies belonging to the C.D.U. who had disapproved
of the Agreement ended by supporting the head of the government.
Doubtless they were as much aware as he of the importance for
Germany of the Paris Agreement and on this point they parted
company with the Socialists. The admission of Germany to
NATO re-introduced her into the Western Alliance and into world

6 *Cf. Verhandlungen des Deutschen Bundestages*, II. 61/3112 *et seq.*, II. 62/3176 *et seq.*,
December 15–16, 1954; and *Journal officiel, Débats parlementaires, Assemblée nationale*,
December 21, 1954.

7 It may be useful to give a few examples. In his speech of December 15 Chancellor
Adenauer recognized that the statement of principles given by the French Government
contained substantial differences in interpretation, not only of important points in the
text of the Agreement, but of its general import. To avoid misunderstanding, he was
planning, he said, to contact the President of the French Council, and if this had no
results, to propose to his colleagues that the problem be submitted to the United Kingdom and United States Governments so that they might try jointly to reconcile these
differing views. The differences of interpretation were also commented on by various
speakers in the National Assembly. Paul Reynaud said : " We are anxious to ratify
the Agreement, but on condition that it be understood the Agreement means the
opposite of what the Germans maintain it means." And he added : " In the light of
Chancellor Adenauer's statements [which, according to him, would have required
re-opening negotiations on the Saar] matters cannot remain as they are, for the result
would be that the Agreement on German sovereignty would come into effect and that
on the Saar would not be implemented." He concluded his argument, saying : " If
there is a new agreement following negotiation, that will be the one we must ratify.
We cannot, as I see it at the moment, ratify a disagreement." Thus, Mr. Mendès-
France was forced in the course of the discussion to give assurances to Parliament that
evoked a heated response in Germany : " I would like to repeat so that there shall be
no misunderstanding, in this country or abroad, that when the time comes the French
Government will demand that the provisions of the Statute be incorporated into the
peace treaty without any changes and that the government will not be a party to any
peace treaty that does not conform to this demand."

politics. Under these circumstances, what was the use of baulking over the Saar question, which would not be finally settled until some time in the future?

The French, too, felt the need to have done with a debate that had already lasted too long. Rejection of the E.D.C. had calmed passions; there was a clear recognition that there was no alternative solution. Mr. Mendès-France had obtained the most that could be hoped for from the autumn negotiations. Should he fail, anything might happen. But the Agreement reached on the Saar seemed to be satisfactory. The opinion which prevailed in Parliament and in the press was that a solution had been reached that was acceptable to both sides. A survey carried out in 1955 by the Institut Français d'Opinion Publique indicated that the people familiar with developments in the Saar believed a fair compromise had been reached. The Germans, however, in reply to a questionnaire in May prepared by the Institut für Demoskopie at Allensbach, were of the opinion that France had been given the advantage.[8]

Several months passed before the Agreement was ratified. It had its second and third readings in the Bundestag only on February 26 and 27, 1955.[9] It was approved on March 18 by the Bundesrat and appeared on March 25 in the *Bundesgesetzblatt*. In Germany the debate continued after this date. The Socialist Party, supported by some deputies of the government coalition, tabled a request to the Federal Constitutional Court that it examine the constitutionality of the Saar Statute. The court's ruling that the Federal law concerning the Saar Statute did not contravene the Basic Law was given on May 4.[10]

In France it was the same; there was a long gap between the vote in the National Assembly on December 23 and the debate in the Council of the Republic, which ended on March 26, 1955, with an affirmative vote.[11]

The French had wanted to wait until Germany had ratified. However, the resistance of opponents of the new Statute was so strong and the indecision of the government coalition so marked that the Chancellor had been compelled to clarify a number of

[8] On the inquiries, see Bibliography and *Analytical Study*, p. 273, notes 4, 5.
[9] *Verhandlungen des Deutschen Bundestages*, II. 71/3859-3877; II. 72/3939-3947.
[10] We do not consider it necessary here to go into details of these controversies.
[11] The Agreement on the Saar was adopted by 368 votes to 145 in the National Assembly and by 217 to 92 in the Council of the Republic. *Journal officiel, Débats parlementaires, Assemblée nationale*, December 24, 1954, p. 6845; *Journal officiel, Débats parlementaires, Conseil de la République*, March 27, 1955, p. 1130.

points and to negotiate not only with the French Government but
with the party leaders and members of the parliamentary group of
the C.D.U. His meeting with Mr. Mendès-France on January 14,
1955, at Baden-Baden, did much to clarify the situation. The heads
of the two governments agreed upon the steps to be taken to
organize the referendum, which was to be supervised by an international commission.[12] They also agreed to settle any future
differences on the Saar within the framework of the Western
Alliance and to make a joint request to the governments of the
United States and the United Kingdom for the guarantee provided
for in Article 8.[13] But this clarification of the methods of implementing the Agreement of October 23 did not touch upon the basic
questions the Chancellor had been insistently urged to clear up by
the leaders of the opposition, influential politicians of the C.D.U.,
and *Minister-Präsident* Peter Altmeier. The result was that this
interview at Baden-Baden was of no particular help to Mr.
Adenauer in his negotiations within the Federal Republic.[14]

There was another reason for delay: the drawing up of a
convention of economic co-operation with the Saar. The two
governments had determined the bases of the convention in an
exchange of letters on October 16. Furthermore, on the day the
Franco-German Agreement was signed, the Saar Government had
made it known that the few changes in the final text did not in any
way affect the letters of October 16.

But the Saar Government made difficulties. It sought to profit
by the situation to free itself from the economic tutelage of France,
and to gain time in order to draw nearer to the Federal Republic
by postponing the drafting and signing of the economic convention
until ratification of the October 23 agreements. Members of the
team of ministers were more and more inclined to pursue their
own individual policies; some of them had recently been in direct

12 The creation of a commission had already been demanded by Mr. Hoffmann soon after
the Agreement of October 23, 1954. *Cf. Saarbrücker Zeitung*, October 26, 1954. This
question had also been the subject of talks between Jean Soutou and Ambassador
Blankenhorn.

13 *Cf. La Documentation française, Articles et Documents, Textes du jour*, No. 0.157,
January 18, 1955, p. 2.

14 It should be noted, however, that an agreement was reached on what persons or
categories of persons could be authorized to take part in the referendum. It was agreed
that the right to take part should be granted, on the one hand, to people who had
been living in the Saar for more than five years, regardless of nationality, and, on the
other hand, to Saar nationals living outside Saar territory.

contact with the Federal Republic. The French negotiators, increasingly on the defensive, were aware of striking collusion, for example, the close resemblance between the conception of the Franco-Saar economic union held by the Minister of Finance, Paul Senf, and that of the Bonn Government.

These dilatory proceedings only partially achieved the results the Saarlanders had desired. The interview of President Hoffmann with Minister Ludwig Erhard on January 31 was fruitless. It was the view of some Saarlanders and of the German Government that these talks should pave the way for negotiations on economic questions with the Federal Republic parallel with those that had been held with France. But apparently, although Johannes Hoffmann was not indifferent to these evidences of attention from the Federal Republic because he saw in them indirect recognition of an existing situation, he became frightened when asked to sign the minute of the interview. He did not intend to hand over a weapon that might be used against him to cut him off from the French.

Ambassador Grandval was following all this closely. Without perhaps being fully cognizant of all the contacts between Saar official circles and those of Germany,[15] he read President Hoffmann's mind, and this the more easily because Mr. Hoffmann had already on a number of occasions indicated his desire to free the Saar from France's economic hold. Thus Mr. Grandval reminded him of the commitments undertaken in the letters of October 16, 22, and 23. There could be no question of raising this issue of the economic union, the continuance of which had been formally provided for in the agreements of October 23. The Ambassador's interventions prevailed over the hesitation of the Saarlanders. Mr. Grandval had at his disposal texts of unmistakable clarity and he was determined. In the absence of a treaty of economic co-operation, it was possible to sign a Franco-Saar protocol on March 21, two days before the opening of the debate in the Council of the Republic. Its essential provisions[16] were in conformity with the

[15] These contacts were many. Chancellor Adenauer openly admitted their existence in a reply to a question put to the Foreign Affairs Committee of the Bundestag by Mr. Mommer. He was quite right to admit them, said the bulletin of the *Saarbund*, for Mr. Mommer was in a position to be very well informed. And the bulletin went on to give certain information at its disposal: between Christmas and the new year, Rudolf Thierfelder met, at his father-in-law's house in Saarbrücken, Karl Burk, President of the *Fédération des gymnastes de Sarre*, and President Hoffmann's head of the Chancellery, Franz Schlehofer. He also saw Minister Senf.

[16] *Cf.* Supplement to *La Chronique sarroise*, No. 50 (April 5, 1955). For the negotiation of this Convention, see Kitzinger, *op. cit.*, pp. 107–118.

principles laid down in the exchange of letters of October 16, and these principles were themselves inspired by those which had governed the drafting of the 1953 Conventions. On May 3 the Convention on Economic Co-operation between France and the Saar was finally signed.[17]

The Saar Government's efforts to regain relative freedom of action were easily explained. The October 23 Agreement had not eliminated the basic contradiction between the policy of euro-peanization of the Saar and the retention of the economic and monetary union with France. The government of the Saar was even more painfully aware of this contradiction because the country was feeling the effects of the fluctuations in the political and economic life of France. Scarcely had they begun to get over the shock of Mr. Mendès-France's advent to power when his government fell. A new ministerial crisis delayed negotiations and further undermined the already rather limited confidence of the Saar Government in France. Ambassador Grandval, who was by now used to this task, endeavoured to heal the breach. But he could not alone make up for all the weaknesses of the central power or make good the inadequacies of the ministers or their ignorance of the problems at issue. The fall of Mr. Mendès-France's Government, which had nothing to do with the Saar question, nevertheless had repercussions on Franco-Saar relations, and these were the more serious because they came at a time when measures were being drawn up to put into effect the decisions taken in October, 1954.

The problems at issue were, in fact, to define the powers of the European Commissioner [18] and to agree on the interpretation of the article concerning the freedom of action of political parties and limitations on the right to criticize.

Furthermore, Mr. Mendès-France's promise to end sequestration raised again, even more actively, the problem of the Roechling factories.

---

17 *Cf. Vertrag zwischen Frankreich und dem Saarland über wirtschaftliche Zusammenarbeit vom 3. Mai 1955. Das Recht des Saarlandes, Blattei für die Praxis der Justiz, Verwaltung und Wirtschaft* (Saarbrücken: 1955).

18 The Franco-German plan, defining the prerogatives of the European Commissioner, provided that individuals, groups, and organizations could, under certain conditions, appeal against a decision of the Commissioner to an arbitral tribunal of the Western European Union. The Saar Government asked what decisions were meant, since the Commissioner had no right to make decisions.

The first group of problems had been the subject of many exchanges of view during the winter.[19] The German Government, subject to the combined pressure of the pro-German parties in the Saar, of the German Socialists, and of members of its own majority, made determined efforts to obtain agreement on a broader interpretation of Article 6 and the prerogatives of the future European Commissioner. But this met with the resistance of the French Government, which itself had to take into account the reservations of the opposition and the opinion of a Saar Government most anxious to retain full power. These problems, indeed, would not have been very hard to resolve if they had not been complicated by the prevailing tension and the general atmosphere of mistrust. Thus, Antoine Pinay, who took over responsibility for the Ministry of Foreign Affairs without any great knowledge of international questions or any practice in the conduct of negotiations, muddled through in a rather undistinguished fashion.

Agreement was finally reached on a few basic points. A letter of March 14, in which Chancellor Adenauer confirmed the interpretation of Article 6 given by Minister Franz-Josef Strauss in an interview he had had a few days earlier with the French Minister for Foreign Affairs, revealed that the German and French points of view had been reconciled in a manner satisfactory to France.[20]

On May 11 the Council of Western European Union, to which the two governments of Paris and of Bonn had turned over the task of arbitrating their differences regarding the prerogatives of the European Commissioner, gave its reply and approved a resolution setting up a commission to supervise the referendum and determine its terms of reference.

The conditions under which the negotiations had been prepared and conducted by the French and the Saarlanders were not, however, very satisfactory. Mr. Pinay's apparently expeditious authoritarianism caused several clashes with Mr. Grandval. President Hoffmann and his colleagues were taken to task in a tone that was sometimes wounding; but, what was even more serious, the Minister for Foreign Affairs did not give those with whom he was

---

[19] After the Adenauer-Mendès-France meeting at Baden-Baden on January 14, conversations took place in Paris on January 18. A plan for a Franco-German agreement had been drawn up and submitted in January to the Saar Government which expressed immediate reservations about the powers attributed to the Commissioner.

[20] For Mr. Pinay's reply on March 22, *cf.* Dischler, *op. cit.*, Vol. II, p. 153.

dealing the impression that he knew enough about the question to put his ideas across. Before the meeting with the Chancellor at the end of April, he had been determined to impose limits on the powers of the European Commissioner, but he returned unsuccessful. Faced with the Saar Government's resistance, he then had to ask the head of the German Government to re-examine the question. As for the settlement itself—the outcome of the Council of Western European Union's arbitration—it was made, to all intents and purposes, in accordance with the German views.

Thus it was not surprising that the Saar Government came out of these negotiations even more uncertain and even more divided than before over the future of its relations with France.[21]

The manner in which the negotiation of the Roechling affair had been carried and the question settled also contributed to an aggravation of tension between those governing the Saar and the French Government.[22]

This problem was one which had long awaited solution. It had scarcely affected Franco-Saar relations in the early years or the Franco-German conflict as such. It was more a controversy that ran parallel to the major issue and got caught up in it from time to time.

The French brandished the name of Roechling as a reminder of the risks Europe was running in allowing the explosive mixture of German nationalism and industrial capitalism to re-form. The Germans, for their part, used the example of the sequestration of Völklingen as one of the most spectacular demonstrations of French imperialism. As for the governments, they had been too occupied with other matters to keep close track of this affair. They became really interested only when they felt there was a danger of it getting out of hand, that is to say, in the decisive stage of the debate over the Saar Statute.

This did not mean that they had entirely neglected the problem until this final phase. On the contrary, everyone knew that

---

21 For all this discussion, *cf.* the parliamentary debates (in the Federal Republic of December 15, 1954, February 25–27, March 31, and May 6, 1955: in France, in the National Assembly, December 24, 1954, March 30, 1955, Conseil de la République, March 23, 24, 25, and 26, 1955) and the bulletins of the *Saarbund*, especially *Informationen und Hinweise*, December, 1954, to May, 1955.

22 The Roechling affair was several times referred to in the French and German newspapers. Drawing their information from the interested parties, they sometimes published very good studies. *Cf.* also the publications of the *Saarbund*.

sequestration was only an interim solution and that a decision would have to be reached on the allocation of assets. From the outset, Michel Debré had tried to free the Roechling industry from sequestration and had proposed the creation of a régime for the iron and steel industries similar to that for the mines. Mr. Grandval appealed to the government more than once to determine its policy towards Völklingen. The Roechling family re-doubled efforts and steps designed either to regain possession of their property or to sell it. They received various offers, especially from groups in the United States. Proposals also naturally came from France; Châtillon-Commentry opened up negotiations with the Roechling family that began in September, 1953, and went on until April, 1954. In December, 1953, another series of negotiations began through the intermediary of the *Crédit suisse*, acting on behalf of Schneider-Creusot. On April 15, 1954, the Roechling family decided to grant an option for the sum of 200 million Swiss francs. It was only after having made their decision that they learned the identity of the would-be purchaser.

The French Government hesitated as to what line to take. It was aware that its proprietary rights to the Völklingen factory were open to question. But it was important for the government to try to retain permanent French control over this enterprise and even more important to prevent the Roechlings from returning to the Saar. There were various possible solutions. One, which had the advantage of simplicity, consisted in deciding to nationalize the industry. But this would alarm French iron and steel concerns and, moreover, it was a costly procedure which would meet with the firm opposition of the Minister of Finance. Another solution might be to encourage private capital. It was with this in mind that the government decided on its attitude to Châtillon-Commentry. But Schneider-Creusot, which was standing by, was no more fortunate than its rival. Despite the extensions of the time-limit which it had been granted, it was unable to submit a concrete offer before the appointed date. Resistance grew. In the Saar the government, warned especially by the Finance Minister, Mr. Senf, tried to oppose a solution which would rob the Saar of any share in the aforementioned enterprise that was still in Saar hands. The German Government, very prudent throughout, nevertheless communicated to the Roechlings its desire to see them retain their business.[23]   The latter took a calculated risk in not pursuing negotiations with private concerns in France.   Might not the French Government have been tempted to resort to a forceful solution which could only be nationalization?

Naturally, the Roechlings were only too pleased to be encouraged.   What was important to them, and they stressed the point continually, was to have the chance of re-assuming the management of their own factories, that is to say, of maintaining their control over the capital shares.   If they could not do this, they preferred to sell out to the highest bidder.

The winter passed in fairly complicated negotiations.   Although November 15 had gone by without the Schneider group having been able to raise the option, all contact was not broken off.   A new French group was formed to further the affair, but it made scarcely any progress.   The Roechlings were in no hurry.   They were even playing for time.

In France, however, anxiety was becoming apparent.   Ambassador Grandval, who was following the affair as closely as he could, urged the government to take a position and if necessary to force a decision.   The question was brought before the public.   On March 17 a long article in *Le Monde*, signed " Albert Duquet," placed the *Roechlingsche Eisen und Stahlwerke* of Völklingen within the Saar economy and " in consequence within the Franco-Saar union and the common market for steel: 855,000 tons in 1954 or a third of the total Saar production and more than 10,000 workmen."   The article recalled " the part played by the Roechlings in the development of nazism and the construction of Hitler's warmachine, also the treatment accorded by these war-mongers to their personnel that had earned several of them terms of imprisonment as war criminals."   The article reaffirmed France's rights, reviewed the series of negotiations that had taken place, and closed with a call to action.   It was definitely not in the interests of the Saar or of France to allow the Roechlings to return.   Such a return would result in the formation within the Franco-Saar economic union of " a dangerous German bastion " and would permit the

[23] The German Government's interest, and also its hesitation, were apparent at the discussion that took place at Bonn on October 22, 1954, between the representatives of the Roechling family and Ministers Franz Blücher and Ludwig Erhard, who were accompanied by Secretaries of State Ludger Westrick and Alfred Hartmann.   After the Agreement of October 23 was concluded, the German Government strengthened its attitude and gave definite encouragement to the Roechlings.

Roechlings an " automatic monopoly of Saar representation in the E.C.S.C."

Such was the thesis, and it was taken up widely. In the Council of the Republic and the National Assembly the President of the Council and the Minister for Foreign Affairs replied to questions put to them on the Roechling affair in the same vein. " I assure you," said Edgar Faure on March 26, " that the government over which I preside will not allow the return of the Roechling family to the head of the Völklingen factories." [24]

A few days later, on March 30, Antoine Pinay in turn declared to the National Assembly: " As far as this matter is concerned, the government has expressed its intention of permanently removing the Roechling family from the management of the Völklingen factories. It is determined to achieve this end, either by an amicable agreement or by imposing its authority." [25]

Finally, on March 31, the Finance Committee of the National Assembly, having heard the Minister for Foreign Affairs and the Minister of Finance, proposed to the Assembly the voting of a law couched in these terms: " The Minister of Finance and Economic Affairs is authorized to take all necessary steps to facilitate the purchase of assets not belonging to the state in the steelworks of Völklingen (Saar) and to re-organize this industry." [26]

The government was now duly authorized to proceed to an authoritarian solution, profiting, as " Albert Duquet " said in his article in *Le Monde*, by the " powers of liquidation legally conferred on the sequestration administration of Völklingen which, subject to authorization, enabled it to proceed to acts of disposal." But it still had to be in a position to do so.[27]

For apart from the financial problem, the importance of which must not be underestimated, there was German opposition, which resolutely strengthened in this last stage of the discussion. The newspapers also took up the question, protesting the attacks in the French press against the Roechlings, criticizing the methods of a

---

[24] *Journal officiel, Débats parlementaires, Conseil de la République*, March 27, 1955, p. 1102.

[25] *Journal officiel, Débats parlementaires, Assemblée nationale*, March 31, 1955, p. 2116. This " authoritarian " solution consisted of relying on French rights to transferable property in order to obtain more than 50 per cent. of the shares so as to ensure French control.

[26] Article 16, section III of Law No. 55347, April 2, 1955.

[27] During the meeting of the Finance Committee, the Minister for Foreign Affairs had remarked that it would be hard for France to acquire the whole of the steelworks of Völklingen.

French Administration which was trying to profit from the influential position it still held to make sure of permanent economic advantages for itself. The far-reaching consequences of a French distraint for the Saar economy and for Franco-German economic relations were brought to light, the arguments of " Albert Duquet " in *Le Monde* turned, as it were, against him.[28]

So the Roechling affair assumed ever greater proportions. In France, Germany, and the Saar it was said that he who controlled Roechling controlled the Saar. The Saar Socialist Party launched a campaign on this theme. It compared the interests of the workers of Völklingen with the big capital interests which were negotiating over the factories without any concern for the potential consequences to the workers of a change in ownership. During March and April, meetings were held to assert the rights of the Saar workers; their protests addressed explicitly to the Roechlings both were aimed at and hit France.[29] The Socialist Party ended by adopting as its own the solution of nationalization, which had been the original idea of the French Ambassador and the French Minister of Finance. On March 30 the party introduced a bill to this effect in the Landtag. During this time the Saar Government was negotiating with both sides to ensure a *présence sarroise* in the final solution. In a letter to Mr. Pinay, Mr. Hoffmann stated very categorically that he was opposed to an " authoritarian " solution. Everyone knew that the arguments on which the French Government based such a solution were of very doubtful legal validity. He therefore urgently requested Mr. Pinay to forgo an act that would be interpreted as an intrusion into sovereign territory and would be certain to have the most unfortunate repercussions.[30]

A copy of this letter was sent to the German Government. Mr. Pinay nevertheless remained firm in his decision. He was bound by the statements Mr. Faure and he had made to the Council of the Republic and to the National Assembly. In order to solve the problem, he demanded, as a condition of the deposit of the instruments

[28] The *Handelsblatt* of Düsseldorf said the following in an article of April 6, 1955: "If majority ownership of Völklingen should pass into French hands, French capitalists would have a rightful claim, in accordance with the weight of their majority position in regard to the entire steel industry of the Saar, to representation in all organizations and institutions, in the joint Franco-Saar committees, in professional bodies of Saar industry, in the Chamber of Commerce and Industry in Saarbrücken as well, of course, after the Saar Statute came into effect—*vis-à-vis* the German Government."

[29] The Socialists were not the only ones to demonstrate. *Cf.*, also, *Analytical Study*, p. 259, note 14.

[30] *Cf.* letter from Mr. Hoffmann to Mr. Pinay, April 22, 1955.

of ratification, a fifty-fifty sharing between France and Germany in the ownership of the Völklingen factories. This was a dramatic session, according to the various accounts that have been given of it.[31] The representatives of the Roechlings were at hand. Chancellor Adenauer, who was determined to settle the matter and who, once again, weighed the long-term advantages that would accrue from signing the agreements, was disposed to pay a fairly high price.[32] He sent Mr. Hallstein to appeal to the Roechlings to give up Völklingen. It was only after a good many attempts to persuade them and a personal overture on the part of the Chancellor that they eventually gave in, but then only after obtaining a letter from Chancellor Adenauer acknowledging that their acceptance of this solution was dictated entirely by their sense of political responsibility.

Mr. Pinay appeared satisfied. He had managed to get the Roechlings out of the way and obtain for the French Government an influence that seemed to him sufficiently strong to offset the presence of Germany. He did not, however, appear to have taken into account the interests of the Saar.

The news of the arrangements agreed upon met with great ill feeling in the Saar and served to confirm the warnings of those who for months now had been pointing out to the Saarlanders that the French considered no interests but their own and were not to be relied on. As for the Roechlings, who had given in under pressure, they knew that henceforth only a rejection of the Statute by referendum would allow them to remedy the situation.

The balance-sheet of the operations involved in completing the Agreement of October 23, 1954, was not so favourable to France as appeared at first glance.

The ratification was finally achieved. Both sides had finally agreed on the method of implementing the Agreement and on the means of putting it into effect. In mid-June, the Council of the Western European Union named the members of the Commission charged with the supervision of the referendum. The Saar Government had prepared draft bills on the organization of the popular

---

[31] *Cf.*, on this subject, the minutes of the meeting of the Bundestag, May 6, 1955: *Verhandlungen des deutschen Bundestages*, II. 81/4463 *et seq.* The accounts are, as usual, contradictory.

[32] The offer Mr. Pinay made had certain advantages for the German Government. Previous solutions had not provided for its participation.

vote. Submitted first for the approval of the Western European
Union, they were voted at a third reading in the Landtag on July 8.
On July 23 the final approval of the Council of the Western
European Union was obtained, the electoral laws promulgated, and
the date of the referendum fixed for October 23.[33]

However, when the election campaign opened—a campaign
in which the political battle was joined to determine the fate of the
Saar—the position of the partisans of the Statute was very weak in
the Saar, that is, on the actual field of battle. The best-informed
French observers who in October, 1954, declared that the Statute
would be approved by 70 to 80 per cent. of the voters, were
much more cautious in their estimates after the conclusion of the
Franco-Saar economic treaty and the Adenauer-Pinay interviews.
The French Government, its attention concentrated on ratification
of the Paris agreements and on maintaining the economic position
it occupied in the Saar, used the Saar Government as an instrument
to be manipulated at will and was content to recompense with fair
words the concessions it imposed. Concentrating on the diplomatic
battle, it had made no preparation for the political one. It had
thought and made its plans in the light of a Statute which it felt
sure would be adopted. Apparently, neither it nor Parliament
anticipated a failure or considered what measures it would take in
such an event. There had been a good deal of talk about the
second referendum without any thought for the fact that the first
one was yet to be won.

As time passed the situation grew worse in the Saar, especially
in government circles. The tendency towards independence from
France, which had become increasingly marked since the 1952 elections, was publicly re-affirmed on various occasions and became
even more pronounced.

Negotiation of the Convention on Economic Co-operation was
only achieved by vigorous pressure from the French Government,
which had threatened Saarbrücken with direct negotiations between
France and Germany. Differences of opinion and personal rivalry
became more serious even within the Saar Government and the
C.V.P., between Minister of the Interior Edgar Hector and the
group of which Paul Senf, Franz Ruland, and Gotthard Lorscheider

---

[33] For further information, *cf*. Dischler, *op. cit.*, Vol. I, pp. 113–120, Vol. II, pp. 229–
285; also " Le problème sarrois," *Chronique de politique étrangère*, Vol. IX, No. 5
(September, 1956); Klaus Altmeyer, " Die Volksbefragung an der Saar vom 23 Oktober
1955," *Europa-Archiv* (August 5, 1956), pp. 9049–9060.

were members. The much-dreaded Mr. Hector, who for years
had been the target of German opposition backed by the press,
was so handicapped by the positions he had held that even some of
the leaders of his own party felt that it would be better if he went.
In the course of the winter, various moves were tried, unsuccess-
fully, to get him out of office. This disintegration of the government team gave rise to general confusion. Everyone began to
negotiate on his own account with the French or with the Germans,
each supplying the others with information at his disposal as it
suited his own interests according to the conviction or whim of the
moment. No one trusted anyone else. No secret could be kept.
Government discussions were almost immediately retailed to a
wider circle, their content filtered abroad, twisted and exaggerated
by imagination and strong feeling. So the government was less and
less able to formulate a policy and it wavered between several.
Johannes Hoffmann himself, though he knew that if the Germans
won he was finished,[34] played off the French against the Germans
and the Germans against the French. During the difficult negotiations in April he pressed Mr. Pinay to oppose a broad interpretation
of the role of the European Commissioner and of freedom of
criticism in the period separating the two popular votes. But at the
same time he let his letter to Mr. Pinay about the Völklingen
factories be sent to the Germans in the hope of strengthening their
resistance.

This disorganization within the Christian People's Party also
affected the Socialist Party. Its leaders, now in opposition again
after a few months of collaborating with the government, tried to
counterbalance the influence of Johannes Hoffmann and to gather
around themselves the many opponents of the man who had been
at the head of Saar affairs for more than seven years; they sought
especially the allegiance of the workers.

They did not succeed, for, in spite of anything they might do,
they remained bound up with a régime, and it was around this
régime, either for it or against it, that the battle was taking place.
Thus their position became increasingly difficult; they were caught
between two fires and more and more cut off from the trade
unions. Although they were in favour of autonomy, they had been

---

[34] It will be recalled that during his speech to the Bundestag on February 25, 1955,
Chancellor Adenauer declared rather brutally that there were two men in the Saar who
would have to be removed—Mr. Hoffmann and Mr. Grandval.

associated with the critics of a French policy tending to define this autonomy within unduly narrow limits. But this did not win for them the approval of the trade union leaders who, since Mr. Kutsch had been removed from office, had joined forces with the German Socialist supporters in the Saar, a group backed by the German Socialist Party.[35] Conversely, the part played by one of their leaders, Mr. Kunkel, in the Kutsch affair widened the gap between the Socialists and trade unionists still further. In the last phase of the negotiations they tried to lead a protest movement against the return of the Roechlings to Völklingen and against the French effort to take over the factories. They organized a vigorous campaign on the Socialist theme of nationalization, but they failed. Worse than this, they, like the government, were forced to admit that the representatives of France did not hesitate to negotiate over their heads and to humiliate them publicly. How were they to defend the Statute henceforth? How were they to reply to the criticisms of their opponents who reproached them at every turn for allowing themselves to be under the influence of Paris? They were bitterly disappointed.

While those who were supposed to lead the battle for the Statute were hesitating, uncertain what policy to pursue, opposition to the government was hardening. For a few weeks after the October 23 Agreement, the opposition had gone through a period of discouragement. But it recovered its drive, carried along by the fervour of a feeling of German nationalism which sprang largely from the rejection of the E.D.C. At the head of the opposition were men who were very sure in their own minds and who had been shaped in their uncompromising attitude by years of struggle. These leaders—Heinrich Schneider, Kurt Conrad, and Hubert Ney—had become more and more sure they could win. They had perceived the weariness which had overtaken the supporters of the régime; the numerous defections from which they had benefited had only served to strengthen their confidence in the outcome of the struggle. They knew they could count on the support of the trade unions and of most of the clergy. They knew they had the sympathy of the important German parties; they knew the Social Democratic Party

---

[35] The strike in the Saar in February had contributed to a further widening of the breach between Socialists and trade unions. It arose out of a wage claim but rapidly evolved into a general strike aimed at the government and also at the Socialist leaders who were preaching moderation. So it was not surprising that it had the result of driving the leader of the *Syndicat des ouvriers métallurgistes* over to the pro-German opposition.

was behind them and that, even in the heart of the C.D.U. itself and in circles very close to the government, there were those who did not consider themselves obliged to show the same reserve towards them as did the Chancellor.

Finally, although their criticism of the restrictive régime in force in the Saar was harsh, at least some of them did not hesitate to use the methods they deplored in others. In their choice of means they showed no great refinement, nor did they resist the temptation of demagogy.

The situation was simplified for them by the departure of the only man of sufficient stature to have stood in their way. Ambassador Grandval, appointed Resident-General to Morocco, left his post at the end of June, 1955. He had played his part. The October Agreement, forbidding any outside interference, would have forced him to be cautious. Perhaps it was better that he should go, for his presence would inevitably have given rise to suspicions and accusations. He was replaced by a very skilful diplomat in the person of Eric de Carbonnel, whose personal influence helped maintain calm. Nevertheless, Mr. Grandval's departure at this time left a void which was the greater because he had been in some measure the incarnation of France in the Saar and had assured a continuity which the governments were not able to provide.

Furthermore, French public opinion did not follow Saar affairs with the same passionate attention that German opinion did. While Rheinland Pfalz was one of the chief centres of support for the campaign against the Statute, Lorraine maintained an attitude of hostility. French attention had shifted to Morocco.

Thus, matters were turning badly for the Hoffmann Government and the supporters of the Statute. They did not seem aware of the fact any more than did French or German government circles. At the beginning of July, the most widely held opinion was still that the Statute had every chance of being accepted, and the leaders of the Saar C.D.U. were still wondering what instructions to give their supporters. To advise rejection was to risk strengthening the hands of Johannes Hoffmann and the C.V.P. in case of a general acceptance of the Statute. Despite counsels of moderation from Germany, however, the decision to advise rejection of the Statute was taken at the beginning of August. The pressure brought to bear by the *Syndicats chrétiens* had something to do with this decision. For them there was no question of hesitation. If the

C.D.U. did not go along with them, then they would go into battle alone.[36]

The three opposition parties now waged one joint campaign.[37] The preparations they had made before they had received the official authorization enabled them to set up their organization with a minimum of delay.[38]

It soon became evident from all sides that the bulk of opinion was in their favour.[39] All the evidence pointed to the same thing: the opposition which had been scattered up till now had crystallized around new centres.   Crowds gathered for every public meeting of the pro-German parties and were carried away by the plain speaking of men like Mr. Schneider.   The new newspapers were in great demand.   An inquiry conducted between August 8 and 13 by the Emnid Institute of Bielefeld revealed that 79 per cent. of those interrogated were against the Statute.   These results, which rapidly came to the attention of the interested parties, could not but encourage opponents of the Statute.

The supporters eventually grew anxious.   They became aware of the impossibility of calling a halt to the opposition's drive.   For the first time, it seemed, they asked themselves what would happen if the Statute were rejected.   No provision had been made for this eventuality.   Might it not be better to abandon the referendum or postpone it to give the French and German Governments time to consult again and find a new compromise?   Steps were taken [40] by moderates who were alarmed at the prospect of the upheavals that

[36] The most decisive intervention of the *Syndicats chrétiens* took place at the meeting in Trier, on July 9, 1955, of the representatives of the C.D.U. of Germany and the Saar to decide on the policy to be adopted.

[37] The formation of the *Heimatbund*, September 2, 1955, was one of the most obvious manifestations of this collaboration.

[38] The C.D.U., slower to start moving, had 7,000 registered members on August 2, 1955, and 15,000 on August 15.   By July 30, 1955, the D.P.S. already had more than 3,000 enrolled members.

[39] For the progress of the campaign, *cf.*, in addition to the Saar, German, and French newspapers, the numerous pamphlets and bulletins of the *Saarbund*, *Informationen und Hinweise*.   Other information on the referendum campaign will be found in the *Analytical Study*, especially the chapter on public opinion.

[40] Much was said at the time about the interventions of Johann Jakob Kindt-Kiefer, a German industrialist, who seems to have striven to obtain either the resignation of Mr. Hoffmann or postponement of the elections.   From the moment his manoeuvres became known denials poured in from all sides.   Mr. Kindt-Kiefer, said the Chancellor, had no brief to speak in his name or, added Mr. Altmeier, any authority to speak in the name of the C.D.U.   In actual fact the moves made by Mr. Kindt-Kiefer were without any importance; they could not be held to have had any influence upon the slight weakening in the opposition observable between the first and the second inquiry carried out by the Emnid Institute.   The second inquiry took place from September 19 to 24, 1955.   It recorded only 72 per cent. against and 28 per cent. in favour of the Statute.

would result from an unleashing of passions over the referendum. Some Saar industrialists, known for their favourable attitude towards a policy of economic co-operation with France, did not hesitate to approach certain high officials in Germany.

Might not the European idea be killed forever and the reconciliation of France and Germany be compromised? The Catholic and Protestant Churches, which throughout this whole campaign had been prudently guarded, called on their parishioners to remain calm. The German Government counselled prudence; one could not be guided by emotion in these matters; the people of the Saar must keep cool, said the Chancellor at the beginning of September at Bochum. The road to a new government must be through the Statute. Europe was in no position to support the creation of a new centre of friction between France and Germany.[41] The Saar C.D.U., in response to efforts to restrain it, declared that it could not reverse the trend. The game was so obviously won that those who had hesitated now rushed to make victory more certain. The many appeals from various European movements had no power to stop this surge towards the German Fatherland.[42]

Johannes Hoffmann still fought on. As for the French Government, bound by its promise not to interfere, it watched powerless while its supporters were routed and its policy collapsed. All it could say was that, if the Statute was rejected, it saw no chance of re-opening negotiations.[43]

On October 23, 67 per cent. of the electors voted against the Statute. Was this the beginning of a new period of trouble? Would Johannes Hoffmann cling to office and take up the fight again? He had neither the strength nor the means. He resigned, leaving to others the task of taking on new responsibilities. This decision cleared the air and indicated the path to be followed.

In Paris as well as in Bonn there was full awareness of the overriding importance of avoiding a crisis in the relationship between the two countries. " Good relations between France and Germany must not be endangered by this vote," said Chancellor Adenauer, and Edgar Faure replied: " Like you I remain convinced that the

---

[41] Chancellor Adenauer renewed his appeal to vote for the Statute on October 21, 1955.

[42] The Central Committee of the European Federalist Union came out unanimously in favour of the Agreement on the Saar on September 27, 1955, in Paris. Heinz Braun, President of the Saar branch of the European Union, received telegrams from the European Federalist Union in the Netherlands, in Switzerland, and from the Central Committee in Paris as well as from the Central Youth Committee.

[43] *Cf. Le Monde*, October 21, 1955.

results of this ballot must not deflect our two governments from the path they have chosen."

In fact, faced with the overwhelming vote of the Saar electors, there was no alternative for those who proclaimed the right of self-determination of peoples but to bow to the inevitable. A question of principle had been decided, one which had been under discussion since 1947: the Saarlanders had expressed their desire to be Germans. Now France and Germany faced one another alone with a " disputed claim " in the Saar that would have to be settled one day.

8

TOWARDS A FINAL SETTLEMENT

SOME months went by before negotiations were resumed. Both sides had been taken by surprise. They needed time to consider the problems in the light of the new situation created by the rejection of the Statute.

The first communiqué published on November 13, 1955, following a meeting between Mr. Pinay and Mr. Adenauer, was restricted to general remarks of a conciliatory nature: the two ministers would try to find a solution that would reconcile the interests of the two countries. A month later, after a meeting of the Committee of Ministers of the Council of Europe and of the Western European Union, the Quai d'Orsay circulated more explicit statements:

> As regards the rumours echoed in the German press concerning the Saar, authoritative circles assert that whatever solution may eventually be found for the Saar political problem, France has basic economic rights and interests in the Saar and these are permanent in character. There can be no solution to the Saar problem unless these are safeguarded.
>
> The Germans, in the course of preliminary conversations in Paris, adopted a positive attitude on the matter, and this crucial point appears to have been won. Thus, the prospects are favourable for the negotiations that are to take place in Paris on a definitive solution of the Saar problem.[1]

The tone was relaxed. It became sharper at the beginning of February, 1956, when the Saar Landtag took its position and formulated its wishes in a much harsher manner. For the elections to the Landtag which followed the referendum [2] had brought the great opposition leaders into power. Heinrich Schneider was elected to the presidency of the Landtag. Hubert Ney became head of a government including, among other ministers, Kurt Conrad and Adolf Blind. It was not surprising, therefore, that on January 17 the Saar deputies approved a resolution demanding the return

---

[1] *Cf. Le Monde*, December 18–19, 1955.
[2] These took place on December 18, 1955.

197

of the Völklingen factories to their former owners, and on January 31 another resolution in which, after stating their firm intention of bringing to an end the separation of the Saar from Germany, they declared that the integration of their country " into the customs and monetary system of the German Federal Republic " was the logical consequence of the political union and that this should be carried out step by step.[3]

This touched the French on a very sensitive spot. Christian Pineau, the new Minister for Foreign Affairs, therefore reminded the Saar deputies that the present situation could be changed only " with the formal consent of the French Government." Mr. Pineau reminded them also that the French Government " could not indeed accept a solution that did not take into account the basic economic interests of France, the volume of trade between France and the Saar, and the balance that must be maintained within European organizations." [4]

Mr. Pineau expressed a feeling fairly widespread in France among those who followed the Saar question closely. They had adjusted quickly to the idea that the Saar should return to Germany and they did not react against this desire which had been so clearly expressed by the Saarlanders. There were very few people who interpreted the plebiscite as a refusal by the Saarlanders to have their territory " europeanized " and who sought a return to the régime preceding the Paris agreements. *Le Monde*, which alluded to this possibility in a rather violent editorial, mentioned it only as a threat to the " politicians of Saarbrücken." [5]

But though the French accepted the political consequences of the referendum, they were determined not to part with anything until they had obtained the guarantees and compensations to which they felt they were entitled on the economic plane.[6] The Economic Council at its meeting of April 26, 1956, unanimously approved the report presented by Emmanuel Mayolle which listed the claims of French business concerns.[7] The Council ended with a resolution

[3] *Bulletin der Bundesregierung* (1956), p. 188; *Le Monde*, February 2, 1956.
[4] *Cf. Le Monde*, February 3, 1956.
[5] February 2, 1956.
[6] See *Analytical Study*, pp. 233–234. *Cf.*, among others, the report of Pierre Eude, Secretary-General of the Chamber of Commerce of Strasbourg, at the meeting of November 24, 1956; *Bulletin de la Chambre de commerce et d'industrie de Strasbourg* (new series), 11th Year, No. 1 (1956), pp. 44–46; *cf.*, also, *Le Figaro*, January 20, 1956; *Le Monde*, February 16, 1956.
[7] *Journal officiel. Avis et Rapports du Conseil économique*, April 22, 1956, pp. 357–361.

affirming its determination not to compromise. First, it was essential to maintain a fairly substantial volume of trade between the Saar and France since the Saar territory was the most important outlet for France next to Algeria. This was one of the points that the representatives of the Chambers of Commerce in eastern France particularly stressed.[8] France's supply of Saar coal was also a problem, for the existence of the Franco-Saar economic union had made it possible to pay in French francs and not in foreign currency.

There was also concern over the balance France wished to preserve between German and French representation in the E.C.S.C.

In addition to these various questions there were two others which took on special importance during the negotiations: the exploitation of the Warndt coal deposit and the plan for a Moselle Canal.

The French demands met with some resistance from the Federal Government. The first discussions took place on February 20 and 21 after an exchange of notes and ended with an encouraging communiqué announcing another meeting on March 3. However, the negotiators had been able to assess the difficulties facing them. Both the French and the Germans were immediately in agreement on the principle of the political union between the Saar and Germany, and they recognized the need for a period of transition during which the monetary and customs union between France and the Saar should be maintained. They also admitted the value of a gradual adaptation of the Saar economy to economic union with Germany. This implied agreement on numerous provisions governing trade between the Saar and Germany in terms of their effect on Franco-Saar trade. The problem of the representation of France and Germany in the E.C.S.C. was easily settled, as was the question of supplying France with Saar coal, since the Saarlanders had an interest in keeping their French market.

---

[8] They conducted an inquiry among industrialists and business men concerned with Saar trade, an inquiry which, according to the previously cited report of Mr. Eude, gave figures that in some cases were "impressive." In the Bas-Rhin, as far as industry was concerned, the Saar market accounted for 5 to 40 per cent. and, in terms of trade, a higher percentage, especially for primary products, food, and textiles. According to Saar statistics, the value of imports from France in 1955 was 160 milliard francs, while Saar exports to France amounted to 120 milliards. The French, although they had doubts about the accuracy of figures that were difficult to check, admitted that the figures reflected adequately the general situation.

There was strong opposition, however, almost unsurmountable at first, in regard to the Warndt coal deposit and to the Moselle Canal. On the first point, French determination to keep the advantages they had obtained for themselves in 1953 and to continue to work the Warndt coalfields during the full term of the contract for their exploitation, met with obstinate resistance in the Saar. When they had been in the opposition, the men now governing the Saar had not failed to denounce the agreements between the Saar and France as acquiescences by the Hoffmann Government in a veritable spoliation of the Saar heritage. Thus they were all the more intransigent because this was a question of prestige and because the Warndt affair had taken on a symbolic importance.

The French plan to construct a Moselle Canal appeared even more fraught with consequences for the Saar economy. It had been conceived in the interests of Lorraine as part of an attempt to improve its contacts with the Rhine-Westphalia area, whence came its coke and where it might find a larger market for its manufactured goods. But the Saarlanders, who were already suffering from inadequate access to the German market, were not willing to consider a plan that favoured their Lorraine rivals and made it possible for Lorraine to conquer the markets of the Rhineland and southern Germany where Saar products still had a preferred position.[9]

These difficulties did not prevent the negotiations from going on and even making progress. Between March and the end of May, Maurice Faure and Walter Hallstein managed to eliminate one obstacle after another and to prepare the ground for the final discussion between Guy Mollet and Chancellor Adenauer on June 5 in Luxembourg. The meeting of the two heads of government took place in an atmosphere that was still strained. Although the communiqués published after the talks between Mr. Faure and Mr. Hallstein had sounded a consistently optimistic note, press commentaries in France and Germany, as well as in the Saar, had stressed the difficulties and exaggerated the opposition over the Warndt and the Moselle.

Mr. Mollet and Mr. Adenauer, however, were both convinced supporters of European integration, which implied close collaboration between France and Germany. They knew that it was to their

---

[9] *Cf. Stellungnahme der Saarwirtschaft zur Moselkanalisierung* (Saarbrücken: December 7, 1955). Memorandum of the Saar Chamber of Commerce and Industry.

advantage to put an end to the struggle. They could do it now more easily because, since the referendum, the question had become less emotional and the issue was essentially the settlement of practical problems.

Germans and Saarlanders had obtained satisfaction, since the French had accepted the outcome of the plebiscite and no longer disputed the Saar's right to return to Germany. They were thus well disposed to make substantial concessions to take account of the economic interests of a France which Germany, as her partner, had no interest in weakening. So agreement was reached. France obtained satisfaction on all essential points. She was granted a period of twenty-five years in which to withdraw from the Warndt, and this gave her the chance of mining 66,000,000 tons of coal. She was also guaranteed delivery by Germany of 1,200,000 tons of coal a year from 1962 onwards from the Warndt or elsewhere, and a third of the total output of the Saar mines. The idea of a Moselle Canal was also accepted in principle; and the German Government further undertook to make a large financial contribution and to agree to an important concession on the toll rights.

The Germans felt that the price exacted from them for the return of the Saar was very high. Some of them, including Mr. Schneider, felt that it was too high. However, they backed the Chancellor's decision on the principle. The title of the article which Joachim Schwelien devoted to the Luxembourg agreement in the *Frankfurter Allgemeine Zeitung* [10] expressed a fairly widespread feeling: " Opfer für die Freundschaft " (" Sacrifice for Friendship ").

In France, where there was good reason for satisfaction, the reception was even less enthusiastic because of a sense of failure. The Saar had gone back to Germany. The Franco-Saar economic union had only three more years to run; the material guarantees that had been obtained were, in the last analysis, no more than compensations. However, the French accepted the situation; they also resigned themselves to the return of Völklingen to the Roechlings—only yesterday war criminals—who had merely been asked to pay indemnities. Three milliards of French francs were all that remained of the Agreement between Mr. Pinay and Chancellor Adenauer that the referendum of October 23 had reduced to ashes.

[10] June 7, 1956.

The debate on the ratification of the Franco-German Treaties finally concluded on October 27, 1956,[11] bore witness significantly to the difference in states of mind in France and in Germany. In France the National Assembly approved ratification by a majority of 354 to 225, and the Council of the Republic, where Mr. Debré bitterly recalled France's lost illusions, by 209 to 66. In Germany, on the other hand, the Bundestag and the Bundesrat gave their unanimous approval, after applauding expressions of gratitude to the French Government which had had enough political good sense after the referendum to bow to the decision of the Saarlanders.

---

[11] This was a group of treaties confirming as a whole the decisions in principle taken by Mr. Adenauer and Mr. Mollet at their meeting in Luxembourg:

    (1) the Franco-German Treaty on the Saar;
    (2) the tripartite Franco-German-Luxembourgeois agreement on canalization of the Moselle;
    (3) a Franco-German Convention of Establishment and Navigation;
    (4) a Franco-German agreement on the Alsace Canal;
    (5) an agreement modifying the Treaty setting up the E.C.S.C.

The instruments of ratification concerning the Treaty on the Saar, the canalization of the Moselle, and the Treaty on the Alsace Canal were exchanged in Luxembourg on December 31, 1956, and came into force on January 1, 1957. *Cf. Journal officiel, Lois et Décrets*, January 10, 1957, pp. 460 *et seq.*; *Bundesgesetzblatt*, II, No. 36, December 24, 1956, pp. 1587–1874. *Cf.*, in this connection, the brochure by Jean-Claude Debray, *Le nouveau statut des échanges franco-sarrois et les perspectives qu'il offre* (Delegation in the Saar of the French Embassy in Bonn, n.p. or d.); Dischler, *op. cit.*

PART TWO

ANALYTICAL STUDY

9

INTRODUCTION: THE KEY DECISIONS

CONSIDERED in its entirety, the conflict between France and Germany over the Saar was dominated by three major decisions.

The first, at the beginning of 1946, was the French Government's formulation of its Saar policy, the essential features of which were economic union with France and political separation from Germany.

The second decision, taken by the German Government and contained in its memorandum of March 10, 1950, publicly and officially acknowledged the existence of a latent conflict by raising the Saar question to the level of relations between two sovereign states.

As for the third decision, that of the Saar population, it was expressed in the referendum of October 23, 1955,[1] in which the majority of the Saarlanders rejected the Statute and by so doing manifested their preference for a return of the Saar to Germany.[2]

One might have been tempted to confine the study of the conflict to the circumstances in which these three decisions were taken. Such an analysis would have furnished useful information, valid not only for the historian of crisis but also for the statesman concerned with the causes of conflict—an analysis all the more useful because conditions varied appreciably from one event to another. Thus, a study of the first decision would bring out the influence of the atmosphere prevailing immediately after the war, an atmosphere dominated by the conviction that the victors and victims of Nazi Germany had their rights, by the ever-present figure of history and a traditionalist concept of French security along the eastern frontier, by the real and decisive importance of the government, or rather of the small group of men who assumed executive responsibility,

---

[1] Fernand Dehousse, who was President of the European Commission for the referendum, pointed out, it is true, that as the referendum was a consultation with those concerned, the reply of the Saar population did not legally constitute a decision. In fact the opinion expressed by the Saarlanders on October 23, 1955, was completely decisive. *Cf.* Fernand Dehousse, " Mission en Sarre," *Bulletin de la Société belge d'études et d'expansion*, March–April, 1956, p. 6.

[2] *Cf.* Appendix III, Map No. 10.

and finally, by the pre-eminence of political considerations—the decision on economic union was taken less for the concrete advantages expected from it than to reinforce the position of France *vis-à-vis* Germany.

A study of the conditions under which the second decision was taken would reveal a far more complex interplay of forces, for it was under the influence of the manifold efforts of the small pro-Saar groups in Germany and pro-German groups in the Saar and as a reaction to negotiation of the Franco-Saar Conventions that Chancellor Adenauer, engrossed in responsibility for the over-all interests of Germany, abandoned the waiting game he was still playing in November, 1949, to take a stand at the beginning of the following year with a suddenness that took his French and even his Saar colleagues by surprise.

The decision of October 23, 1955, was of another kind. The popular vote took place only after an election campaign in which emotional arguments prevailed over a cool appreciation of the situation and an assessment of interests, with the result that the real object of the referendum was gradually lost to sight. A study of the electoral campaign would reveal the emotional nature of the arguments.

However, these three decisions are not explicable solely in terms of the immediate circumstances; they are equally the product of various elements which had made themselves felt previously. Thus the explanation of the October 23, 1955, vote does not lie merely in the electoral campaign which preceded it. Rather this campaign, despite its discernible fluctuations, seems to have been shaped, not to say determined, by prior acts and debates. Similarly, the play of forces that drove Chancellor Adenauer to take a position can be grasped only to the extent that it is possible to follow their evolution from the very beginning.

However vital these decisions were, they do not form the core of all the possible explanations. They indicate the starting point of the conflict and its point of arrival, at least for that phase which is the subject of this study, but they do not make it possible to understand the evolution of the conflict. For it is not enough to know the origins of the conflict, why and how it began. One must also be in a position to follow its evolution, which was not pre-determined but, on the contrary, was shaped by events in which chance played its part and by the grouping of forces; these forces were individuals or groups swayed by emotional reactions, by considerations of self-interest or what they believed to be their interests. The decision of October 23, 1955, was not the only possible one. At various times between 1950 and 1955 other solutions had been envisaged at various times and had even come close to being adopted. Why were they abandoned? What obstacles had they encountered? Was their failure expressed in the form of a clearly identifiable decision? Was it not rather the effect of the absence of a decision or even of indecision which cannot simply be dismissed as a form of decision?

The historical reconstruction of the entire debate on the Saar problems seems therefore to have served a useful purpose. It was a necessary prelude to the analytical study of those forces whose interaction constitutes the warp of the conflict.

10

THE MEN AND THEIR ACTIONS

THERE were certain men who stood out, whose decisions counted, or more exactly, who took decisions by virtue of the powers invested in them through their office.

Such men were few. On the French side there were Georges Bidault, Robert Schuman, succeeded for a short time by Pierre Mendès-France and Antoine Pinay. On the German side, there was one outstanding personality, Chancellor Adenauer.

This simple list emphasizes a major fact: the continuous presence of Chancellor Adenauer, not only at the German Foreign Ministry but also at the head of the government, gave German policy a continuity, a possibility of coherence, that French policy never had to the same degree.[1]

France had four Foreign Ministers, very different from one another as much in training and political philosophy as in temperament, character, and intellectual capacity. Mr. Bidault and Mr. Schuman, who belonged to the same party, pursued in principle the same general policy. They were borne along by the hope, so widespread after the war and characteristic of the new party to which they belonged, of building something new and not allowing themselves to be bound by antiquated historical moulds or the rivalries of the past. So they called themselves "Europeans." But Mr. Bidault, being an historian, found it harder to escape from the pressure of the past because he held the post of Minister for Foreign Affairs immediately after the war; this was the period of strongest reaction against Germany, during which France—or at least the group of men who, under Charles de Gaulle, ruled her—sought to regain her place as a Great Power and made her claims the more strongly because she sensed her own weakness. Thus, there was a certain rigidity, a sharp insistence upon the political aspect of the problem, in France's attitude towards and negotiations over the Saar. Mr. Schuman, on the other hand, less affected by the phase of " *politique de grandeur,*" less intellectual, too, and more

[1] *Cf.* Appendix II.

practical, was more flexible in negotiation and more inclined to make concessions. Because of his own past he had greater awareness of the problems of frontiers and he well knew their complexity and seriousness.

As for Mr. Mendès-France and Mr. Pinay, who came into the affair for short but decisive periods, they were very different, not only from those who had preceded them but from one another, in temperament, general policy, and methods, so much so that even if their Saar policy was not perceptibly different from that formulated by Mr. Bidault and adapted more or less satisfactorily to circumstances by Mr. Schuman, their term at the ministry nevertheless resulted in a certain lack of continuity in French policy on the Saar.

How could it have been otherwise? The influence of the permanent departments, however considerable it may be, nevertheless has limits—their permanence only partially moderates the inevitable reactions that follow when a head of ministry is changed. There comes a moment when only the minister can take a decision; and a permanent official is not always at hand to remind him in the final review, before the decision, of those components of the problem he would not normally think of for himself. At such times it is immediate considerations that count. As circumstances and men change, these considerations cannot be those of one's predecessor. Likewise, the calculations that enter into sometimes subtle bargaining during the last stage of a negotiation—when phrases are weighed more in terms of their contribution to an understanding of the moment than of their permanent meaning—do not necessarily guide the next negotiator, who thus abandons tactics that have already been mapped out. This break in continuity was to be especially manifest during the transition from Mr. Mendès-France to Mr. Pinay, the more so as the latter's attitude towards the Saar Government and the French Ambassador at Saarbrücken was one of aloofness bordering on casualness.

As a result of all this, Chancellor Adenauer's position became stronger and his opportunities for manoeuvring greater.

He played the German hand alone for the whole period of the conflict. He knew the problem every bit as well as Mr. Schuman and better than Mr. Mendès-France and Mr. Pinay. These latter were never able to acquire more than a limited familiarity with the Saar question. They worked from the files; they were short of time and they were needed elsewhere, so they formed a cursory view of the state of the Saar question, learning only as much as they needed to carry on negotiations.

For Konrad Adenauer, a German and a Rhinelander, the Saar was a living reality, a familiar problem with which he had dealt long before he became head of the Government of the Federal Republic. He knew not only the facts but all the elements and all the finer meanings, thanks in particular to certain contacts with public opinion and to the information he obtained from his colleagues. The advantages that stemmed from remaining in office and from his knowledge of the question, which was much more profound than that of his French opposite numbers, were further enhanced by his qualities as a statesman and a diplomatist. However valid the criticisms that might be directed against him after the various negotiations on the Saar, it is nonetheless clear that he made himself felt in these negotiations by a combination of firmness of views, tenacity in the struggle, and flexibility of tactics. None of the French Foreign Ministers, with the possible exception of Mr. Mendès-France, whose term at the Foreign Ministry was too short for an adequate judgment of his policy, was of sufficient stature to measure up to him. This did not mean that the Chancellor was victorious on all occasions. Quite the contrary, his French opponents were several times able to pride themselves on concessions they had won from him, thanks to Mr. Schuman's quiet firmness or to what amounted to ultimata from Mr. Mendès-France or Mr. Pinay.

The attitude of all concerned was influenced by the role they attributed to the Saar problem.

This role was inevitably but a secondary one. When in 1946 Mr. Bidault laid down the French Government's Saar policy, he was embarked on much broader negotiations concerning the whole German problem, the outcome of which, in his opinion, would determine the future of France. " The nature of the régime in the Saar will depend upon what we do in Germany," he had already declared in 1945, " and those who are under French rule will have no cause to complain." [2] The debates on the future political organization of Germany and on the control of the Ruhr Basin

---

[2] Statement made to the press in London, May 2, 1945. *Cf. L'Année politique 1944–1945, op. cit.*, p. 220.

preoccupied him more than did the status of the Saar. He maintained that the opportunity to wipe out the consequences of the defeat of 1940 must be seized. France must recover the position she had occupied in Europe before the war.[3]

For Robert Schuman the settlement of the Saar problem also took second place. Despite the arguments he addressed to his adversaries or to critics of his Saar policy, it was nonetheless clear that this question was subordinated to his policy of *rapprochement* with Germany and of European co-operation.[4] Manifest proofs of this were his capitulation on the double signature and the exchange of letters of March 20, 1951. " We do not want the Saar to become the stake in a competition between two rival neighbours," he said in a speech in the National Assembly in November, 1953. " On the contrary, the Saar both can and wishes to become the concrete expression of reconciliation and future co-operation between France and Germany."

When Mr. Bidault returned to the Ministry for Foreign Affairs from the beginning of 1953 until June, 1954, the Saar was not his chief preoccupation. He had on his hands not only the whole question of the E.D.C. but the crisis in Indo-China, where he had to do all he could to maintain a *présence française*, an essential condition, as he saw it, of France's remaining in the ranks of world Powers. Thus, despite the pressure exerted by the European Consultative Assembly and the support that body gave to the Van Naters Plan, he took only a limited interest in the discussions over the actual drafting of a Saar Statute. The Statute was so closely bound up with ratification of the E.D.C. that it became difficult to discern the true motives behind points of view and to know whether the Saar was the end or the means of a policy.

As for Mr. Mendès-France and his successor, Mr. Pinay, each had a major preoccupation; for the former, it was the drafting and signing of the Paris agreements, and for the latter, their ratification. It was on Franco-German relations that their attention was concentrated and it was in the light of their ideas on this subject and the

---

[3] This does not mean that Mr. Bidault neglected the Saar problem. On the contrary, from his speeches in the Council of Foreign Ministers it is evident that he strove with great energy to obtain the agreement of the Allies to France's Saar policy. *Cf. Déclarations de M. Georges Bidault, président de la délégation française au Conseil des ministres des affaires étrangères, Session de Moscou, mars–avril, 1947* (Paris: 1947), p. 41.

[4] *Cf.* Pierre Gerbet, " La genèse du Plan Schuman, des origines à la déclaration du 9 mai 1950," *Revue française de science politique* (July–September, 1956), pp. 525–553.

importance they attached to it that they both approached the Saar problem. This subordination was expressed in a very obvious form in the casualness shown by Mr. Pinay towards the Saar " ally," with what consequences for Franco-Saar relations we have already seen.

Chancellor Adenauer's attitude was even more clear-cut. From the time he took over as head of the Government of the Federal Republic until the referendum of October 23, 1955, Konrad Adenauer was determined never to let the Saar question become an obstacle to the establishment of good relations between France and Germany. His main objective was to have conquered Germany once again take her place in the concert of nations and participate in the system of European and Western security. It was within the framework of this policy that a solution to the Saar problem had to be sought. " Considered in proper perspective," he said in a statement over the *Nordwestdeutsche Rundfunk* on January 30, 1953, " the Saar problem is only part of a greater problem and a solution to it must be found within the scope of solutions to wider problems." This did not mean that he was not interested in the fate of the Saar, despite the accusations of his German opponents. The vigour of his interventions, the tenacity he showed in negotiation, the arguments he used, all indicated that he would accept the idea of europeanization of the Saar only on certain conditions: it must be, first and foremost, the expression of a clearly-voiced preference on the part of the Saarlanders [5]; it must not serve as a mask for French domination or influence; it must not imply any break between the Saar and the *Deutschtum*.

The subordination of the Saar question to the general aims of foreign policy ought to have made agreement possible. It did

[5] Mr. Adenauer had already expressed this opinion in an article that appeared in the *Kölnische Rundschau*, January 7, 1947: " The Saar question can only be clarified on the basis of international law. This, however, precludes any annexation. As for the rest, the right of the Saar population to self-determination is undeniable. This also holds for the so-called economic separation. This right of self-determination can only be exercised by means of a free and secret popular vote."

Jakob Kaiser, who took up this theme in his memorandum of January 12, 1950, made the following very interesting observation: " On the other hand, such a plebiscite would considerably ease the position of the German Republic because, if the majority of Saarlanders decided in a free and secret ballot in favour of maintaining the present situation without change, the German Republic would have to respect this expression of the popular will because of the international legal principle of self-determination, and would thus escape the accusation by nationalistic circles of having surrendered without a fight a German territory with 880,000 inhabitants. This is the very accusation that weighs most heavily on political discussion of the Saar question. It is susceptible not only of burdening German policy but also of poisoning the whole relationship with France as it once did in the Alsace-Lorraine question."

indeed seem on several occasions as though a compromise solution was very near; this was true during the negotiations of the summer and above all of the autumn of 1952, later during the discussions on the Van Naters Plan, and during the Adenauer-Teitgen meeting. The Statute agreed to on October 23, 1954, by the Chancellor and the President of the French Council, represented the compromise solution around which discussions had been revolving for years. But despite the fact that the Agreement was signed, this final compromise remained a subject of debate among those who signed it. Discussion revealed the limits placed on concessions and hence also revealed the basic objectives.

As has been pointed out, the Germans resigned themselves to europeanization only on condition that it entail a real europeanization that would enable Germany to recover a position analogous to that held by France in the Saar on the political, economic, and cultural planes. Any other solution that did not ensure Germany's rights and did not respect her cultural links with the Saar was excluded. Similarly, Chancellor Adenauer accepted the temporarily privileged position of France on the understanding that this was not permanent and that a final decision would be deferred until the second referendum. He was aware that time was on Germany's side. But, however uncompromising he may have seemed on these few points, he always left the door open for an agreement.

The French position was less flexible. Europeanization was accepted only to the extent that it did not involve termination of the economic and monetary union. It is more difficult, if only for the sake of prestige, to give up what one has than to abandon the idea of regaining what has been taken away. But even more powerful were the recollection of the inter-war experience, the failure of the 1935 plebiscite, and the feeling that time was short, that it was vital to settle the problem once and for all and to secure, while it was still possible, certain economic advantages. All this hampered French policy and governed the reactions of those ministers responsible for the conduct of foreign affairs during this period; it also explained the obstinacy with which they all came back to the idea that there must be an " irreversible " agreement.

In the conduct of the negotiations and above all in the actual decision, what was the role of the minister and that of his colleagues?

The reply to this question, posed in general terms, is not easy for an obvious reason: the difficulty of getting information. How is it possible to get near enough the sources of the decision to be in a position to define by a knowledge of a man's methods of work the character of the relations that exist in his immediate *entourage* and to penetrate the subtle inter-play of influences at the crucial moment? It was sometimes possible, with the help of private correspondence, departmental memoranda, or studies for internal use, to reconstruct the successive stages of the preparation of the decision. But nothing, except perhaps oral witness or a private diary giving a day-by-day, hour-by-hour account of the evolution of the final deliberations, could enable us to achieve that degree of knowledge requisite for an evaluation of responsibilities. Oral testimony, even when obtainable, is not always reliable. Time distorts the view of events. Details—sometimes essential—become blurred. The mind introduces a logical order into things where there was perhaps no more than a succession of disconnected reflections. The witness who was a participant in the events casts himself in a role. As for diaries, obviously a valuable source of information, they must be kept and written while the memory is still fresh.

No, an analysis of the evolution of a decision, however tempting from a theoretical point of view, is faced in practice with formidable obstacles, even if one has the ambition to carry it through as far as may be necessary. With a little luck it is possible to find valid and sufficiently accurate sources of information in some cases. But the number of such cases is limited, and the nature and value of the information at one's disposal varies from one to another; thus discretion is needed in drawing conclusions.

Moreover, who are the men who co-operated with the minister? How can they be identified? How can one circumscribe a group that may vary from year to year, month to month, or between one event and another? Certain officials who are not normally close to the minister may through circumstances be led to furnish him with information or make proposals that will be adopted.

Let us now turn to the specific subject under consideration: the Saar conflict. There is one basic observation to be made. The continuous presence in office of Chancellor Adenauer gave him the same advantage in relation to his own colleagues that it gave him in relation to France. The role which devolved on the Chancellor under the Basic Law, the freedom left him to choose his colleagues, who were then responsible to him, emphasized the hierarchy in relationships. Thus, the influence of those around him was reduced.[6] This did not mean that the Chancellor did not consult his close colleagues, such as Walter Hallstein and Herbert Blankenhorn, or that he did not take their opinions into account. His authority was tempered with prudence. He made his own decisions but he tried first to be fully informed; he was skilful in using his colleagues to take the necessary soundings, to collect information, and to prepare negotiations. It is enough to follow the goings and comings of Mr. Hallstein and Mr. Blankenhorn and at times even of Rudolf Thierfelder to measure the degree of activity of German diplomacy. It is also true that the Chancellor did not try to manage everything himself, that he knew how to delegate authority when necessary. From the way in which Mr. Hallstein conducted certain negotiations, one has the impression that he had some freedom of action and that he negotiated with the tranquillity of a man who knows he can commit himself with no fear of being contradicted.

It remains to be seen whether this method of work was fruitful. There might have been hesitation. It does not appear that Mr. Adenauer was always as well informed as he would have liked. Mr. Hallstein, for example, much concerned with the cultural aspect of the problem, seems to have been influenced by the criticisms of French policy in the Saar concerning the role of the university and the composition of the faculty. It is also known that the Chancellor underestimated the strength of the pro-German movement in the Saar[7] and that he, like many others, was surprised, if not by the result of the referendum, at least by the turn taken by the electoral campaign.

However, if the conflict is considered as a whole, there can be only one conclusion: the policy pursued by Germany was the policy of the Chancellor, who from beginning to end kept the Saar question within the framework of his European policy.[8]

---

[6] The biography of the Chancellor by Paul Weymar is useful not only for the information it supplies but also because of its semi-official character. It is a pity, however, that the author did not develop the analysis of the methods of work of the Chancellor and his colleagues. *Cf. Konrad Adenauer, die autorisierte Biographie* (Munich: 1955).

[7] Apparently Chancellor Adenauer had been influenced by the results of the November, 1952, elections.

[8] We are not concerned here with the effectiveness of his policy but with his intentions. One might argue about the results: some would say the Saar returned to Germany despite the Chancellor; others would reply that the final settlement with France in

In France the relationships between minister and colleagues seem even more difficult to define. The ministers changed. So did some of their colleagues, even if only the members of their cabinets. From 1947 to 1955, the post of *sous-directeur de la Sarre*, at the Quai d'Orsay passed from Jacques de Bourbon-Busset to Etienne Burin des Roziers, Jacques Delarüe Caron de Beaumarchais, Pierre Maillard, and then to Tanguy Courson de la Villeneuve.[9] The only person who held office throughout the entire period was Gilbert Grandval.[10]

Amid so many changes this permanence in what might be called a key position of a man of the temper and political intelligence of Mr. Grandval resulted in giving him an influence disproportionate, perhaps, to his function, but incontestable. True, his strong personality aroused opposition. The central administration always fears a proconsul who has a real sense of government. Tension at times verged on crisis. Twice Mr. Grandval handed in his resignation to Mr. Schuman: Mr. Pinay had a very violent scene with him. But these passing difficulties had no lasting consequences. They did not diminish the influence of the Military Governor who became High Commissioner and subsequently Ambassador. It was perceptible throughout the ten years of the *présence française* in the Saar. It was Mr. Grandval, together with Michel Debré who played a key role in the years 1946–1947, who developed French foreign policy towards the Saar; a policy that the Minister for Foreign Affairs, preoccupied with international conferences, sponsored and adopted. It was also Mr. Grandval who initiated the moves towards broadening Saar autonomy which resulted in the 1950 Conventions and later in those of 1953. Some of the speeches on matters relating to the Saar in the National Assembly or the Council of the Republic, whether delivered by the Minister for Foreign Affairs, a deputy, or a general *rapporteur*, adopted, even if they did not actually say so, views and suggestions put forward by Mr. Grandval. All this was quite in order; no one knew the Saar problem better than he and it was to him that people appealed for reliable information and advice.[11]

1956 was only possible because of the atmosphere of co-operation that Mr. Adenauer had established between the Federal Republic and France.

[9] November, 1947–July 29, 1948; November, 1948–September 1, 1950; September 1, 1950–January 5, 1953; January 8–July, 1953; July 2, 1953–end of 1955.

[10] *Cf.* Appendix II.

[11] It should be noted, however, that Mr. Grandval was not able to take part directly in the negotiations with Germany.

There were times when Mr. Grandval's influence was decisive, for example, during the attempted negotiations between Mr. Schuman and Mr. Adenauer in October, 1952. It was his intervention that made Mr. Schuman break off the negotiations, just as he was on the point of reaching agreement. This episode is an interesting one. Mr. Schuman and Mr. Adenauer, straining towards their vital objective, which was the political integration of Europe, were anxious to be rid of the obstacle represented by the Saar. Though he was cautious, Mr. Schuman was disposed to trust a German colleague who was, he felt, anxious to transcend strictly national concerns. But Mr. Grandval, whose whole attention was concentrated on the Saar and who knew the pressure to which the Chancellor was subjected from the pro-German opposition in the Saar and from the " Saar Party " in Germany, was inclined to be mistrustful. In the apparently harmless formulae of the agreements proposed by Germany he perceived ambiguities he was convinced would be used to re-open the question of France's position in the Saar. So he intervened obstinately with the minister; he used all his power to remove from the text of the agreement the " diplomatic " phrases that were designed to please everyone but that, as he saw it, merely weakened the French case when it was essential that it should be explicitly recognized by the Germans. In this discussion the rigorous logic of Mr. Grandval finally won through and stopped the negotiations. A year and a half later, when Pierre-Henri Teitgen and Chancellor Adenauer met in Strasbourg, Mr. Grandval's intervention was equally decisive. During the days preceding and following the negotiations, the French Ambassador to Saarbrücken increased his activities and interventions with Mr. Teitgen and Maurice Schumann to prevent the former from entering into negotiations and to obtain a statement expressing disapproval of the agreement. The Foreign Minister, Mr. Bidault, then attending the Conference on Asian Affairs in Geneva, followed the affair only from a distance and did no more during a flying visit to Paris than to encourage Mr. Grandval in his resistance.

The role of the French Ambassador to Saarbrücken was decisive in these two cases; there were other occasions when it was not effective, as, for example, on April 18, 1951, when Robert Schuman abandoned the idea of the double signature and engaged in an exchange of letters with Chancellor Adenauer, and again during Mr. Pinay's term of office at the Ministry for Foreign Affairs. The minister acted without heeding the advice or the opinions of those of his colleagues who were best informed on the Saar question.

What conclusions can be drawn from these few facts? Obviously the intensity of influences varied.[12] This was due not only to the change in composition of the group taking the decision—for example, when a new minister took office—but also to circumstances. From the two crises which can be studied closely, during the period when Robert Schuman was at the Ministry for Foreign Affairs, it is clear that the relationship of the influences at work was reversed; in the first crisis, the minister's view prevailed; in the second, the tenacious resistance of an active colleague apparently overcame the hesitancy of the man responsible for making the decision. It should be noted in passing that in April, 1951, Mr. Schuman was negotiating privately with Mr. Adenauer and Mr. Grandval's interventions were those of an outsider. In October, 1952, however, Mr. Grandval was present while Mr. Schuman was in communication with the Chancellor only by letter.

In both these cases the subject under discussion was the same. The question was whether French policy towards the Saar should be modified in the light of the demands of a policy of Franco-German co-operation and of European integration. This implied the sacrifice of some of the economic advantages France had gained for herself. Mr. Schuman and Mr. Pinay, given the choice, opted for Franco-German co-operation. They found themselves up against the intransigence of Mr. Grandval, who was the incarnation of France in the Saar and was striving to hold the positions that had been won.

Beyond the immediate circle of the minister's colleagues there were certain individual influences at work that must now be studied.

Individual influences—the term is subject to misconstruction, for the more or less rapid succession of these individual actions sometimes led to a co-ordination of effort that tended to result in the formation of groups. Hence it is hard, as we well know, to

---

[12] These few examples further underline the difficulty of reconstructing the inter-play of influences. We can consider ourselves fortunate to have been in a position to reconstruct in certain cases the sequence of events leading to a decision. But the number of such cases is limited and the conclusions that can be drawn from them scarcely go beyond hypothesis.

distinguish sufficiently clearly between the action of an individual
and that of a group.

In the period in which France was developing her Saar policy,
there were many individuals who, without holding any political
power, tried to make their voices heard and to direct the thinking
of people in government circles. We have identified some of them:
Saar refugees in France or elsewhere who were anxious to return to
their country to take their revenge for the persecutions from which
they had suffered, or, more simply, to work for the rehabilitation of
their Saar Fatherland. Some of them, like Mr. Hector, sought to
exert an influence in France and were in contact with groups particularly sensitive to the problems of the Rhine frontier or with
those Frenchmen who had already shown an active interest in the
strengthening of bonds between France and the Saar.[13] Such men
were Abel Verdier, Robert Herly, and certain members of the
Association française de la Sarre. Their activities, dictated by
various motives—material interest, desire for compensation, love of
country—had a certain importance. They helped to direct towards
the Saar the attention of a French public opinion preoccupied with
more pressing concerns and to familiarize it with the idea that the
Saar might be prepared to accept close association and union with
France. It was around this concept of union that men rallied,
organized themselves, and tried for a year or two to persuade their
fellow citizens in the Saar to join with them and to convince the
French Government. But the *Mouvement pour le rattachement de
la Sarre* was not formed until February, 1946, that is to say, at a
time when the decision in principle to proceed to economic union
had already been taken and had been publicly announced by the
French Government.

In Germany, the first attempts to react against French policy in
the Saar were also the work of isolated individuals. There were
some whose interests or emotions were directly affected by French
policy. There were others who took a position in the name of the
general principle of self-determination or who set themselves up as
defenders of the national integrity of the territory. Some drew
upon their memories of experiences before 1935 and of their subsequent struggles as reasons for taking up the French challenge.
They were not numerous, but their activity, as we have seen,[14] was

[13] *Cf. Historical Study*, pp. 7–11.
[14] *Ibid.*, pp. 50–55.

considerable and to some extent decisive. This was because, in the
first place, they were the only ones in Germany during the period
preceding the creation of the Federal Republic to express any
opposition to the Franco-Saar economic union and the rupture of
the political bonds uniting the Saar with Germany. They were not
satisfied with expressing opposition; they organized themselves.
From them came plans or proposals for a solution of the Saar
question. It was through their agency and on their initiative that
criticism of French policy and information on the Saar were transmitted to newspapers and politicians. Finally, it was thanks to
them that links were forged between Saarlanders and Germans,
and that various groups were set up outside the parties, like the
Saarbund, or within the parties and inside Parliament. There is no
doubt that the combined efforts of an Eberhard, a Strohm, a
Hellwig, of a Father Bungarten, or of *Minister-Präsidenten* like
Peter Altmeier and Karl Arnold, and their collaborators, helped to
keep the Saar question alive in the down-trodden Germany of the
post-war period. Their efforts were the more praiseworthy because
they met with nothing but indifference on all sides. A tally of the
sum total of personal overtures, oral or written, and of studies and
circulars,[15] reveals more acutely both the passivity of German
opinion, even in those circles that presumably should have shown
an interest in the Saar in view of the union of this German province
with France, and the vital importance of the activities of a few individuals who compelled their compatriots to take an interest in the
problem and who were behind the German resistance which in
turn created the actual conflict.

This does not mean that their attitude towards France was
aggressive. A study of the available sources reveals, on the contrary, a constant willingness to seek agreement, a desire to see

[15] Here are some examples. In September, 1948, for instance, a study was requested on
the subject of "Lorraine steel–Ruhr steel" for a meeting of industrialists, trade
unionists, and economists from Germany and France. At other times they busied
themselves with translating and sending out the American memorandum on the Saar,
the distribution of which was not always easy when it had to be sent across the Saar
frontier. They also approached certain Saarlanders who had taken refuge in Germany
to propose the founding of an association to protect their rights as German citizens of
Saar origin. Saarlanders living on pensions or investments on the territory of the
Federal Republic were also encouraged to join together. A list of German firms with
interests in the Saar was also drawn up. At the same time, the attention of certain
industrialists and deputies in the Bundestag was drawn to the French plan to lease the
Saar mines. It is easy to imagine the amount of work that each of these undertakings
entailed.

co-operation established.[16]   All were as well aware as was Fritz Hellwig of the interdependence of French and German economic interests and were equally convinced of the need to transcend national quarrels.

After the establishment of the Federal Republic, when Chancellor Adenauer was formulating his European policy, the influence of these few isolated individuals was decisive.   The Chancellor tended to be cautious and to play a waiting game.   He favoured not taking a position until Germany had been admitted to the Council of Europe, which would give him relative freedom of action.   The problem therefore was to overcome this regrettable caution to outwit the man responsible for the decision through the intermediary of Parliament so as to bring him to modify his position.   Thus it was that, through a series of moves establishing links between those acting as private individuals and officials close to the Chancellor,[17] the events of January 13, 1950, came about.   This day was notable for two meetings that were decisive for the future of the Saar: one included Richard Becker, Heinrich Schneider, Eduard Martin, and other influential Germans, the other was between Chancellor Adenauer and Mr. Schuman.   Mr. Strohm, Mr. Hellwig, and others made a major contribution to the statement that day by Chancellor Adenauer to Mr. Schuman.

They continued the struggle.   They did not consider that the intervention of the German Government relieved them of the responsibility they had assumed.   They were too deeply committed to withdraw.   Moreover, as far as the Saar was concerned, their confidence in the Chancellor was limited.   So they kept a close watch on the government and subjected it to constant pressure, which was irritating even to the Chancellor if one can judge by his reaction to Mr. Strohm in the spring of 1952.   At the same time Mr. Hellwig, Father Bungarten, and the few Saarlanders in Germany whom they had managed to contact, pursued their efforts to

16 *Cf.*, for example, in addition to the previously mentioned memorandum of Gustav Strohm, the outline drawn up at the end of 1948 entitled *Programmpunkte für eine deutsch-französische Industrie-Entente*.   In a letter of December 16, 1949, Mr. Strohm said, in connection with a recent incident, that the other camp no doubt preferred violent attacks to offers of co-operation.   But he had no wish to give way to this temptation.   "We are men of good will and understanding.   In my case this is even a conviction.   That is why I asked . . . two years ago for a study of the interrelationship of the Saar with its neighbouring regions."

17 It will be recalled that at the end of 1949 Mr. Strohm went to the *Bundeskanzleramt*. On the very day when Mr. Schuman arrived, Chancellor Adenauer sent for Mr. Strohm to prepare for the interview he was to have with his French colleague.

form an organization, and the *Saarbund* was the result.[18] A parliamentary group was also established uniting the members of various parties in a common policy towards the Saar. But the task was not easy. Despite support from the Ministry for All-German Affairs, the *Saarbund* got off to a slow start. It was up against indifference and passivity; the industrialists to whom appeals were made for funds gave them very grudgingly. Progress was made only by ceaseless effort and constant activity.

In the Saar, too, the influence of certain individuals was of capital importance. No one would question the influence of Johannes Hoffmann who dominated the political scene from 1947 to 1955. Similarly, the first resistance in the Saar came from isolated individuals. Heinrich Schneider, Richard Becker, Eduard Martin, Karl Walz, and Egon Reinert, and also Ernst Roth, Kurt Conrad, Friedrich Regitz, Hermann Trittelvitz, Karl Hillenbrandt, Aloys Schmitt, and Paul Kutsch, who were among the first to show their opposition and to take up the struggle in the Saar itself, experienced some difficulty in winning over opinion to their side.[19] This was probably due to resistance from the government and the control it exerted over political life, perhaps even more to the timidity and passivity of the people. It was several years before individual action could set in motion a solidly based movement. The fact that these men did not become discouraged was often because they had burned their bridges and also because the contacts they had established with the Germans brought them the encouragement they failed to find in the Saar. These individual efforts were mutually helpful. The few Saarlanders who resisted their fellow countrymen were used by Germans as evidence of an opposition in the Saar that should be supported. In the same way the Saar opposition used, in the Saar, the attitude of their German friends as conclusive proof of the German desire to win back the Saar. From these exchanges across the frontiers, increasing as time went by, there developed a dense and intricate network of relationships that contributed decisively to moulding public opinion in Germany and in the Saar, to upsetting the calculations of governments, and to playing havoc with their agreements.

[18] *Cf. Historical Study*, pp. 101 *et seq*.
[19] In the *Historical Study* we have stressed sufficiently the part played by some of these men and it is unnecessary to reiterate it here. *Cf.* pp. 13–15, 83–85. See also Johannes Hoffmann, *Am Rande des Hitlerkrieges* (Saarbrücken: 1948).

11

GROUP INFLUENCES IN FRANCE AND GERMANY

INDIVIDUAL actions, as has been observed, tended to converge and develop into collective action, itself led by an organized group. Those Saarlanders who wanted the union of their country with France transformed their *Mouvement pour la libération de la Sarre* into a *Mouvement pour le rattachement de la Sarre*. And the Saarlanders in Germany ended by creating the *Saarbund*.

It has also been indicated that individuals endeavoured to work within already constituted groups and modify their policies, while at the same time undergoing the influence of these groups by a strange process of interaction often difficult to reconstruct.

It is therefore worth while studying more closely the attitude and behaviour of groups—political parties, trade unions, economic groups of various kinds, diocesan clergy—who in one form or another in France, Germany, and the Saar took part in the debate over the Saar.

IN FRANCE

The Political Parties

It was only to be expected that the political parties should be led by circumstances to take a position regarding France's policy in the Saar. Perhaps it might even be said they were forced to do so. The rarity of their interventions is as striking as the vagueness of their proposals. The Saar was not their primary concern. Their attention was taken up first by problems of internal policy. In discussions on foreign policy, the place accorded to the Saar was necessarily small in relation to that reserved for Franco-German relations, various aspects of the struggle between the Soviet Union and the non-Communist world, and the problems of France's overseas possessions. There was little or no interest in the Saar as such or in the Saarlanders. The Saar was not likely to enrich France's economic, spiritual, or intellectual life. It represented a *quid pro quo*, and they approached it from the point of view of security and of reparations. France needed Saar coal; she had a right to reparations. On this point all the political parties were agreed in 1945—M.R.P., Socialists, and Communists alike.[1]

In this same spirit, the economic union was approved. If the Communists opposed it after the Moscow Conference and stood solidly behind a total rejection of France's Saar policy, it was under orders from the U.S.S.R. who had just broken off relations with those who had been her associates in the struggle against Hitler's Germany. But the other parties, supported by the Radicals and the R.P.F., upheld the policy of economic union between France and the Saar.

A *quid pro quo* and a means of reparation the Saar may have been, but it was also an instrument of French policy towards Germany. Members of the M.R.P., Socialist, Radical, and R.P.F. parties were agreed in maintaining that the economic union with France and the political separation from Germany were indissolubly linked and that this solution offered France an essential guarantee, at the same time re-establishing a vital, if relative, balance between the industrial potential of the two countries. This theme of balance recurred constantly in the arguments of both sides, especially after the Schuman Plan was launched and after the formation of the E.C.S.C. when the place of the Saar in this new Community was under discussion. On many occasions deputies belonging to various parties stressed that a return of the Saar to Germany would give the latter too much weight in the E.C.S.C. and consequently put her in a position to exert an influence that would compromise Franco-German co-operation. It was this concern for the preservation or re-establishment of balance that led to the formula of Saar autonomy, to which all the parties rallied, or to the idea of europeanization on which they were less in agreement. The R.P.F. and Radicals viewed this kind of solution with the same mistrust they showed for Robert Schuman's policy.

The introduction of the idea of the " Saar settlement as a prerequisite " also appeared to be an expression of that attitude which chose to see in the Saar an instrument of policy. This was not true for everyone, however. There were some among the first of those to conceive the idea—Mr. Grandval for one—who saw in it a means

---

[1] This more or less unanimous opinion of the parties echoed statements emanating from the most diverse groups—C.G.T. or *Union française des associations des combattants de la Libération victimes des deux guerres.*

of forcing the Federal Government to relinquish its claims to the Saar. Others made a German concession on this point the touchstone of German sincerity. But there were many—Radicals, members of the R.P.F., and Socialists—who used the Saar-settlement-as-a-prerequisite formula to bar the way to the E.D.C. without thinking of the consequences that introduction of the " prerequisite " might have on the solution of the Saar question.

If the ten-year period under review is considered as a whole, it will be seen that the political parties, with the exception of the Communists, were not so far removed from one another as might at first seem. The positions they adopted according to circumstances were scarcely distinguishable from one another. There were, of course, fine shades of distinction. In the early years, the M.R.P., or some of its members, seemed more conscious of the historical factor than were the Socialists, which was not surprising. The Saar had been French in the past; the bonds established at that time justified the policy adopted in 1945. The Socialists, on the other hand, had a keener awareness of the fact that the Saar was by nature German, and this put them on their guard. They were the first to take a position explicitly against any form of annexation. Léon Blum was suspicious of a policy that tended to insist on an autonomous status for the Saar; Félix Gouin, in a speech on March 24, 1946, in Strasbourg, when he was President of the Provisional Government, emphasized that though the French were unanimous in demanding international control of the mining and metallurgical production in the Saar, this did not mean that they had decided to demand the political separation of the Saar from Germany.[2] A few months later, on July 18, 1946, Salomon Grumbach, speaking at a working session of the Socialist group, was still more categorical:

> We are opposed to the official view of the French Government that provides for the definitive amputation of a large area of German territory in the West, Ruhr, and Rhineland. We opposed this in the first place on principle and then on a conclusive, factual ground, namely, that we felt it would be impossible to obtain the indispensable agreement of our Allies on this point.[3]

The Socialists adopted, however, the idea of the unity of the Saar-Lorraine Basin and the theme of French security.

[2] Cf. *L'Année politique 1946, op. cit.*, p. 370.
[3] *Ibid.*, p. 404.

The fact that from 1950 onwards the M.R.P. returned more insistently than the other parties to the idea of "europeanization" might, it is true, indicate a more fundamental divergence of policy, all the more so because the term embraced sometimes widely differing concepts of European co-operation.[4] But if on the strength of its European convictions the M.R.P. was better disposed than the other parties to modifications in France's policy in the Saar, it was nevertheless firm on the subject of the Franco-Saar economic union. We should not forget that it was Mr. Bidault who, as Minister for Foreign Affairs, refused to sign the Teitgen-Adenauer agreements. His inflexibility was not merely the manifestation of a personal policy or solely the result of Mr. Grandval's intervention, however decisive that may have been. It reflected the general state of mind of the influential members of the M.R.P., and it also reflected the prevailing mood in the National Assembly, a mood that was itself conditioned by a defensive complex nurtured by the consciousness that the balance of strength was being upset.

Economic Interests

Through the intermediary of Parliament, political parties had an opportunity to exert direct or indirect influence on the decision either by their participation in the government or by their support, by their interventions in the debates on the negotiations, or because those in office modified policy in accordance with their concept of the probable reaction of Parliament. The influence of the political parties was therefore generally exercised openly enough to enable an outside observer to be aware of it and to analyse it.

The problem raised by our study of organized economic interests was much more complex; the inter-play of influences worked in much more unobtrusive, if not more devious, ways. Economic publications and the discussions of Chambers of Commerce or of professional groups certainly furnished useful information, as did some of the annual reports of large business firms. General attitudes as well as main lines of policy can be perceived from these. But however sharply positions may sometimes be taken, there is a tendency not to delimit interests in too obvious and brusque a manner; the objective is cloaked in more general considerations; for

---

[4] Thus, the R.P.F. countered the M.R.P.'s idea of a "supranational" Europe with its own concept of an "allied" Europe.

reasons easily understood, it is only in private that the concrete objectives which are to be discreetly achieved are clearly set out.[5]

One basic observation must be made: the decision in principle in favour of economic union preceded consultations with representatives of economic interests and of trade unions. The government, in the person of Mr. Bidault, announced its position at the beginning of January, 1946, and it was on the basis of this first decision that in the course of 1946 studies were made of the means of implementing French policy in the Saar.

At this time, politicians and responsible officials had a clear concept of the reasons that had governed the decision.[6] One has only to recall the comments made by one of them in 1946:

> Economic union between the Saar and France has an obvious political virtue. It will, in fact, make it possible for French influence in the Saar to be exerted to the detriment of Germany by weakening Germany's links with the Saar and, as far as the Saar itself is concerned, to break up the politico-economic block it constitutes, symbolized, for example, by the Roechling group. It will thus be brought closer to France.
>
> The realization of these aims essential to French policy should take precedence over all other considerations and lead to bringing about economic union with the Saar even if there were no economic advantages in the operation in addition to political interests.

The political considerations were predominant. Economic union was perhaps less a way of strengthening France economically than a way of weakening Germany and thus of altering the balance of relative strength between the two countries in France's favour. But the purely economic interests were not entirely overlooked: "The chief wealth of the Saar, its coal," noted the author of the observations quoted above, "must contribute to France's recovery, either by being sent directly to France or by being used to manufacture products intended for France. Similarly, Saar labour must work for France by producing goods directly useful to France or which, sold for export, will bring in the foreign currency that the French economy needs." Once the principle of the subordination of the

---

[5] The study of pressure groups now in progress will make it possible, we hope, to reconstruct the operation of these influences in a more satisfactory manner than is possible at the present time. *Cf.*, on this subject, the work of Georges Lavau, especially his report presented to the Round Table of the International Political Science Association at Pittsburgh in September, 1957, on "Political Pressures by Interest Groups in France," in Henry W. Ehrmann, ed., *Interest Groups on Four Continents* (Pittsburgh: University of Pittsburgh, 1958). Other useful sources are the numerous studies of Jean Meynaud and his recent book, *Les groupes de pression en France* (Paris: 1958). *Cf.*, also, Henry W. Ehrmann, *Organized Business in France* (Princeton: 1957).

[6] *Cf. Historical Study*, pp. 21–23.

Saar economy to the general interests of France had been laid down, it remained to solve the more delicate question of how to fit this into the over-all pattern of the French economy. Some of the industries—mining, tubing, ceramics—were competitive with French ones. Measures would have to be taken that would be elaborated during the course of 1947, particularly within the framework of the *Commission du Plan de la Sarre*. It is, however, interesting to note that on this point, too, long before they officially consulted the representatives of the industries concerned, the government departments had already decided in principle not to carry the subordination of the Saar economy to the point of closing down production by Saar industries which were in competition with French industries. The author of the previous remark wrote:

> There is no reason to envisage the slowing down or cessation of corresponding branches of Saar industry; on the contrary, this activity must continue, under conditions to be determined, in the general interests of France. To this end the Saar economy must be directed towards exports and this implies, as we are fully aware, the maintenance of certain economic links with Germany.

When some of the industrial representatives were consulted, they had difficulty, as we have already seen,[7] in accepting this view. Reactions varied, naturally, according to the sectors under consideration and to the individuals. In the case of Saar agriculture, agreement was reached fairly quickly. There was no competition to fear. The Saar market, it was felt, would remain open to the agricultural products of eastern France. Industry was another matter entirely. From the moment that there was any question of competition, there was always the temptation to liquidate the awkward rival. This was the case with the French tube industry which felt it was quite capable of reaching the targets assigned to it by the Monnet Plan for the reconstruction and modernization of French industry (prepared by the *Commissariat général du Plan de modernisation et d'équipement*). All it lacked was raw materials and manpower. It would therefore be best to close the Saar factories as soon as possible or, if this could not be done, to integrate them into the over-all plan for supplying French needs during the transitional period. In the case of ceramics, where there was greater anxiety because the Saar competitors were better equipped, a solution was sought in the integration of the Saar

[7] *Ibid.*, p. 30.

industries into the professional groups of the various branches of the French ceramic industry and into the trading bodies. The ceramic industry, moreover, could be directed towards the German market.

Discussion was even more bitter over Saar iron and steel. This was because of the importance of this industry in the Saar, its influence on the French market, the place it held in the German market, and, finally, the diversity of the conditions of ownership of the chief factories: Völklingen was in the hands of the Roechling family; Neunkirchen belonged 50 per cent. to the Stumm group and 50 per cent. to the Wolf group, both German; Dillingen and Brebach were divided—40 per cent. of the capital was German and 60 per cent. French. Finally, as far as Burbach was concerned, 30 per cent. of the capital was French, 40 per cent. Belgian, and 30 per cent. Luxembourgeois. There were two opposing factions. Some, whose opinion was expressed in the report of the Sub-committee for Iron and Steel,[8] within the *Commission du Plan de la Sarre*, were in favour of restrictive measures. Though they agreed, rather reluctantly, that the factories of Burbach, Dillingen, and Völklingen should re-open, they wanted to keep the Neun-kirchen factory closed. Moreover, they considered it necessary to prevent the flow of Saar steel to France. Their opposition was based on the fact that the cost price of products delivered to France from the Saar was higher than that of products made in Lorraine, and that because of the cost of transport. While orienting Saar production to the markets of southern Germany, they also sought to ensure that French factories would be kept informed concerning Saar exports.

This policy did not meet with the approval of the *Commissariat du Plan* whose representative declared categorically that it was in complete contradiction with the objectives drawn up by the *Conseil du Plan* for the French iron and steel industry. In his opinion, in the programme for the expansion of the French iron and steel industries, there was room for Saar iron and steel. It would be a great mistake to close the French home market to Saar products. The only valid criterion must be free competition. It was also false reasoning to try to avoid competition in exports between the two iron and steel industries and at the same time to maintain the

[8] These Sub-committees, in accordance with a principle laid down by the *Commissariat du Plan*, were made up of representatives of technical organizations, French employers' and workers' organizations, French administrative services, and of French administrators of Saar industries (when there were any). There were no Saar representatives.

principle of conserving Saar outlets. The *Commissariat's* representative further stressed the necessity for the Saar factories to work at full capacity in the next three or four years in the interests of French industry, which was itself limited by inadequate fuel supplies. Finally, he was opposed, if not to the Sub-committee's decision in principle to prohibit any modernization in the Saar factories in the next five years, then certainly to the form in which it was expressed.

The views of the *Commissariat du Plan* won the support of those in charge of Saar affairs. Mr. Grandval and Mr. Baboin, Director-General of the *Régie des mines*, who were both dealing with concrete problems, were in a position to assess the economic, political, and social consequences of restrictive measures towards Saar iron and steel. It was therefore not surprising that they opposed the Sub-committee and in fact stressed the importance of making clearly evident both the satisfaction felt at the integration of the Saar iron and steel industries into those of France and the desire to see them on an equal footing. The principle of the modernization of the iron and steel industries must be laid down at once, but its application might be deferred, as might the anticipated allocation of materials and dollars.

The joint efforts of the *Commissariat du Plan*, the representatives of the government and of the French Administration in the Saar, were successful in leading the *Commission du Plan de la Sarre* to modify the proposals of the Sub-committee for Iron and Steel. The final decision, as we have seen, merged the Saar iron and steel industry with that of France and provided that the same rules concerning production programmes, programmes of work to be undertaken, allocation of raw materials, and commercial policy should be applied to both.[9]

Thus considerations of the over-all interests of the French economy prevailed over a narrower concept which would have limited French policy to the protection of individual interests and confined it to a defensive attitude. In other words, the statesmen triumphed, confirming the decisions taken in principle in 1946.[10]

[9] On this last point a reservation was made in regard to the future: if for the time being there was no fear of competition, it had to be borne in mind that in a few years Saar iron and steel, with a productive capacity greater than the needs of the French market, would once again be in a position to export. At that point, there would have to be a re-distribution of outlets.

[10] It is interesting to note in this connection that the Commission, while maintaining its reservations about re-opening the Neunkirchen factories, nevertheless admitted that

These decisions in principle, however, met with resistance in practice. Inside the French Administration, in the *Direction de la sidérurgie*, certain reservations still persisted. Some officials felt that Saar iron and steel would be a burden on France. They mistrusted the Saarlanders, whom they still thought of as Germans. So they deemed it was essential to take precautions to ensure that France was in a position to take the lead. This mistrust partly explains some of the opposition and interventions from the ministerial offices of which Mr. Grandval complained later. It may also have been at the root of the complications which arose from the allocation of Marshall Aid. It is a known fact that the Saarlanders complained frequently they had been passed over. From 1949 to 1951 there were many complaints in the Saar press and in the Landtag. Even the most pro-government Saarlanders considered that, if the population figures were taken as a basis of calculation, they had the right to one-forty-sixth of France's Marshall Aid. The Saar, said Deputy Kunkel, for example, in July, 1950,[11] had had 2,379 million francs of Marshall Aid allotted to it and had received 1,980 million francs; whereas, if the scale of one-forty-sixth had been adopted she would have been entitled to 7,560 million. The French explained [12] that, though valid for branches of the national industry other than coal and steel, the proportion of one-forty-sixth could not be used, since the share for the colonies, the allocations to the monetary stabilization fund, and those to the coal and steel industries had to be deducted. In fact, they said, the Saarlanders were better off than they thought because the Saarlanders occupied in industries other than coal and steel represented only 1·75 per cent. of the total population of metropolitan France. They added, on the basis of calculations the details of which it is unnecessary to enter into here, that the Saar had in reality received the full share to which it was entitled, that the Saar *Régie des mines* had been in a position to modernize its equipment much more quickly than had been the case in the mining valleys in France, and that the

political considerations beyond its scope might bring the government to a contrary decision. Thus the Commission formulated certain conditions which should be met if the situation arose.

[11] *Volksstimme*, July 8, 1950. *Cf.* also *Volksstimme*, May 18, 1951, and May 3, 1952. In this last issue, Dr. Lion protested vigorously against the decision taken by the Pinay Government to reduce the credits intended for investment more sharply in the Saar than in France. He asked whether the French Government were not afraid that the day might come when a europeanized Saar would reveal to the world and to the United States the extent to which it had been deprived of the Marshall funds intended for it.

[12] *La Chronique sarroise*, No. 0 (March 1, 1952).

Dillingen factories had received substantial help from the part of
Marshall Aid funds allocated to coal and steel.[13]

Indeed, there appears to be a fairly substantial difference
between the decisions taken in 1947 and the policy practised
between 1949 and 1951 in the matter of the allocation of Marshall
Aid. Priority seems to have been given to French industry, despite
the appeals of the High Commissioner [14] and protests from the
Saar. What exactly was the influence responsible for this? It is difficult to say. At best, in the present state of our knowledge, one can
draw certain conclusions from comments on the 1947 discussions.

The guarded attitude towards the Saarlanders and towards the
French Government's Saar policy was also manifest on other
occasions. The heads of the iron and steel industries continued to
show a certain mistrust of the Saar iron and steel industries, fearing
competition. The tendency to economic Malthusianism in matters
concerning Saar industries was so apparent that the High Commissioner was led to propose that the state, rather than a private
group, should take over Völklingen and Neunkirchen because the
latter might decide to slow down production or bring it to a stand-
still without thought for the disastrous consequences of such a
decision on the economic and social equilibrium of the Saar. In
quite a different field the High Commissioner's efforts met with
the opposition of employers that stemmed from the same attitude.
In fact, the integration of Saar professional organizations into those
of France, sought by Mr. Grandval, did not seem to suit the leaders
of French employer groups. The Saarlanders were kept at arm's
length and were only allowed to join professional organizations as
corresponding members.

Should we therefore conclude from this that there was an over-
all opposition on the part of employers to the principle of a Franco-
Saar economic union? This would be exaggerated. We must bear

---

[13] *Cf. Historical Study*, pp. 162–163; François Muller, *L'économie sarroise, op. cit.*,
pp. 334–351.
[14] Mr. Grandval was very active and in April, 1949, made the following remarks: "In
these circumstances, I cannot but draw attention once again . . . to the systematic
resistance we encounter among the various relevant administrative services in regard to
financial and economic questions affecting the Saar. Whether it is a question of delivery
of equipment under the [European Recovery Programme], general matters of foreign
trade, food, or problems of industrial production, it is clear that the administration as
a whole manifests a characteristic defeatism towards the aims of French policy in the
Saar. It is high time that the government gave categorical instructions to put an end
to this impossible situation which completely paralyses the High Commissioner's Office.
. . . Economic union brings with it both rights and duties; we can no longer continue
to demand that the Saarlanders respect the former if we consistently evade the latter.'

in mind that the information at our disposal is incomplete and this makes any generalization impossible. However, one must also bear in mind the diversity of interests that conditioned a diversity of attitudes. Some were not concerned at all; others were seeking to strengthen their position on the Saar market. Schneider and Châtillion-Commentry were even competing with one another for Völklingen. Finally, the rejection of the Statute and the debates on the settlement of the Franco-Saar dispute provoked among employer circles a lively reaction in favour of the preservation of the *status quo*, which they believed to be favourable to France. The report submitted to the Economic Council on April 19, 1956, by Emmanuel Mayolle is a veritable plea for the Franco-Saar economic union. The union, he said, met political and moral conditions which no one had thought to contest when the E.C.S.C. Treaty was signed. It was geographically and economically justified, for the prosperity of the Saar had never been as great as since the economic union between the two countries. This union moreover had become a "must" for France since the formation of the E.C.S.C., for it was the prerequisite to maintaining the balance within the Franco-German community. Mr. Mayolle also advanced France's legal title to reparations which gave her rights of ownership over certain industrial equipment. He set aside the Roechling claim, upheld the French official position on the canalization of the Moselle and on the Warndt, and ended by declaring that there should be no changes in the 1953 Conventions. "Any arrangement likely to end or reduce commercial, industrial, or worker exchanges between France and the Saar must be expressly avoided. But, at the same time, necessary measures must be foreseen to avoid abuse of the facilities afforded to Saar goods on the French market." [15]

There could be no more vigorous defence of the Franco-Saar economic union. But by this time the political die was cast.

If organized economic interests as such did not play a decisive role in the period when French policy towards the Saar was being developed between 1945 and 1947, and if at that time political considerations prevailed, it would appear that subsequently the defence

[15] *Journal officiel, Avis et Rapports du Conseil économique*, April 22, 1956, p. 361.

of strictly French economic interests motivated certain groups of employers and even the action of some of the government departments. This attitude and the decisions to which it drove people did not perhaps have any direct and apparent effect on diplomatic negotiations between the French and German Governments. Their influence was nonetheless important on relations between France and the Saar. The economic union and the principle of equality of treatment implied on the part of the French an acceptance of the Saarlanders as partners and a recognition of their rights. The guarded attitude adopted towards them in circles which should, on the contrary, have been striving to win them over, together with the tendency towards centralization of the ministerial departments, helped to prevent the development of any real Franco-Saar co-operation, and in so doing weakened France's position in the dialogue with Germany.

The Frontier Region

The inhabitants of the frontier regions, that is to say, of Lorraine exerted their influence in the same direction.

One might have imagined, remembering Lotharingia or listening to the appeals launched on the theme of the unity of the Saar-Lorraine Basin, that the people of Lorraine would play a decisive role in the integration of the Saar with France. But the fact was that these close neighbours had very different sentiments. For them, the Saarlanders were Germans and would remain Germans. There were unhappy memories of the behaviour of some of them during the occupation. The theme of the economic unity of the Saar-Lorraine Basin was nothing but a myth. A report submitted to the Chamber of Commerce of Metz in the spring of 1946 [16] said that the history of economic relations between France and the Saar since 1870 had been falsified by exaggerating the benefits that accrued to Lorraine and to France. The report referred to the criticism already voiced by the Chamber of Commerce of Metz between 1920 and 1935 and the opposition it had always shown to economic union. [17] On the present state of the problem the report

[16] *Cf.* report presented to the plenary session, May 11, 1946; see also *Historical Study*, pp. 24–26.

[17] Thirty-nine replies to an inquiry held in 1929 among members of the Chamber of Commerce were in favour of the Statute. Those who declared themselves satisfied were retailers and wholesalers on the frontiers, the clothing, shoe, wood, and food trades, salt works and some transforming industries. Plaster and electrical construction industries were not interested; glass, china, metallurgical transforming, machine, paper, and

was scarcely more encouraging. As the metallurgical industries of Lorraine had particularly strong reservations, it was not surprising that the motion adopted by the Chamber of Commerce at the conclusion of its debates stressed the disadvantages of economic union with the Saar and recorded its opposition.

With the passage of time this attitude changed but little. The press in Lorraine continued to express scepticism of French policy in the Saar and as to the possibility of co-operation with the Saarlanders. *Le Républicain lorrain* wrote on January 20, 1950:

> For the people of eastern France the Saar is something other than the orphan whom others are trying to take from us and to whom France has been a generous guardian since 1945. True, it represents a certain number of economic advantages, but, humanly speaking, it is a vast unknown quantity. Thus, the closer we get to the frontier, the more does enthusiasm give place to caution, even to downright reluctance. The game of diplomatic prestige should not blind us to the practical facts of a situation that is evolving rapidly.

These remarks were typical expressions of the general tone of the press in Lorraine.

The Chamber of Commerce of Metz in a further report of this same year, 1950, repeated the conclusions of its previous report and maintained its reservations. While admitting that application of the principle of the integration of the Saar into the French economy should avoid some of the disadvantages which had been manifest in the years 1920–1935, it nevertheless asserted that the Saarlanders enjoyed a much more favourable situation than their competitors in the Moselle. The political autonomy of the Saar placed at the disposal of the government means and powers which the neighbouring French provinces did not have. The government could obtain information directly—without going through Paris—on the development of economic activity in the Saar. It could also, thanks to its representatives in Paris or through the intermediary of Saarlanders attached to certain French consular posts, make its interests known and thus promote measures that discriminated in its favour.

pharmaceutical producers demanded protection. The Chamber of Commerce concluded by requesting that a political union with Germany should put an end to the economic union with France.

In 1934 a further inquiry gave only seven replies in favour of the *status quo*, and these came from flour mills and the salt works. The coal mines and the iron and steel industry were in favour of union with Germany. The Chamber of Commerce requested union with Germany while recommending that measures be taken to protect the interests of agriculture, milling, and salt.

The report therefore demanded an equalization of production in the Saar and in France and the conclusion of agreements within various occupational sectors, particularly in machinery, cement, and glass industries. The general tone was less negative than in 1946–1947. But there was no enthusiasm. "It is fairly difficult to draw up an objective balance-sheet of advantages and disadvantages for the Moselle, because the representatives of the Lorraine economy do not have the same facilities for acquiring information as do their colleagues in the Saar."

There was agreement, however, on the usefulness of the Economic Commission for Lorraine, Alsace, and the Saar, set up on April 24, 1948.[18] The report declared that this organ of "co-ordination and conciliation" constituted a "notable improvement" over the previous period; it had already "rendered great service during the first stage of adaptation of the economic union and it was well worth maintaining and preserving."

This wish was not fulfilled. The Commission ceased to meet after the signing of the Franco-Saar Conventions of 1950. No more was heard of it until the summer of 1953 when, at Mr. Grandval's instigation, serious consideration was given to reviving it. The conclusion of the Franco-Saar Conventions of 1953 had aroused in the Moselle the mistrust and hostility that was only semi-dormant, and the representatives of small- and medium-sized industries became, as we have seen, the mouthpiece of these feelings.[19] Their opposition was expressed in categorical terms by an influential group [20] and it aroused Mr. Grandval, who was the special target, to suggest that the Commission which had been so useful between 1948 and

---

[18] "Organ of co-ordination charged with the task of studying and watching the effects of the economic union between the Saar and France on the economy of the departments of the north-east and upon that of the Saar territory, with particular reference to the application of the principles and measures envisaged by the plan for modernization and equipment in matters of common concern to the two economies." Cf. *Journal officiel, Lois et Décrets*, April 26–27, 1948, p. 4068 (*Décret* No. 48–715). The Commission's headquarters was Metz. Michel Debré was made president.

[19] For a summary of the complaints of the small- and medium-sized industries, cf. *Historical Study*, pp. 137–139.

[20] Cf. on this subject, Georges Lavau, "Note sur un 'pressure group' français: la Confédération générale des petites et moyennes entreprises," *Revue française de science politique*, No. 2 (April–June, 1955), pp. 370–383. Mr. Lavau gives useful information: this organization, founded in 1944, claimed in 1954 that it represented 50 per cent. of production, 48 per cent. of manpower, and 95 per cent. of distribution. Its leaders made no secret of their aims or of their interventions with the administration and the political parties. They let it be clearly understood that they had played a decisive role in Mr. Pinay's coming to power. They were violently opposed to the E.C.S.C. and demonstrated constantly in favour of a protectionist policy for French commerce and industry.

1950 be re-formed. The government agreed readily enough in principle, but discussion on the actual composition of the Commission dragged on for months because of the resistance of the Chamber of Commerce of Metz to the presence of officials representing the French Diplomatic Mission in the Saar. It was not until December 21, 1954, that the final composition of the French delegation was determined by decree. At the end of January, 1955, the Commission was still without a president. Meanwhile the small- and medium-sized business interests and the Chamber of Commerce pursued their campaign of protest against the advantages accorded to the Saar.[21]

They continued to pursue it in 1955, especially when the Convention on Economic Co-operation between France and the Saar was signed, which gave rise to a new wave of criticism. These agreements " considerably expanded the rights conceded to the Saar in foreign trade," noted the Chamber of Commerce of Metz at its meeting of May 6, " particularly as far as import quotas are concerned." Thus the Saar " will reap substantial benefits " while the Moselle Department " will suffer injurious consequences." This study of the situation then ended with protests against the new arrangements for road transport which favoured Saar carriers to the detriment of those of the Moselle; there were also protests against the lowering of the postal rates between the Saar and Germany. Simultaneously, demands were made that fiscal and social obligations be brought into line with those in France, though it was admitted that this was more and more difficult to achieve as the Saar extended its autonomy.[22]

Thus, from the beginning to the end of the attempt to integrate the Saar into the French economy, economic groups in the Moselle were constantly on the defensive. Their reactions were those of competitors who had definite interests to consider and who, after unfortunate experiences in the past, trusted neither their government nor their own strength. They therefore accepted without too much regret a defeat they had seen coming and to which they had contributed to some extent by their resistance.

[21] Cf. *Information*, special issue of September 12, 1954; *Le Républicain lorrain*, July 6, 20, 22, 1954; *L'Economie mosellane*, May 15, July 24, 1954.
[22] Cf. also *Bulletin de la Chambre de commerce et d'industrie de Strasbourg*, No. 1 (1956), No. 1 (1957). These contain an expression of the anxiety felt at the concessions made to the Saar as well as the desire to retain the Saar markets.

In Germany

The Political Parties

The silence which brooded over conquered Germany was not of long duration. As early as the autumn of 1946, newspapers and political parties profited from the freedom granted to them to express their opinions on the decisions taken about German territory. On September 23, 1946, Kurt Schumacher declared that he could not approve the statement of Secretary of State Byrnes that the Saar territory should go to France. On March 13, 1947, the Committee of the Social Democratic Party publicly took a similar position. The bulletin of the C.D.U./C.S.U. did likewise at the beginning of June of the same year.

From then on, statements followed one another, all to the same effect. There was no question about it: the German political parties had come out against the political separation of the Saar from Germany and its economic union with France. Before acting, they had not waited until the German Federal Republic had been constituted or until the Bundestag had met.

Behind their unanimity, however, there were fairly significant divergences of viewpoint. They may have been agreed on the final aim—the return of the Saar to the German Fatherland—but they were less in accord on the means to bring this about. In this disagreement over the means, there could be seen reflected the sharply-defined firmness of their purposes. While the Socialists trod the path laid down for them by Mr. Schumacher and continued to proclaim themselves adamant in their determination to make a favourable settlement of the Saar question (which meant a return of the Saar to Germany) a condition of European co-operation, the C.D.U. was less rigid and more inclined to consider a compromise solution.

The opposition of the two parties was fairly obvious and the reality of which it was an expression was just as straightforward. It is not true, as some Socialists have tried to claim, that the Socialist Party was the only one to fight for the return of the Saar which the opposing party was quite prepared to sacrifice. For even within the C.D.U. positions varied. Fritz Hellwig, for instance, was an active member of the C.D.U.; from his pen came the memorandum of this party's economic committee, showing how closely the Saar economy was bound up with that of its two neighbours. Peter Altmeier, *Minister-Präsident* of Rheinland-Pfalz, one of the most active fighters in the struggle for the return of the Saar to Germany, was also one of the most influential leaders of the C.D.U. A list drawn up at the end of July, 1954, by the *Saarbund* [23] of its members from the Bundestag and the Bundesrat gave the following figures for the various parties: C.D.U./C.S.U., 13 deputies; F.D.P., 13 deputies; S.P.D., 11 deputies; G.B./B.H.E., 11 deputies; D.P., 5 deputies. The *Saarbund* thus gave proof that it relied on all parties and that the policy it advocated had a truly national character.

As a matter of fact, the disagreement over the Saar did not so much set one party against another—or against others—as oppose those who were responsible for the conduct of affairs to those who were not. As we have seen, the government could not build its whole foreign policy round the Saar. The primary considerations were to re-establish contacts that had been broken, to restore confidence between Germany and her neighbours, and to win back for the Federal Republic a place that would enable her to exercise an influence proportionate to her interests and her resources. For Mr. Adenauer, who thought in terms of Germany's over-all position, who was particularly conscious of the power of the Soviet Union, the most important objective was the re-establishment of Franco-German co-operation and the organization of a system of European security. The Saar came after this; in his view, it would be a major error, which might well result in the disappearance of Germany and of Europe, to jeopardize European co-operation merely to satisfy the demands of national pride.

But those whose eyes were fastened on the Saar, those who did not have the responsibility of office and therefore were not faced with basic policy alternatives, could not understand the reservations or the reluctance of the government. Their failure to understand grew the farther they were away from power. Those members of the C.D.U. who did not approve of Chancellor Adenauer's Saar policy and would have liked to see him take a firmer attitude were nevertheless compelled to support him when it came to a vote involving the authority of the government and even its very existence. They might increase their personal efforts and endeavour to

[23] *Deutscher Saarbund, Bundesgeschäftsführung*: "Mitgliedschaft von Mitgliedern des Bundesrats und Abgeordneten des Bundestages" (Bonn: July 31, 1954). The list does not include the names of some of the deputies who intervened most often against a policy of compromise.

exert an influence inside the party or to work on the government, but when it came to a vote they were bound by the requirements of loyalty dictated by their political sense. During the winter of 1954–1955, Peter Altmeier made various proposals and representations to the Chancellor with some vehemence stemming from his anxiety to defend the interests of Rheinland-Pfalz and to ensure that the C.D.U. was not alone in taking responsibility for approving the Statute. But when it came to the vote, Mr. Altmeier could only support the government, while the opposition parties could criticize more freely and use the Saar as evidence of their greater patriotism, because they knew the government party was about to pass an unpopular measure. They were not the only ones to take advantage of this freedom. If, for example, the F.D.P. thought it could and should split from the government and thus win popularity for itself, was this not because it believed the Statute could be approved without its help? [24]

The role of the opposition parties and of those who did not play a decisive part in the coalition was easier. They could cloak themselves in the mantle of intransigence. It was they who doubtless most frequently proclaimed the rights of Germany or, in more general terms, the right of self-determination of peoples. Chancellor Adenauer, relying on previous experience, replied to this that Germany, even if she felt she had right on her side, could not count on outside support for a Saar policy whose only aim was to satisfy national interests, nor could she compel France to withdraw.[25] Compared with the Socialist Party with its insistence on Germany's rights, the position of the C.D.U. became characterized by the frequency with which the theme of European unity and of a " European " solution for the Saar recurred. The F.D.P. also took

[24] " The C.D.U. cannot be the only one to ratify the Saar agreement," remarked a member of the C.D.U. " This is especially true as regards the F.D.P. Since France has made the four agreements interdependent, the partners of the coalition must recognize that their approval of only three of the agreements is worthless. To be sure, the rejection of the Saar agreement by these people was made very easy by the unfortunate publication of the resolution of our party council. Now they can justly say: ' Why should we continue to burden ourselves with the " Saar betrayal " when the majority of the C.D.U.—with a few outsiders from among us—makes acceptance certain. The coalition parties . . . must be forced to assume responsibility. . . .'"
[25] Statement made on April 29, 1954, to the Bundestag: " We Germans have no means to force France against her wishes into a renunciation of her position in the Saar. Here unfortunately it is irrelevant whether France assumed this position justly or unjustly. . . . Let me tell you today frankly that these efforts taught us that a policy which merely satisfies our own national interests in the Saar question cannot expect to find support outside of Germany, even if justice is on our side." Cf. *Verhandlungen des Deutschen Bundestages*, II. 26/1070, April 29, 1954.

up the European theme but abandoned it gradually, perhaps under the influence of the Saar opposition parties. It declared instead that the Saar's road towards Europe ran through Germany rather than through France.

There was one common meeting ground, however, for all parties, and this was the question of democratic freedoms in the Saar. Christian Democrats, Socialists, and Liberals alike all adopted the same uncompromising attitude: they all abandoned themselves to outbursts of indignation which might seem exaggerated to the outside observer. This was quite probably the outcome of the efforts of the most active members of the Saar opposition. There is no doubt that the Saar régime, aware of its own weakness, tried to protect itself by keeping a close watch over the opposition and by restrictive measures such as those taken against the opposition parties or against newspapers coming in from Germany. But the opposition, engaged in an increasingly bitter struggle, did not stop at denouncing abuses; it succumbed to the temptation of expressing more and more positive opinions and falling, consciously or unconsciously, into the kind of distortion which consists in presenting only one aspect of a situation until it becomes a caricature. The opposition had described a reign of terror in the Saar and had given Germany a picture which, when passed on from one to another in conversation, in the *Saarbund*, and in the press, became generally accepted, especially since its acceptance made easier the justification of positions already taken. This distorted picture was nonetheless the basis on which the various political parties and even the government itself worked, and this in turn limited their freedom of action. The sacrifice of the Saar to Europe was already considered by the opposition as a betrayal by Germany, all the more blameworthy because it meant abandoning a German population to the domination of a tyrannical régime.[26]

Economic Interests

At a meeting of the Committee for Economic Policy held on January 26, 1955, Fritz Hellwig pointed out, by way of introduction to his analysis of the proposed Saar Statute, that it was not possible to reach a satisfactory settlement of the problem because the economy on which the political solution was dependent had not

[26] *Cf.*, on this subject, *infra*, pp. 283–286.

been able to develop according to its own dynamic impulse. If this " dynamism " could again exert its influence on the economy and if the Saar could once more let the larger part of its products flow into the south German market, then the time would be ripe for a solution of the Saar problem. This was how things had been prior to 1935. In fact, when in 1926 Saar products had been able to take their place on the German market, it had been plainly apparent to all those acquainted with the problem that the way was henceforth open for the political decision of 1935. Mr. Hellwig therefore added that care must be taken not to drift into adopting at this point a political solution that would make it impossible to re-orient the Saar economy towards the German market.[27]

A few years earlier, in the autumn of 1947, when this same Mr. Hellwig had received a mandate to draw up a memorandum on the economic relations between the Saar and its neighbours, he had been clearly given to understand that his inquiry must lead to the conclusion, on the political plane, that any unilateral solution must be avoided in the interests of the Saar, the Saar economy, Franco-German economic relations, and the new Europe. Any advantages which one side might seek to obtain temporarily could only be a burden on the other party concerned, with the Saar hemmed in between France and Germany.

Thus, from the beginning to the end of this debate, the consciousness of the interdependence of the economies was apparent, as was the anxiety to oppose the attempt on the part of France to break economic ties to her own profit. This is what Mr. Hellwig watched most particularly, following step by step France's policy of integrating the Saar's economy. He declared more than once that this integration amounted to a distraint put by France and the French on the Saar economy.[28] Mr. Hellwig was not the only one who was concerned with this problem. Dr. Strohm and those at the *Friedensbüro* and elsewhere who followed Saar affairs very closely in no way underestimated the importance of economic

---

[27] *Sitzung des Ausschusses für Wirtschaftspolitik* (*21. Ausschuss*), January 26, 1955. (Mimeographed.)

[28] We have mentioned several times the bulletins of the *Deutsches Industrieinstitut* entitled *Material zum Zeitgeschehen*. Here we refer especially to a study entitled *Die Behandlung des deutschen Wirtschaftsvermögens im Saargebiet seit 1945* (No. 1, mimeographed), which analyses in turn the position of the mines, of the sequestrated industries (iron and steel, metallurgy, cinema, banking), of the insurance companies, and of the railways, and concludes by noting the advantages accruing to France from the banks, insurance companies, savings banks, and public funds in the Saar. The study was made after the Agreement of October 23, 1954.

questions. Proof of this was to be found in the plans for Franco-German economic co-operation which were drawn up by various and sundry individuals between 1948 and 1950.[29]

It is important to know whether these efforts had any results, and in particular what the attitude was of business and industrial circles. Would not the German industrialists react against a French policy which robbed Germany of an important industrial centre? As Germans, did they not feel affected, their interests damaged? Would they not be the ones to protest most vigorously? Such was not the case. On the contrary, it seems, at least from the sources at our disposal, that industrial circles, far from pursuing an active course, remained passive. Some of them, it is true, sought information on the economic situation of the Saar, especially on those firms or groups that most concerned them. But they did not commit themselves, at least not in the beginning. It was only with some difficulty that they made up their minds to give material support to the activities of the *Saarbund*, the organization and development of which were held back by lack of funds as well as by the difficulties the promoters experienced in building up membership. Those who had the most immediate interests in the Saar were every bit as slow to move as the others.

Wherein lay the explanation of this attitude? Some of the industrialists would merely have said that they had more pressing tasks to attend to. Their attention was concentrated on the reconstruction of their own factories and the reconstitution of the economic infra-structure inside the Federal Republic. The Saar had been considered a marginal area. It was no longer a part of Germany. So, for the time being it was pushed to one side.[30] The difficulties German industry was encountering were not merely technical and financial; they were bound up with the political situation in Germany and the burden laid upon industry by decisions concerning reparations or by the intervention of the occupying Power. One large German firm with interests in the Saar refused

[29] Along with the plan for Franco-German co-operation drawn up by Mr. Strohm, *cf.* *Programmpunkte für eine deutsch-französische Industrie-Entente*, *op. cit.* See also a study at the end of 1949 for the Economic Committee of the European Movement entitled *Deutsch-französische Industrieverständigung*, to which are appended two other studies entitled *Die wirtschaftliche Seite der Saarfrage* and *Bemerkungen zur Frage einer französischen Kapitalbeteiligung*.

[30] "The problem was simply not an immediate one for the German economy," notes one of the representatives of Ruhr industry. "There was hardly money enough to carry out even the most urgent work in the Ruhr territory."

to provide the financial support for which it was asked because of
its own precarious situation as a result of the decision of the Military
Government to liquidate it.　Others were a little more generous.
They gave some money towards the launching of the *Saarbund*, for
instance, but they made it clear that their names must not be mentioned in connection with it in case it proved embarrassing to them.
Thus the Roechlings, who had every reason to see the status of the
Saar modified and a settlement reached permitting them to return
to Völklingen, showed themselves disposed to support certain
activities; they did so, but remained carefully in the background
and confined their help within very modest limits.

The worst difficulties were overcome in Germany, and in time
some firms came to modify their attitudes.　The economic and
political prospects were more hopeful.　The influence of the Federal
Republic was increasing.　The government could now speak with
the Allies, its recent conquerors, on equal terms.　So the risks were
less and there was again hope of being able to regain some of the
positions they had lost and of compelling the French to abandon the
monopoly they held.[31]　News from the Saar encouraged this hope,
not only the opposition's reports on its own activities but increasing
manifestations, publicly evinced by the Hoffmann Government, of
a desire to develop economic relations between the Saar and
Germany.　However, activities went forward cautiously.　The
Roechlings, who remained till the last minute under the threat of
nationalization held over them by Saarbrücken and Paris, negotiated with representatives of French industrial groups as though
they had lost all hope of going back to the Saar.　It was only after
they had been persuaded by Chancellor Adenauer to abandon their
share in Völklingen completely that they decided on a sustained
struggle against the Statute.　Even so, this position, dictated by a
natural reaction against a decision harmful to their interests, was
not typical of the attitude of German industrialists in the last phase

[31] The president of a German firm who in 1946 had had to give up his rights to an
important factory in the Saar to a French firm wrote these remarks at the end of
October, 1951, which he accompanied with a cheque to help the work of the *Saarbund*:
" It is clear to me that, from the viewpoint of prevailing civil law, such property
changes are almost unassailable.　But it is conceivable that if the Saar returned to
Germany, there might be an over-all revision of all actions taken on the assumption
that the *de facto* annexation of the Saar by France in 1945 would be ratified legally.
In any case, in my opinion an effort should be made to create the possibility of such
a revision in which naturally the interests of the participants must be justly considered
and weighed, as in the case of the restitution laws imposed upon Germany by the
occupying Powers.''

of the conflict. In the Ruhr, noted one of their representatives, the surprise caused by the result of the referendum of October 23 was complete and resulted in considerable confusion. How was the Saar economy to be integrated into that of Germany?

Mr. Hellwig stressed the dynamism of a Saar economy which was naturally oriented towards Germany. Were the German industrialists conscious, as he was, of the interdependence of interests? Judging by the detachment they showed, it would not seem so. Their caution was only equalled by that shown in economic circles in France. So we come to this paradoxical conclusion—that the Saar, united economically with France for political reasons, ran foul of the lukewarm reception of economic groups, a reception which flung it back into the arms of reluctant German industrialists.

The Role of Rheinland-Pfalz

The widely adopted slogan of the unity of the Saar-Lorraine Basin tended to distract attention from the Saar's neighbouring " country " of Rheinland-Pfalz. And yet this *Land*, or rather its inhabitants and those who governed it, played a part which should not be underestimated in the development of relations between Germany and the Saar and in the formulation of the Federal Republic's Saar policy.

This is not surprising. Rheinland-Pfalz, as we have seen,[32] was the only one of the *Länder* to have a common frontier with the Saar. Between these two countries, both German-speaking and with a German culture, there were close bonds. It was no mere chance that the United States, during her brief period of authority in the Saar, set up an administrative unit known as *Mittelrhein-Saar*.[33] The proximity of the two areas also encouraged constant economic exchanges; the Saar provided an outlet for agricultural products from the neighbouring Palatinate, whose metallurgical industries used Saar coal. Finally, and this was important, most of the inhabitants were Catholic, as were the Saarlanders, and like them were in the dioceses of Trier and Speyer.[34]

[32] *Cf. Historical Study*, pp. 52–53.
[33] *Cf.* Georg Kratz, *Mittelrhein-Saar*, *op. cit.*, pp. 9–12.
[34] *Cf.* the memorandum drawn up by the chancellery of Rheinland-Pfalz and published under the title *Der Saargrenzgürtel* (Mainz: 1954), p. 4. This memorandum, protesting against the separation of the Saar, said: " (a) That its concept amounts politically and administratively to nothing more than the amputation of parts of the communes of Trier, Coblenz, and Pfalz; (b) that, as for its population, the Saar is German and its inhabitants are of the same stock as those of the neighbouring German territory of

It was therefore not surprising that the reaction of Rheinland-Pfalz to the breaking of political ties between the Saar and Germany and to the economic orientation of the Saar towards France was immediate and vigorous; it was even less surprising because this new *Land* itself had to struggle for existence within a Germany in the process of rehabilitation, and the sacrifice [35] of territory exacted from it was weakening it in a most inopportune manner. Mr. Altmeier, who occupied the post of *Minister-Präsident* of Rheinland-Pfalz from 1947, was, moreover, born at Saarbrücken. Like many of the inhabitants of his " country " who numbered relatives and friends in the Saar, he was particularly attached to it; he considered himself the defender of the interests of the whole of Germany. But this mission, assumed on behalf of Germany, was not the only reason for his action. In his struggle for the return of the Saar, the existence of his own state was at issue, and also the future of a " Christian and conservative " policy. Rheinland-Pfalz had active enemies determined to eliminate a state which, as Mr. Altmeier said, was the fortress of what used to be called " ultramontanism " and which is now defined as political Catholicism or clericalism. Union with a Saar re-united with Germany would effectively consolidate its threatened position.

The *Minister-Präsident* for Rheinland-Pfalz thus led the struggle for the Saar with extraordinary energy. He was not one of the first to take a position publicly,[36] for, as we have already seen, Mr. Zimmer led the way in this.[37] But he was active. He returned ceaselessly to the charge with the Chancellor, afraid that the latter would allow himself to be persuaded to make too many concessions. It was not that Mr. Altmeier wanted to follow in the footsteps of Kurt Schumacher and abandon himself to chauvinist patriotism. He refrained from this and was very careful to keep his distance from the Socialists. But he was convinced that with firmness the

Rheinland-Pfalz; (c) that with the separation of the Saar an organically developed economy would be wilfully destroyed as well as its trade relations; (d) that at the same time there would also be the danger of fostering a separate cultural and political development in a region where close cultural ties with the neighbouring districts of Germany find expression, for example, in the field of church organization by belonging to the same dioceses and parishes."

35 *Ibid.*, pp. 5 *et seq.*

36 *Cf.*, in particular, the statements made on July 16, 1949, at Mainz at the C.D.U. Congress; also Mr. Altmeier's speech of August 9, 1949, at Trier.

37 According to some sources, there was no clearly formulated Saar policy in Rheinland-Pfalz until the autumn of 1948. But certain individuals, among them Mr. Zimmer, were very active in organizing an opposition.

problem could be resolved without calling into question Germany's European policy.

The influence of the government at Mainz made itself felt through various channels. A frontier province, Rheinland-Pfalz was in constant contact with the Saar. A centre of information, it was at the same time a base of operations. The *Deutsche Saarzeitung*, the *Freie Saarpresse*, and other illegal newspapers were printed there and sent secretly into the Saar. It was also in Rheinland-Pfalz that various demonstrations designed to impress the Saarlanders were organized; among these was the " Westricher Heimattag " at Coblenz and political conferences which brought together Germans and Saarlanders opposed to the régime.[38] Moreover, Karl Walz and Hermann Trittelvitz,[39] both Saarlanders, were chosen from the electoral lists of the C.D.U. and the S.P.D. for Rheinland-Pfalz as candidates for the Bundestag. Elected in 1953, they took their seats as " opposition deputies." [40]

The government of Rheinland-Pfalz was also in touch with one of the most ardent fighters in the struggle for the Saar, namely, the Bishop of Trier. It received from him information and encouragement in the struggle and was able to give the same to him in return. Through him and through the clergy, information and instructions were given.

The activities of Rheinland-Pfalz also made themselves felt within Germany. The *Saarbund* had received valuable moral and financial support from it. Inside the C.D.U. Mr. Altmeier and his companions in the struggle were not idle, and they stiffened the backs of certain leaders, such as Mr. Gerstenmaier, who were, they felt, too much inclined towards compromise. Finally, the Mainz Government made its views known to the members of the Federal Government and to the Administration. Its *chargé d'affaires* in Bonn, Mr. Hermans, was a remarkably well-informed man who made a point of keeping in close touch with the colleagues of the Chancellor, especially with high officials in charge of Saar questions, like Rudolf Thierfelder, or Wilhelm Bodens who was

---

[38] Mr. Altmeier, to quote one example, presided over the conference on July 9, 1955, at Trier, at which were present representatives of the C.D.U. of Germany and of the Saar, and of the *Syndicats chrétiens*; at this conference the decision was taken to vote against the Statute.

[39] There had been some question of Mr. Conrad at first. But he gave up the idea of being a candidate so as to be able to continue his work in the Saar.

[40] After their election these two men were deprived of their Saar nationality and expelled from the Saar.

particularly concerned with the Saar affairs in the Ministry for All-German Affairs. Thanks to him, Mr. Altmeier was able to follow closely the increasingly frequent negotiations between Mr. Adenauer and one or another of his close colleagues, such as Mr. Hallstein or Mr. Blankenhorn. He also had the opportunity of bringing his ideas directly to the attention of the Chancellor and of intervening when he wished, either to advise against recourse to a plebiscite and against negotiation with members of the Saar Government, or to suggest to the C.D.U. that it become not too committed in favour of the Statute, or, finally, to participate in drafting the provisions concerning the Saar and the referendum within the framework of Western European Union.

The advice or suggestions of the spokesmen of Rheinland-Pfalz were not always heeded. But their role was nonetheless decisive. It is a fact that their firmness on various occasions counterbalanced the influence of those in favour of compromise, and that this encouraged the Chancellor to take a stiffer position towards France and the Saar. It is still more clear that the rejection of the Statute on October 23, 1955, represented both a political defeat for Mr. Adenauer and a great victory for the government of Rheinland-Pfalz. Mr. Altmeier, who had voted out of party discipline for a Statute that he did not approve of, found in the rejection both revenge and the reward for his labours.

It in no way reduces the importance of the contribution of Rheinland-Pfalz to stress the contrast in the attitude of the two frontier regions, for the reservations of the people of Lorraine towards the Saarlanders facilitated the action of the Saar's neighbours in Rhineland Germany.

12

GROUP INFLUENCES IN THE SAAR

IN the struggle between France and Germany over the Saar, the role of the Saarlanders themselves should not be underestimated. The right of self-determination which was constantly invoked by both sides placed those who could take advantage of it in the position of arbiters. The attention with which both Germany and France followed the various polls that took place in the Saar between 1946 and 1955, the efforts made to influence them, the impassioned discussions to which they gave rise, were all proof of the importance attached to them. The governments of Paris and Bonn, which were fighting the diplomatic battle, were aware that no solutions could be implemented unless they obtained the sanction of the Saarlanders.[1] Their acceptance of the referendum of October 23, 1955, as a decision against which there was no appeal was logically consistent with their attitude throughout the previous years. They were bound more perhaps than they had realized, more than anyone thought at the time, by a principle which had acquired political force through constant use.

What were the factors in the Saar itself that governed the Saar decision? What was the part played by political, economic, and religious groups in a position to exert an influence on the life of their country? This is what must now be examined.

The Political Parties

The diffident resumption of political life in the Saar had been characterized at the beginning of 1946 by the formation of political parties. To be accurate, it was rather a question of re-construction, for the groups which were formed were naturally inclined to resume the political traditions that had been suspended under National Socialism. Despite the profound disturbances created by

[1] The Saarlanders were equally well aware of this. It should be noted in this context that 80 per cent. of Saarlanders questioned in April, 1955, declared that the decision on the future of the Saar was one for the Saar people. The inquiry was undertaken by the *Institut für Demoskopie. Cf. Jahrbuch der Oeffentlichen Meinung: 1947–1955* (Allensbach/Bodensee: 1956), p. 327.

the war, the structure of Saar society had not been destroyed. The same contrast persisted between the fragmentation of land and the concentration of industry; there was the same juxtaposition of peasant workers and a middle class consisting mainly of white-collar workers and officials stamped with Prussian tradition, of artisans and tradesmen. The influence of the Church had not weakened in this country where the Catholics represented 75 per cent. of the population and where the Protestant reaction was always that of the watchfulness natural to a minority.

Moreover, the men who presided over this fresh start were all, or almost all, old hands at politics who had served their apprenticeship under the Weimar Republic. The former members of the *Zentrum* chose the Christian People's Party approach, which was dominant after the war, while Socialists and Communists re-formed their parties which had been dissolved, parties they considered still part of the Social Democratic and Communist Parties of Germany.

It was not until after the parties had been formed that the problem of the status of the Saar arose as French plans became clearer. Divergences of opinion immediately began to appear. Within the C.V.P. there were three groups. The one led by Bartholomeus Kossmann, to which Father Bungarten belonged, stressed the Saar's links with the German Fatherland and maintained an aloof attitude which sometimes turned into outright opposition towards French policy. The weakest group was that of the members of the M.R.S., and the third group was the one led by Johannes Hoffmann. The struggle was short. The election of Mr. Hoffmann as leader of the party on February 10, 1946, assured victory for his policy, which henceforth became that of the party as a whole. Those who, like Father Bungarten, were not willing to conform were excluded. Mr. Kossmann, who was a very sick man, faded in the background. In any case he had not won the sympathy of the Military Government. The others approved or followed without protest. The few stray impulses towards independence evident among the *Junge Generation* had scarcely any influence on the party as a whole. This youth organization was dissolved in 1952 and replaced by a new group, *Jeune Sarre*, more tractable to the orders of the party leaders.

Within the Saar Socialist Party the struggle went on for some years between those who, like Ernst Roth, Kurt Conrad, and Friedrich Regitz, were trying to find a form of co-operation that did not entail a break in the bonds between the Saar and Germany and those who, like Peter Zimmer, Richard Kirn, and Heinz Braun, accepted not only economic union but autonomy. All were agreed in opposing the policy envisaged by the M.R.S. But once this solution had been abandoned, they fought with increasing asperity among themselves until the break that came in the spring of 1952. The S.P.S., like the C.V.P., had created youth organizations which initially were little concerned with political questions. However, tension did exist and it found expression in a clear-cut statement of position by the *Bund der Sozialistischen Jugend* in favour of its president, Friedrich Regitz, when he was engaged in openly opposing the policy of the S.P.S. The Committee of the Social Democratic Party tried in vain to bring back the *Bund* within its sphere of influence. When it realized that this could not be done, it decided to set up the *Sozialistische Arbeiterjugend* for which it obtained government authorization; at the same time the *Bund* was refused a licence.

In 1952 the situation was as follows: on the one hand there were the two parties—Christian People's and Socialist—in favour of an autonomous status. Despite the sometimes serious and disturbing differences of opinion that divided them on the subject of home affairs, they were nonetheless united in their common adherence to a foreign policy they knew was the mainspring of their existence. On the other hand, still fighting in scattered ranks were the opponents of a status implying a break with Germany. These opponents would have liked to join forces and organize themselves into a party in order to create a political force strong enough to dislodge the two parties currently in power. But Johannes Hoffmann, aware of their intentions and apprehensive at the idea that they might form within the existing framework an opposition designed to destroy the régime, worked unceasingly to keep them out of the electoral struggle and to limit their influence. He thus maintained a sort of monopoly which he shared with the S.P.S. Other centres around which opinion crystallized might well exist. But as long as they were excluded from the electoral struggle the two parties advocating the existing régime were the only ones to wield power and to maintain a legal existence. As the only official catalysts of public opinion and of the will of the people, they carried out a policy elaborated and implemented essentially by one man.

In this case the group was the instrument of the individual who inspired and dominated it.

There was nothing new in this method and it could be effective. For some years it seemed to work for Mr. Hoffmann. But though the President of the Saar Government knew how to defend himself against opposition at home, he was in no position to resist blows dealt from without. He had little or no influence in the diplomatic field where the Governments of France and the Federal Republic met; the decisions that concerned the Saar were taken independently of him, almost in spite of him. His prestige suffered in consequence. The fluctuations in French policy and the concessions to Germany could not but weaken the position of the defenders of the régime set up in 1947. Initially a source of uncertainty, these factors after the autumn of 1954 became the agent of disintegration. At the same time the recovery of Germany could not fail to strengthen the German opposition which found in this change in relative strength outside the Saar the means of increasing its own influence in the Saar despite the government. Also it was by means of an international agreement that this opposition found its place in the political life of the Saar. It was a triumphal entry, as we know, for in a few weeks the balance of strength was reversed. Thus the progress of the diplomatic struggle contributed to change the situation within the Saar, and, as a result, there was a decision contrary to what the diplomatists had hoped or foreseen and to which they were forced to yield.

What were the reasons that led people to take a position for or against an autonomous status? Wherein lay the explanation? Did the opposition of the anti-government political parties stem from differences in their social structure? Was it a question of the age of the members or the part of the country from which they came? Apparently not.

The social composition of the C.D.U. was virtually identical with that of the C.V.P. The two rival Socialist parties drew their members from the same lower-middle and working class circles. As for the re-modelled D.P.S., if it differed from the party founded in 1946, it was in the diversity of its membership. As an opposition party it had, in the space of a few years, rallied to itself the opposition forces from circles that did not normally adhere to it.

Age perhaps played some role in this. In the two parties favourable to the régime, the majority of members were over the age of forty. Both parties had difficulty with their younger groups. But this did not mean that the young people were won over in any numbers to the opposition. They reserved their position and did not commit themselves until the campaign for the referendum. In this their attitude was no different from that of most of the population. It must be stressed that the political parties represented only a small minority of the electorate: 10 per cent., according to some estimates.

Would a comparative study of the elections to the Landtag in 1947, 1952, and 1955, and of the referendum of October 23, 1955, provide additional information? At best the conclusions drawn from it might be less imprecise.[2] It appears that those regions with a constant tendency to opposition were of mixed faiths. In the east, there were the areas that had been most recently added to the Saar (the districts of Kusel and Birkenfeld) and the two communes of Webenheim and Brenschelbach. The Warndt area, very strongly opposed, was also of mixed faiths. In addition, there was a hard core of opposition in the Catholic west (Haustadt and the surrounding area) composed primarily of workers who, because they worked at some distance from home, came into contact with opponents of the régime. It was also apparent that areas in which miners represented more than 14 per cent. of the total population voted in 1955 more solidly against the Statute; they voted chiefly for the C.D.U. and then for the D.P.S. The regions more or less steadily favourable to the government were either near the French frontier or under the influence of some outstanding personality.

[2] *Cf.* Appendix III, Maps 7, 8, 9, 10, 11. An article by Fernand Dehousse published in the *Saarländische Volkszeitung* of February 9, 1956, contains some useful information: " *Wer sagte Nein, wer Ja?*" "Faced with these figures one cannot but draw a series of conclusions. For instance: the large majority participating in the elections, 96·5 per cent. of the voters went to the polls voluntarily and unhindered. This influx unquestionably reveals a deep-seated popular sentiment. The result: 67·72 per cent. No, 32·48 per cent. Yes. With the exception of a few electoral districts, these percentages were roughly constant throughout the territory. A somewhat more penetrating analysis shows—and this is very remarkable psychologically—that the lowlands (the clergy had not intervened) voted massively in the negative. But the working class also voted No. Proof of this is the fact that under the régime of free suffrage they had already formed a pro-German trade union and that this trade union captured more than three-quarters of all organized workers within a period of a few weeks. That a majority of the workers voted No seems all the more striking because this No ran counter to their closest and most obvious interests. The intellectuals by and large also voted No. Who then voted Yes? Largely the cities, the middle classes, those circles who have benefited from the customs and economic union with France." *Cf.* also Dehousse, " Mission en Sarre," *Bulletin de la Société belge d'études et d'expansion, op. cit.*

These personal influences were only to be expected in a country of such limited area with such a stable population. They were not, however, necessarily exerted in favour of the régime or of the Statute. Here are a few examples: Habkirchen and the neighbouring communes of Bliesbecken voted for the government; this was not only because of proximity to France but because of the influence of Erwin Müller, who came from Habkirchen. The commune of Schwarzerden, in the district of St. Wendel, voted for the S.P.S. from 1947 to 1955. In December it was the only commune in which the S.P.S. was still the strongest party. This was due to the activity of the Socialist deputy for the area. The faithful allegiance of Otzenhausen was also attributable to the influence of one man, Heinz Braun. Similarly, Neunkirchen, which gave 20–30 per cent. of its votes to the S.P.S., was the home of two S.P.S. deputies. Schiffweiler, the native heath of Richard Kirn and of an editor of the *Saarbrücker Zeitung*, gave 15–20 per cent. of its votes to the S.P.S. Another interesting case was that of the commune of Webenheim in the extreme south-east of the Saar, which steadfastly showed its opposition by voting for the D.P.S. or for the Communist Party and which, in 1952 and 1955, returned among the highest percentages of abstentions (*i.e.*, in 1952 more than 45 per cent. were abstentions, and in 1955, 90–100 per cent. were negative votes). The reasons behind the opposition of this agricultural population were not to be found solely in proximity to Germany but in a reaction against the competition of agricultural products coming in from Lorraine. The inhabitants of Brenschelbach, largely Protestants and mostly in the opposition, voted in December, 1955, for the C.D.U. The reason for this was that Julius von Lautz, a Protestant deputy in the Landtag, had convinced them that it was essential for the Christian forces to unite. We will give one more example of the influence of personality, in this instance that of the industrialist Luitwin von Boch-Galhau, which was the determining factor in Mettlach and the surrounding area, as is proved by the results.

But if it is possible to single out certain personal influences, it is harder to distinguish satisfactorily the more general factors in the complete reversal of relative strength. All that can be said is that, at a given moment, the west, mostly Catholic, swung over from the C.V.P. to its rival, the Christian Democratic Union, and that the D.S.P. took the place of the S.P.S.; also that the D.P.S. found most of its support in urban centres where, however, it had to reckon with the D.S.P. and the Christian parties. There were very varied motives at the root of this opposition of the parties. Above all, there were emotional reactions. The majority of Saarlanders felt themselves to be Germans; they were aware that they belonged to the *Deutschtum*. If some of them felt that economic co-operation with France was useful and were even prepared to pay for it by breaking political ties with Germany, there were others, more attached to their native country, who viewed the new policy as a betrayal. According to their individual temperaments, they either joined the battle immediately or waited to see what would happen. Personal background and circumstances chiefly explained the positions taken. If the flux included mainly the victims of National Socialism who had hoped to find in economic co-operation with the victor a remedy for an almost desperate situation, the reflux contained all those who waited in the beginning to see what would happen and those who, for various reasons, had had trouble with the French authorities or with the Hoffmann Government. There were also those who foresaw or counted on the reversal of the balance of forces between France and Germany.[3]

As for the Communist Party, it played scarcely any part in the struggle. Its position, like that of the Russian Government, did not change after 1947. Compelled, as was the S.P.S., to sever its connections with the German Communist Party, it nonetheless remained resolutely opposed to a policy of economic union with France. This opposition persisted through the years. It did not, however, prevent the Saar Communist Party from pursuing objectives that seemed to it more important or from vainly trying to win the working classes over to the Communist cause.

Economic Interests

Unconditional surrender placed Germany at the mercy of the Allies who could draw on the resources of the conquered country for compensation for the damage inflicted on them. Therefore, when the French installed themselves in the Saar, they considered they had the right to take over German possessions and assume control of the country's economic life. This operation was made easier by the fact that the Germans, whether owners or managers of the

---

[3] Further information on this can be found, *infra*, pp. 290 *et seq.*

industries, fell beneath the blow of the Allied provisions for de-nazification, even if, unlike Hermann Roechling, they were not labelled as war criminals.

After the first measures had been taken, a course of action had to be determined. This took more time because uncertainty over the future of the Saar and the contradiction between a policy of reparations and dismantling and one looking toward economic union complicated the working out of any plans and delayed their implementation. But once a decision had been taken in principle, the policy of economic union was methodically pursued. Sequestrations and the re-organization necessary to implement the economic union inevitably resulted in giving the French a controlling influence over the whole of the Saar economy. Mines, steelworks, the iron and steel and metallurgical industries, banks, insurance companies, and the railways all came directly or indirectly under French control. Frenchmen were also to be found at the head of the employers' federations that were being formed. Thus the president of the *Saarländischer Industriellen-Verband* was Georges Thédrel and its director was another Frenchman, Mr. Siedler. These two men held similar offices in the *Fédération sarroise des Chambres syndicales des métaux*, which included the *Chambre syndicale de la sidérurgie de la Sarre* (also headed by Mr. Thédrel and Mr. Siedler), and three other *Chambres syndicales* dominated by French interests: the *Chambre syndicale de la première transformation de l'acier en Sarre*, the *Chambre syndicale des fabricants de tubes en fer et en acier soudés, sans soudure et rejoints*, and the *Chambre syndicale des industries métallurgiques mécaniques et connexes*.[4] Mr. Thédrel was also president till 1950–51 of another employers' organization, *Arbeitsgemeinschaft der Arbeitgeber-Organisationen des Saarlandes*, and, in addition, he was naturally on the council of the Chamber of Commerce of Saarbrücken with another Frenchman, Frédéric Schlachter, representing

[4] In the *Chambre syndicale de la première transformation* . . . were sequestrated factories such as Georg Heckel, St. Ingbert and Luisenthal. For some years its president was a Frenchman. The *Chambre syndicale des fabricants de tubes* . . . also included some works which had been sequestrated, such as Bous and Homburg, as well as Brebach which was under French control; its president was a Frenchman. As for the fourth *Chambre*, in which were grouped approximately 400 Saar firms, it was presided over by a Saarlander who was an ardent supporter of economic union. It should be noted that this preponderance of Frenchmen in the *Fédération sarroise des Chambres syndicales des métaux*, that is, in the most powerful group because of the importance of the industries it represented, assured French influence within the *Saarländischer Industriellen-Verband*.

banking, who was in turn president and vice-president until the elections of 1952.[5]

So the French grip on the economic life of the Saar was such that the most powerful economic groups were beyond the control of the Saar Government. But they were not outside that of the High Commissioner. Does that mean they were instruments of his own policy? To say this would be going too far. For, however active Mr. Grandval may have been in the re-organization of the Saar economy, however careful to put his own men into positions of authority, he nevertheless had to take into account the opinion of his government, the interventions of the French Government departments, and the reactions of employers' organizations in France.

As for the Saarlanders who might have had reasons to protest against this *présence française,* they remained mute for a long time. It has been said that this was a question of temperament; it was more a question of a conscious recognition that resistance was useless. The great leaders of industry had been eliminated. Many owners of middle- and small-sized enterprises were compelled to be careful because of the threat of being accused of collaboration with the National Socialist régime. Thus they preferred to work for the recovery and developments of their own businesses rather than run risks in the political field where the opponent had the advantage over them. This same caution prevailed amongst those in charge of the banks and insurance companies. Economic union, moreover, presented certain advantages. For some it might even be said that the opening of the French market was a source of valuable profit and gave rise to high hopes.

The situation changed in time. The French gradually withdrew from the positions they held, either on their own initiative and in conformity with a policy designed to give full autonomy to a europeanized Saar, or under the pressure of circumstances or of opposition from the Saar and from Germany. From 1950 onwards, Saarlanders began to occupy posts in economic institutions previously held by Frenchmen. In the Chamber of Commerce of Saarbrücken, for example, Frédéric Schlachter exchanged the presidency for the vice-presidency and he left the Council at the end of

---

[5] Mr. Schlachter was not unknown to the Saarlanders. He was director and co-owner of a private bank in the Saar from 1920 and a partisan of the *status quo* on Mr. Hoffmann's side. He did not leave Saarbrücken until after the plebiscite of 1935.

1952.[6] Georges Thédrel faded gradually into the background. Theodor Jansen, who was reputed to be in favour of economic union, in 1954 gave up the presidency of the Chamber of Commerce which he had held since 1950. And it was under the auspices of his successor, Kurt Lenhard, that the manifesto was published in the spring of 1954 in which this institution demanded the opening of the German market.

A comparable development took place in other institutions. In the artisans' association (*Handwerkskammer*), founded in 1946, Louis Arend, a member of the M.R.S. sympathetic to the policy of economic union, was replaced as president in January, 1951, by Wilhelm Maurer,[7] an independent who had differences of opinion with the French director. The tendency to opposition, already noticeable at the end of his term of office, increased during that of his successor, Alois Keller, and the new director, Karl-Heinz Buchholz, a member of the D.P.S.

Certain influential posts in the administration of the workers' association (*Arbeitskammer*), which during the early years had been in the hands of men connected with the S.P.S., were taken over by trade unionists opposed to the government.[8]

In the middle classes, the opposition was also gaining ground. The *Bloc sarrois des classes moyennes*,[9] formed on July 8, 1952, rose almost immediately against the Hoffmann Government. Its programme, as set out in the *Saarhandwerker* of July 15 and October 15, 1952, included the setting up of an economic council, fiscal reform, and the drafting of a joint financial policy, especially as far as credit was concerned. According to its president, Hermann Wildt, who represented the retail trade, the Franco-Saar economic union placed this trade in a very difficult situation. Quotas and licences were shackling business. The people wanted German

---

6 According to some sources, groups in close touch with the Chamber of Commerce apparently had already manifested their opposition during the electoral campaign of 1952.

7 Mr. Maurer was *elected* president, while his predecessor had been *appointed*. Thus this first election, judging by the comments in the *Saarhandwerker* of July 31, 1950, December 20, 1950, January 15, 1951, assumed the character of a show of independence towards the authorities.

8 *Cf.* Robert Schmidt, *Saarpolitik 1945–1947*, Vol. III, Pt. III.

9 *Saarländischer Mittelstandsblock*. This *Bloc* included various organizations representing the wholesale and retail trades, the artisan classes, and the co-operatives. The *Saarhandwerker* of November 30, 1952, gave some information on the aims, if not on the importance, of this group. It gave what amounted to an analysis of the structure of this middle class which it claimed to represent and which, according to its reckoning, comprised 80,000 to 100,000 electors.

goods.[10] The skilled workers, for their part, complained that the market open to them was much too restricted; they were cut off from Germany and had no real opportunity to penetrate the French market. They also felt the inadequacy of medium- and long-term credits.[11] Their demands were presented in a fairly vigorous manner in the plan for immediate action approved at the end of the demonstration of October 12, 1952, in Saarbrücken. The leaders of the *Bloc* demanded with special insistence the "real" integration of the Saar into the European economy. This implied recognition of the interdependence of the markets of the Saar, Germany, and France, and consequently the establishment of supplementary quotas of German goods in the transition stage towards europeanization.[12]

The influence of the *Bloc sarrois des classes moyennes* is hard to assess. Some who underlined the break at the very beginning with the peasant group which had joined it [13] pointed out that actually the *Bloc* was known only for the one demonstration it organized on October 12, 1952, in Saarbrücken.[14] These observers believe that the divergent interests of the tradesmen and the artisans doomed the *Bloc* to failure from the outset. This judgment seems somewhat arbitrary. If the *Bloc* could not engage in constant political activity along with the political parties, it nevertheless served as a rallying point for the opposition. Its leaders were active in the opposition. Hermann Wildt and Manfred Schäfer, director of the *Bloc* from

---

[10] The Saarlanders had profited from the lessening of trade restrictions to make purchases in Germany where they found goods answering their tastes. So they must have been even more conscious of the trade restrictions when France re-imposed the quota system in January, 1952.

[11] *Cf.*, among others, *Zur Kreditlage der saarländischen Wirtschaft* (Deutsches Industrie-institut, n.d.). (Typed memorandum.)

[12] " 1. Re-organization of the economic administration of the Saar in the sense of a true integration with the economy of Europe as a whole;
  " 2. Sufficient consideration of the fact that the Saar economy has its market oriented both towards Germany and towards France;
  " 3. During the transition period before europeanization, creation of supplementary import quotas covering German investments and consumer goods within the framework of foreign exchange surpluses in the Saar."

[13] *Saarländischer Bauernverein*. Robert Schmidt, author of *Saarpolitik 1945–1957, op. cit.*, points out that, according to information given him, the break took place because of the intervention of Mr. Kurtz, at the time Secretary of State and president of the *Landwirtschaftskammer*. According to the same source, the *Bauernverein* was less loyal in 1954; reactions to the policy of the Hoffmann Government began to be manifest. Furthermore, Mr. Kurtz left the presidency of the Chamber of Agriculture, and his successor did not seem to be so favourable to the government.

[14] *Cf. Saarhandwerker*, November 30, 1952. Two demonstrations which took place at Völklingen on October 27, 1954, and April 28, 1955, to protest against French attempts to take over the Roechling factories, were organized by the retail trades' association (*Landesverband des Saarländischen Einzelhandels*) directed by Mr. Wildt.

1953, belonged to the C.D.U.; Mr. Buchholz to the D.P.S. The *Bloc's* newspapers, *Saar-Handel* and the *Saarhandwerker*, regularly took the Hoffmann Government to task for its policy.[15]

The modifications that took place within some of the important economic groups and the resultant change in trend obviously contributed to a reversal in the relationship of forces favourable to or against an autonomous status and economic union. To what extent this was so it is very difficult to say, particularly as the groups themselves were subjected to the influence of developments that took place on the political plane, both within the Saar and abroad.[16] Opinion, moreover, was not unanimous: some wanted the opening of the German markets [17]; others feared that a modification of the régime might jeopardize outlets they had already obtained for themselves in France.[18] The Saar ceramic industry had managed to supply the French market with almost 65 per cent. of its wall tiles and 40 per cent. of its floor tiles. Thus it is not surprising that there were certain moves [19] during the election campaign to put off the referendum. There was a diversity of material interests and a diversity of reactions. While the Roechling family supported the partisans of rejection, others feared their victory. But however powerful either side might be, it could exert only a limited influence, given the wave of feeling on which the Saarlanders were borne along during the summer and autumn of 1955.

Should we conclude from this brief analysis that Saar employers as a body, especially the employers' federations, played almost no part in the struggle for the Saar? This would be exaggerated. Their potentiality for influence in this industrial country must have weighed in the balance of political forces. We have noted that, in the beginning, their influence was exerted in favour of economic union, the activities of employers or of economic organizations having been in some ways both an extension of and a support to

15 The *Saarhandwerker*, from its first number of January 20, 1949, was extremely critical of the government. From the beginning it mingled with its demands of a professional nature political opposition directed to Johannes Hoffmann and the C.V.P., but aimed at the régime set up in the Saar by France. Apparently, Heinrich Schneider played a role in this group of skilled workers, and a memorandum criticizing the fiscal system in the Saar, which was distributed in October, 1948, came largely from his pen. The *Saar-Handel* was much more moderate in tone.
16 Mr. Wildt in an interview with Robert Schmidt pointed out that the opposition became more and more centred in economic and occupational groups because it could not find expression on the political level through a political party.
17 This was the position of wholesalers and retailers of textiles and furniture.
18 For instance, the transforming industries and ceramics.
19 *Cf. Historical Study*, p. 194.

the High Commissioner. Subsequently, as the French hold on the
Saar slackened, a change took place within employer and professional organizations, sometimes in the direction of strong opposition to France and the régime, sometimes in the direction of
favouring greater autonomy for the Saar in order to reflect more
accurately the inter-penetration of the economic interests of the Saar
and its two great neighbouring countries.

The Trade Unions

Of all the organized interest groups in the Saar, it was unquestionably the unions that played the most important, or rather the
most decisive, part.

Why was this? First, because the unions represented a major
element in this industrial country: some 240,000 workmen out of
a total population of 980,000. Of these 240,000, more than 60,000
were mine workers and almost 40,000 were iron and steel workers.[20]
Another reason for the decisive role of the unions was the sound-
ness of an organization based on traditions which, while they did
not go back very far, were nevertheless very strong.[21]

The post-war atmosphere was favourable to trade unionism.
The unions were soon authorized to re-form: in 1945 permission
was given to the *Syndicat unitaire,* which included workers, white-
collar workers, and civil servants, grouped by type of work. The
strongest and most dynamic of these was the *Syndicat unitaire des
mineurs.* The *Syndicats chrétiens de Sarre* were formed a little
later in 1947, with the support of the C.V.P., and they also classified
their members by types of activity.

The attitude of the two trade union organizations was not
unfavourable to economic union. The first president of the
Syndicat unitaire, Heinrich Wacker, had returned to the Saar after

[20] *Cf. Saarländische Bevölkerungs- und Wirtschaftszahlen, op. cit.* The figures given
here are as of December 31, 1954. Number of inhabitants: 987,650, of whom 242,997
were workmen and 68,982 white-collar workers; the mines absorbed 65,519 and the
iron and steel industry, 39,986.

[21] In his *Etude sociologique sur la Sarre* (unpublished ms.), Georges Goriély recalls the
paternalist policy of the Stumm era which, for a long time, kept the Saar workers docile.
But, as he also points out, they made up for lost time during the inter-war period and
energetically sought to achieve their emancipation. *Cf.,* also, Muller, *op. cit.,* p. 149.
Mr. Muller makes the following observation: "It is noteworthy that the Saar miner
has the benefit of an exceptionally good organization. At the slightest dispute, one
comes up against a host of bodies and associations of a social nature which equip,
house, hospitalize, and even bury the miner. Historically, this organization was an
expression of the strong reaction to the repressive measures taken by the Prussian
Government." Also Francis Roy, *Le mineur sarrois* (Paris: 1954).

years of exile and was in favour of Franco-Saar co-operation. Hans Ruffing, president of the *Syndicat chrétien*, had a similar attitude. The workers, like their leaders, had more urgent concerns than the future status of the Saar. They had their living to earn; in order to do this, they had to rebuild their factories and get them working again. Collaboration with France offered an opportunity of doing this. Above all, it enabled them to escape the dismantling of their plants, a disaster particularly dreaded by a traditionally sedentary population of workers who were attached to their own trade and to the bit of earth they cultivated.[22]

However, the shock produced by the crisis following the introduction of the French franc and of the various measures involved in economic union destroyed over-optimistic illusions and compelled a change of attitude. The protests heard at the time were perhaps not numerous; the crisis and the tension to which it gave rise calmed down. Nevertheless, as we have noted, some of the grievances that were to be developed later had already become manifest. Hence, for example, the complaint of the *Syndicat unitaire des mineurs* which had agreed to approve the policy of economic union because it had been promised that the mines would be nationalized.[23]

The feeling of having been tricked remained. It explained the unwavering opposition, in 1948 and 1950, to leasing the mines to France and the open break when the first Franco-Saar Conventions were being negotiated. Aloys Schmitt, who was then the representative of the *Syndicat unitaire des mineurs*, was not opposed to a joint Franco-Saar administration of the mines on condition that Saarlanders were placed on an equal footing with Frenchmen.[24] But he was categorically opposed to leasing the mines, which meant, in effect, a " leasing out of the miners." He also pointed out that the Saarlanders spoke German and thought in German. If France were sole owner of the mines, he said, one would not need the gift of prophecy to forecast as of now which way the " spirit of the people " of the Saar would go once national feeling had been

[22] This observation applies essentially to the miners. (Sixty-five per cent. of them lived in places having less than 10,000 inhabitants and 35 per cent. in places of less than 5,000 inhabitants. *Cf.* Muller, *op. cit.*, p. 139.) The iron and steel workers were grouped in urban centres near their factories.

[23] This promise is supposed to have been made to the Military Government by the man responsible for trade union affairs, Mr. Rieth.

[24] He had started by demanding that the presidency of the *Conseil des mines*, one of the major bodies, be given to a Saarlander. Later he agreed to an alternating presidency.

aroused by increased pressure from Germany.[25] Others were also of this opinion. Among these was Paul Kutsch. The representatives of the *Syndicat chrétien des mineurs*, though more moderate in tone, also agreed with this position. The government, however, did not follow their example.

From then on, the gap between the Saar Government and the *Syndicat unitaire des mineurs* widened. The measures taken by Johannes Hoffmann to bridge the gap proved vain. This first revolt acted as a catalyst. The miners' opposition won over other unions. Their resistance was encouraged by the German unions with which contacts developed, while the language barrier, and also Communist influence in the C.G.T., made co-operation with the French unions more difficult. The opposition found perpetual fuel in the difficulties of everyday life and these provided a source of constant complaint against the government and, through the government, against France.[26]

Trade union opposition also contributed to the break-up of the S.P.S. Mr. Conrad and Mr. Regitz found in the unions the basic staff organization and the personnel they needed for the struggle on the political as well as on the professional level. The government was thus gradually driven to the defensive. The measures it took for its own protection were virtually useless. The dissolution of the *Syndicat des mineurs* which followed the sanction against Mr. Kutsch could not check the forward thrust of the opposition. On the contrary the measures taken by the government seemed to act as a stimulus.

Mr. Hoffmann should have been able to count on the support of the *Syndicats chrétiens*, but even there he ran into increasing difficulties, despite the withdrawal of Karl Hillenbrand who was the first to oppose the policy of Franco-Saar economic union. The leaders of the *Syndicats chrétiens* also had to take into account the wishes of their members; they could support the government only to the extent they were sure their men would follow them. Some of the moves made by the *Syndicat unitaire* compelled them to take similar positions. There was nothing surprising, for example, in the previously mentioned letter [27] from Hans Ruffing to Mr. Schuman

[25] *Pariser Verhandlungen* (February, 1950), p. 23. (Typed memorandum.)
[26] *Cf. Historical Study*, pp. 102 *et seq.* It has already been pointed out that the trade union press was generally characterized by its opposition frame of mind.
[27] *Cf. Historical Study*, p. 83, note 22.

after the signing of the Franco-Saar Conventions, demanding modification and expansion of Saar autonomy. How could the president of the *Syndicat chrétien des mineurs* accept an agreement the *Syndicat unitaire des mineurs* was openly combating as contrary to the interests of the Saar workers? It was not surprising either that there should develop in the Christian trade union press an increasingly vigorous criticism of the government. There was a moment when the intervention of the *Syndicats chrétiens* contributed to a decisive stand. At the beginning of July, 1955,[28] the C.D.U. was still hesitating as to what course to take. Should it recommend a negative vote? Trade union leader Peter Hahn, representing the *Syndicat chrétien des cheminots* and the public utilities and metallurgical unions, intervened to assert that the *Syndicats chrétiens* could support the C.D.U. only if it came out in favour of a negative vote.

The Clergy

An analysis of the results of the November, 1952, elections to the Landtag made by a French observer contained the comment that the influence of the clergy was decisive throughout: where the clergy was good, so were the results; where the clergy was bad, the results were bad.

This observation reflects a fairly widely held view. Mr. Grandval, in particular, constantly asserted that the intervention of the clergy had considerable weight in Saar policy and that its influence was exerted to the detriment of France: hence the desperate struggle on the diplomatic level as well as within the country to win over this potential influence or at least to prevent the incursions of the clergy into politics.

To what degree did this opinion correspond to reality? Was the role of the Saar clergy as decisive as has been claimed?

One basic fact must not be overlooked: 75 per cent. of Saarlanders were Catholics.[29] But what was even more important, their Catholicism was not merely *pro forma*, existing only in statistics. Saar Catholics for the most part faithfully observed their religious duties and consequently the influence of the Church upon them was strong.

[28] A meeting took place at Trier, and there were some forty leaders of the Saar and the German C.D.U. present.

[29] *Cf.* Appendix III, Map No. 5.

The fact that the Saar was included in the dioceses of Trier and Speyer also played a part.[30] The Bishop of Trier, Monsignor Franz Bornewasser, had already taken a position during the campaign which had preceded the plebiscite of 1935, as indeed had his predecessor.[31] The Bishops of Speyer and Trier had stepped in more than once to remind the Saarlanders of their duty towards their German Fatherland. In this connection, the telegram of July 29, 1934, sent to President Hindenburg is worthy of note: " Fifty thousand young Catholic men and women of the territory of the Saar, meeting in Saarbrücken together with the Bishops of Trier and Speyer to demonstrate their Catholic faith, present to the head of the German Reich their unshakable confidence in Germany's westward march." [32]

After the war, Monsignor Bornewasser reminded the Saarlanders of the ties binding them to their German Fatherland in a very firm pastoral letter which, as we have seen,[33] provoked a very strong reaction on the part of the Military Government in the Saar. His successor, Monsignor Mathias Wehr, adopted a similar attitude. Although his tone was more moderate, there was no doubt as to his opinion. More than once he approached the Hoffmann Government on behalf of the opposition which was trying to band together in the Saar C.D.U.

To what must one attribute this determined opposition of the Bishops to French policy in the Saar? The fact that the Saar territory comprised the richest part of the bishopric of Trier must doubtless have been a major consideration. The Bishop of Trier could not remain unmoved when faced with a policy designed to establish a Saar bishopric, thus amputating his diocese and diminishing its resources. There were also other motivations besides this one: an instinctive reaction to change, the weight of tradition—heavier in the case of a bishop of Trier who could claim to be heir to the far-off Prince-Electors of the Holy Roman Empire. That men like Monsignor Bornewasser and Monsignor Wehr were convinced of

---

[30] *Ibid.*, Map No. 6.
[31] *Cf.*, on this subject, Maxime Mourin, " Le Saint-Siège et la Sarre," *Politique étrangère, op. cit.*, pp. 411–426. The author refers to the statement made in 1919 by the Bishop of Trier, Monsignor Korum: " We must at all costs keep strong the faith of the Saarlanders. They must know that now, as before, I am still their bishop. Religious unity must be preserved whatever happens. It is the solid link which unites the faithful people of the Saar with the German Fatherland." *Ibid.*, p. 413.
[32] *Ibid.*, p. 415.
[33] *Cf. Historical Study*, p. 53; also Mourin, *op. cit.*, p. 419. Father Franz Bungarten has included the text in his pamphlet, *Ich darf nicht schweigen* (Cologne: 1951), pp. 49–54.

the close link in this region between Catholicism and Germanism, that they felt imbued with a mission to defend the German Fatherland, was scarcely surprising.[34]

This intervention of the Bishop of Trier endangered the realization of Mr. Hoffmann's plans. Thus Mr. Hoffmann did all in his power to win the Saar clergy to his cause, either by hastening the rebuilding of churches and presbyteries, by subsidies, or, in some cases, by the elimination of those like Father Bungarten who opposed him.

The President of the Saar, however, does not appear to have been very successful. According to Father Bungarten, this was because almost all the Saar clergy considered themselves to be German. In his opinion, not more than seven priests refused to sign the petition he addressed to the Pope at the beginning of 1947 asking that the Saar be retained within the bishopric of Trier.[35] Father Bungarten conceded that some of the priests did not draw the logical conclusion and thought that a policy of autonomy was compatible with their attachment to Germany. In fact, the opposition to Mr. Hoffmann's policy was not as great as his adversaries declared or would have liked. Though the resistance we have already referred to[36] hardened, hesitations and fluctuations were nonetheless manifest, attributable probably to personal reactions and circumstances and to the reserve shown by the Holy See throughout the whole of this period.

The attitude of the Vatican to the appeals from both sides is well known. Following a tradition that had guided it between 1918 and 1935, it refused to create the Saar bishopric asked for by the French Government and merely appointed an " Apostolic Visitor " in the person of Monsignor Schulien.[37] The decision

---

34 A French observer makes the following remarks on the psychological and human background in the Saar: " The first major factor, the most basic naturally, is the German one. . . . The second major factor is Catholicism." " Let us not forget," he adds, " that in the Saar we are at the entrance to the famous *Pfaffengasse*. The human infra-structure of the Saar belongs historically to the lands bordering the Rhine. These are, without any doubt, the most Catholic in Europe, not only in terms of spiritual dogma but of temporal activity in a specific area that is the essence of political life." *L'évolution de l'opinion publique en Sarre de 1945 à janvier 1949* (March 15, 1949). (Unpublished manuscript.)

35 *Cf.* Bungarten, *op. cit.*, pp. 44–48. According to him, 351 priests signed this petition.

36 For example, that of Dean Braun. Among the active opponents should also be mentioned Father Fassbender, almoner of Saar youth. Administrative correspondence obviously contains the names of a certain number of ecclesiastics who manifested their opposition with particular vigour. But it is not possible to name them, any more than it is to draw up lists of those for and against the Statute.

37 The Apostolic Visitor was not a diplomatic representative. He had no mandate to speak or act in the name of the Vatican but had to refer back to Rome. He had no diplomatic privileges but was allowed to use the cipher.

contributed indirectly to a weakening of the French position, for it emphasized the provisional nature of the régime instituted in the Saar. Yet it could not be interpreted as open approval of the attitude of the Bishop of Trier and the priests in favour of the return of the Saar to Germany. Monsignor Schulien was extremely cautious; he tried to exercise a soothing influence and to prevent the clergy from slipping into politics. He succeeded only imperfectly because he did not have the authority to intervene directly with those priests who were being incited to opposition by their superiors in the hierarchy.[38] Nothing revealed the limits of his influence more than the episode of the November, 1952, pastoral letter; the Holy See forbade that it be read, but the contents were nonetheless known before the interdict was announced and were widely disseminated afterwards without any move by the Bishop to ensure respect for the Pope's instructions.

In 1955, however, during the campaign for the referendum, Monsignor Schulien intervened with greater success. At the end of September he made a statement reminding people that " in the opinion of the Church, all electors are free to vote according to their conscience. . . . Let them not forget that it is their religious duty to protect the rights of the Church and that they bear their share of responsibility in all that concerns the well-being of their native land." [39] The appeal did not fall on deaf ears. The Saar clergy, which was not this time encouraged to act by the Bishops of Trier and Speyer, remained aloof or apparently so. Was this out of discipline or because the arrival on the scene of unauthorized parties and their rapid development gave promise that final success was sure—hence the clergy had no need to commit itself openly?

The Apostolic Visitor's efforts at restraint may have had some effect, but only in the final phase. In the preceding years, when the struggle was at its height, they had little influence against the constant pressure exerted by a clergy largely committed to the

---

[38] Other efforts were made to exert influence on the Saar people from outside by using the clergy as a go-between. Here is an example of a programme planned at a later date, at the beginning of 1955, taken from private correspondence, *Aktion zur Unterrichtung der Geistlichkeit*: " The plan is that every fourteen days a ' personal letter from the former Catholic Party Deputy Diel' should be printed in an attractive format. About 2,800 copies of it will be needed for the Catholic clergy in the Trier and Speyer dioceses (including the Saar) and another 1,000 copies for the Protestant clergy in the same territory. The campaign should run from now until the end of the elections to the Landtag.''

[39] *Cf.* Mourin, *op. cit.*, p. 422. The statement was published on September 27, at the request of Monsignor Schulien, in the *Saarländische Volkszeitung* and the *Neueste Nachrichten*.

return of the Saar to Germany and supported by the top officials in the hierarchy. At the most, the aloofness of the Holy See and its refusal to take sides could but serve to encourage Catholics favouring an autonomous status or europeanization to hold firm against the appeals which came, via the clergy, from Germany. These supporters of Johannes Hoffmann were neither as few nor as weak as their opponents maintained: the December 18, 1955, elections to the Landtag gave twelve seats to the C.V.P., as against fourteen to the C.D.U., thirteen to the D.P.S., and seven to the S.P.D. The communal elections of May 13, 1956, gave 23·3 per cent. of votes to the C.V.P. as against 26·9 per cent. to the C.D.U. The division of votes between the two parties, which opposed each other not on religious or denominational but on political grounds, is a valuable indication, even if only an approximate one, of the attitude of the Catholic voters towards the Statute. One might conclude that the influence of the clergy had not been brought to bear in favour of Germany in a manner as decisive as was claimed by those endeavouring to restrain it.

The Evangelical Church

The Evangelical Church did not have much influence in the Saar, judging solely by the number of its adherents. But the circles in which this influence was exerted were not without contacts or power.

However, the attitude of the Church was characterized by an intentional aloofness from politics. At the outset, its leaders [40] stated that the Church as such had no business interfering in a political struggle; the Christian, solely in his capacity as a citizen, took responsibility for his own decision. This was a basic principle to which the Evangelical Church remained faithful; it was reiterated on various occasions, particularly in a broadcast on October 22, 1955, in which it was made clear that opinions expressed by pastors committed only themselves.

Certain pastors felt that it was their right, even their duty, to take a position. Some of them expressed their opinion at the time of the elections of November, 1952. Still more did so during the campaign for the referendum and the majority opted to reject the

---

[40] Most of the Evangelical Church of the Saar (formerly Prussian) was attached to the *Rheinische Landeskirche*, the seat of which was at Düsseldorf. The other section of it belonged to the Church of the Palatinate with its seat at Speyer.

Statute. This was true of Superintendent Zickwolf of Dillingen, at a meeting of the synod of the district of Völklingen on July 4, 1955. At the beginning of 1955, Superintendent Zickwolf, along with thirty-three Saar pastors, had signed an appeal published in a tract urging people to vote against the Statute.

The number of signatures was impressive.[41] It showed where the sympathies of most members of the Evangelical Church lay.

There are certain conclusions to be drawn from this analysis of the structure of the development of the various political, economic, and denominational groups which were in a position to influence and crystallize public opinion in the Saar.

One can see how the government, which initially could legitimately claim that its policy was founded on consensus, was gradually forced into isolation or on to the defensive. In 1947 the only active opposition came from the clergy under the influence of the Bishop of Trier. Apart from this, there were several critics, not very many, apathetic, resigned, or inclined to sit on the fence. After 1950 the situation changed. The trade unions changed sides. The French hold on the country's economy loosened. The opposition, kept out of politics, took refuge in professional organizations where it set up cells and extended its influence over the whole country. It was all the more effective because it operated out of the most varied centres. In 1954 the government had against it not only the clergy but the trade unions and professional organizations[42] which represented, or claimed to represent, trade and the artisan classes. The Chamber of Commerce of Saarbrücken came out publicly in favour of the expansion of trade with Germany, which implied a loosening of the economic union with France. Johannes Hoffmann was so conscious of his isolation that he sought to modify a policy that no longer had majority support. But he no longer had the authority necessary for success. The man had worn himself out at the same time as the policy he embodied.

---

[41] The only pastor to take a position in favour of the Statute was Pastor Roederich-Richter of Saarlouis, who published his opinion on October 18, 1955, in the *Saarländische Volkszeitung*.

[42] The opposition had even won over the Administration as was seen in the autumn of 1952 in the critical attitude of the *Beamtenbund* (set up in October, 1950). On the other hand, the ex-servicemen's associations remained under the influence of the C.V.P. Apparently, however, they were not interested in political activities.

13

PUBLIC OPINION

THIS is a problem that can never be approached without some uneasiness. What is "public opinion," this half-sleeping monster that everyone seeks to chain or unleash according to his interests? How can one grasp or guess what it is? How measure its influence? Despite numerous studies of public opinion and the substantial progress made in public opinion polls and in carrying out press inquiries and analyses, the findings are still very tentative.

Work in progress on "pressure groups" and on various kinds of associations which are foci of certain sections or currents of public opinion has undoubtedly provided useful information, as has been seen in the case of the Saar. But these studies relate only to limited circles. Such groups or associations represent only a small fraction, even if perhaps the most active or the most turbulent, of public opinion. Alongside these "organized congeries" there is the great mass of the silent population which, nevertheless, continues to exist; its opinion, even though not openly expressed, is a force all the more formidable because there is no way of knowing where its sympathies lie.

There are those who claim to express it or to describe it; this is one of the hopes and pretensions of the journalist. But when a journalist describes a situation, expresses opinions, reconstructs currents of thought or trends, he can in fact speak only for himself. It is his own view of men and problems that he is giving, and his own interpretation of events and attitudes. And sometimes this interpretation is more influenced by the traditions, techniques, and orientation of his professional background than by the society he observes or the instructions he receives.[1] The conditions under

[1] There is a tendency, in our opinion, to overestimate the influence of the owner of a newspaper on the editor. No doubt the position varies from one paper to another. In the case of those with which we are concerned, the number of papers where the degree of material dependency takes the form of an intellectual and moral subordination of the journalist to the owners or their representatives is very small. The influence of the owner shows much more in the selection of managers and chief editors whose views are in line with his own than in actual instructions given. An increasingly marked tendency is noticeable in the press in recent years to assert the rights of the journalist, to defend his ideas and convictions against the owner. Thus the tendencies of a newspaper cannot be adequately defined merely by identifying the owners or the

which a newspaper is put together, the strain under which a journalist works, wherein he is pressed for time, compelled to comment even if he has nothing to say, obsessed with the need to give something striking to the reader, and therefore inclined to dramatize, to look for catch phrases and for the most salient subjects and characteristics—all this leads to loss of contact with reality, a phenomenon frequently discussed though its importance and implications are not always given sufficient weight. Between the fact and the representation of the fact there is often a complete gulf; the very men responsible for this are duped because they are deluded by the interweaving of commentary and fact, hypothesis and statement; they are victims of a perpetual slipping from conditional to actual and of a confusion between reporting and direct quotation.

Thus the picture of reality presented by the press becomes reality for those who look at it and even for those who paint it. Men argue and order their conduct not on the basis of what really happened but on what they are told happened. Just as the picture given of the fact becomes " the fact," so, too, the version given of public opinion becomes public opinion. This may be termed an allegation that cannot be proven, but it may be less questionable than appears at first sight, since the opinion of the man in the street about an event is inevitably conditioned by the version of it given to him. Obviously, the identification is not complete. The number of newspapers, the often contradictory opinions of some of the commentators who have penetrated the surface imagery to get to the sources, all contribute, as does social background, to keep a certain critical spirit alive among the " silent population," or at least to maintain a reserve or a defence mechanism towards those who claim to be the embodiment of public opinion. But this defence mechanism operates only in relatively scattered areas. The vast majority of people seem to be drowned in the waves of dispatches and accounts of events, incapable of protecting themselves against slogans and myths; they are, in fact, prisoners of the opinions attributed to them.

Public opinion polls may make it possible to get a clearer picture and to get into direct contact with the man in the street. Experience has made it possible to perfect methods and techniques that

group (difficult in any case to determine) of readers to whom it appeals, at the risk of neglecting the conditions under which the information is produced; conditions which, in our opinion, constitute a much more important factor in the distortion of information.

give some hope for the future.[2] But the number of such polls at our disposal for the study of even the recent past is too limited to provide more than indications of a state of mind.

Nevertheless, despite the gravity of these difficulties, it is worth trying to assess the influence of public opinion on the progress of the struggle for the Saar and to analyse reactions and trends.

FRENCH AND GERMAN OPINION ON THE SAAR

One of the first questions which arises is the degree of interest aroused in France and Germany by the struggle over the Saar.

A survey of the principal newspapers in the two countries has enabled us to give a preliminary answer to this question: the Saar occupied only a very secondary place in the minds of the Germans and the French. As we have seen, both had more urgent economic, political, and social problems to resolve. Their attention was primarily concentrated on domestic affairs and on debates on foreign policy in which the Saar figured but intermittently. For the Germans, one has only to remember the importance of the Berlin blockade and, later, of the question of their eastern frontier or that of their inclusion in the system of Western security; and for France, the seriousness of the crisis in Indo-China, which lasted from 1948 to 1954, and the North African problems.

There is, however, a second point to be noted: the Saar question seems to have been followed more attentively in Germany than in France. We have noted, for instance, that Chancellor Adenauer gave the impression of being dogged not only by the Socialist opposition but by papers of various persuasions which drove him to take a firmer stand *vis-à-vis* France's Saar policy. We have noted how, on the contrary, the French papers showed an aloofness amounting almost to indifference. The contrast was very marked at the time the Treaty creating the European Coal and Steel Community was signed.[3]

---

[2] *Cf.*, in this connection, the excellent study of J.-B. Duroselle giving a very valuable account of the present state of this question: *De l'utilisation des sondages d'opinion en histoire et en sciences politiques* (Brussels: Institut Universitaire d'Information Sociale et Économique, 1957).

[3] *Cf. Historical Study*, pp. 90–91. In a public opinion poll carried out in June, 1951, in Germany by the Institut für Demoskopie of Allensbach, 46 per cent. replied " Yes " to the question of whether Germany should subordinate her collaboration in the Schuman Plan to a return of the Saar. Sixteen per cent. replied in the negative, 38 per cent. had no opinion.

Can one verify this impression and reach more valid conclusions? The few public opinion polls taken furnish scarcely any information on this point. At the most, one can record the relatively high proportion of those who had no opinion at all or who confessed to ignorance, according to the comparative study made by the Institut Français d'Opinion Publique in April, 1955, and by the Institut für Demoskopie of Allensbach the next month,[4] that is to say, during the period following ratification of the Paris agreements and preceding the campaign for the referendum. Of those queried in France, 51 per cent. declared they had no answer to the following question: "France and Germany have recently been discussing the question of the Saar. Do you know whether an agreement has been signed?" Fifteen per cent. declared that no treaty had been signed. In Germany 45 per cent. of those questioned did not know the answer.[5]

Can one hope to obtain further information by a comparison between the place given to the Saar in the French press and that in the German press? Existing doubts about quantitative analyses of the press are well known: the diversity among newspapers of the same country in format, number of pages, typographical arrangement, allocation of material, is too great to permit compilation of comparable data. It is even more difficult to draw conclusions from a quantitative analysis of the press of two countries. However, we made an attempt to measure the space given to the Saar by certain French and German newspapers during the "turning points" and "crises" in the Saar question.[6] The conclusions drawn from this

---

[4] This inquiry was made among 2,170 persons in France and among 2,222 persons in Germany, including West Berlin. *Cf.* List of public opinion polls carried out in France, Germany, and the Saar between 1944 and 1955.

[5] Another inquiry, conducted in Germany in September, 1955, by the Institut für Demoskopie of Allensbach revealed that 22 per cent. of the people questioned did not know that a referendum was imminent. One-fifth of those concerned knew the purposes of the referendum; 56 per cent. said they could not tell what the outcome would be; 53 per cent. were not in a position to say whether the rejection of the Statute would be a good or bad thing for Germany.

[6] (*a*) Elections to the Landtag, October 5, 1947.
(*b*) Introduction of the French franc and French laws, November 15–20, 1947.
(*c*) Visit of Robert Schuman to Bonn and publication of the Federal Government's memorandum, January–March, 1950.
(*d*) Signing of the Treaty setting up the E.C.S.C., April 18, 1951.
(*e*) Schuman-Adenauer decision to negotiate the europeanization of the Saar, March 19–20, 1952.
(*f*) Elections to the Landtag, November 30, 1952.
(*g*) Acceptance of the Van Naters Plan as a basis of negotiation, March 9, 1954.
(*h*) Signing of the Saar Agreement, October 23, 1954.
(*i*) Adenauer-Pinay meeting in Bonn. Settlement of the Roechling affair, April 30, 1954.
(*j*) Referendum, October 23, 1955.

[*continued*

analysis are, we admit, very tenuous for the reasons already given. The number of dispatches and articles of all kinds on the Saar in *Le Monde* and *Le Figaro* was considerably less than in the *Frankfurter Allgemeine Zeitung* and the *Süddeutsche Zeitung*.[7] Moreover, these two German newspapers gave substantially more space to the Saar than did either of the French.[8]

A similar analysis was made of the debates in the Bundestag and the French National Assembly for 1944–1955. Although this analysis does not give the position of the man in the street, it does serve to complete and to corroborate the fragmentary information at our disposal. Moreover, parliaments may be said to reflect as well as to form the opinions of the electors. The results are given in the three following tables.

Tables 1 and 2 are based on the verbatim records of the National Assembly debates in the *Journal officiel de la République française*; Table 3 is based on the verbatim records in the *Verhandlungen des Deutschen Bundestages*. The explanations of the break-down in these tables are as follows:

"Number of Lines."—The number of lines printed in a column and the number of columns on a page vary. To equalize these discrepancies, we calculated an arithmetical mean for the number of lines printed in a column. As for the total number of lines printed on a page, we have divided the number of lines so calculated by the number of columns. To permit comparison of these figures with those given by calculations made in the analysis of the Bundestag, we have added 20 per cent. to the number of "French" lines to compensate for the difference in German printed characters. In fact, the French verbatim records as compared with the German on a basis of "equal lines" contains one-fifth more text. As a check on our method, we made counter-tests on one hundred pages: the margin of error was never more than 5 per cent.

"International Questions."—We considered as international questions the political problems that arose between France and one or several sovereign states; thus debates on matters relating to territories of the French Union have not been included.

The survey covered the same period. But it is worth noting that a comparison, if possible at all, can be made only from the moment when there was a German press, *i.e.*, after 1950.

[7] For the two French newspapers, respectively, 130 and 108; for the two German newspapers, respectively, 251 and 161.

[8] For the two German newspapers, 3,325·2 and 2,460 square centimetres, against 1,510·5 and 1,684·8 square centimetres for the two French.

" The German Problem."—It was extremely difficult to separate the German problem from " international questions " generally. This remark applies with particular force after the " European " problem arose. These two categories become almost inseparably involved with one another.

" The Saar Question."—All questions concerning the Saar (economic, political, financial, and administrative).

KEY TO TABLES 1–4

N.B.—The following is a list of items which appears as letters *a* through *m* in Tables 1, 2, 3, and 4.

(*a*) Number of lines relating to international problems.
(*b*) Number of lines relating to budget for foreign affairs.
(*c*) Total of *a* and *b*.
(*d*) Proportion (per cent.) of debate on international questions to total debate.
(*e*) Number of lines relating to German question.
(*f*) Number of lines relating to the budget of the High Commissioner's office.
(*g*) Total of *e* and *f*.
(*h*) Proportion (per cent.) of debate on the German problem to total debate.
(*i*) Proportion (per cent.) of debate on the German problem to total debate on international questions.
(*j*) Total number of lines relating to the Saar question.
(*k*) Proportion (per cent.) of total debate.
(*l*) Proportion (per cent.) of total debate on international questions.
(*m*) Proportion (per cent.) of debate on the German problem.

Table 1

QUANTITATIVE ANALYSIS OF THE DEBATES IN THE NATIONAL ASSEMBLY
(1944–1948)

		1944	1945	1946	1947	1948	Total
Number of Lines		33,075	74,651	141,785	193,018	241,575	684,104
International Questions	(*a*)	3,948	—	8,443	9,174	17,393	38,958
	(*b*)	—	3,487	768	1,663	1,333	7,251
	(*c*)	3,948	3,487	9,211	10,837	18,726	46,209
	(*d*)	11·9	4·7	6·5	5·6	7·8	6·8
The German Problem	(*e*)	312	—	4,046	2,445	7,565	14,368
	(*f*)	—	159	192	991	288	1,630
	(*g*)	312	159	4,238	3,436	7,853	15,998
	(*h*)	0·9	0·2	3·0	1·8	3·3	2·3
	(*i*)	7·9	4·6	46·0	31·7	41·9	34·6
The Saar Question	(*j*)	—	—	755	2,034	1,156	3,945
	(*k*)	—	—	0·5	1·1	0·5	0·6
	(*l*)	—	—	8·2	18·8	6·2	8·5
	(*m*)	—	—	17·8	59·2	14·7	24·7

Table 2

QUANTITATIVE ANALYSIS OF THE DEBATES IN THE NATIONAL ASSEMBLY
(1949–1955)

		1949	1950	1951	1952	1953	1954	1955	Total
Number of Lines		235,589	430,791	445,133	306,029	316,743	305,089	262,397	2,301,771
International	(a)	19,446	7,630	14,812	14,112	16,800	40,632	2,130	115,562
Questions	(b)	779	8,738	5,760	1,860	1,202	2,064	192	20,615
	(c)	20,245	16,368	20,572	15,972	18,002	42,696	2,322	136,177
	(d)	8·6	3·8	4·6	5·2	5·7	14·0	0·9	5·9
The German	(e)	11,287	7,440	8,126	11,376	16,522	16,252	—	71,003
Problem	(f)	223	3,216	1,968	864	279	288	—	6,838
	(g)	11,510	10,656	10,094	12,240	16,801	16,540	—	77,841
	(h)	4·9	2·5	2·3	4·0	5·3	5·4	—	3·4
	(i)	56·9	65·1	49·1	76·6	93·3	38·7	—	57·2
The Saar	(j)	269	732	828	39	2,988	1,982	1,170	8,008
Question	(k)	0·1	0·2	0·2	—	0·9	0·6	0·4	0·3
	(l)	1·3	4·5	4·0	—	16·6	4·6	50·4	5·9
	(m)	2·3	6·9	8·2	0·3	17·8	12·0	—	10·3

Table 3

QUANTITATIVE ANALYSIS OF THE DEBATES IN THE BUNDESTAG
(1949–1955)

		1949	1950	1951	1952	1953	1954	1955	Total
Number of Lines		42,012	179,712	187,317	220,536	154,440	165,132	171,882	1,121,031
International	(a)	5,156	6,932	10,638	40,318	14,826	16,848	15,526	110,244
Questions*	(d)	12·3	3·9	5·7	18·3	9·6	10·2	9·0	9·8
Saar Question	(j)	177	2,412	3,907	3,014	931	2,614	4,898	17,953
	(k)	0·4	1·3	2·1	1·4	0·6	1·6	2·8	1·6
	(l)	3·4	34·8	36·7	7·5	6·3	15·5	28·5	16·3

* These debates were concerned principally with the reintegration of Germany into international life. Debates in NATO, E.D.C., Council of Europe, E.C.S.C., etc., did not begin until 1950.

It is obvious that the Bundestag [9] gave more attention to the Saar than did the National Assembly. A comparison of the number of lines devoted to this problem in the verbatim records is indicated in Table 4.

[9] Here again the attempt at comparison may seem open to discussion, given the differences in the organization and conduct of debates. However, one may assume that official minutes of public debates provide a common basis from which it is possible to estimate the relative importance of debates on the Saar in the two assemblies.

Table 4

COMPARATIVE QUANTITATIVE TABLE ON DEBATES ON THE SAAR
IN THE NATIONAL ASSEMBLY AND THE BUNDESTAG
(1949–1955)

		1949	*1950*	*1951*	*1952*	*1953*	*1954*	*1955*	*Total*
National	(*j*)	269	732	828	39	2,988	1,982	1,170	8,008
Assembly	(*k*)	0·1	0·2	0·2	—	0·9	0·6	0·4	0·3
	(*l*)	1·3	4·5	4·0	—	16·6	4·6	50·4	5·9
Bundestag	(*j*)	177	2,412	3,907	3,014	931	2,614	4,893	17,953
	(*k*)	0·4	1·3	2·1	1·4	0·6	1·6	2·8	1·6
	(*l*)	3·4	34·8	36·7	7·5	6·3	15·5	28·5	16·3

Another and more accurate approach is through this comparison:

	Bundestag	*National Assembly*
Number of sessions *	403	1,863
Sessions in which the Saar problem was discussed	54	46
Place given to the Saar (per cent.)	13·4	2·5

* The difference in the number of sessions of the Bundestag and the National Assembly is explained by the fact that in Germany the total number of debates in any day is counted as one session while the National Assembly can have several sessions in one day

A study of the debates on the Paris agreements confirms the above observations:

	Bundestag	*National Assembly*
Date of Sessions	Dec. 15–16, 1954 Feb. 24–27, 1955	Dec. 20–23, 1954 Dec. 27–29, 1954
Number of sessions	6	15
Number of lines covering debates	23,230	19,680
Number of lines referring to Saar	4,378 (18·8%)	1,743 (8·9%)
Number of speeches	87	72
Number of speeches on the Saar	30 (34·5%)	14 (19·4%)

These few quantitative analyses have no value as proof but the information they supply reinforces what we had already obtained from a careful survey of the newspapers on the relative importance attached to the Saar question in France and in Germany.

It is even more important to analyse the motives of the individuals or groups taking part in the struggle.

We have already made some observations on this point. The question now is whether it is possible to distinguish trends or currents of opinion that were not confined to groups but transcended them.

Public opinion polls, rare though they are, might provide some indications.[10] The first at our disposal for France, carried out in Paris in December, 1944,[11] gives a high proportion (75 per cent.) of affirmative answers to the question: " In the peace treaty, should France ask for permanent annexation of the Saar and its coal-fields? " Ten years later,[12] when the question asked was " Do you consider that France has rights in the Saar? " the reply was less certain. Thirty-five per cent. asserted that France had such rights; 45 per cent. did not know; 20 per cent. replied in the negative. The divergence in replies is not surprising. It reflects the weakening that had taken place in the French viewpoint. In 1944, at the time of the Liberation and with the end of the war near, there was a strong feeling concerning France's right to reparations and to compensation for the damage she had suffered. In 1954, this was not felt so sharply.

These two surveys also provide useful information on the composition of French public opinion, but we must beware of overestimating their importance. In both, the liberal professions and those groups belonging to a so-called " higher " cultural level were more hesitant about demanding France's rights. As far as the 1944 poll was concerned, a higher proportion of workers and artisans wanted annexation of the Saar (80 per cent. of those queried) as compared with 70 per cent. of those engaged in liberal professions. The 1954 poll, covering the entire country, indicated that in the so-called " primary " category the number of those asserting France's rights in the Saar was twice as high as those denying them. In the " upper " category, there were as many opponents as partisans. It should also be noted that the proportion of " Noes " increased from one category to another while that of

[10] Of interest in this connection are the surveys of French opinion concerning Germany and the E.D.C. *Cf.* the chapter by Alain Girard and Jean Stoetzel, " L'opinion publique et la C.E.D.," in *La Querelle de la C.E.D.*: Raymond Aron et Daniel Lerner, eds. *Cahiers de la Fondation nationale des sciences politiques*, No. 80 (Paris: 1956), pp. 127–155.

[11] *Bulletin d'information* of the Institut Français d'Opinion Publique, No. 6, December 16, 1944, p. 10.

[12] Survey carried out by the Institut Français d'Opinion Publique in July, 1954, at the request of the Institut für Demoskopie of Allensbach.

" Don't know " decreased.[13] Finally, it must be pointed out that, in the classification according to age, the highest proportion of positive and the lowest of negative replies were in the 55–64 age group.

The poll held in Germany in January, 1952, also provides some interesting data.[14] What the pollsters wanted to find out was whether the Germans were prepared to give up the Saar permanently if by so doing they might hope to forge a lasting friendship with France, or whether they were unwilling to relinquish the Saar under any conditions, even if this meant the impossibility of establishing friendly relations. The trend revealed by the answers is very clear: 71 per cent. of those questioned did not want to give up the Saar, and 10 per cent. were prepared to do so. The answers did not vary in any marked degree from one political party to another with two exceptions: that of the *Bayernpartei*, with 33 per cent. of the replies in favour of relinquishing the Saar, and that of the *Deutsche Partei*, with only 4 per cent. in favour, the smallest figure of all. The distribution by social classes presented a picture similar to that observed by France: of those who were prepared to give up the Saar, 22 per cent. were in the " upper class " (*Obere Schicht*), 12 per cent. in the middle class (*Mittelstand*), 8 per cent. in the working classes (*Arbeiter Kreise*),[15] and 5 per cent. in what the poll describes as the lower classes (*Untere Schicht*).

These few inquiries thus agree on one point of some interest: they underline the tendency of the upper categories to make concessions to the adversary's viewpoint. At first sight this is not surprising. But the classifications used are too vague to permit firm conclusions. In each case one should know what kind of people were questioned and what were not only their training and their income but also their profession, their place of residence, and the particular circumstances of their lives.[16]

[13] Distribution on the educational level was as follows:

	Yes	No	Don't know
Primary	33%	15%	52%
Higher primary	40%	21%	39%
Technical	37%	28%	35%
Secondary	41%	30%	29%
Upper	37%	37%	26%

[14] Survey carried out by the Institut für Demoskopie of Allensbach.

[15] The workers who were members of a trade union were more attached to the idea of Germany's rights than were the non-union members: 5 per cent. "Yes" and 80 per cent. "No" for the former, and 4 per cent. "Yes" and 70 per cent. "No" for the latter.

[16] It should be noted that the survey of attitudes towards Franco-German *rapprochement* in the various sociological categories carried out in France in July, 1954, revealed that

These polls are unfortunately so few as to make all generalizations open to question and, moreover, they provide only vague indications as to motives: consciousness of a right, tendency not to compromise, willingness to make concessions. But there is one poll that is worth particular mention. In August, 1952, the following question was put to a number of Germans: "Why does Germany take such an interest in the Saar?" Of those questioned, 58 per cent. replied it was for economic reasons while 53 per cent. thought Germany was guided by broader national considerations.[17]

A study of the parliamentary debates gives fuller information which, taken as a whole, supports the observations that had emerged from the survey of the press and of administrative and private correspondence.

For France, for example, it reveals that between 1944 and 1947 emotional reactions and economic and political considerations were given equal weight. We endeavoured to study the problem more closely, to tally the formulations expressing primarily an emotional reaction and those in which economic or political reasons or considerations were apparent. The results were as follows: formulations expressing an emotional reaction amounted to 51 per cent., while those containing economic or political reasons or considerations amounted to 49 per cent. But this is only a very rough approximation because of the interweaving of approaches, indicative of the ambivalence of those using them. During those three years, the relationship between the two types of formulation varied; expressions such as "Germany is guilty," "Germany must be punished," "Germany must pay," and "We have conquered Germany," gradually gave way to such phrases as that of Mr. Grumbach: "Let us not annex the Saar, but let us annex its sub-soil."

The idea which finally took over and prevailed until the end was naturally that of economic union with France, linked with the idea of political separation from Germany. The importance attached to these ideas, which we have had occasion to emphasize throughout our study, perhaps appears more clearly in Figure 1,

81 per cent. of those belonging by cultural level to the upper category were in favour of *rapprochement* as compared with 46 per cent. in the primary category. In the classification by professions, among industrial circles and the liberal professions, 70 per cent. were in favour as compared with 43 per cent. of agricultural workers and 49 per cent. of labourers. *Cf.* Alain Girard and Jean Stoetzel, *loc. cit.*, p. 154.

17 *Cf. Jahrbuch der Oeffentlichen Meinung 1947–1955, op. cit.*, p. 324.

which endeavours to present the relative importance of the arguments used by speakers in the National Assembly between 1944 and 1955.

Figure 1

<small>RELATIVE IMPORTANCE OF ARGUMENTS USED IN
DEBATES IN THE NATIONAL ASSEMBLY</small>

N.B.—This attempted evaluation of opinions is based on an analysis of 150 speeches in the National Assembly. Figures in parentheses indicate number of references to the argument.

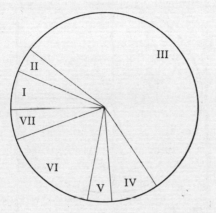

I.   *The Saar is French territory.* (10)
     Opinion expressed mainly just after the Liberation.

II. *The Saar must be " independent and sovereign."* (6)
     Point of view held by those who demanded primarily the permanent political separation of the Saar from Germany, but without any definite plan for the future of the region.

III. *Economic union with France, political separation from Germany.* (82)

IV. *Europeanization.* (13)
     This opinion still bears "traces" of the ideas expressed under III. In general III and IV were inter-connected.

V.   *Active opposition to integration.* (6)
     Mostly centred on the interests of Lorraine. The principal concern was to eliminate the competitive economic strength of the Saar.

VI. *" The Saar has become the victim of bloc politics."* (25)
     Communist and progressive opinion put forward in opposition to any proposed solution.

VII. *The Saar is German.* (8)

A similar study of the debates in the Bundestag (Figure 2) brings out how weak the response was to the idea of europeanization of the Saar. The sentiments voiced most often were those protesting against the weakness of the government, against the French attempt to take over the Saar under cover of autonomy or of europeanization, and against the fact that there was neither liberty nor democracy in the Saar. Beyond these objections the firm conviction was apparent that the Saar was German and that no solution to the problem was valid which did not recognize this fact.[18]

Figure 2

RELATIVE IMPORTANCE OF ARGUMENTS USED IN
DEBATES IN THE BUNDESTAG

N.B.—This attempted evaluation of opinions is based on an analysis of 75 speeches in the Bundestag. Figures in parentheses indicate number of references to the argument.

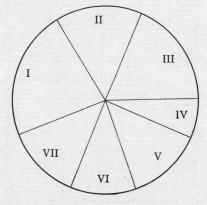

I. *The Saar is German.* (33)
   Key phrases:
   " Teil des Deutschen Reiches im Bereich seiner Grenzen vom 31 Dezember 1937 " (A part of Germany within the scope of its December, 1937, borders).

II. *Denunciation of French policy.* (23)
   " . . . Anerkennung Völkerrechtswidriger Loslösung der Saar vom Reich " (Acknowledgment that the separation of the Saar from Germany contravenes international law).
   " Einseitige Bindung des Saarprotektorats " (Unilateral link of the Saar protectorate).
   " Verhüllte Annexion " (Annexation in disguise).
   " Verschleierte Annexion " (Veiled annexation).
   " Junktimpolitik " (Interdependent policy).

III. *Against the absence of " democratic freedoms " in the Saar.* (27)
   Cf. Table 5 and comments.

IV. *" Justification of German Unity."* (10)
   " Was im Westen gültig ist, ist es auch im Osten " (What is valid in the West, is also valid in the East).
   " Parallelität zwischen Saargebiet und Oder-Neisse Grenze " (Parallelism between the territory of the Saar and the Oder-Neisse border).

[18] It should be mentioned that the opposition was not alone in protesting against French policy or against the régime set up in the Saar any more than did it have the monopoly in reminding people of the German character of the Saar. Division showed up largely over the europeanization of the Saar. Here the government found itself alone. However, it should be pointed out that the inquiries made by the Institut für Demoskopie in April and August, 1952, and in November, 1953, reveal that the percentage of replies definitely opposed to europeanization of the Saar weakened between 1952 and 1953 (60 per cent. and 57 per cent. in 1952, then 48 per cent. in 1953), while there was a rise in the percentage of those in favour (21 per cent. and 22 per cent. in 1952, then 28 per cent. in 1953). *Cf. Jahrbuch der Oeffentlichen Meinung, op. cit.*, p. 322. However, another inquiry made in 1954 by the same institute gave 66 per cent. in favour of union with Germany and 11 per cent. for europeanization. *Ibid.*, p. 324.

V.   *The Statute is not final; we must await the peace treaty.* (20)
VI.   *Europeanization is a mistake or at least premature.* (17)
  " . . . Saargebiet durch Europäisierung auf kaltem Wege von Deutschland losgetrennt wird " (Through europeanization the territory of the Saar will coldbloodedly be separated from Germany).
  " Missbräuchliche Anwendung des Begriffs: Europäisierung " (Misuse of the concept of europeanization).
  " Wir halten es für bedauerlich, dass die Saarfrage überhaupt mit der Europafrage verknüpft worden ist " (We consider it most unfortunate that the Saar question has been completely intertwined with the question of Europe).
  " . . . Europäische Gedanke nicht reif genug " (The European idea is not ripe enough).
  " . . . Europäisierung wäre ein Verzicht " (Europeanization would be renunciation).
VII.   *Let us europeanize in a positive way.* (20)
  " Lösung im Rahmen unserer gesamteuropäischen Politik " (A solution within the framework of our over-all European policy).

It has already been pointed out that there are grounds for certain reservations about the value of information on trends of public opinion as supplied by parliamentary debates. One must therefore be cautious about drawing conclusions. We have limited ourselves to setting out the facts revealed concerning the various arguments used in debates and their relative importance, and to establishing the striking similarity in Germany, as well as in France, between parliamentary debates and the discussions in newspapers and periodicals, both as to subject-matter and as to allocation of space. To give just one example, that of the period during which the ratification of the Paris agreements was under discussion: both in the French press and in the National Assembly the same emphasis was given to the argument that this was to be a definitive agreement[19]; in the German press and in the Bundestag there was the same emphasis on the provisional character of the Statute, and on the question of democratic freedom in the Saar we find the same reaction against agreements considered to be disadvantageous to Germany.

The problem of democratic freedoms played an important role. This was not surprising if one thinks of the importance given to it in the German press. Even before the creation of the Federal Republic, protests had been raised against some of the measures taken first by the Military Government and then by the Saar Government. Criticisms were addressed not only to the expulsions but to the obstacles placed in the way of entry of German newspapers into the Saar and to certain measures affecting the world of

---

[19] It is worth stressing again how little space the press gave to the Saar question during this period.

sport. Kurt Schumacher, who called for a plebiscite in the Saar
under international supervision, specified that there should be a
guarantee of free elections.

These first reactions were still sporadic. But after the Federal
Government had taken its position in March, 1950, the theme of
democratic freedoms appeared over and over again in the press until
1955. What was the particular target? It was certain measures
taken by the Hoffmann Government to put up a protective screen
in the Saar against the infiltration of German influence and, even
more, government activities against the opposition. Sources of
information for this early period were very few, stemming most
frequently from Heinrich Schneider alone; complaints and accusations were transmitted to the press and to representatives of various
political parties by the channels previously mentioned. But soon,
as the number of opponents grew, the flood of information swelled
and in Germany protests against the absence of democratic freedoms
in the Saar increased in scope. The banning of the D.P.S., on May
21, 1951, aroused a wave of indignation.[20] The great debate that
took place on May 30 in the Bundestag provoked in the press a new
spate of critical comments on the Saar Government in which even a
moderate paper like the *Rheinischer Merkur* joined. The protests
lessened in the months that followed, only to flare up again at the
end of the year; they were intensified by the resistance of the Hoffmann Government to attempts to organize opposition parties and
by its refusal to grant them the authorization they requested.
Throughout 1952 the theme of democratic freedoms in the Saar
recurred regularly in the German press, punctuating the tentative
moves made in March by the Chancellor *vis-à-vis* the Council of
Europe and the ups and downs of the struggle unfolding in the
Saar. In 1953 the pressure relaxed, but this was because of other
events: the electoral campaign for a new Bundestag relegated the
Saar question to second place. It was not, however, forgotten, and
criticism of the régime of Johannes Hoffmann was expressed from
time to time, as, for example, when the Germans lodged their

[20] From May 22 to May 26, we noted fourteen articles in the newspapers studied:
*Süddeutsche Zeitung, Kölnische Rundschau, Frankfurter Neue Presse, Frankfurter
Allgemeine Zeitung, Rhein-Neckar Zeitung, Neue Ruhr-Zeitung, Die Welt, Industrie-
kurier, Münchner Merkur, Neuer Vorwärts.* The tone throughout is firm, even sharp.
The *Rhein-Neckar Zeitung* speaks of "kurzsichtige Saarpolitik" (shortsighted Saar
politics), *Die Welt* of "Saar-demokratur," "Unbegründet und unangebracht"
(Groundless and unsuitable), said the *Industriekurier*. "Verleugnung der Demokratie"
(Denial of Democracy), wrote the *Neuer Vorwärts*.

complaint with the Council of Europe. Criticism became sharper in 1954, when the Van Naters Plan was being discussed, and after the signing of the Paris agreements; it developed parallel to the discussions on the organization of the referendum which were going on between the French and German Governments and within the Council of the Western European Union.

We have already pointed out that this criticism was excessive. Though it is true that the Hoffmann Government and the French Diplomatic Mission in the Saar took steps to control and restrain the opposition and to fight a propaganda hostile to the régime, it is quite false to maintain that a reign of coercion and even of terror had been established. The number of people affected by the expulsion orders was relatively small. Provisions for police surveillance were aimed at only a small proportion of the population. But those who were affected reacted violently; they raised the issue of principle, thus aggravating the tension and broadening the debate, giving it a scope that went far beyond its original limits and conferring upon it a political importance out of all proportion to reality. It was to their image of the situation that the readers of the German papers reacted. This was also true for the deputies in the Bundestag, as indicated in Table 5.

Table 5

ATTACKS IN THE BUNDESTAG ON THE ABSENCE OF
DEMOCRATIC FREEDOMS IN THE SAAR

Year	Government	C.D.U./C.S.U.	F.D.P.	S.P.D.	K.P.D.	Various	Total
1950	1	1	1	3	2	3	11
1951	1	4	2	2	1	3	13
1952	3	1	2	6	4	3	19
1953	1	2	1	7	—	1	12
1954	2	2	3	6	—	1	14
1955	3	3	2	6	—	1	15
Total	11	13	11	30	7	12	84

In twenty-nine out of fifty-four sessions a recrudescence of criticisms of anti-democratic methods was observable. The debate of October 22, 1952, was devoted entirely to a consideration of this problem. Eight speakers took part and they all denounced the situation in the Saar. On this point, government and opposition were in agreement.

A few phrases will illustrate the violence of these speeches:

Adenauer: "Im Saargebiet herrscht weder Freiheit noch Demokratie" (In the territory of the Saar neither freedom nor democracy prevails).

Strauss (C.D.U./C.S.U.): "Undemokratische, sogar diktatorische Massnahmen zur Unterdrückung jeder Opposition" (Undemocratic, even dictatorial measures to quell any opposition).

Mayer (F.D.P.): "Polizeistaatliche Willkür im Saargebiet" (Arbitrariness of a police state in Saar territory).

Mayer (F.D.P.): "An der Saar herrscht Unrecht" (In the Saar injustice reigns).

Eichler (S.P.D.): "Forderung: Aufhebung des politischen Terrors" (The demand: Abolition of political terror).

Mommer (S.P.D.): "Marokko Methoden Frankreichs an der Saar . . ." (France's Moroccan methods in the Saar . . .).

Let there be no mistake however: if the theme of democratic freedoms played the part we have described in Germany, this was not solely the consequence of propaganda or of an official effort to exaggerate. The repercussions of the situation in the Saar, the increasingly bitter battle between the government and the opposition, periodically gave it a new impetus. Its powers of attraction and suggestion rested upon a certain relationship between image and reality.

The study of another theme—that of the unity of the Saar and Lorraine—provides a similar example. Between 1944 and 1946 this theme recurred on various occasions in France and in the Saar.[21] It was referred to in order to justify France's claims on the Saar and to convey the feeling that France had history on her side, as well as

21 According to Abel Verdier, in his memorandum re-edited in 1945 and published in part in May, 1946, the Saar and Lorraine "form an economic whole." Some of the speakers in the provisional National Assembly used the very same argument when taking part in the debates on January 15, 16, and 17. In his speech at Bar-le-Duc in July, 1946, General de Gaulle spoke of the coalfields of the Saar "the development of which goes naturally hand in hand with that of our iron mines." The economic and political press spoke constantly of this economic unity or of the traditional economic orientation of the Saar towards France. Similarly, in the Saar this thesis was often quoted: for example, Peter Zimmer, in his article in the *Neue Saarbrücker Zeitung* of December 8, 1945, entitled "Saarländische Kohle und lothringisches Erz." Mr. Zimmer also spoke, on April 4, 1946, at a conference for business men, skilled workers, and industrial workers in the Saar, of the "natural inter-connections of Saar coal, Lorraine iron ore, and Saar foundry works." A resolution of May 5 of the Chamber of Commerce and the Workers' Association of Saarbrücken referred to the "natural connections that link the Saar with the neighbouring territories of France."

geographical and economic considerations. Arguments were borrowed from the Germans and used to support the French thesis. The measures the National Socialist Government had had to take in the Saar between the plebiscite of 1935 and 1939 had emphasized the marginal position of the Saar economy and the unfortunate consequences for it of an over-dependence on the German market.[22] The Germans had considered that the inter-penetration of the economic interests of the Saar and Lorraine—an inter-penetration that had persisted despite the numerous changes that had taken place on a political plane—justified an attempt to co-ordinate and unify their economic development.[23] In 1940 Lorraine was included in an administrative district which also comprised the Palatinate and the Saar and which, by a decree of the *Führer* of March 11, 1941, took the name of *Westmark*.

The theme of the unity of the Saar-Lorraine basin, with its most popular slogan the " marriage " of the mineral ores of Lorraine to Saar coal, came up repeatedly in succeeding years until 1953. As time went by, however, references to Lorraine became less frequent. Emphasis was placed rather on the links between the French economy and the Saar economy, and it was the policy of economic union between the Saar and France which people tried to justify. Gradually, too, the theme of europeanization was introduced and repeated along with the idea that the French and the Saar economies were complementary; it died away in its turn in the Saar, and disappeared completely the moment the Chamber of Commerce of Saarbrücken and the Saar Government openly took a position in favour of trade with Germany.

The conclusion of the Paris agreements, and above all the referendum of October 23, 1955, caused a revival of the Saar-Lorraine theme. Indeed, it seemed that the moment the French, especially business circles in the eastern departments, became conscious of the danger of losing the Saar market, they abandoned the reservations and criticisms so frequent in preceding years and stressed the inter-dependence of the two regions. The resolution

[22] *Cf.* the report of a commission of economic studies, in Berlin, at the end of 1938, *Bericht des Reichskuratoriums für Wirtschaftlichkeit, Die Wirtschaft des Saarlandes* (Saarbrücken: Service d'information du gouvernement de la Sarre, 1951): "The economic realities of the union with the Saar," it concluded, "have considerably cooled the fervor of political sentiment."

[23] *Cf.*, on this subject, Fritz Hellwig, "Die geschichtlichen Beziehungen zwischen der saarländischen und lothringischen Eisenindustrie," *Westmärkische Abhandlungen zur Landes-und Volksforschung*, Vol. IV (Kaiserslautern: 1940).

adopted by the Economic Council, after a hearing of the Mayolle Report, stated that " trade between France and the Saar amounting to some 275 milliard francs a year is equally profitable for both as a result of the natural geographic features that complement one another and have created between the Saar and neighbouring areas in France ancient and permanent ties."

A study of the few public opinion polls carried out in the period which concerns us, a survey of the most representative newspapers, and a methodical analysis of the contents of debates in the Bundestag and the National Assembly have afforded corroborative evidence of the interest taken by the public both in France and in Germany in the Saar question, and of some of the most characteristic reactions.

Public Opinion in the Saar

What was the state of public opinion in the Saar? Some of the authors or observers who claim to know the Saarlanders well have given a cautious reply to this question. According to their oral or written statements, the Saarlander is by nature passive and malleable. This sedentary and peaceful population, it is noted, is very conservative. The methods of Prussian administration, the paternalism of the Stumm period, had accustomed the Saarlanders to respect authority. The events of the post-1919 era were not of a kind to encourage initiative. What else could they do in 1945 but accept the consequences of an historic decision which had implications that extended far beyond them? How could they resist the policy advanced, not without determination, by the victor? Why not allow themselves to be led? [24]

With time this attitude changed, but not immediately. Fits of bad temper in 1948 did not lead to any real opposition to government policy. The few " resisters " were isolated and knew it. They complained of the fact, as did those who, in Germany, were working to modify the situation created by the 1947 decisions. It was only from 1954 on, and particularly after the spring of 1955,

---

[24] There are interesting comments in the previously cited typed memorandum, *L'évolution de l'opinion publique en Sarre de juillet 1945 à janvier 1949*. The author remarks that in 1945 the Saarlander, a good German, associated with the Hitlerian venture, could not help having a guilt complex towards the Allies and the French; moreover, he could not fail to see the material advantages offered to him by France at a time when Germany had gone out of existence, and he did not know when or how she might be reborn.

that the movement speeded up and that opposition grew and stiffened with surprising strength as soon as the electoral campaign opened. This reversal of an attitude, it was said, was further proof of the adaptability and opportunism of the Saarlanders who rushed to the side of victory in 1955, as they had done ten years earlier.

This judgment is a little hasty. It is generally agreed that the Saar population tries to avoid complications for itself and that it has an accommodating nature. But was not this passivity rather more widespread than has been generally realized? The Second World War and the post-war years gave too many proofs of the adaptability of men and the versatility of peoples to warrant attribution of a kind of monopoly to the population of one controversial area.

An analysis of the development of public opinion in the Saar, at least as it appears to us through the newspapers, parliamentary debates, and administrative and private correspondence, reveals, moreover, that the change was more gradual than has been maintained. This analysis also furnishes useful information on motives.

A previously cited French observer,[25] who made a study of Saar public opinion early in 1949, wrote:

> Ten months have passed since November 20, 1947. This day was considered by the Saarlander as marking the end of the war because it was the day on which he ceased to be hungry.
>
> Materially he is content; he is hard-working and can now live and work, but he considers that he owes his prosperity to no one but himself and his own efforts. It is well known that a good digestion leads to good feelings, and the Saarlander is regaining confidence in his own worth.
>
> In the analysis of his daily life, he can no longer distinguish and give credit to the consequences of economic union.
>
> In 1946, with an empty stomach and a threadbare coat, he would set out on foot for an unheated office and return home in the evening uncomplaining. Today, he has his breakfast coffee, puts on a good suit, takes a new trolley-bus or his little four-horsepower Renault to the office, does business for eight hours with a French industrialist, returns to his warm home in the evening to eat his sausage, and falls asleep listening to the radio. It is a French make and he is already beginning to think it does not work as well as a German set.
>
> The average Saarlander depicted here, who is one of 150,000 others, does not remember that what seems to him normal since union with France was previously just a dream. Striving, like the Germans, towards the future and, like all Germans, quick to forget the past, the years of suffering have faded from his mind. He does not compare the value of the material benefits he enjoys in 1948 with the supreme blessing which

---

[25] *Cf. supra*, note 24.

would allow him in 1952 to become again a citizen of the Reich while
continuing to live just as comfortably; to do this would appease his guilty
conscience, which, deep within him, knows that he has sold his birth-
right for a mess of pottage.

He would be so pleased to have the French give him back the sense
of self-respect he feels he has lost that he would be willing to see them
leave the Saar in 1952 without asking them for any reckoning.

This French observer went on to point out the effect on the Saar
of Germany's revival in the international sphere. The Saarlander,
even if he still accepted economic union, remained " faithful to the
German spirit." But, as he " admits to himself, albeit confusedly,
his fear of too sudden a return to Germany which would fling him
into more trouble," he nursed deep down inside himself the hope of
a reconciliation between his two great neighbours with his country
serving as a " bridge."

Even if these observations are somewhat caricatured, they are
nonetheless interesting for the light they shed on the way in which
a Frenchman from the Saar summed up the psychological situation
and also on the actual situation. There is no doubt that some of
the remarks are highly pertinent.

It is incontestable that even in 1948 the Saarlanders' frame of
mind had changed and that two factors in particular had contributed to this: the improvement in living conditions, which had
made the population more exacting and the presence of the French
less necessary and even less bearable; the recovery of Germany,
which was beginning to be apparent, as well as her emergence as
an active element once more in the play of international forces.

The interaction of these two factors was felt even more strongly
in the years that followed. Mention has already been made of the
sensitivity of the Saarlanders to fluctuations in the French economy,
the reactions that were manifest in 1951 and 1952 to the rise in
prices, and in 1953 and 1954 to the stabilization and even to the
slight drop in production and sales in France.[26] We have pointed
out the increasingly marked opposition from 1952 onwards of the
small traders and artisans who complained that economic union was
injurious to them.[27] We have also noted the inter-penetration of
social claims and nationalist opposition to the French presence. It
is quite clear that the economic recovery of Germany, which went
hand in hand with her political revival, could not fail to increase

[26] *Cf. Historical Study*, pp. 143–144.   [27] *Cf. supra*, pp. 258 *et seq*.

her powers of attraction for the mass of the Saarlanders, the more so because, as time went by, personal contacts increased.

The importance of the change which had taken place in the public mind was not realized before the beginning of 1955. True, no one was ignorant of the existence of an opposition and of the attempts it was making to organize itself. In 1952 it was possible to follow the ups and downs of the struggle between the Hoffmann Government and the political parties which were demanding permission to organize legally. The activities carried on by Heinrich Schneider as well as those in which Mr. Kutsch engaged have already been discussed. But the elections to the Landtag in November, 1952, gave supporters of the régime a majority which was still very large; the results, however much they may have been contested by those who were defeated, are nevertheless the only available indication of the relative strength of the government and opposition forces.[28] After the signing of the Paris agreements there were very few who thought that the Statute would be rejected. The most ardent fighters in the pro-German opposition in the Saar had little hope of winning. And yet a review of the various centres of opposition reveals the real strength they would be able to acquire as soon as they were grouped into new parties. Proof of this was obvious from the beginning of 1955.

By that time, positions had been taken. A public opinion survey conducted by the Emnid Institute in Bielefeld[29] indicated that 74 per cent. of those asked whether they preferred to retain the Franco-Saar economic union or return to Germany replied in favour of union with Germany; only 5 per cent. wanted to keep the Franco-Saar economic union. The difference was overwhelming. Questioned on their attitude regarding possible Saar autonomy or europeanization, these same people gave much more evenly divided answers: 35 per cent. were in favour of autonomy, 34 per cent.

[28] It should be noted, however, that a poll conducted in November, 1952, by the Institut für Demoskopie of Allensbach seemed to confirm the reservations of the electors towards Germany. The question asked was: " Do you think that, in case of a complete union of the Saar and Germany, your own personal position would be economically improved? " Of those questioned, 38 per cent. replied that their position would be worse; 18 per cent., that it would be better; and 26 per cent., that it would make no difference. *Cf. Jahrbuch der Oeffentlichen Meinung, op. cit.,* p. 323. To another question relating to the status of the Saar, 33 per cent. of the Saarlanders favoured union with Germany; 15 per cent., union with Germany in conjunction with a special economic agreement with France; 33 per cent., an independent status under European supervision with freedom to negotiate economic agreements; 9 per cent., an independent status under European supervision with economic union with France. *Ibid.*

[29] Inquiry made in 1955. *Vor Volksabstimmung und Wahlen im Saarland.*

against, 24 per cent. for europeanization, and 28 per cent. against.
The survey also provides interesting information on the question of
democratic freedoms; of those questioned, 52 per cent. felt that
democratic freedoms were not fully assured, while 30 per cent.
stated that they were. A poll on the political parties revealed clear
majorities in favour of the C.D.U. and the D.S.P. against their
rivals, the C.V.P. and the S.P.S.

An analysis of the press and of propaganda material used in
connection with the referendum confirms, completes, and clarifies
the conclusions of the poll. A classification of the major themes of
the campaign, in the order of their importance, results in the
following list in so far as the opposition parties are concerned [30]:

The C.D.U.

1. Propaganda in favour of the C.D.U.[31]
2. The Saar is part of the German nation. Evocation of the Reich.
   Appeal of the Fatherland.
3. Against MM. Hoffmann, Kirn, Hector, and the C.V.P.
4. In favour of a negative vote without giving specific reasons.
5. Against separation and the separatists.
6. In favour of democratic freedoms.
7. Against the French régime.
8. In favour of an increase in pensions. (Theme used primarily in
   pamphlets published jointly by the three *Heimatbund* parties.)
9. Against Mr. Grandval.

The organ of the C.D.U., the *Neueste Nachrichten*, which we
studied exhaustively for the month of August and the month of
October, the period preceding the plebiscite, put forward similar
arguments but in a different order of priority:

1. Against Mr. Hoffmann, by far the most frequent theme.[32]
2. For the C.D.U.

---

[30] Only the major themes have been considered. This does not mean that the political
parties did not make use of others, as for example, the C.D.U., of Europe, and the
Communist Party, of the rejection of the Paris agreements. This analysis was carried
out according to quantitative criteria and we have selected only those themes expressing
preoccupations of the Saar itself.

[31] Based on tracts, pamphlets, and printed matter. The classification of posters is a
rather delicate matter. Often, a poster merely bore the word "No." Reference should
especially be made to a significant poster that aroused a strong reaction: it showed a
wolf in sheep's clothing with the caption: "Nein, zu weiterer verkappter Ausbeutung.
Nein, zu den französich-saarländischen Wirtschaftskonventionen" (No to Further Disguised Exploitation. No to the Franco-Saar Economic Conventions).

[32] This is attributable to the fact that Johannes Hoffmann was particularly well known.
The poll carried out by Emnid Institute in August showed that 73 per cent. of those
questioned knew Mr. Hoffmann, while the name next best known obtained only
36 per cent. votes.

3. For Germany.
4. Against an affirmative vote and against the parties and papers in favour of it.
5. Against the separatists.
6. In favour of a negative vote.
7. In favour of democratic freedoms.
8. Against France.
9. Propaganda in favour of the pro-German parties.

The D.P.S.

1. Propaganda in favour of the D.P.S.
2. Propaganda in favour of a negative vote without giving specific reasons.
3. The German Fatherland.
4. Against Mr. Hoffmann and the C.V.P.
5. Against the French régime.
6. In favour of democratic freedoms.
7. Violent attacks against those in favour of the old régime and intending to vote for the Statute.

The newspaper of this party, the *Deutsche Saar*, always had sensational headlines and was violent in tone. The same themes recur:

1. Against Mr. Hoffmann.
2. In favour of a negative vote.
3. In favour of the German nation and Fatherland.
4. Against the separatists.
5. In favour of the D.P.S.
6. Fall of the French régime.
7. For democratic freedoms.
   Against the parties fighting for an affirmative vote. ⎫ Of equal importance
   Against the French franc, which was falling. ⎭
8. Against the French Customs. ⎫
   Against the French laws. ⎬ Of equal importance
   Against Mr. Grandval. ⎭
9. Against indirect taxation.

The *Deutsche Saar* frequently attacked the French régime. Here are some of their headlines: " Sensationelle Enthüllungen: Grandval bescheinigt Hoffmann den Bankrott. Der Dicke muss weg " (Sensational revelations: Grandval affirming that Hoffmann is bankrupt. The fat man must go)—one of the favourite slogans in the struggle against the " autonomists " and one of the most successful. " Skandal um die Botschaft. C.V.P.—Korruption vor der Abrechnung. Separatisten wollen nicht weichen " (Scandal in the Embassy. C.V.P.—Financial corruption. Separatists won't yield).

The D.S.P. (S.P.D.)

This party engaged in less propaganda than the other two big pro-German parties, for its means were limited and it exhausted them in the beginning setting up its printing press. Pamphlets and tracts from the D.S.P. were therefore quite rare during the campaign for the plebiscite. It was different during the electoral campaign preceding the December 18, 1955, elections. An analysis of these few pamphlets and of an election leaflet entitled *Die Wespe* indicates the following:

1. Propaganda for the D.S.P.
2. Attempt to ridicule Mr. Hoffmann and his régime.
3. Fidelity to the German Fatherland.[33]

The themes in the German Social Democratic paper, *Saarbrücker Allgemeine Zeitung*, were as follows:

1. Against Mr. Hoffmann.
2. In favour of a negative vote.
3. In favour of the German nation.
4. Against the separatists.
5. Rejection of French laws.
6. Against the parties in favour of the Statute.
   For the parties fighting against the Statute.
7. Against France.
8. For democratic freedoms.

The Communist Party

The Communist Party held to its usual policy, systematically attacking all the other parties. In its pamphlets and tracts,[34] which

---

[33] Here are a few typical titles of this kind of propaganda: "Separatistenverrat am Vaterland." "Treue zu Europa setzt Treue gegenüber dem eigenen Volk voraus." "Jeder anständige Deutsche sagt Nein zu diesem Regime." "Der Unheilige Johannes." "Unliebsame Erinnerungen" (Ruland). "Ein Zeugnis geistiger Umnachtung" (Richard Kirn). "Die Luft muss endlich besser werden." "Hoffmanns letzte Klage." "Wanderung durch den separatistischen Herbst." "Wenn Separatisten in die Stratosphäre wirbeln." "Dafür haben Sie Geld," etc.

[34] Communist posters were: against a *colonial status* (argument of the French Communist Party), against *separatism* ("Ihre Zeit ist um"), in favour of a negative vote ("Nein zum Saarstatut"; "Das Nein der Arbeiter entscheidet"), and, above all, in favour of the *unity of Germany* and for Germany in general ("Richtig wählen, deutsch wählen, für deutsche Einheit—Nein"; "Beitrag zur deutschen Verständigung"; "Für Verständigung der Deutschen aus Ost und West"; "Nein, Dein Bekenntnis für Deutschlands Einheit und kollektive Sicherheit in Europa"; "Für gesamtdeutschen Vorschlag zur Genfer Aussenministerkonferenz am 27 Oktober").

were fairly numerous and frequently very suggestive, by far the most important place was taken by:

1. Propaganda in favour of a negative vote, followed by:
2. The German Fatherland and nationalist sentiment.
3. Propaganda for the Communist Party.
4. Attacks against all other political parties.
5. Against the separatists.
6. Attacks against MM. Hoffmann, Kirn, and Adenauer.
7. Attacks against Mr. Schneider.
8. In favour of democratic freedoms.
9. Against Mr. Grandval.

The same order is observed in the party newspaper, *Die Neue Zeit*:

1. In favour of a negative vote, followed at a considerable distance by:
2. Propaganda for the K.P. and its paper.
3. Against separatism and chauvinism.
4. Nationalist sentiment.
5. Against Mr. Hoffmann and Mr. Hector.
6. Against parties and newspapers favourable to the Statute.
7. Propaganda for the U.S.S.R.
8. Against Mr. Adenauer. } Of equal importance
   For democratic freedoms. } Of equal importance

A similar study of the arguments employed by *parties favourable to the Statute* produced the following findings:

The C.V.P.

1. Propaganda against parties which favour a negative vote, coupled with endorsement of an affirmative vote without giving much explanation.
2. For Europe, followed closely by:
3. Propaganda on the economic advantages that the union with France and the Statute ensure for the Saar.
4. Propaganda for the C.V.P. and in favour of Mr. Hoffmann, but in a rather discreet manner.

The paper of the Christian People's Party, the *Saarländische Volkszeitung*, carried the following themes:

1. Against the opposition parties.
2. In favour of an affirmative vote.
3. Encouragement to members of the party.
4. In favour of Europe.
5. Economic advantages of the Statute.
6. In favour of Mr. Hoffmann.

7. In favour of France in general.
8. Reminder of the Second World War.

The S.P.S.

The pamphlets and tracts of the Saar Socialist Party,[35] particularly a series entitled *Unter der Lupe*, give roughly equal importance to:

1. Propaganda for an affirmative vote and attacks on the parties opposed to the Statute, followed by:
2. Propaganda for the S.P.S.
3. Against the C.V.P., the C.D.U., and the D.S.P.
4. Propaganda for Europe.
5. Economic advantages of the Statute.
6. Hostility to Mr. Schneider.
7. Support for Mr. Hoffmann, which did not imply approval of his party or of his domestic policy.

The *Volksstimme* took the same line:

1. Against the parties unfavourable to the Statute, against their nationalism and their newspapers.
2. In favour of an affirmative vote.
   In favour of Europe.
3. Propaganda for the S.P.S.
4. Propaganda for Mr. Hoffmann.
5. Propaganda on the economic advantages of the Statute.

Alongside the political parties, the European organizations also embarked upon large-scale propaganda in favour of the Statute with many posters and pamphlets. Western European Union edited a broadsheet, *Europa ruft*, which emphasized the following themes:

1. Against the parties in favour of a negative vote, their nationalism, and their newspapers.
2. In favour of an affirmative vote.
3. In favour of Europe.
4. Propaganda on the economic advantages of the Statute.
5. In support of Mr. Hoffmann.
6. Reminder of the Second World War.

---

[35] The posters of the S.P.S. were fairly typical for a Socialist party: " S.P.S. soziale Gerechtigkeit, macht die Linke stark . . . wählt sozialdemokratisch." " Die S.P.S. kämpft gegen Reaktion, gegen Ausbeutung, gegen Kriegspolitik." There was, naturally, the theme of *Europe* (pole with the flags of Europe including that of the S.P.S.—" Deine Stimme S.P.S. für Europa "). Another poster showed an atomic explosion with the caption: " Darum wähle europäisch S.P.S." Still another poster showed a mother and son on a pile of ruins: " S.P.S., dann Ja."

These themes came up again in the major Saar newspaper, the *Saarbrücker Zeitung*, which declared itself:

1. In favour of an affirmative vote.
2. In favour of Europe.
3. In favour of the economic advantages of the Statute.
4. Against the parties favouring a negative vote.
5. In favour of the C.V.P. and Mr. Hoffmann.

This brief study reveals that the campaign concentrated on very simple issues: Yes or No. But it also reveals that the argument most employed by the opposition parties was that of the German Fatherland.[36] This was not surprising, if we remember the nature of a campaign of this type which appeals to sentiments rather than to material interests. Faced with this evocation of a Germany to which the Saarlanders were attached by traditional ties, Europe was powerless. Supporters of the Statute often sought to appeal to reason to show the advantages of the Statute. But the majority of the Saarlanders were not convinced of the economic advantages and, on the other hand, they knew that a return to Germany, their native land, would also satisfy their material interests.

PUBLIC OPINION AND THE DECISION

In concluding this effort at analysis—and let it not be forgotten how tentative the conclusions are—an attempt will be made to evaluate the influence of public opinion on the final decision.

One observation must be made at the outset: that is, the limited interest in the Saar question in Germany as well as in France. In comparison with problems of domestic policy—problems raised by the Berlin blockade or reunification, the re-armament of Germany, the E.D.C., or the war in Indo-China—the Saar occupied only a very secondary place. At no time did the French and Germans give the impression that the absence of a satisfactory agreement could have a serious effect on relations between the two states. Never for a moment did the idea of recourse to arms appear to occur to them. There was no suggestion of a move towards armed resistance. No one seems to have thought of a break in diplomatic relations.

A second observation is this: the French followed the affair even less closely than did the Germans. So the government, or rather

[36] *Cf.*, also, Dehousse, *op. cit.*, p. 19.

the Minister for Foreign Affairs, had considerable freedom of action, at least in the years 1950 to 1952. In April, 1951, Robert Schuman was not harried by an opposition, as was his German opposite number, nor was he swept along by public opinion. It was easier for him to make concessions than it was for Chancellor Adenauer. The difference in the response of public opinion played an important part in the decision on this occasion.[37]   Mr. Schuman's successors had much less chance to manoeuvre. But this was not because of a re-awakening or a hardening of public opinion. It was because they were bound by the concept of the "Saar as a prerequisite."

Chancellor Adenauer also had relative freedom of action as far as public opinion was concerned. His decision at the beginning of 1950 to take a public position on the Saar question was not forced on him by any visible pressure of opinion expressed through a press campaign or by especially vehement parliamentary speeches. It was more in the action of his followers and the small group of men concerned with the Saar question that an explanation was to be found. It lay even more in considerations of a tactical nature (the need to answer the French move to create a *fait accompli* by negotiation of the Conventions) or of a political order (*Gesamt-deutsche Legitimation*). By March, 1952, German public opinion was undoubtedly more attentive to the Saar problem than it had been two years earlier. The parliamentary opposition intervened several times very sharply and the newspapers protested against the Hoffmann "régime." In spite of this, the Chancellor decided in the course of the negotiations with Mr. Schuman to withdraw the complaint lodged with the Council of Europe concerning the "violation of democratic freedoms" in the Saar. This was because he had seen more profitable possibilities of manoeuvring in the diplomatic field. In 1954, when the Agreement of October 23 was concluded, and then in 1955, during the electoral campaign pre-ceding the referendum, the Chancellor kept to the general line of policy he had laid down for himself, despite the growing pressure of German opinion and despite the obvious opposition of the majority of the Saarlanders which was apparent by August, 1955.

In the Saar, on the other hand, the relationship between public opinion and the decision was more apparent. The influence was

[37] *Supra*, p. 272.

much more the result of a mood than of an active demonstration of public opinion or of pressure.

The mood was one of acceptance or of indifference in the early years when the French were formulating the policy aimed at economic union. In general, the Saarlanders were either well disposed or passive. In the proposed solution they perceived certain advantages which they were the more inclined to consider because there was no alternative. Limitations on the freedom of the press, furthermore, made it difficult to express an opinion. Later, the mood altered. Acceptance was tinged with reserve, indifference with criticism. The hope of fruitful co-operation gave place to scepticism, even to hostility. The state of mind gradually became one of opposition. The relation of light and shade changed imperceptibly. The advantages of the present situation faded into the background and the spotlight focused on the things that were wrong; people were all the more inclined to exaggerate, because to do so justified their wish to return to a Germany which was on a rising tide of prosperity. Everything became an excuse for protest and rejection.[38]

There was no valid argument which the government could oppose to this emotional reaction. In the mood of 1955, considerations of material interests were no longer compelling; Europe had no power of attraction.

[38] It is interesting to note that, later, some of the men who had been the most energetic critics of French policy and of the Hoffmann Government indirectly paid homage to the régime which they had brought down by stressing the advantages that French social legislation had brought to the Saar people. The D.P.S. deputies abstained from voting at the session of the Saar Parliament on December 13, 1956, when the decision was taken concerning the return of the Saar to Germany. By so doing they showed solidarity with their leader, Heinrich Schneider, who had declared that the German Government had not given sufficient guarantees that it would maintain their *Sozialer Besitzstand*.

14

INTERNATIONAL INFLUENCES

THE Franco-German conflict over the Saar developed in an international context. To what extent was it influenced by this fact?

We have already tried to give an answer by pointing out the importance of the turning-point of 1947 and that of 1950–1951, recalling briefly the changes that had taken place in international relations and their effect on the Saar question.[1]

The development of relations between the Russians and the British, American, and French Allies influenced, as we have seen, initial decisions concerning the Saar. The French Government had sought, after the war and especially during the period of the tripartite agreement, to follow a middle course between the Anglo-American powers and the U.S.S.R., without committing itself too far on one side or the other, and it had hoped to find support for, or at least some understanding of, its German policy from the Moscow Government. It met with an evasive attitude which gradually changed into open opposition. In the beginning, there was the possibility that French and Russian aims might converge to some extent: internationalization of the Ruhr might offer the U.S.S.R. the chance to obtain a footing in Western Germany after obtaining control of Eastern Germany. But the break-down of the tripartism and the realization of the differences in concepts as to methods of international control held by France and by the U.S.S.R. led to a hardening of positions. At the Moscow Conference in the spring of 1947, Mr. Molotov refused, despite the repeated appeals of Mr. Bidault, to agree to the French proposal to detach the Saar politically from Germany and unite it economically with France. A new attempt in 1947 was equally fruitless.

From then onwards the Soviet Government, followed by the Communist parties, expressed its disapproval of the policy France had adopted towards the Saar.

This Soviet opposition, merely a manifestation of an over-all policy aimed at splitting up the Western Allies and preventing the

[1] *Cf. Historical Study*, pp. 39, 70–73.

consolidation of Western Germany, had a twofold consequence. It led the French Government to be more flexible in its German policy in order to anticipate the desires of its Allies. And it led the British and Americans to make their attitude towards the French proposals for the Saar more explicit.

At a moment of mounting tension with the U.S.S.R., neither London nor Washington could afford to have France, herself a battlefield for influence, slide over to the Russian side. There was a greater disposition to make a few diplomatic concessions because her demands concerning the Saar did not raise any fundamental questions of principle and because the Allies were still in a period in which the right to carve up Germany was assumed and the demands of European security justified the severest measures towards the defeated. In the various American plans for Germany, the case of the Saar was treated along with that of the Rhine-Westphalia basin, and the possibility was envisaged of treating it as a separate entity and setting up a state under international control.[2] The creation of the state of Mittelrhein-Saar during the period of American occupation, although not the implementation of a definite plan, stemmed from the same political reasoning.

But if the United States Government appeared willing to agree to the solution proposed by Mr. Bidault, as evidenced by the statements of Mr. Byrnes to his French colleague early in 1946[3] as well as his oft-quoted speech of September of the same year, in Stuttgart, it nevertheless withheld its agreement in order to make France abandon her opposition to the formation of a central German administration.

The result was that the whole affair dragged on and it was not until the Moscow Conference in the spring of 1947 that the United States definitely took a position. General Marshall expressed

[2] The Morgenthau Plan provided for the same economic régime in the Saar as in the Ruhr. As for Sumner Welles, he had envisaged either a south German state, of which the Saar would be a part, or the formation of three international states under United Nations control: Ruhr, Rhineland, and Saar. *Cf.*, respectively, his *The Time for Decision* (New York: 1944), p. 352, and *Where are we Heading?* (New York: 1946), p. 126.

[3] Mr. Byrnes assured Mr. Bidault, in a personal letter of February 6, 1946, that he fully sympathized with French claims in the Saar but at the same time he was not willing to go along with French opposition to the Allied plans for Germany. *Cf.* James F. Byrnes, *Speaking Frankly* (New York: 1947), p. 170. When at the end of the year General Clay protested against the establishment of the French customs barrier on the Saar-German frontier, he was informed by Dean Acheson that Mr. Byrnes had secretly agreed to this French decision some months previously ". . . while our government would not approve such action neither would it oppose it." *Cf.* Lucius DuBignon Clay, *Decision in Germany* (Garden City, New York: 1950), p. 133.

himself clearly: after reiterating the idea of Saar-Lorraine unity and stressing the importance for France of Saar coal, the Secretary of State referred to the statements of his predecessor at Stuttgart and concluded by declaring that the United States backed the French request for the political separation of the Saar from Germany and its incorporation through a customs and monetary union into the economic and financial system of France. The status envisaged at the time was very close to that given to the Saar in the inter-war period with, however, one basic difference: the Saar territory was not to be placed under the control and protection of an international body. Nevertheless, measures would have to be taken to guarantee its political autonomy and the right of the Saarlanders to manage their own affairs. Was this intended as a provisional solution? Was that what General Marshall seemed to suggest when, at the end of his statement, he recalled that " the definitive determination of its boundaries will have to be decided by the German peace settlement which will also have to decide many details relating to the ownership of property, debt, and other matters "? [4] " Definitive determination "—did not this indicate that in the mind of General Marshall the régime for the Saar to which he gave his approval was destined to stand, and that all that was lacking was the sanction of the treaty? A few months later, at the Conference of Foreign Ministers which met in London from November 25 to December 15, the Secretary of State returned to the attack stressing several times in the face of Soviet opposition that three delegations were in agreement that the Saar should be politically separated from Germany and united economically with France.

Three delegations. England had indeed followed the same policy as the United States on the Saar question. At the end of 1947 the French Government could go forward in the certain knowledge that she had the support of her British and American Allies for her Saar policy.

The governments of Washington and London did not deviate from the attitude they had adopted in 1947. From then until the plebiscite of 1955 they continued to support France and they officially rejected attempts on the part of Germany to re-open the question of the Saar's status. The statement of Mr. Acheson on

---

[4] *Cf.* " Moscow Meeting of the Council of Foreign Ministers, Statements by the Secretary of State," Department of State *Bulletin*, Vol. XVI, *op. cit.*, p. 696.

January 18, 1950, in reply to a question from a correspondent concerning the Saar left no room for doubt. Even more categorical and curt was the reply of the Allied High Commissioners on August 3, 1951, to Chancellor Adenauer's note of May 29: " The Saar Statute is not in contradiction with the Allied declarations of June 5, 1945." Moreover, " the jurisdiction of the Federal Republic does not extend beyond its own territorial limits." [5]

This official severity [6] did not prevent the discussion from cropping up again. The Anglo-American guarantee was, in fact, given only to a provisional status. The fact that the final decision was expressly deferred till conclusion of the peace treaty provided the opponents of French policy with an opportunity to call into question the solutions adopted. The English and the Americans could no more prevent this than could the French. Their insistence in stressing that a final decision could not be taken until later, within the scope of an over-all settlement, was interpreted as encouraging discussion or as an implicit disowning of French policy. The shift in alliances and the recovery of Germany, moreover, added further weight to this interpretation. By 1950 the Federal Republic had become not only a possible and useful ally but a necessary one who must be treated with consideration. Requests that she might make could no longer be dismissed outright. The memory of the war was fading as a new threat grew. The demands of France and her attempts to give permanence to a status which the governments accepted as provisional met with an increasingly lukewarm response in London and in Washington. They did not officially go back on the commitments they had made, but they let it be more and more clearly known that they would be glad to see an amicable settlement between France and Germany in the interests of Europe.

The change of attitude was gradual, even subtle, but it was nonetheless evident. Though in March, 1950, after a conversation between Mr. Bevin and Mr. Schuman, the Foreign Office gave very firm instructions to its High Commissioner in Germany to inform the Chancellor that it was pointless to try and set the United States and Britain against French policy in the Saar, and though in August, 1951, the High Commissioners replied in the negative and

[5] *Cf. Historical Study*, p. 100.
[6] Helmut Hirsch received from the State Department a letter dated May 29, 1956, reiterating the United States Government's intention of keeping out of the discussions.

very curtly to the Adenauer note of May 29, in the autumn of 1952 Mr. Eden agreed to act as intermediary for Chancellor Adenauer in the attempted negotiation that preceded the elections to the Saar Landtag.

In the spring of 1953 when René Mayer and Konrad Adenauer visited Washington in turn and each raised the question of the Saar, the United States Embassy in Paris intervened in regard to the new Franco-Saar Convention.[7] In the autumn of this same year when the French Government was preparing to re-open discussions with the German Government on the Saar, it found that its efforts to obtain public support from its British and American Allies met with considerable lack of enthusiasm. Once again they made it clear that there was no question of their going back on promises they had made; but they manifested their hesitation by emphasizing the importance of getting rid of the Saar barrier to the ratification of the E.D.C.

Even more important than the Allied shift from firm support to an increasingly marked reserve was the change in attitude that could be observed in the press and in certain statements made by associations or groups representing segments of opinion.[8] Despite a natural sympathy for France and doubts about Germany, there was manifest in various quarters, both in the United Kingdom and the United States, a growing anxiety about the tension aroused by the discussions between France and Germany on the subject of the Saar. There was also apparent some impatience with the over-rigid position adopted by France. It is noteworthy that *The New York Times*, which after the 1947 elections to the Landtag was favourable towards French policy, was more critical in its comments on the measures taken by the French at the beginning of 1950.[9] The Saar affair was deplored as endangering European peace unnecessarily and very definite reservations were expressed in regard to the Conventions and to a " but thinly-disguised annexation of the Saar." [10] At the same time, it was asserted, Germany's protests, coming from a nation which had subscribed to its own conquests,

---

[7] *Cf. Historical Study*, p. 133, note 6.

[8] We were not able to make a systematic survey of the American and British press, but, in the case of the United States, we have made use of research done at our request by Helmut Hirsch and we have supplemented it with certain polls. *Cf.* Preface.

[9] *Cf.* Hans Rothfels, " The Saar Problem in 1950," *American Perspective*, Vol. IV, No. 3 (Summer, 1950). Mr. Hirsch was able to study the cuttings from *The New York Times*—35 in all—used by Mr. Rothfels for the period January–March, 1950.

[10] *The New York Times*, March 6, 1950.

were out of place. The only possible justification for a German protest, said the writer of the editorial in *The New York Times*, lay in the fact that the final status could not be determined until conclusion of the peace treaty and that, as a result, it was the duty of any German government to reserve its country's rights.[11]

The opinion expressed by *The New York Times* on this occasion was similar to that in other newspapers and it recurred more and more frequently in the American press [12]; especially after 1952 the press reflected the growing anxiety and irritation caused by increasing French opposition to certain forms of European integration, particularly to the E.D.C. Criticism varied in intensity according to the influences at work.[13] It should be noted that it was particularly strong in trade union circles, which adopted the arguments of the German Socialists. In fact, it was in the statements of the American Federation of Labor that French policy towards the Saar was most openly criticized. Thus, a mid-September, 1952, report by its Executive Council to the Seventy-first Convention of Trade Unions condemned the arbitrary decision to separate the Saar from Germany as a move that weakened the West in its struggle against the Soviet Union and against the Oder-Neisse line. The statement declared that French policy must be revised if the confidence of the German workers was to be won and the participation of the German people in the defence of Europe and democracy ensured.[14] At the beginning of 1955, the American Federation of Labor returned to the attack, requesting the government not to guarantee the unreasonable and anti-democratic status proposed for the Saar.[15]

The British press, or rather those few among the most influential papers and periodicals we studied,[16] showed an increasingly marked reserve towards the French Government's Saar policy.

[11] *Ibid.*

[12] *Cf.*, for example, a commentary by Ned Stanford, Washington correspondent for the *Christian Science Monitor*, January 19, 1950, on Dean Acheson's statement. We also had at our disposal a mimeographed study by Lawrence H. Goldberg, *The Saar Problem as Discussed in Two Editorials of the Christian Science Monitor*, which is based on a survey of twenty-five articles in that newspaper.

[13] The Saar and French Governments, on one side, and the Federal Government, on the other, did their best by active propaganda to win American opinion to their way of thinking.

[14] *Cf. International Free Trade Union News*, October, 1952.

[15] *Ibid.*, March, 1955.

[16] Newspapers such as *The Times* and the *Manchester Guardian*, and periodicals such as *The Economist* and the *New Statesman and Nation*, interested us particularly because they are read abroad and because they are held, rightly or wrongly, to be representative of British opinion.

True, the commentators took great care not to offend France and to avoid anything that might seem like interference in the Saar crisis. They also showed little sympathy for certain violent speeches from the German opposition. The memory of the disturbances preceding the 1935 plebiscite and of the Hitlerian era was still too fresh for them to observe without anxiety the outbreaks of nationalist fever among some of the Saarlanders or the Germans.

But they did not hesitate to criticize the interventions of Mr. Hoffmann's police [17] and the all too obvious limitations on democratic freedoms.[18] They also showed a polite but growing impatience [19] with the French resistance to a compromise solution that was, they felt, absolutely essential to Chancellor Adenauer, who had to hold his own against a dangerous opposition. What they were trying to make France understand was that consideration of her interests in the Saar—for which they showed a good deal of understanding—must not be allowed to prejudice Franco-German *rapprochement* [20] and solution of the major problems facing the whole Western community. *The Economist* of September 19, 1953, wrote: "If the French refuse to compromise on the Saar, important though it be to their weakened economy, they will be helping to frustrate any hope of a peaceful handling of the eastern frontier question." It went on to remind the British and American Governments that they, too, must shoulder their responsibilities if they wanted France to assume all the risks of a compromise with Germany. This last remark indicates that, although France's

---

[17] *Cf.*, for example, an article in *The Times*, November 26, 1952.

[18] *Cf. New Statesman and Nation*, December 6, 1952.

[19] A somewhat acid politeness, judging by some of the comments in *The Economist* on the proposal that there be a Saar contingent in the European Army (January 20, 1951); or later, when Mr. Grandval was appointed Ambassador, "The appointment of Mr. Grandval was neither patient nor intelligent" (*ibid.*, February 9, 1952).

[20] "Developments seem therefore to be proceeding with the same disastrous inevitability that marked similar disputes after the First World War. The British and American Governments approved the economic attachment of the Saar to France and its political detachment from Germany at a time when German nationalists dared not raise their voices. They are now faced with the distasteful fact that the French have had to take undemocratic measures to protect their acquisition from German agitators. Unless a concerted effort is made to prevent history repeating itself further, it is to be feared that the concessions that are being denied to Dr Adenauer will one day be granted to some nationalist demagogue successor to the German chancellorship." Or again: "The Franco-German dispute over the Saar has gone from bad to worse, as each side takes up new positions in public from which it will be hard to retreat. This is particularly unfortunate, as the best hope of reaching a settlement lay in postponing action until M. Schuman and Dr. Adenauer could come to terms, and the federation of Europe could take shape." *The Economist*, November 22, 1952.

allies may have been critical of her policy, they had no intention of leaving her to stand alone.

There is still a further question: What was the influence of the Council of Europe and of the Van Naters Plan on the development of the Saar conflict? At first sight one is tempted to reply that in fact, despite all the efforts made, the Van Naters Plan played only a secondary role and was swept aside when France rejected the E.D.C. A more considered view, however, suggests other conclusions. First, it should be recognized that the intervention of the Council of Europe and the decision in the autumn of 1952 to re-examine the problem as a whole had a calming influence and strengthened the position of those in France and in Germany who were working for the *rapprochement* of the two countries. A heated debate on the violation of democratic freedoms in the Saar and on the intervention of Germany was avoided and attention was concentrated on a plan for europeanization. From the moment this plan was formulated and submitted, the governments could not ignore it. The bilateral discussions which started again in the autumn of 1953 took place under the indirect pressure of a " third party " which was working all the more enthusiastically because it was inspired by the desire to achieve victory for a cause. For Mr. van der Goes van Naters, and perhaps even more for his collaborators, members of the Secretariat of the Council of Europe, it was essential to obtain the French Parliament's ratification of the treaties setting up the E.D.C., and this meant abolishing the obstacle created by " the Saar prerequisite." But the Government of the Federal Republic could not accept a European status for the Saar that gave France a privileged position. Thus, the initial project of Mr. van der Goes van Naters providing for the preservation of the Franco-Saar economic union was not acceptable. Hence they did their best to modify it by introducing what might be called a kind of " balance " into its economic clauses. It was with this in mind that in October, 1953, the Gerstenmaier-Pfleiderer amendment was submitted providing for an arrangement that would gradually open the Saar market to German products. We know that the Economic Sub-committee, meeting in Brussels at the beginning of December, 1953, took this proposal into consideration and without accepting the whole Gerstenmaier-Pfleiderer amendment it did introduce modifications designed to make the Plan more acceptable in Germany.[21] During the vote on April 26, 1954, in the General Affairs Committee, Mr. Mommer maintained his opposition and Mr. Pfleiderer abstained; Mr. Gerstenmaier, after being in touch with Mr. Adenauer, ended by giving his approval. Meantime, moreover, the French and German Governments had decided to accept the Van Naters Plan as a basis of negotiation.[22]

The intervention of the Council of Europe was therefore helpful, and its influence apparent even before the Consultative Assembly was called upon to act on the final version of the Plan. We know that it never did so, since the rejection of the E.D.C. by the National Assembly meant that the problem then had to be reconsidered on a different basis. The effect of this parallel action by the Council of Europe was felt for some time, however, despite the failure of the E.D.C. and the abandonment of the plan for europeanization, because of the growing interrelationship between the Franco-German bilateral negotiations and the discussions relating to the final draft of the Plan. However different the mood in which the Paris agreements were concluded in the autumn of 1954, it was nonetheless clear that French and German negotiators had benefited from the work done by Mr. van der Goes van Naters and his colleagues. The inclusion in these agreements of provisions for the development of economic relations between Germany and the Saar, towards the " balance " requested by the Federal Republic, was fairly significant.[23]

21 *Cf.*, in this connection, Kitzinger, *The Economics of the Saar Question, op. cit.*, pp. 26 *et seq.* The author was not in a position to give detailed information, but one cannot fail to be struck by the fact that it was Mr. van der Goes van Naters himself who, at the meeting of December 3 following private discussions, proposed a modification which he qualified as decisive in his speech of May 25, 1954. A passage from this speech is given below as a matter of interest :
" By finding a solution to the economic problem, the Sub-committee which met in Brussels under the chairmanship of Mr. Struye has perhaps made a decisive contribution which will allow these European solutions to be put into effect.
" It will be seen from paragraph 29 of the statement of principles governing the report how this solution was reached. My initial report of July, 1953, clearly expressed our intention of finding an economic solution, European in character, but I lacked the technical means at that time. Economic experts of the Secretariat, helped by the researches of the Saar experts, gave conclusive replies to these questions." Council of Europe, Consultative Assembly, 6th Ordinary Session, Part I, May, 1954, *Minutes of Debates*, Vol. I, p. 179.
22 This did not mean that the two governments were disposed to accept the formula proposed in the plan. *Cf. Historical Study*, pp. 157–159. Mr. van der Goes van Naters and his collaborators maintained, it is true, that the formula they had drafted safeguarded the interests of all three countries involved. *Cf.*, in this connection, the interview given by Mr. Federspiel, Chairman of the Economic Committee of the Council of Europe, to *Le Monde* and published in that paper on June 6–7, 1954.
23 Mr. Kitzinger compared the economic clauses in the various agreements. *Cf.* Kitzinger, *op. cit.*, Chapters VII, VIII, Appendix II.

The influence of Europe, or more exactly, of the European idea, was not exercised merely through the Council of Europe. The Western European Union, hastily created in the autumn of 1954, also performed a service that must not be underestimated; it was responsible for the vital decision to create the European Commission for the Saar referendum. As soon as the Saarlanders were given an opportunity to express their opinion, an opinion that would be binding, it was vital to ensure, in so far as possible, freedom of the Saar citizens. The struggle in the Saar itself had become more and more impassioned. There was a danger that it might degenerate from verbal battles to fisticuffs. There is no doubt that the activities of the European Commission for the referendum, and particularly of its chairman, Fernand Dehousse, kept the electoral campaign within reasonable bounds and thus helped to make it easier for France to accept the results of the referendum.[24]

As we have said, some mistrust of Germany lingered in the United States and in the United Kingdom, a mistrust that was not allayed by the violence of the German opposition's attacks on Chancellor Adenauer. The weakening of France's position was caused particularly by contradictions in her own policy; contradictions that became more apparent as the international climate changed. What seemed possible—even legitimate—immediately after the war became questionable from the moment an attempt was made to give the Federal Republic a place within the Western Alliance and, through European federation, to transcend national antagonisms.[25] Germany's protests, timid and questionable henceforth, found a response. Her claim was justified by the very

---

[24] *Cf.* Dehousse, *op. cit.*, pp. 13 *et seq.*

[25] Mr. Grandval was aware of the problem for France inherent in the change in international climate. His comments on this subject during 1950 are worth mentioning: "When the main lines of French policy in the Saar were laid down between 1945 and 1948, it was not impossible to consider a solution of the Saar problem based on the classic type of peace treaty. . . . Our intention at the time was to impose on the Saar a tutelage limiting its autonomy, using its international status as a basis; we therefore tried to instil this idea into Saar institutions as well as into its way of life. . . . Developments indicated that it would be wiser not to count on a classic type of peace treaty. . . . On the other hand, the supremacy of the traditional notion of sovereignty tended to become blurred by the efforts to pool European purposes and resources. Any idea of annexation or of hegemony in Europe is gone today. For its part, the French Government has for some years given up any idea of this kind, and any German attempt to re-integrate the Saar could only be regarded as a display of nationalism and as the expression of a desire for hegemony contrary to the very foundations of European Union."

principles proclaimed by the conquerors who now sought alliance
with her. It was Germany who made her demands in the name
of the right of peoples to self-determination and in the name of
Europe. It was Germany who demanded that democratic freedoms be respected. It was she who based herself on the
fundamental concepts upon which the twentieth century intended
to build an international society. The relation of moral forces had
changed. On the international level a transformation had taken
place analogous to that in the Saar. Just as the Saar Government
found itself gradually driven to the defensive by an opposition
whose development it could not stop, so the French Government
found itself little by little caught in a dilemma, partly of its own
making, between a policy of European and international co-operation in conformity with what it considered to be France's vocation
and the instinctive desire—inherently restrictive—to protect her
security. The struggle to escape from this impasse, the efforts of
the French Government to reconcile defence of its interests in the
Saar with its policy of European integration, far from giving the
hoped for results, only afforded its critics new opportunities to
underscore the contradictions in its policy. How could anyone
fail to be struck by the fact that the conclusion of the Franco-Saar
Conventions of 1950 and 1953, resulting in a broadening of Saar
autonomy, produced not only a hardening in German opposition
but coolness on the part of the British and American Allies?

Neither the shift in alliances nor the changes that had come
about in the international climate would have sufficed to create a
change in the balance of moral force between France and Germany
had there not been a parallel change in the balance of material
force. The fact is too evident to need stressing. After the
monetary reform, Western Germany recovered with disconcerting
rapidity and force. Scarcely had the Federal Republic been constituted when she took her place in the concert of European nations,
and her influence did not cease to grow. This economic and
political recovery served not only to give Germany back her power
of attraction over the Saar. It also conferred on her demands in
the international field a weight impossible for a state of more
modest resources. The means at her disposal, her ever-increasing
power, and the dynamism of her economy, forced those with
whom she dealt to give her a hearing and to take her desires into
consideration. Those managing the affairs of the Federal Republic

moreover found renewed confidence in a consideration of her power and a conviction that the change in the balance of strength would lead almost inevitably to a solution of the Saar problem favourable to Germany.[26]

The French also were conscious of the change that was taking place, a change that was to their detriment. They therefore suffered a contrary reaction. As against German confidence there was anxiety in France, and as against the dynamism of Germany there was a tendency to withdraw into her shell. Very soon, even before the Federal Republic was officially established, those responsible for France's Saar policy made it apparent that time was working against their country.[27] Hence the oft-expressed desire, even haste, to take steps to consolidate while there was still time and to create something definitive out of a régime that was officially regarded as provisional. Hence the defence reflex in regard to Germany, expressed in rejection of the E.D.C. and also in the introduction of the " Saar prerequisite." French policy became frozen, thus leaving to the Federal Republic the advantage of diplomatic initiative and the benefit of arguments in favour of European federation.

[26] *Cf. Historical Study*, p. 105.
[27] *Ibid.*, pp. 56 *et seq*.

15

CONCLUSIONS

AT the end of 1945 the French Government had decided to integrate the Saar into its economy. This decision was dictated by a desire to overcome the economic difficulties of the post-war period as quickly as possible. Its justification was based on a faith in the right of the French to reparations for the damage they had suffered. It was inspired equally if not more so by the political advantage to France of having the economic balance between the two neighbouring countries tipped in her favour.

This policy of the French Government was carried out in the Saar by a man who had the stature of a great administrator. When it was formulated, the policy corresponded to the relative strength of a Germany beaten and disorganized and a France associated with the Allied victory. It was based on the support of the political parties in France and on the explicit or tacit adherence of most of the Saar population.

There was scarcely any opposition, to say nothing of resistance. At the very most there were certain reservations in France towards any policy of annexation. The sensitivity of the French to the idea of the right of self-determination of peoples and to the principles proclaimed during the war acted as a brake on their own activities and offered grounds for eventual criticism of a French policy that sought to free itself of these restrictions. The silence that hung over Germany implied neither approbation nor lasting acceptance. Isolated protests arose that were perhaps the forerunners of others.

A few years later the situation had completely changed; France, facing a dynamic and demanding Germany, seemed uneasy and isolated. The Saarlanders were going over to the opposition in increasing numbers and they saw in the return of their country to the German Fatherland the opportunity of reconciling their interests with their feelings. The British and American Allies were lukewarm. The memory of the war had faded, as had that of the German occupation, of the conquerors' rights to reparations and to precautionary measures against a possible return to power of a warlike Germany. The victims under discussion were no longer Frenchmen in territory occupied by the National Socialist régime but Saarlanders demanding restitution of their democratic liberties. It was in the name of the spirit animating the Schuman and Pleven Plans and of European co-operation that the German Government asked the French Government to find a solution to the Saar problem in conformity with the principle of self-determination of peoples.

How are we to explain this reversal of the situation? First of all, what was the source of the conflict? What was its nature? If consideration were limited to the resources of the Saar, there might be a temptation to concentrate attention on the economic factor, to assert that France and Germany had quarrelled over Saar coal and some of the large iron and steel companies. This explanation, as has been seen, is superficial. The conflict was, in fact, primarily political. One has only to recall the comment made in 1946 by one of the men responsible for shaping French policy in the Saar: economic union had obvious political advantages, he said; and after defining the objectives, he asserted that their fulfilment should take precedence over all other considerations and should result in bringing about economic union with the Saar, " even if there were no economic advantages . . . in addition to political interests." [1] Nor should the negative attitude of representatives of the French iron and steel industry and of groups in Lorraine be forgotten.

This obviously does not mean that economic considerations played no part. On the contrary, they were always present in the actions of the French Government. In 1945 France needed Saar coal. Her rulers admitted the fact. They wanted to ensure control of an important industrial region and they defended tenaciously to the end the economic union they had achieved. But the quest for economic advantage never distracted them from the political aim underlying all their actions: economic union was a means of reducing Germany's industrial potential and inversely of increasing that of France and, consequently, of lessening the imbalance of strength between the two countries.

On the German side, economic arguments seemed to have even less weight. Industrial circles, as we have seen, showed themselves

[1] *Cf. supra*, p. 227.

very lukewarm and even indifferent. They had no part in Chancellor Adenauer's decision in the beginning of 1950 to raise the Saar question officially. Despite repeated appeals they gave only limited support to the activities of the *Saarbund*. They were fully occupied first in reconstructing and then in developing their own businesses, and the Saar played only a marginal role. The overriding concern of the Federal Government, as well as of Parliament and the mass of public opinion, was political and national. Preoccupation with what has been called the *Gesamtdeutsche Legitimation* contributed to the decisive 1950 move Chancellor Adenauer was encouraged to take by pressure from the little group led by Gustav Strohm. The Federal Government would have committed a bad tactical error had it given way on the Saar; it would have compromised its chances in the more difficult and delicate negotiations that would have to be undertaken one day on the subject of the eastern territories. The government had no right to abandon a German territory. For the Germans there was no question about it: the Saar was German. Opinion was unanimous on this point. As early as 1946, long before the Government of the Federal Republic came into being, all the statements on the Saar took the same line and this unanimity continued to the end. The only area of disagreement was on the possibilities of a compromise with France or the method of accomplishing it—which meant by implication a special status for the Saar. Opposition to economic union with France was all the more determinedly uncompromising because this union implied the Saar's political separation from Germany, which the Germans refused to accept. Rejection of europeanization stemmed from the same attitude. The Germans' Saar policy was thus dominated by a nationalist reflex and the settlement of the Franco-German dispute after the referendum was one more proof of this. Significantly, the French Government, forced to bow to the decision of the Saarlanders, fell back on the economic concessions that the Government of the Federal Republic granted with a generosity based on the fact that it had obtained satisfaction on the crucial issue. The Saar was German; the French, who had to be satisfied with compensation, were as well aware of this as the Germans who granted it.

In explaining the reversal of the situation in the Saar an important element was the fact that the Saar belonged to the *Deutschtum*. This impediment to the implementation of a French policy designed to detach the Saar from Germany could be surmounted only to the extent that France was able not only to offer the Saarlanders compensations for a change of nationality but also to provide a gravitational pull strong enough to turn them away from their native country. The possibilities of success which seemed to exist in the beginning dwindled away as time went on. Why? Was it because the material advantages that the Saarlanders hoped for turned out to be less than they had thought? Was the "economic factor," then, perhaps more important than has been said? Was nationalist sentiment a factor only when it coincided with material interests? There is some force in this argument. Certainly in the beginning most of the Saarlanders turned towards France because there was little to be gained from a crushed and dismembered Germany. It is also true that when these same Saarlanders declared themselves to be German they were spurred by considerations of material interest. The influence on the attitude of the Saarlanders of rising prices in the Saar and the instability of France's economic policy contrasting with the recovery and spectacular expansion of the German economy, have rightly been emphasized, but this does not mean that the economic factor was paramount. Did not the European Statute proposed in 1955 also offer material advantages? And yet it was for the German Fatherland that the majority of the Saar electors opted. The atmosphere of the campaign, the arguments put forward by the various parties, all showed that when the moment came to take the final decision, the Saarlanders did not reason but allowed themselves to be guided by their feelings.

Can the change that had taken place in the relative strength of France and Germany be considered the decisive factor?

All those historians or political scientists who attribute a dominant role in international affairs to power relationships must be tempted to interpret the evolution of the Saar conflict in the light of their own theories. This would lead to a delightfully simple formulation: France, profiting from Germany's disaster, took over control of the Saar, a German province, and instituted an economic union which the Saarlanders accepted because it seemed to be to their advantage to do so. But Germany recovered. She took her place in Europe and in the concert of Powers again; for the Saarlanders she regained her magnetism, all the greater because France had meanwhile grown weaker. France, therefore, failed because she was not able to ensure implementation of her policy and because she did not have the necessary strength to restrain the centrifugal forces set up by Germany's recovery.

This explanation is certainly not without merit. It indicates one of the essential elements in the reversal that occurred between 1947 and 1955. It is supported by comments made at various times by some of the principal actors in the drama, as, for example, the previously cited remark by a German minister concerning the change in the relative strength of France and Germany and its influence on the outcome of the Saar conflict.[2] Mention must also be made of Gilbert Grandval's observations on the "ineluctable degradation" he had to suffer in the Saar because of a "policy too exacting for the weakness of the régime."[3]

But this type of formulation, however thought-provoking, has the disadvantage of over-simplification. It does not follow the winding paths of history. It takes no account of the many and various forces that contribute in one way or another to the development of a situation and that have to be analysed separately if their importance is to be assessed. It passes over in silence the activities of a Grandval, a Debré, or a Schuman. It does not indicate how the skill and level-headedness of an Adenauer paved the way for a peaceful settlement of the conflict. It does not reveal, as it should, the significance of the contribution of men like Strohm, Hellwig, Zimmer, Altmeier, Mommer, Bornewasser, Schneider, Kutsch to the final victory of the German case. It does not make it possible to measure the influence of individuals who embodied a Saar policy in France and in Germany, of groups involved in the conflict, or of the underlying forces and collective emotions; nor does it make it possible to estimate the importance of economic interests, the outreach of emotional reactions, or the effects of diplomatic negotiations in which men of unequal capabilities whose decisions dictated the sequence of events faced one another. It also ignores the influence of the changes in the political climate in France, Germany, and Europe on the circumstances in which the Saar problem was broached.

Each one of these elements deserves to be taken into consideration. This is what we have tried to do in the second part of our study. However, when we come to assess their relative importance,

[2] Cf. *Historical Study*, p. 105.
[3] *Ma mission au Maroc* (Paris: 1956), p. 8.

we are forced to conclude that not one of them can explain the development of the conflict. They are but component parts of an explanation that must be sought within a wider frame of reference, in the combination and interaction of all these individual elements. The political and sociological study, indispensable for widening the field of investigation, is fruitful only to the extent that it is located in time and integrated into a reconstruction of historical evolution.

In seeking to discern the first manifestations of the development of Franco-Saar relations, this effort at reconstruction reveals the precariousness of the French position from the very beginning. France's Saar policy was based on the rights of the victorious victim to reparations and security. Nothing could be more transitory, more affected by the passage of time, than the status of victim or victor and hence of the rights that spring from it—all the more so because those rights were in conflict with other rights of more general import, such as the right of peoples to self-determination, and because the compromise solution arrived at (economic union, political separation) was inherently ambiguous. This ambiguity stemmed from the confusion between an autonomous régime and a protectorate, in the contradiction between the political objective and the ostensibly economic measures to achieve it, in the ambivalence of the Saarlanders who turned towards France for material reasons while remaining more or less consciously German at heart, in language, temperament, and taste. Strength might, perhaps, have attenuated the ambiguity and made more enduring the legal foundations of a status resulting from a unilateral decision. But France, an associate in the victory of the Great Powers, had only limited means to act abroad; her international influence was measured by the authority of the government inside the country. Throughout this period, France certainly had at her disposal military means superior to those of Germany. But this obvious superiority was of no benefit. Not a single one of the governments that followed one another into office in Paris ever thought of using it. They were convinced that the Saar problem was not the kind to be settled by force. The interests at stake did not justify a recourse to arms that would arouse in France, in Europe, and in the whole world an immediate and powerful opposition. The

Faure Government was well aware of this when it accepted the results of the referendum.

The fragility of the political system built by France in the Saar was at the root of the uneasiness that became apparent as soon as the régime for the Saar came into being and of the anxiety felt by certain of its promoters and defenders. The crisis following the introduction of the French franc banished some of the Saarlanders' illusions on the material advantages to be gained from economic union. The subsequent improvement in living conditions, which ought to have drawn the Saarlanders closer to France, seemed, on the contrary, to encourage aloofness. In the one case as in the other, the French were the losers. They were so conscious of this latent hostility in the Saar that they concluded they had to retreat. But the measures they took to consolidate their position while there was still time resulted in the failure of their effort to substitute a régime founded on joint agreement for a status born of a unilateral decision. These measures aroused open resistance, which was exactly what the French had been trying to avoid, and led to the internationalization of the conflict.

From then on French policy seemed to be caught in the cogs of a machine. The more France tried to stop them from turning or to free herself from them, the more she became enmeshed. The request that the Saar mines be leased to France alarmed the trade unionists because of the double threat to their occupational interests —*i.e.*, fear of losing control over their livelihood—and to their Saar patrimony. This helped to link together economic and social demands with nationalist protests, crystallizing against France a reflex in defence of material interests while stimulating people to seek support from the only available protector: renascent Germany. The growth of Saar opposition, which included not only isolated individuals but organized groups, decided the Saarbrücken Government to take repressive measures, which in turn generated more opposition and produced what might be called a constraint-resistance spiral. The concessions granted had much the same results; they, too, encouraged the opposition to come out into the open and to challenge the whole situation the French were endeavouring to stabilize. Scarcely were the first Conventions signed when their revision was already being discussed. Those of 1953, which gave rise to almost as much criticism as the first ones, were contested in diplomatic negotiations before they had even been put into force.

In the same way, the launching of the Schuman Plan, far from consolidating the French position in the Saar, helped to call it into question again by underlining the contradiction between a policy of European integration and one of economic union inspired by an apparently anachronistic preoccupation with nationalism. This gave Chancellor Adenauer not only a new argument but a weapon in the diplomatic negotiations: the Federal Republic would co-operate on the European project only in exchange for French concessions on the Saar.

Moreover, the recovery of Germany stimulated the Saar opposition, whose activities in turn encouraged the Bonn Government to act. Under the twofold impulse of these combined forces the Governments of Paris and of Saarbrücken not only gave way but were pulled away from each other, since contradictions are sharper in a defensive position.

In Paris it was not possible to escape from the initial confusion between autonomy and protectorate. The intention was, certainly, to strengthen the autonomy of the Saar and to obtain for it the recognition of a European status. But consideration of France's own interests led to subordination of this recognition to friendly collaboration with Germany. Acceptance of this subordination implied, as a corollary, admission of the principle of negotiation with the Federal Republic on the Saar question, which had been excluded until then, and the elimination of the Saar Government from the negotiations. Thus France allowed herself to be trapped in a tête-à-tête with Germany, which lowered the prestige and lessened, both in Europe and the Saar, the authority of those who supported her and whom she, in her turn, purported to uphold. Once caught up in the discussion, France was induced to consent in the name of her partner to concessions she had later to convince or even compel her partner to accept. This was the case when the Paris agreements were negotiated and later when Mr. Pinay went to Bonn. The Saar Government was thus more and more isolated at home and abroad by the diplomatic action of its protector; this led to the disintegration of the forces supporting it and led the government itself finally to re-open the question of the Franco-Saar economic union.

Thus, the economic union broke down—and here the study of the Saar conflict makes it possible to verify certain observations made in a wider field—under the pressure of a combination of forces whose cumulative thrusts produced a phenomenon of auto-aggravation and acceleration. The contradictions in French policy, caught between European co-operation and the defence of national interests, highlighted by the launching of the Schuman Plan, were aggravated both by the change in the international climate, which left France out of step, and by the reversal in the relative material and moral strength of France and Germany, a reversal which lent weight to the German claims. This very change in relative strength encouraged opposition in the Saar and by so doing indirectly stimulated the " nationalist " reaction in France and the mistrust towards European organizations as well as towards the Saar partner, thus serving to underline and aggravate the initial contradictions in French policy.

France, we have already noted, was caught up in the cogs of the machine.

And yet the development of the conflict seemed at moments to be turning in the opposite direction from the one it eventually took. At various times an agreement was almost concluded on a solution quite different from the one that finally emerged from the referendum of October, 1955. One has only to remember the October, 1952, negotiations on the Teitgen-Adenauer agreement of May, 1954. Mr. Mendès-France even managed to get the Chancellor to accept a status in accord with the fundamental aims of France's Saar policy. His success was so complete that for a time those in favour of the Saar's returning to Germany hovered in a state of indecision and discouragement.

This was because Mr. Mendès-France, like Napoleon on the battlefield, instinctively sought to " create the event " or, to use an expression more commonly heard, to produce a psychological shock. He did it in the same spirit as Jean Monnet, who some years earlier had also sought to " unravel " the knotted forces.[4] Breaking with the defensive tactics of his predecessor, he impressed a rhythm on his activities that disconcerted those with whom he was dealing. By reversing the roles he changed the combination of forces.

---

[4] *Cf.* Gerbet, " La genèse du Plan Schuman . . . ," *op. cit.*

The intervention of Mr. Mendès-France did not achieve the results he might have expected. It had only a passing influence; Mr. Mendès-France, too, suffered the effects of the " weakness of the régime." But the experience is nonetheless significant and rich in lessons. Does it not call attention to the liberating power of initiative? [5]

[5] Interview with Mr. Maurice Merleau-Ponty, in *L'Express*, July 3, 1958: " If the Mendès-France Government was able for a short time to pull French political life out of despair and doldrums, as *no* other government has been able to do since 1944, it is because he conceived of government as a rallying force, of action as a movement not to be harassed at every second but to be free to go before the nation, organize its own pedagogy, and justify itself by its evolution."

APPENDICES

APPENDIX I

DEVELOPMENT OF POLITICAL INSTITUTIONS
IN THE SAAR, 1945–1955

ORGANIZATION CHARTS

WE have tried in the charts appearing below to represent the inter-penetration of French and Saar institutions in the four phases which made up their development during the period under consideration. An arrow indicates, on the one hand, the right of the French Republic to oversee certain domains within the scope of the Saar's sovereignty and, on the other, the power delegated by the Saar Government to the Government of the French Republic.

Chart I. 1945–1947

The *supreme authority* is retained by the Allies and partially and gradually delegated to the German authorities.

BASIC TEXTS:

1. *Allies*

Declaration regarding the defeat of Germany and the assumption of the supreme authority with respect to Germany by the Governments of the United States of America, the Union of Soviet Socialist Republics and the United Kingdom and the Provisional Government of the French Republic (U.S. Dept. of State *Bulletin*, Vol. XII, No. 311, p. 1051); Potsdam agreement of August 2, 1945 (*ibid.*, Vol. XIII, No. 319, p. 153), and Control Council Proclamation No. 1 (Allied Secretariat, *Official Gazette of the Control Council of Germany*, October 29, 1945).

2. *France*

Decree of June 15, 1945, creating the office of Chief of Command of French Forces in Germany (*J.O.*, June 27, 1945), of December 26, 1945, creating the office of *Commissariat général* of German and Austrian Affairs (*J.O.*, December 27, 1945); Orders of the Commander-in-Chief of French Forces in Germany, nos. 1 and 2 of August 21 and 22, 1945 (*J.O.*, C.C.F.A., September 3, 1945); Decision no. 1 of August 30, 1945, and Order of September 5, 1945, concerning the creation of a *délégué supérieur* for the Military Government in the Saar (*J.O.*, C.C.F.A., October 8, 1945); Order of September 14, 1945, concerning the organization of delegations for the provincial governments (*J.O.*, C.C.F.A., October 11, 1945).

3. *Saar*

Decree of July 31, 1945, creating the *Regierungspräsidium* (*Amtsblatt des Regierungspräsidiums Saar*, 1945, p. 5); Ordinance no. 68 of October 8, 1946, creating a provisional Administrative Commission for the Saar Territory (C.A.T.S.) (*J.O.*, C.C.F.A., October 20, 1946).

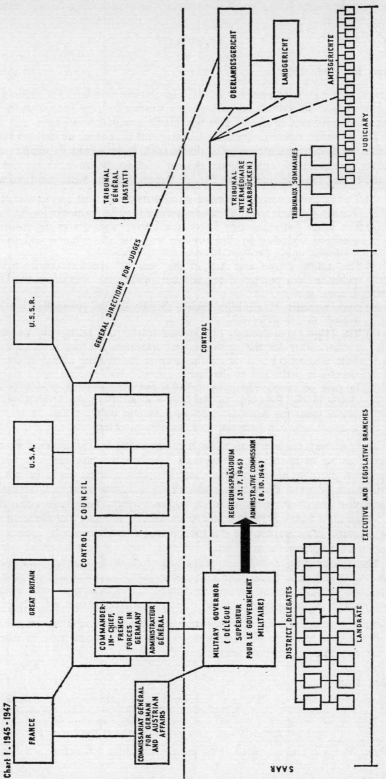

Chart I . 1945 - 1947

Chart II. 1948–1950

The Saar *legislative power* is limited, on the one hand, by the application of French laws in matters of customs and finance and, on the other, by the High Commissioner's right to give his official sanction to all laws.

The *executive power* of the Saar Government is limited, on the one hand, by the delegation of its powers to the French Government in matters concerning foreign affairs and national defence and, on the other, by the powers of the High Commissioner of the French Republic in the Saar, that is to say:

(1) The High Commissioner assures the publication and application of all French legislative and statutory measures to be enforced in the Saar;

(2) The High Commissioner determines by order or decree the measures rendered necessary by the customs and monetary union and by the economic union between France and the Saar;

(3) The statutory laws and Acts of the Saar Government can be neither published nor put into force without the official sanction of the High Commissioner;

(4) Appointments of all high Saar officials and all naturalizations are subject to his approval;

(5) The High Commissioner can include in the Saar budget the necessary credits either for the application of measures relating to the Franco-Saar economic union or for the normal functioning of public services necessary to the life of the Saar;

(6) In case of events likely to threaten the fundamental principles laid down in the Preamble to the Saar Constitution, the High Commissioner takes the necessary steps to maintain public order.

He is also limited in financial and customs questions.

The *judiciary power* is assured by the Saar tribunals. However, a Franco-Saar Chamber of the Court of Appeal of the Saar is empowered to rule on appeals on decisions of courts of first instance (1) in matters where French law is directly applicable; (2) in all matters where Saar law must be brought into line with French law. It likewise has within its jurisdiction crimes and cases of offences in which a French official or soldier is either the defendant or the plaintiff. The decisions of the Franco-Saar Chamber may be appealed to the French Supreme Court.

The Administrative Tribunal of the Saar (which, in fact, was not set up until 1951) has jurisdiction in matters of taxation and customs in all cases where the French Administrative Tribunals are competent. The *Conseil d'Etat* takes cognizance of appeals against decisions of the Administrative Tribunal of the Saar and of claims against the French Administration.

Directly or indirectly, France exercises full power in the Saar in matters of finance, customs, foreign affairs, and defence.

Basic Texts:

Laws of November 15, 1947 (*Amtsblatt der Verwaltungskommission des Saarlandes*, no. 62, November 28, 1947, pp. 903–924); Decrees Nos. 47–2436 and 47–2447 of December 31, 1947, on the prerogatives and powers of the Saar High Commissioner (*Amtsblatt des Saarlandes*, no. 4, January 26, 1948, pp. 79–81); Constitution of the Saar of December 15, 1947 (*Amtsblatt des Saarlandes*, no. 67, December 17, 1947, p. 1077); Agreement of January 3, 1948, relating to the organization of the judiciary in the Saar (*Amtsblatt des Saarlandes*,

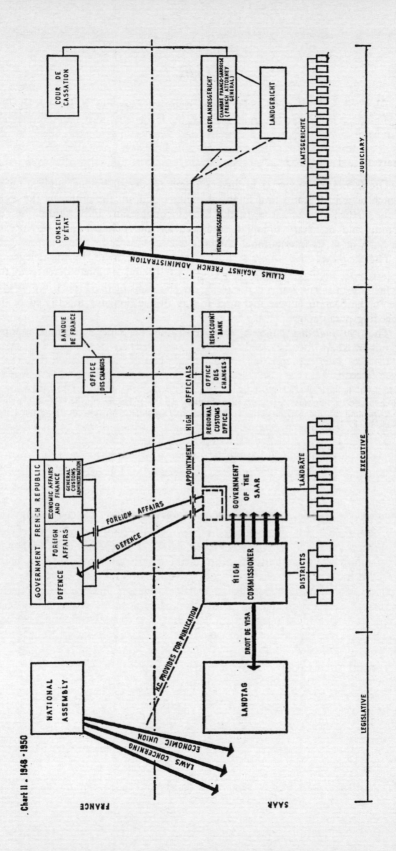

Chart II . 1948 - 1950

no. 23, April 5, 1948, p. 380); Fiscal and budgetary agreement of January 13, 1948 (*Amtsblatt des Saarlandes*, no. 4, January 26, 1948, pp. 82 *et seq.*); Ordinance 144 of January 10, 1948, relating to the Military Government in the Saar (*J.O.*, C.C.F.A., January 13, 1948).

Chart III.   1951–1953

The *legislative power* is limited, on the one hand, by the application of French laws in customs and financial matters and, on the other, by the right of the French representative in the Saar to oppose any bills contrary to the customs and monetary union, to the security and political independence of the Saar, or to its international obligations.

The Saar *executive power* is limited, on the one hand, by the delegation of power in matters concerning foreign affairs and national defence to the French Government and, on the other, by the right of the French representative in the Saar to oppose measures in any of the domains mentioned in the preceding paragraph.[1]

The Saar *judiciary power* is exercised under the same conditions as those set out in Chart 2.

BASIC TEXTS:

Judicial, budgetary, and fiscal agreements of January 3 and 13, 1948; Agreements of March 3, 1950 (*Amtsblatt des Saarlandes*, January 5, 1951); Decree no. 52–309 of March 5, 1952, relating to the jurisdiction of the French Diplomatic Mission in the Saar (*J.O.*, March 16, 1952).

---

[1] In fact, the representative of France used his right to oppose only five times.

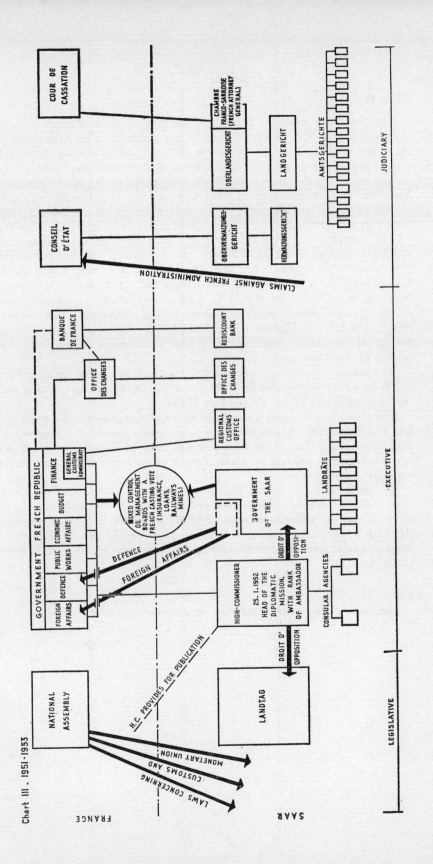

Chart III . 1951 - 1953

Chart IV. 1954–1956

The *legislative power* is limited by the application of French laws in customs and monetary matters. Further, the Commission of Arbitration or the Court of Arbitration set up by the General Convention can decide the total or partial abrogation of a law contrary to the Franco-Saar Conventions or suspend a law if it is not within the competence of the Saar authorities. Moreover, the French Government may request the President of the Court of Arbitration to put into force in the Saar a text which the Saar Government may not have published, although required to do so by the Conventions.

The *executive power* of the Saar can have no cognizance of matters relating to foreign affairs and defence. A state of siege can be declared by the French Government after consultation with the Saar Government. Furthermore, the Commission of Arbitration and the Court of Arbitration have the same power in regard to *actes réglementaires* in financial and customs matters as those mentioned above for *actes législatifs*. International treaties concluded by France in the name of the Saar must henceforth be ratified by the Saar. Mixed Control and Management Boards exist for matters of credit and exchange.

The *judiciary power* is re-organized. Two jurisdictions are instituted for the Franco-Saar economic union: the Court of the Franco-Saar Union and the Supreme Court of the Franco-Saar Union.

The Court of the Union (three Saarlanders, one of whom is the president, and two Frenchmen) has authority to hear appeals against the decisions of Saar courts which have ruled in the first instance in customs and monetary matters and penal offences in which French soldiers or customs officials are involved or wronged.

The Supreme Court (three French members, one of whom is the president, and two Saarlanders) is empowered to hear appeals against decisions of the Court of the Union. It hears first and last resort civil actions against the French State, cases relating to contracts passed to the Saar by the French Administration, and disputes concerning damage done by the French army in the Saar.

Basic Texts:

Agreements of May 20, 1953 (*Amtsblatt des Saarlandes*, December 15, 1953).

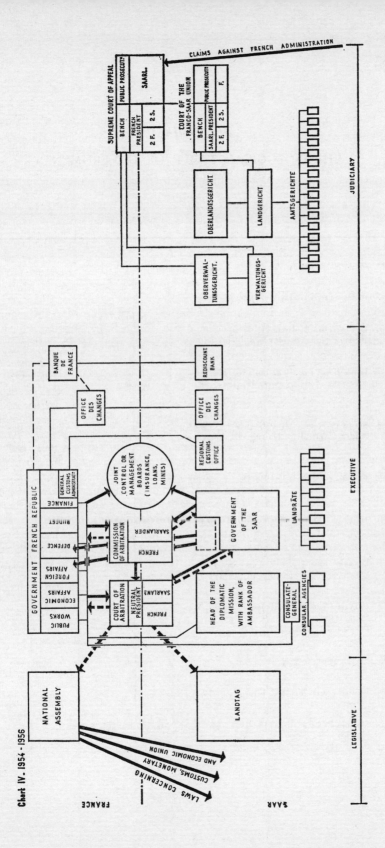

Chart IV. 1954 - 1956

APPENDIX II

CHRONOLOGICAL TABLE OF GOVERNMENTS AND SERVICES, 1944–1955

FRANCE

Year	Government	Foreign Affairs	
1944	DE GAULLE (Sept. 9, 1944)	BIDAULT	
1945	DE GAULLE (Nov. 13, 1945–Jan. 20, 1946)		
1946	GOUIN (Jan. 23–June 11, 1946) BIDAULT (June 19–Nov. 28, 1946)		DEBRÉ (Dec. 1946) *Co-ordination Commission*
1947	BLUM (Dec. 16, 1946–Jan. 16, 1947) RAMADIER (Jan. 28–Nov. 19, 1947)	BLUM BIDAULT	*Sous-Direction de la Sarre*
1948	SCHUMAN (Nov. 22, 1947–July 19, 1948) André MARIE (July 24–Aug. 27, 1948)	SCHUMAN	BOURBON-BUSSET *1st Deputy-Director* (Nov. 1947– July 29, 1948)
1949	QUEUILLE (Sept. 17, 1948–Oct. 6, 1949)		BURIN DES ROZIERS (Nov. 1948– Sept. 1, 1950)
1950	BIDAULT (Oct. 28, 1949–May 24, 1950)		
1951	PLEVEN (July 11, 1950–Feb. 28, 1951) QUEUILLE (Mar. 13–July 10, 1951)		DE BEAUMARCHAIS (Sept. 1, 1950– Jan. 5, 1953)
1952	PLEVEN (Aug. 8, 1951–Jan. 7, 1952) FAURE (Jan. 18–Feb. 29, 1952) PINAY (Mar. 6–Dec. 23, 1952)		
1953	MAYER (Jan. 6–May 21, 1953)	BIDAULT	MAILLARD (Jan. 8–July, 1953)
1954	LANIEL (June 26, 1953–June 12, 1954)		DE COURSON (July 2, 1953– end, 1955)
1955	MENDÈS-FRANCE (June 18, 1954–Feb. 5, 1955) FAURE (Feb. 23–Nov. 29, 1955)	MENDÈS-FRANCE PINAY	

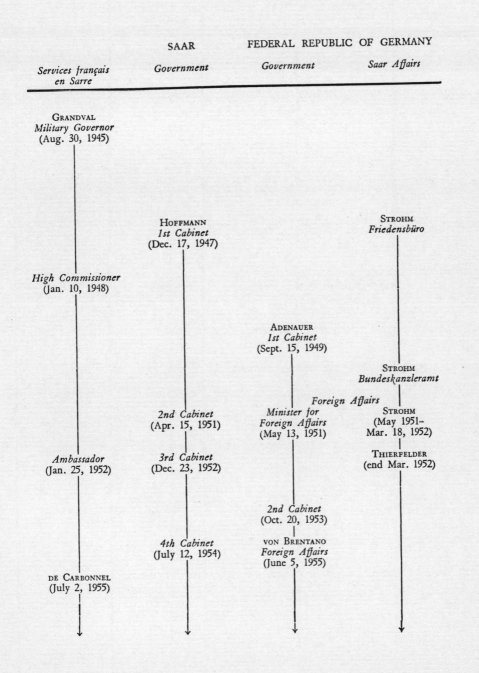

	SAAR	FEDERAL REPUBLIC OF GERMANY	
Services français en Sarre	*Government*	*Government*	*Saar Affairs*

GRANDVAL
Military Governor
(Aug. 30, 1945)

HOFFMANN
1st Cabinet
(Dec. 17, 1947)

STROHM
Friedensbüro

High Commissioner
(Jan. 10, 1948)

ADENAUER
1st Cabinet
(Sept. 15, 1949)

STROHM
Bundeskanzleramt

Foreign Affairs

2nd Cabinet
(Apr. 15, 1951)

Minister for
Foreign Affairs
(May 13, 1951)

STROHM
(May 1951–
Mar. 18, 1952)

Ambassador
(Jan. 25, 1952)

3rd Cabinet
(Dec. 23, 1952)

THIERFELDER
(end Mar. 1952)

2nd Cabinet
(Oct. 20, 1953)

4th Cabinet
(July 12, 1954)

VON BRENTANO
Foreign Affairs
(June 5, 1955)

DE CARBONNEL
(July 2, 1955)

APPENDIX III

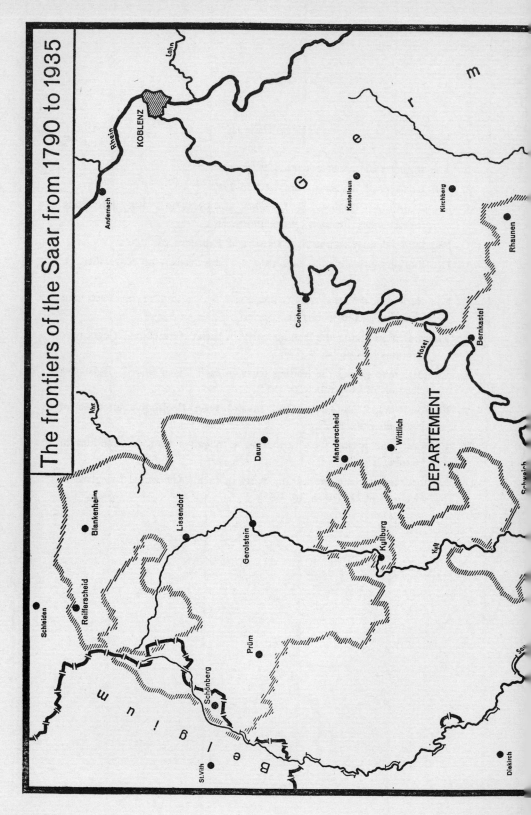

The frontiers of the Saar from 1790 to 1935

Map No. 1

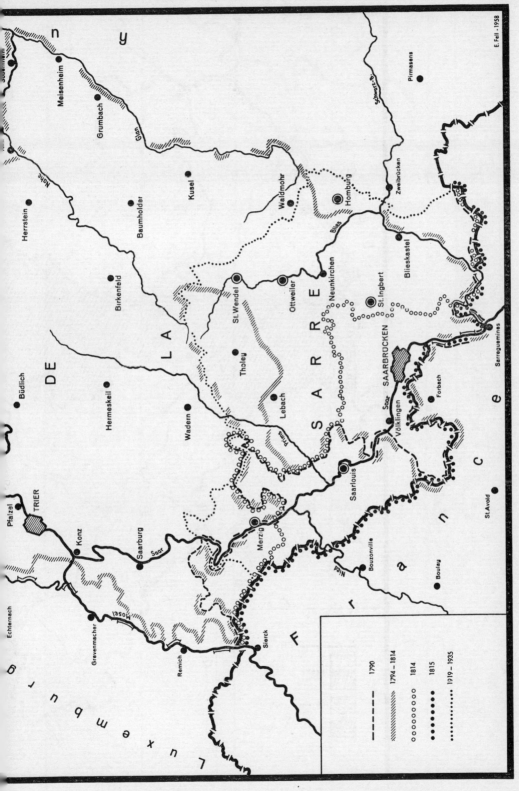

E. Fell - 1958

n y

DE

LA

SAARRE

F r a n c e

Luxemburg

TRIER

SAARBRÜCKEN

Herrstein
Büdlich
Pfalzel
Echternach
Konz
Saarburg
Hermeskeil
Waden
Grevenmacher
Remich
Sierck
Merzig
Saarlouis
Thotey
Lebach
Völklingen
Forbach
St.Avold
Bouzonville
Boulay
Sarreguemines
St.Ingbert
Neunkirchen
Ottweiler
St.Wendel
Waldmohr
Homburg
Zweibrücken
Blieskastel
Pirmasens
Kusel
Baumholder
Birkenfeld
Grumbach
Meisenheim

Saar
Soar
Nied
Mosel
Blies
Schwarz Bi.
Nahe
Glan

1790
1794 – 1814
1814
1815
1919 – 1935

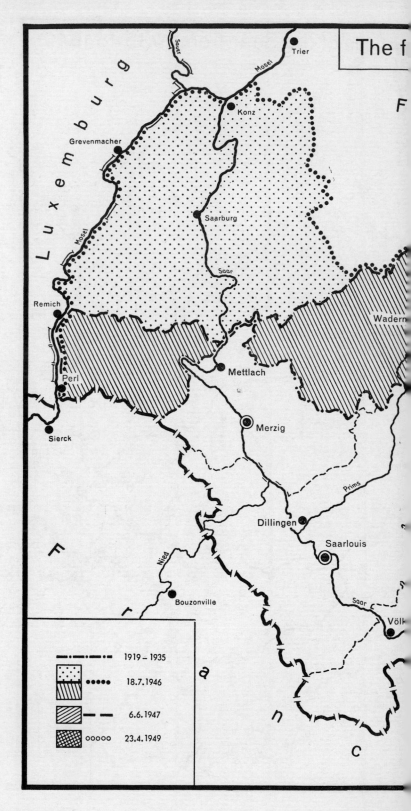

The f

F

Trier
Sauer
Mosel
Konz
L u x e m b u r g
Grevenmacher
Mosel
Saarburg
Saar
Remich
Wadern
Mettlach
Perl
Merzig
Sierck
Prims
Dillingen
Saarlouis
F
Nied
r
Bouzonville
Saar
Völk
a
n
C

		1919 – 1935
	●●●●●	18.7.1946
	▬▬	6.6.1947
	ooooo	23.4.1949

Map No. 2

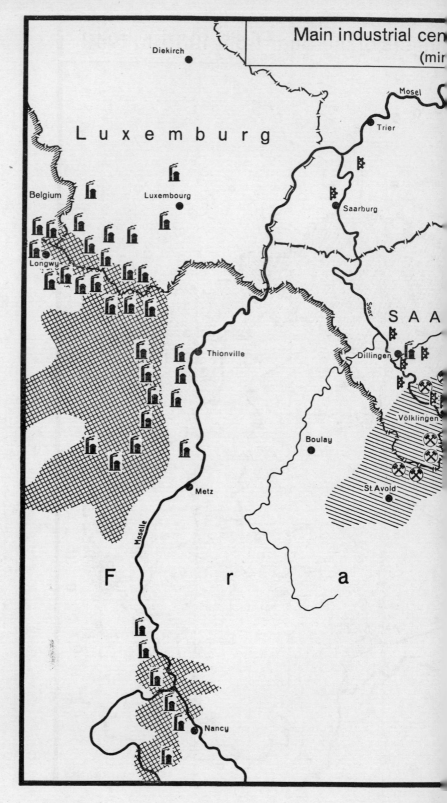

Map No. 3

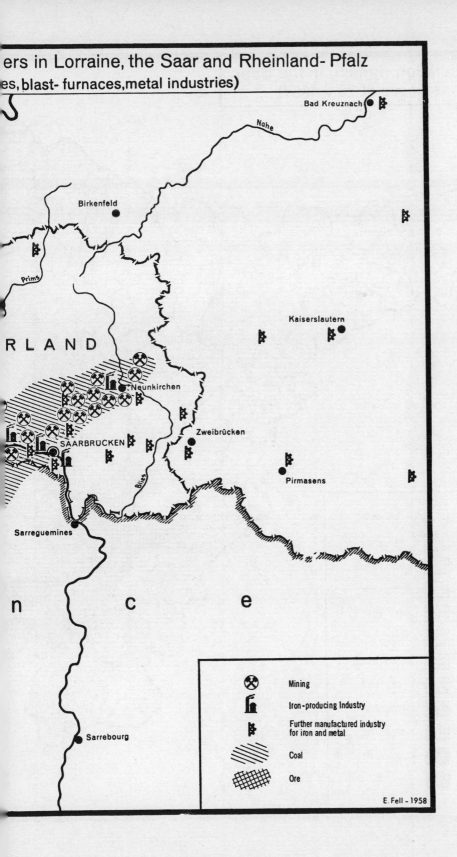

...ers in Lorraine, the Saar and Rheinland- Pfalz
...es, blast- furnaces, metal industries)

Bad Kreuznach

Nahe

Birkenfeld

Prims

Kaiserslautern

RLAND

Neunkirchen

SAARBRÜCKEN

Zweibrücken

Blies

Pirmasens

Sarreguemines

n   c   e

Sarrebourg

	Mining
	Iron-producing Industry
	Further manufactured industry for iron and metal
	Coal
	Ore

E. Fell - 1958

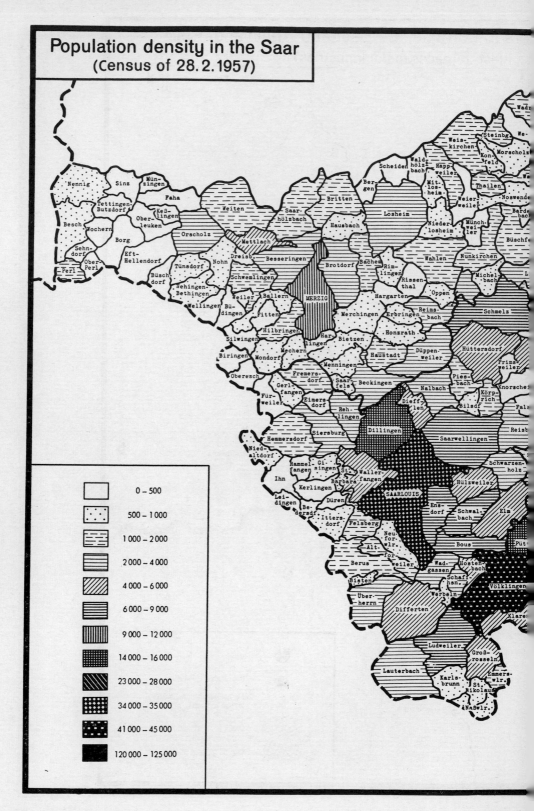

Population density in the Saar
(Census of 28. 2. 1957)

	0 – 500
	500 – 1 000
	1 000 – 2 000
	2 000 – 4 000
	4 000 – 6 000
	6 000 – 9 000
	9 000 – 12 000
	14 000 – 16 000
	23 000 – 28 000
	34 000 – 35 000
	41 000 – 45 000
	120 000 – 125 000

Map No. 4

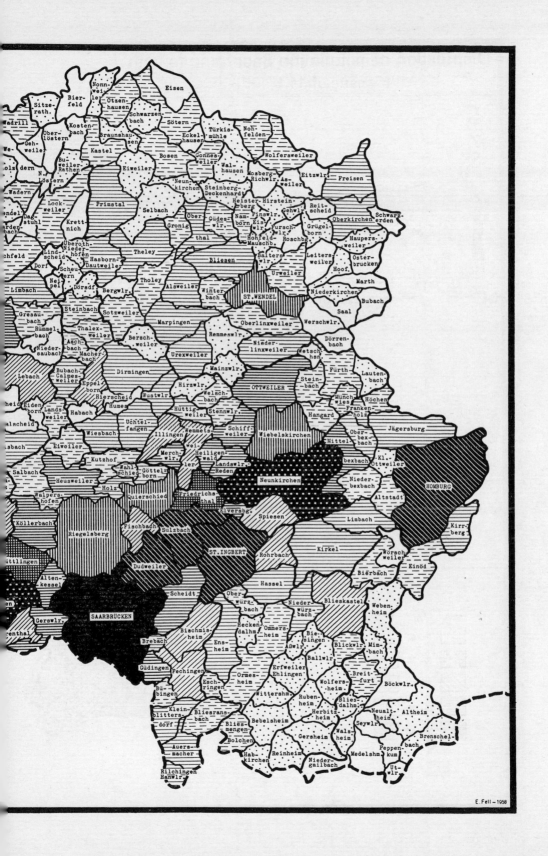

E. Fell – 1958

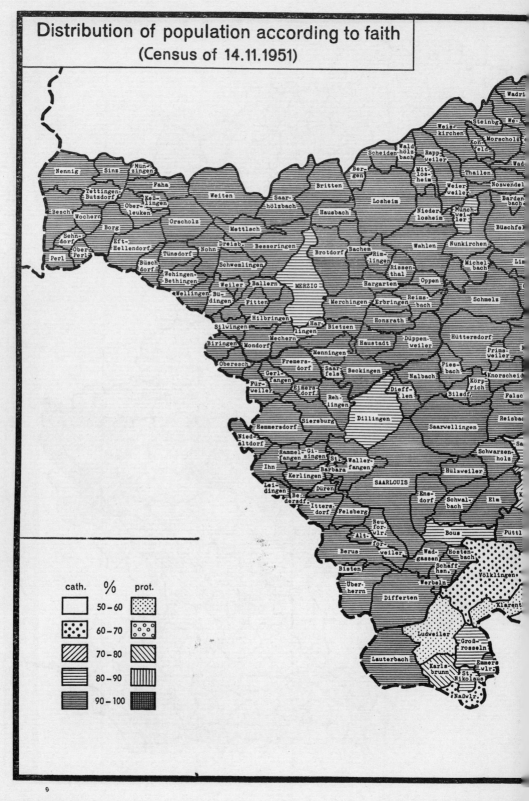

Distribution of population according to faith
(Census of 14.11.1951)

cath.	%	prot.
	50 – 60	
	60 – 70	
	70 – 80	
	80 – 90	
	90 – 100	

Map No. 5

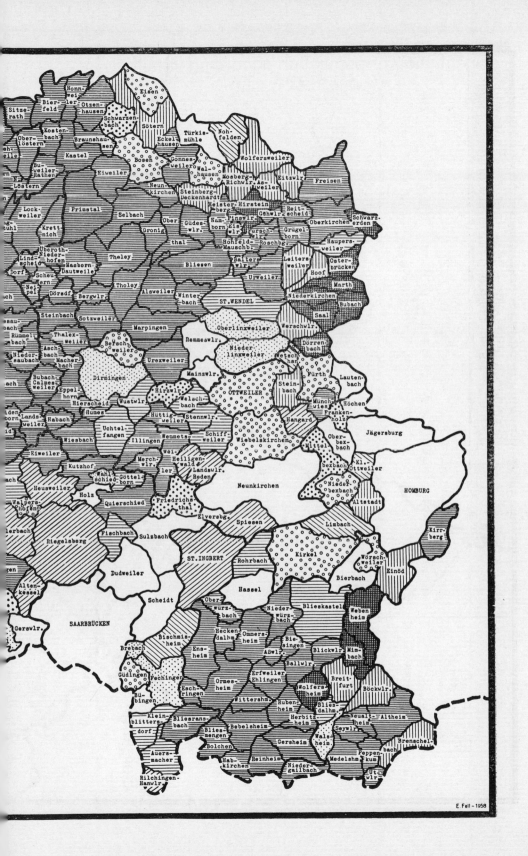

E. Fell - 1958

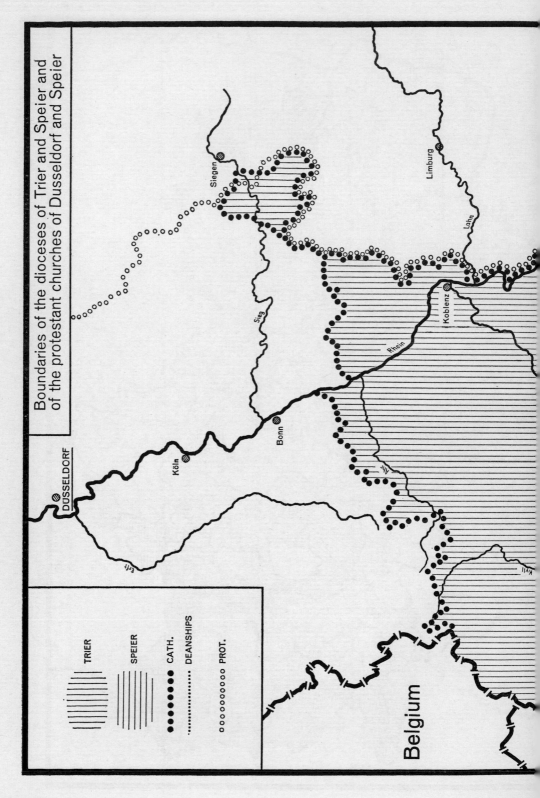

Boundaries of the dioceses of Trier and Speier and of the protestant churches of Dusseldorf and Speier

Legend:

TRIER	
SPEIER	
•••••• CATH.	DEANSHIPS
∘∘∘∘∘∘∘∘∘ PROT.	

DÜSSELDORF

Köln

Bonn

Siegen

Sieg

Rhein

Koblenz

Lahn

Limburg

Ahr

Erft

Kyll

Belgium

Map No. 6

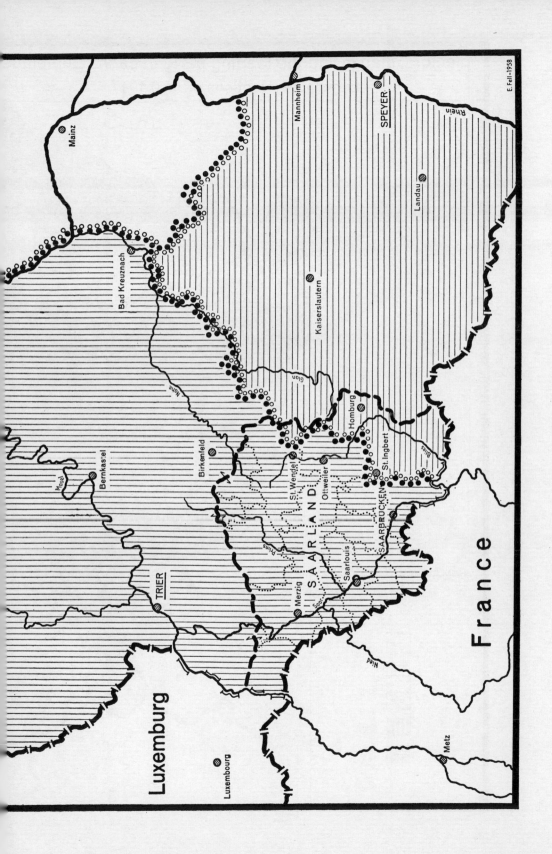

Luxemburg

Mainz

Bad Kreuznach

Mosel

Bernkastel

Nahe

Birkenfeld

TRIER

Merzig

Prims

Saar

SAARLAND

St. Wendel

Ottweiler

Saarlouis

SAARBRÜCKEN

St. Ingbert

Homburg

Glan

Kaiserslautern

Blies

Mannheim

SPEYER

Rhein

Landau

Luxembourg

France

Metz

Nied

E. Fell - 1958

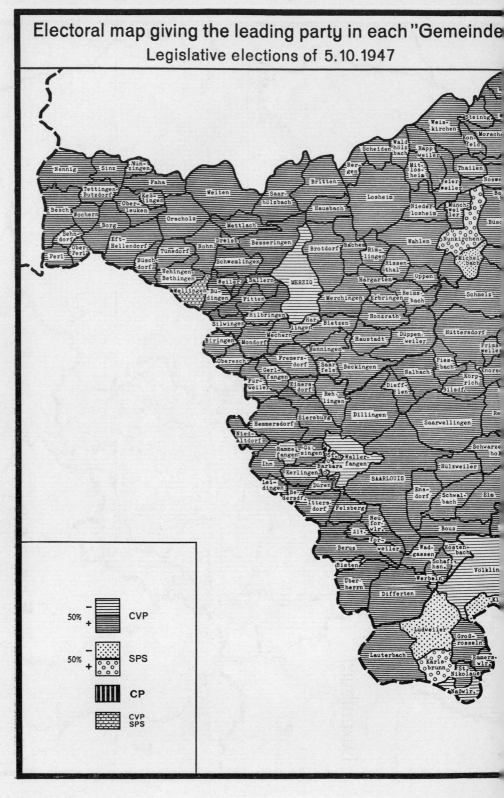

Electoral map giving the leading party in each "Gemeinde"
Legislative elections of 5.10.1947

Nennig Sinz Nün-zingen Faha Weiten Britten Weis-kirchen Steinbg Morsche Kon-feld
Tettingen-Butzdorf Keß-lingen Scheiden-bach Wald-hölz-bach Rapp-weiler Mit-los-heim Thailen
Besch Ober-leuken Saar-hölzbach Bergen Weier-weiler Noswe Ba
Wochern Oracholz Hausbach Losheim Nieder-losheim Münch-weis-ler Büsc
Sehn-dorf Borg Mettlach Dreisb Besseringen Brotdorf Bachen Wahlen Nunkirchen
Ober-Perl Eft-Hellendorf Nohn Rim-lingen Michel-bach
Perl Tünsdorf Schwemlingen Rissen-thal Oppen
Büsch-dorf Wehingen-Bethingen Weiler Ballern MERZIG Hargarten Reims-bach Schmelz
Wellingen Bü-dingen Fitten Merchingen Erbringen
Hilbringen Honzrath
Silwingen Har-lingen Bietzen Düppen-weiler Hüttersdorf
Biringen Mondorf Mechern Haustadt Prims-weiler
Oberesch Fremers-dorf Menningen Pies-bach Knorsc
Für-weiler Gerl-fangen Saar-fels Beckingen Nalbach Körp-rich
Eimers-dorf Dieff-len Bildsf.
Roh-lingen
Hemmersdorf Siersburg Dillingen Saarwellingen Re
Nied-altdorf
Rammel-fangen Gi-singen Waller-fangen Schwarze-ho
Ihn Barbara Hülzweiler
Kerlingen SAARLOUIS
Lei-dingen Düren Ens-dorf Schwal-bach Elm
Be-dersdf. Itters-dorf Felsberg Bous
Neu-for-wlr. Alt-for-weiler
Berus Wad-gassen Hosten-bach
Bisten Schaf-hsn. Völklin
Über-herrn Werbeln
Differten Kl
Ludweiler Groß-rosseln
Lauterbach Karls-brunn Emmers-wlr.
St. Nikolaus
Naßwlr.

Legend:

- 50% −/+ CVP
- 50% −/+ SPS
- CP
- CVP SPS

Map No. 7

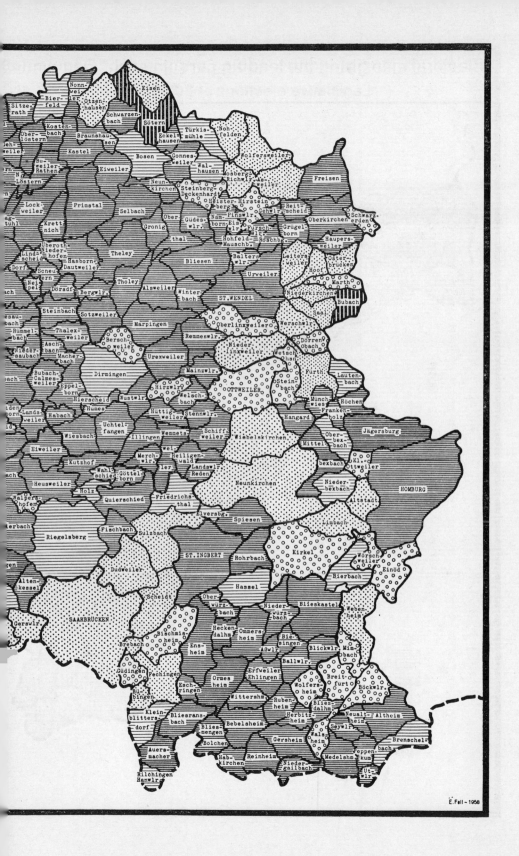

E. Fell - 1958

Electoral map giving the leading party in each "Gemeinde"
Legislative elections of 30.11.1952

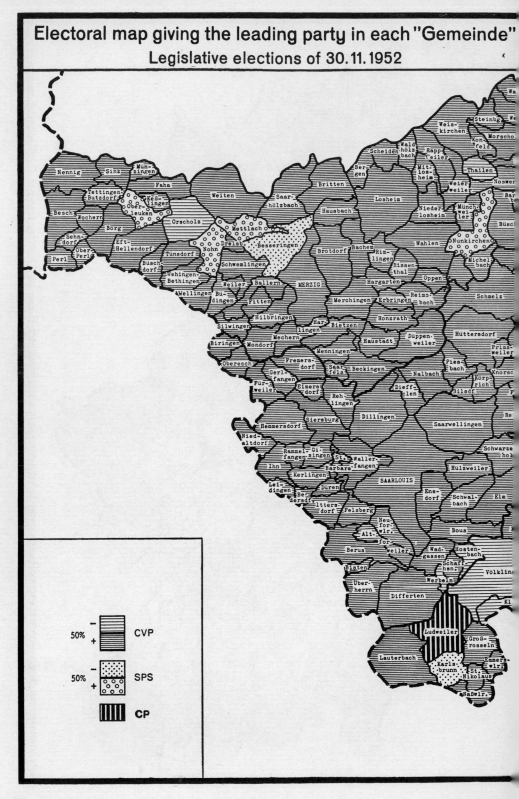

Legend:

50% CVP

50% SPS

CP

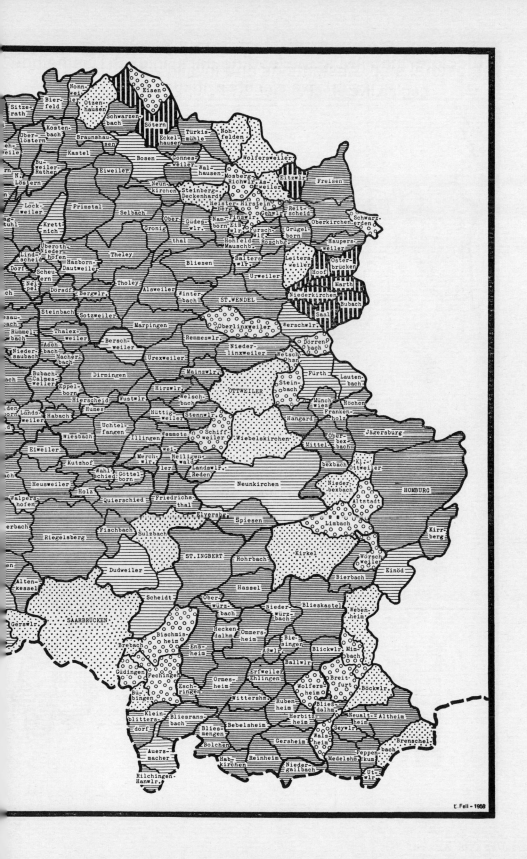

E. Fell - 1958

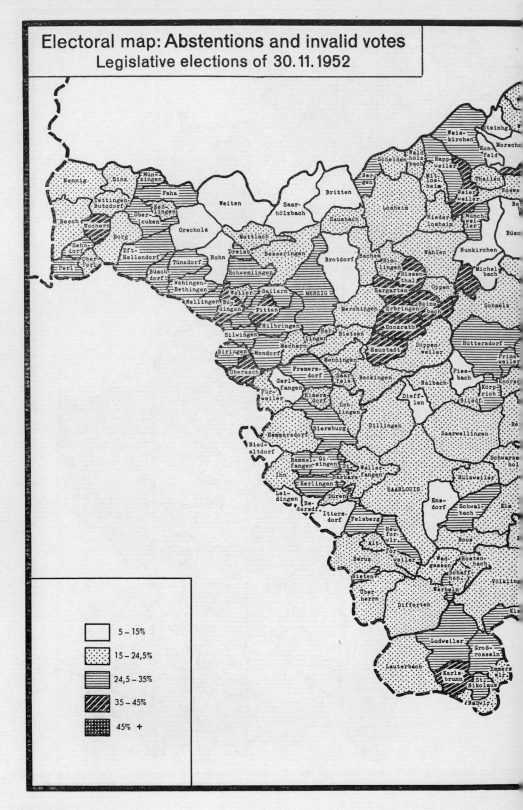

Map No. 9

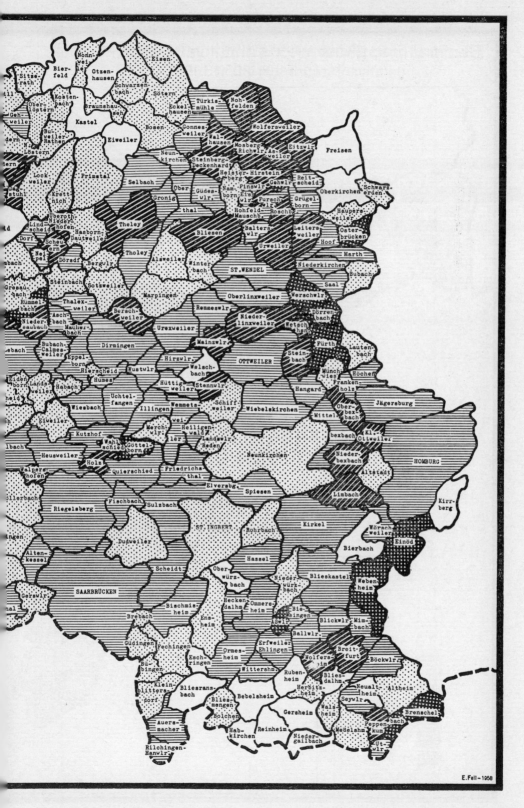

E. Fell - 1958

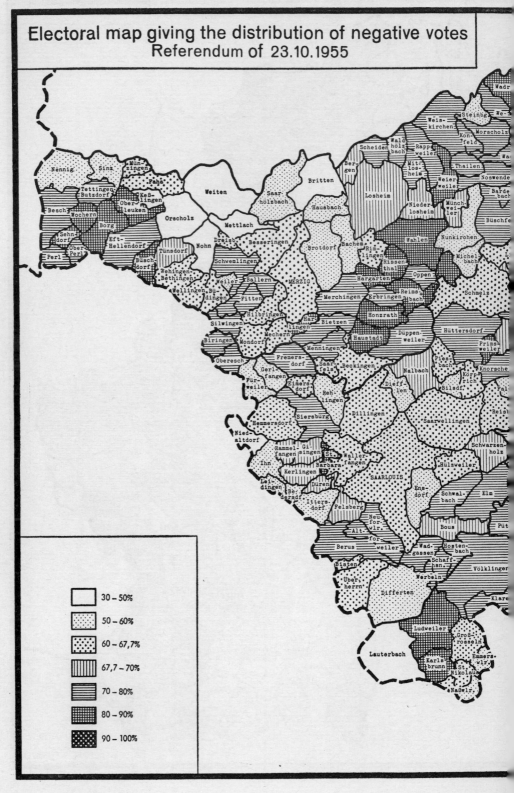

Electoral map giving the distribution of negative votes
Referendum of 23.10.1955

Legend:
- 30 – 50%
- 50 – 60%
- 60 – 67,7%
- 67,7 – 70%
- 70 – 80%
- 80 – 90%
- 90 – 100%

Map No. 10

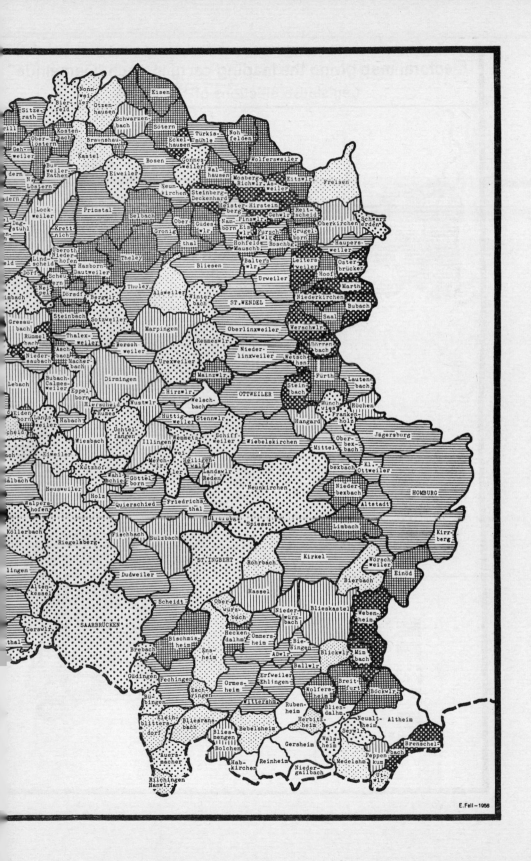

E. Fell – 1956

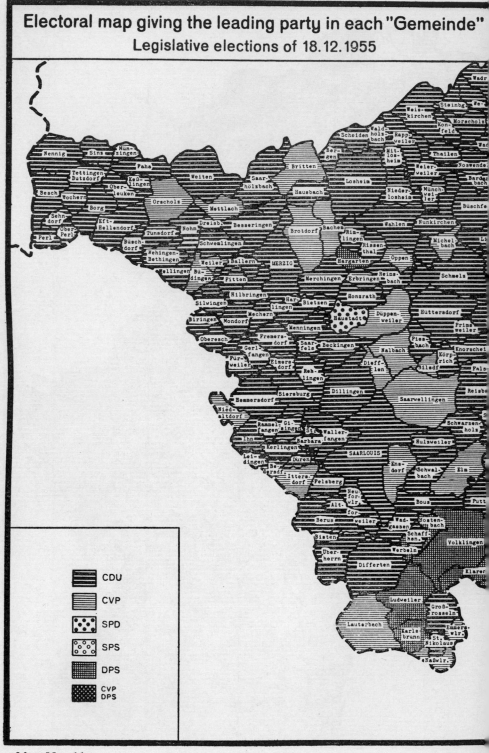

Electoral map giving the leading party in each "Gemeinde"
Legislative elections of 18.12.1955

Legend:
- CDU
- CVP
- SPD
- SPS
- DPS
- CVP DPS

Map No. 11

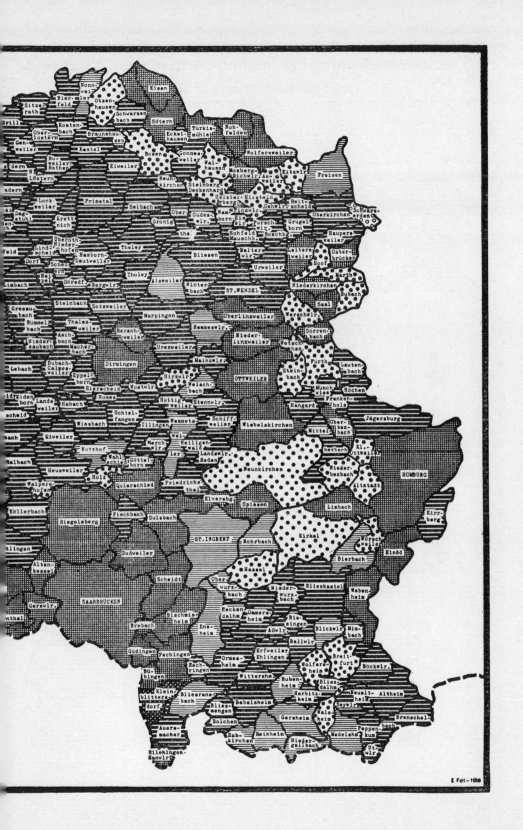

BIBLIOGRAPHY

359

BIBLIOGRAPHY

I. *SOURCES*

1. Manuscript Sources [1]

A. France

Official Texts

Haut Commissariat. Mission diplomatique française en Sarre. Speeches by Gilbert Grandval (documents).

Minutes, Memoranda, Reports

Archives of political parties in France: M.R.P., S.F.I.O., Radical and Radical-Socialist Parties, R.P.F., and Communist Party.

Chambre de commerce et d'industrie de la Moselle. Minutes of proceedings, 1945–1946; pp. 47–69.

Reports presented to the plenary session of the Chamber of Commerce of Metz, May 11, 1946, and June 27, 1946.

Report, 1950: *Par rapport à l'Union douanière franco-sarroise créée par le traité de Versailles, l'Union économique franco-sarroise est-elle avantageuse pour le commerce et l'industrie de la Moselle?*

L'évolution de l'opinion publique en Sarre de 1945 à janvier 1949. Typed, unpublished; 103 pp.

Le problème sarrois, 1945–1955. Paper for the use of lecturers at the Ecole nationale d'administration, 1955; 19 pp.

Verdier, Abel. *France et Sarre.* Unpublished memorandum, 1946; 15 pp.

B. Federal Republic of Germany

Minutes, Memoranda, Reports

Allgemeiner Zeitungsdienst West (AZW).

Deutscher Saarbund. *Aufruf zur Gründung.* March 2, 1951, mimeographed; 1 p.

Koreferat, gehalten von Dr. Heinrich Lietzmann, Essen, I. Vorsitzender des Deutschen Saarbundes, am 27. Januar 1956 vor dem Rhein-Ruhr Klub e.V. in Düsseldorf. Typed; 5 pp.

Kulturelle Notizen; Kulturpolitik. Mimeographed.

Material zur Saarfrage.

Informationen und Hinweise. Mimeographed.

Deutsches Industrieinstitut. *Material zum Zeitgeschehen.* No. 1, "Die Behandlung des deutschen Wirtschaftsvermögens im Saargebiet seit 1945." Mimeographed; 18 pp.

No. 20, "Das Kreditwesen an der Saar." August 10, 1953. Mimeographed; 11 pp., five appendices.

Vertrauliche Sonderinformation zur Kreditlage der saarländischen Wirtschaft. Mimeographed; 5 pp.

---

[1] In a considerable number of cases, manuscripts cannot be cited, *cf.* in this connection, comments made in our introduction regarding sources.

Die Deutsche Aktion. *Mitteilungen des Sekretariats Wiesbaden und der Aktionsgruppen in Südhessen und Rheinland-Pfalz.* Mimeographed.

Deutsches Büro für Friedensfragen.

    Materialien zur Saarfrage. " Frankreich und das Saarland." Stuttgart: 1949, mimeographed; 38 pp.

        " Die französische Saarförderung auf den internationalen Konferenzen seit 1945." Stuttgart: 1949, mimeographed; 34 pp.

        "Die Grundlagen der französischen Stellung im Saarland." Stuttgart: 1949, mimeographed; 61 pp.

        "Memorandum der Regierung des Saarlandes und die Entgegnung der Kommunistischen Partei des Saarlandes." Stuttgart: 1949, mimeographed; 44 pp.

        "Die Saargruben." Stuttgart: 1949, mimeographed; 17 pp.

Sozialdemokratische Partei Deutschlands. *Die Sozialdemokratie und das Saarproblem.* N.p. or d. Mimeographed; 99 pp.

    Die Verletzung Sozialdemokratischer Grundsätze durch die Sozialdemokratische Partei Saar. Memorandum presented to the Büro der Partei Deutschlands. Bonn: February 23, 1953. Mimeographed; 60 pp.

Hellwig, Fritz. *Aufzeichnung zum gegenwärtigen Stand der Saarfrage, an die Unterzeichner der Saar-Interpellation.* No. 2115. Bundestagsdrucksache, April 12, 1951. Mimeographed; 7 pp.

    Referat, gehalten vor der 21. sitzung des Ausschusses für Wirtschaftspolitik. January 26, 1955. Mimeographed; 5 pp.

Kaiser, Jakob. *Die Saarfrage.* January 12, 1950. Typed, unpublished; 18 pp.

Die S.P.D. zur Saarfrage. N.p. or d. Mimeographed; 251 pp.

Strohm, Gustav. *Skizze für ein deutsch-französisches Abkommen betreffend das Saarland.* 1949. Mimeographed, unpublished; 19 pp.

C. Saar

Minutes, Memoranda, Reports

Christlich-Demokratische Union des Saarlandes. *Einheit und Menschenwürde. Der Weg der Christlich-Demokratischen Union des Saarlandes.* Mimeographed; 30 pp.

Deutsche Sozialdemokratische Partei Saar. *Die Gründung der Deutschen Sozialdemokratischen Partei im Saargebiet.* N.p. or d. Mimeographed; 15 pp.

Industrie-und Handelskammer des Saarlandes. *Wie sieht die Saarwirtschaft die Auswirkungen des Saarstatuts vom 23. Oktober 1954 auf die Wirtschaft an?* Saarbrücken: 1955. Mimeographed; 59 pp.

    Mémoire du Mouvement pour le rattachement de la Sarre à la France concernant le règlement du problème de la Sarre. February, 1947. Typed; 11 pp.

    Die neue Lage an der Saar. Vortrag des Herrn Landtagspräsidenten Dr. Heinrich Schneider, Saarbrücken, am 27. Januar 1956 vor dem Rhein-Ruhr-Klub e.V. in Düsseldorf. Typed; 22 pp., appendix.

    Pariser Verhandlungen. Memorandum by the president of the *Syndicat unitaire des mineurs,* Aloys Schmitt. February, 1950. Typed; 37 pp.

Sozialdemokratische Partei des Saarlandes. *Eine Antwort an die Denkschrift der Sozialistischen Partei Deutschlands.* Saarbrücken: March 14, 1950. Mimeographed; 32 pp.

2. Printed Sources

A. France

Official Texts

Journal officiel de la République française. Débats parlementaires.
Lois et Décrets.
Avis et Rapports du Conseil économique.
Déclarations de M. Georges Bidault, président de la délégation française au Conseil des ministres des affaires étrangères, Session de Moscou, mars-avril 1947. Paris: Imprimerie nationale, 1947; 61 pp.
Documents relatifs à l'Allemagne, août 1945–février 1947. Paris: Imprimerie nationale, 1947; 64 pp.
Gouvernement militaire de la Sarre. *Documentation sur le statut de la Sarre.* Saarbrücken: November, 1946; 30 pp.
Renaissance de la Sarre. Saarbrücken: September, 1947; 75 pp.
Gouvernement militaire de la zone française d'occupation. *Journal officiel du Commandement en chef français.*

Pamphlets, Minutes, Memoranda

Association française de la Sarre. *Le verdict sarrois.* Paris: Imprimerie Mazarine, 1953; 56 pp.
Gebelein, Gauthier. *La France et le problème sarrois.* Paris: Office français d'edition, 1946; 47 pp.
Hector, Edgar. "L'intégration de la Sarre à la France," *Le Rhin.* Statement of policy of the Association. Paris: Imprimerie Krémer, February, 1945; pp. 3–4. (Information bulletin of the Comité d'études pour les frontières françaises de l'Est et le problème de l'Allemagne occidentale.)
Chambre de commerce et d'industrie de la Moselle. *Bulletin.*
Chambre de commerce et d'industrie de Strasbourg. *Bullletin*: 1951, No. 1; 1952, No. 2; 1954, No. 1; 1956, No. 1 (in particular, "Le futur régime économique de la Sarre et ses répercussions sur l'économie française," pp. 37–48); 1957, No. 1 (in particular, "Questions sarroises," pp. 38–42).
Les données actuelles de la question sarroise. N.p., January, 1952; 12 pp.
Grandval, Gilbert. *Ma mission au Maroc.* Paris: Plon, 1956; 273 pp.
Institut national de la statistique et des études économiques. Simon, Claude and Dircks-Dilly, Jacques. *L'économie de la Sarre.* Paris: Presses universitaires de France, 1947; 147 pp., maps.
Mission diplomatique française en Sarre. Service de l'information. *Le dialogue franco-allemand sur la Sarre, essai de définition des thèses en présence.* 1954; 6 pp.

La Documentation française

Notes documentaires et Etudes (later, *Notes et Etudes documentaires*). No. 582: "Documents français relatifs à l'Allemagne" (August, 1945–December, 1946). March 27, 1947; 15 pp.

No. 620: "A la Conférence de Moscou. Documents relatifs à l'Allemagne" (March 21–April 11, 1947). May 12, 1947; 44 pp.

No. 762: "Les réalisations françaises dans la Sarre" (Press conference by Colonel Gilbert Grandval, Military Governor of the Saar, October 17, 1947). November 17, 1947; 9 pp.

No. 773: "Constitution de la Sarre." December 6, 1947; 10 pp.

No. 855: "Accords franco-anglo-américains sur le charbon de l'Allemagne occidentale" (April, 1947–February, 1948). March 19, 1948; 8 pp.

No. 991: "Trois ans de présence française en Sarre." September 13, 1948; 79 pp.

No. 1135: "Principaux documents relatifs au statut de l'Allemagne occidentale." May 21, 1949; 52 pp.

No. 1310: "Accords franco-sarrois du 3 mars 1950." April 8, 1950; 20 pp.

No. 1756: "Conventions franco-sarroises" (Paris: May 20, 1953). Speech by President Georges Bidault. June 25, 1953; 51 pp.

No. 1951: "Accords sur le statut de la Sarre" (October 23, 1954). November 23, 1954; 4 pp.

No. 2038: "Echange de lettres relatives à la Convention de coopération économique entre la France et la Sarre." June 28, 1955; 15 pp.

Bulletin quotidien. Textes du jour. No. 2336: "Lettre de M. Robert Schuman, ministre des Affaires étrangères, au président du Conseil sarrois sur la révision des Conventions franco-sarroises" (November 26, 1952). November 28, 1952.

Articles et Documents. No. 0.98: "Communiqué sur les conversations franco-sarroises de Sarrebruck" (August 23-24, 1954). August 26, 1954.

No. 0.106: "Communiqué relatif à l'entretien entre les présidents Mendès-France et Hoffmann" (Paris: September 12, 1954). September 14, 1954.

No. 0.120: "Communiqué sur les entretiens franco-sarrois" (October 13, 1954). October 16, 1954.

No. 0.157: "Communiqué final des entretiens de Baden-Baden" (January 15, 1955). January 18, 1955.

No. 0.179: "Communiqué du Ministère français des affaires étrangères relatif à la Sarre" (March 4, 1955). March 10, 1955.

No. 0.185: "Protocole d'accord franco-sarrois" (March 21, 1955). March 24, 1955.

No. 0.243: "Aide-mémoire du gouvernement de la République fédérale d'Allemagne relatif au referendum en Sarre" (July 21, 1955). August 11, 1955.

No. 0.275: "Echange de télégrammes entre le chancelier Adenauer et le président Edgar Faure et entre M. Pinay et le chancelier Adenauer" (October 24-25, 1955). October 27, 1955.

B. Federal Republic of Germany

Official Texts

Bundesgesetzblatt.
Bulletin der Bundesregierung.

Bundesanzeiger.
Denkschrift der Bundesregierung zur Saarfrage. Bonn: Bonner Universitäts-Buchdruckerei, Gebr. Scheur. March 9, 1950; 29 pp.
Die gegenwärtige Lage des Saarlandes. Cf. Printed Sources: D. Council of Europe and United States, U.S. Department of State, "The Present Status of the Saar."
Die Rechtslage an der Saar, Gutachten des Justizministeriums von Rheinland-Pfalz. Mainz, 1954; 55 pp.
Der Saargrenzgürtel, die Folgen der Abtrennung des Saargebietes und die Notwendigkeit überregionaler Hilfe. Memorandum of the government of Rheinland-Pfalz. State Chancellery. Mainz: 1954; 24 pp.
Deutscher Bundestag. *Verhandlungen.*
Landtag von Rheinland-Pfalz. Verbatim records, especially the following meetings: No. 3: June 13, 1947, pp. 14–15; No. 8: August 28, 1947, pp. 63–68; No. 22: February 25, 1948; No. 38: August 19, 1948, p. 941; No. 47: March 20, 1949, pp. 1192–1196; No. 55: March 24, 1949, pp. 1468–1469; No. 21: April 18, 1952, pp. 684–687; No. 55: March 22, 1954, pp. 1861–1862; No. 67: November 5, 1954, pp. 2253–2269; No. 73: March 2, 1955, pp. 2483–2486; No. 74: March 15, 1955, pp. 2510–2524.
Reichskuratorium für Wirtschaftlichkeit. *Die Wirtschaft des Saarlandes.* Berlin: 1938.

Pamphlets, Minutes, Memoranda
Arbeitsgemeinschaft Demokratischer Kreise. *Die Wege zur Lösung der Saarfrage* (Communication No. 5). Bad Godesberg: 1954; 26 pp.
Deutsche Aktion. *Schriften der Deutschen Aktion.* Published by Amorbacher Verlagsbuchhandlung.
Der Weg der Deutschen Aktion, ein Rechenschaftsbericht; das Reichssekretariat. Amorbach-im-Odenwald: n.d.; 7 pp.

Deutscher Saarbund
Beckmann, Herbert. *Wahlmanöver an der Saar, die Landtagswahl vom 5. Oktober 1947.* No. 5. Cologne: Comel Verlag, 1952; 165 pp.
Brenner, Ludwig. *Freie Wahlen, ein Nachwort zu den saarländischen Landtagswahlen 1952.* No. 7. Cologne: Comel Verlag, 1952; 48 pp.
Bungarten, Franz. *Ich darf nicht schweigen.* No. 1. Cologne: Comel Verlag, 1951; 67 pp.
Hoffmeister, Martin. *Wer regiert die Saar.* No. 3. Cologne: Comel Verlag, 1952; 118 pp.
Pistorius, Ludwig. *Der Hohe Kommissar und die D.P.S.* No. 4. Cologne: Comel Verlag, 1952; 85 pp.
Schneider, Georg. *Die Wahrheit über die Saarwirtschaft.* No. 2. Cologne: Comel Verlag, 1951; 48 pp.

C. Saar
Official Texts
Amtsblatt des Regierungspräsidiums Saar. From No. 1 (June 5, 1945). Saarbrücken.

Amtsblatt der Verwaltungskommission des Saarlandes. From No. 49 (October 21, 1946). Saarbrücken.

Amtsblatt des Saarlandes. From No. 67 (December 17, 1947). Saarbrücken.

Landtag des Saarlandes. *Bericht des vom Landtag des Saarlandes durch Beschluss vom 7. Juli 1953 gemäss Art. 81 der Verfassung und gemäss Art. 21 der Geschäftsordnung eingesetzten Untersuchungsausschusses.* N.p. or d.; 24 pp.
   Drucksachen.
   Handbuch. Saarbrücken: K. Funk, 1957.
   Sitzungsberichte.

Regierung des Saarlandes. *Das Saarland, Memorandum der Regierung des Saarlandes.* 1st ed., September 1, 1949; 16 pp.; 2nd ed., September 1, 1952; 31 pp.; 3rd ed., May 1, 1953; 35 pp.
   Informationsamt. *Saarbuch 1955.* Saarbrücken: 1955; 127 pp.
   Saarland, Leben, Landschaft, Leistung. Saarbrücken: 1952; 34 pp.
   Saarland. Illustrated pamphlet with contributions by Dr. Goergen, Prof. E. Meyer, Dr. J. Keller, Richard Kirn, Th. Jansen. Foreword by Johannes Hoffmann. N.p. or d.; 24 pp.
   Saar-Problematik in Dokumenten. Saarbrücken: 1951; 36 pp.
   Wille und Weg des Saarlandes. No. 1. Brochure on the 100th session of the Saar Landtag on April 6, 1951, with speeches by Peter Zimmer, President of the Landtag (pp. 3–12), and by Johannes Hoffmann, Minister-Präsident (pp. 13–18); 18 pp.
   Wille und Weg des Saarlandes. No. 2. Suppression of the D.P.S. Speeches of Minister-Präsident Johannes Hoffmann at the C.V.P. party congress in Wiebelskirchen on May 6, 1951, and over Radio Saarbrücken on May 21, 1951.
   Wille und Weg des Saarlandes. No. 3. "Wir rufen zur christlichen Solidarität." Speech of Minister-Präsident Johannes Hoffmann at the 6th Land congress of the C.V.P., December 7–9, 1951, in Saarbrücken.

Vertrag zwischen Frankreich und dem Saarland über wirtschaftliche Zusammenarbeit, vom 3. Mai 1955. Das Recht des Saarlandes. Blattei für die Praxis der Justiz, Verwaltung und Wirtschaft. Saarbrücken: Saarländische Verlagsanstalt und Druckerei, 1955.

Publications of Public or Semi-Public Bodies

Industrie- und Handelskammer. *Economie sarroise et européisation de la Saare.* Saarbrücken: Saarländische Verlagsanstalt und Druckerai, 1954; 131 pp.
   Aus dem Fabrikationsprogramm der saarländischen Industrie. Saarbrücken: 1954; 24 pp.
   Mitteilungen der Industrie- und Handelskammer. Saarbrücken: from 1949.
   Nachrichtendienst der Handelskammer zu Saarbrücken. Saarbrücken: 1945–1948.
   Stellungnahme der Saarwirtschaft zur Moselkanalisierung. Saarbrücken: December 7, 1955.

Régie des mines. *Vom Saarbergbau und seinen Bergleuten.* Saarbrücken: 1948; 103 pp.
   Die Kohlengruben an der Saar. Saarbrücken: 1953; 44 pp.

Statistisches Amt des Saarlandes. *Amtliches Gemeinde- und Ortsverzeichnis des Saarlandes.* 8th ed. Saarbrücken: 1950.

Amtliches Gemeinde- und Ortsverzeichnis. 9th ed. Saarbrücken: 1954.

Amtliches Gemeinde- und Ortsverzeichnis des Saarlandes mit Übersichtskarte. Saarbrücken: 1948.

Gemeindeverzeichnis. Saarbrücken: 1947.

Das Saarland in Zahlen. Heft 1: *Gebiet und Bevölkerung.* Saarbrücken: 1948.

Erste Landtagswahl, 30. November 1952, und andere wichtige Angaben 1952–1954. Saarbrücken: 1954.

Saarländische Bevölkerungs- und Wirtschaftszahlen, 1949–1955. Saarbrücken.

Statistisches Handbuch für das Saarland. Saarbrücken: 1950, 1952.

Die Wahlen zum Saarländischen Landtag am 5. Oktober 1947. Saarbrücken: 1948.

Kurzbericht. No. IV/13, April 13, 1956, *Das Sozialprodukt des Saarlandes in den Jahren 1952 bis 1954;* 10 pp.

No. IV/39, October 16, 1957, *Die Entwicklung des Franken in der Nachkriegszeit;* 8 pp.

No. IV/74, September 24, 1954, *Das Sozialprodukt des Saarlandes im Jahre 1951;* 12 pp.

Pamphlets, Minutes, Memoranda of Political Parties

Christlich-Demokratische Union Saar. *Die C.D.U./Saar im Abstimmungskampf.* Opinions and reports about the plebiscite on October 23, 1955. Saarlouis: Hausen, 1955; 78 pp.

Christliche Volkspartei des Saarlandes. *Christliches Saarland im christlichen Europa, 5. Landesparteitag der C.V.P. vom 23.–26. November 1950 in Saarbrücken.* Saarbrücken: 1950; 52 pp.

Ja oder Nein zum Europäischen Saar-Statut. Die Antwort des christlichen Gewissens, eine Viertelstunde allein mit Dir selbst. Edited from authoritative sources. Saarbrücken: 1955; 24 pp.

Klare Fronten! Warum Koalitionsbruch, das geht uns alle an. Saarbrücken: 1954; 39 pp.

Der Wahrheit eine Bresche, die drei Ziele des Europäischen Saarstatuts. Abstracts from a report by H.M. Goergen. St. Ingbert: 1955; 14 pp.

Wir wollen Europa. Speech by Minister-Präsident Johannes Hoffmann, Land party chairman, at the 9th Land congress of the C.V.P., January 16, 1955. Saarbrücken: 1955; 21 pp.

Demokratische Partei Saar. *Begründung des Verbots der Demokratischen Partei Saar.* Oberverwaltungsgericht. February 16, 1952. 1952; 12 pp.

Das wollen wir, das 8 Punkte Programm der D.P.S. 1955; 10 pp.

Joho: Das bin ich. 1955; 24 pp.

Saarfrage in Dokumenten, die Beweise gegen das Verbot der D.P.S. Essay by Dr. Schneider, edited by Richard Becker. Saarbrücken: 1952; 144 pp.

Warum sagen die Saardeutschen " Nein zum Saarstatut." 1955; 19 pp.

1. Letter to President Heuss of March 14, 1955.
2. Letter by R. Becker and Dr. Schneider to Chancellor Adenauer dated January 31, 1955.
3. Memorandum on constitutional objections to the Paris agreements.

Kommunistische Partei, Landesverband Saar. *Unser Nein zum Saarstatut.* Report of First Secretary Fritz Bäsel at the Land conference on July 31, 1955. 1955; 46 pp.

    10 Jahre Kampf für den Sieg des Nein, Für Frieden, Einheit und Demokratie. Position of the Communist Party from 1945–1955. 1955; 40 pp.

Sozialdemokratische Partei des Saarlandes. *Bericht der S.P.S.-Delegation bei den Pariser Verhandlungen über die neuen Staatsverträge.* Saarbrücken; 1953; 28 pp.

    Bericht über die Verhandlungen des 9. Parteitages vom 25–28. März 1954. Saarbrücken: 1954; 163 pp.

    Bild des Staatshaushalts 1953 mit Vergleichszahlen aus den Jahren 1950, 1951 und 1952. Saarbrücken: 1953; 21 pp.

    Die Rentenleistungen im Saarland, in der Bundesrepublik und in Frankreich. By Richard Kirn, Land party chairman. Saarbrücken: 1955; 15 pp.

    Die Saarfrage. A documentary collection. 2nd enlarged ed. 1954; 72 pp.

    Sozialdemokratie—Saarfrage—Saarwirtschaft—Sozialpolitik. Abstracts from speeches by Land party chairman Richard Kirn. Saarbrücken: 1955; 93 pp.

Pamphlets, Minutes, Memoranda

Becker-Schneider. *Warum Nein zum Natersplan.* Stimmen der deutschen Saaropposition, Heft 3. Cologne: Comel-Verlag, 1954.

Eberhard, Walter. *Wer kaufte Joho; dreimal an der Saar.* Paris: Selbstverlag, 1951; 56 pp.

Hoffmann, Johannes. *Am Rande des Hitlerkrieges.* Diary. Saarbrücken: Saarländische Verlagsanstalt und Druckerei, 1948; 133 pp.

Saarkorrespondenz. *Die Saarwahlen.* Saarbrücken: 1952.

Schneider, Heinrich. *Lösungsvorschläge zur Saarfrage.* Stimmen der deutschen Saaropposition, Heft 2. Bonn: Deutscher Saarbund, 1953; 27 pp.

    Die rechtlichen Probleme einer Saarlösung. Baden-Baden: Jus-Verlag, 1954; 47 pp.

    Die Saar, deutsch oder europäisch? Cologne: Comel-Verlag, 1954; 63 pp.

    Zusammenstellung von drei Artikeln des Verfassers. Stimmen der deutschen Saaropposition, Heft 2. Cologne: Deutscher Saarbund, 1952; 22 pp.

Stöber, Robert (pseudonym). *Die saarländische Verfassung vom 15. Dezember 1947 und ihre Entstehung.* Cologne: Comel-Verlag, 1952; 566 pp.

D. Council of Europe and United States

Council of Europe. *Le statut de la Sarre, index des documents du Conseil de l'Europe relatifs à la question sarroise, septembre 1952-janvier 1955.* Consultative Assembly, 7th Ordinary Session, General Affairs Committee. Strasbourg: February 7, 1955. Mimeographed; 12 pp. (Restricted AS/AG (6) 90.)

Letter of March 29, 1956 addressed to Helmut Hirsch in the name of the
Secretary of State by John P. Meagher, *Jahrbuch für internationales
Recht,* Vol. VII, No. 1; pp. 84–85.

Office of the U.S. High Commissioner for Germany. *Chronology July 1951–
1953: Documents on the Saar.* Vol. II. Bad Godesberg: February 16,
1953; 266 pp.

United States Department of State. *Bulletin,* Vol. XV, No. 359 (July 28, 1946)
and Vol. XVI, No. 407 (April 20, 1947).

" The Present Status of the Saar," *Documents and State Papers,* Vol. I,
No. 7 (October, 1948); pp. 435–450. Also published in German: *Die
gegenwärtige Lage des Saarlandes, eine Denkschrift des amerikanischen
Department of State, mit einem Vorwort von Karl Arnold, hrsg. von
der Regierung des Landes Nordrhein-Westfalen unter Mitwirkung des
Deutschen Büros für Friedensfragen in Stuttgart.* Düsseldorf: 1949;
20 pp.

3. Newspapers, Periodicals, Public Opinion Polls

A. France

Dailies

L'Aube. Paris.
L'Aurore. Paris.
Combat. Paris.
Le Courrier de Metz. Metz.
Le Figaro. Paris.
L'Humanité. Paris.
Information. Paris.
Le Monde. Paris.
Le Populaire. Paris.
Le Républican lorrain. Metz.

Periodicals [2]

*Allemagne: Bulletin d'Information du Comité français d'échanges avec l'Alle-
magne nouvelle.* Paris.
L'Année politique 1944–1946. Paris: Presses universitaires de France, 1946–
1947.
Documents. Paris.
L'Express. Paris.
Le Fait du jour. Paris.
L'Observateur, later *France-Observateur.* Paris.
Perspectives. Paris.
Le Rassemblement. Paris.

Economic Publications

Actualités industrielles lorraines et du Nord. Paris.
L'Agence économique et financière. Paris.
Bilans hebdomadaires. Paris.

---

[2] It was not considered necessary to list here the titles of all the political journals used
in the preparation of this study. In the bibliographical section entitled "Studies"
will be found the titles of articles to which particular reference has been made.

Bulletin du Conseil national du Patronat français. Paris.
Le Commerce international import-export. Paris.
Les Echos. Paris.
L'Economie. Paris.
Economie et politique. Paris.
L'Economie mosellane. Metz.
L'Economiste européen. Paris.
Entreprise. Paris.
L'Exportateur français. Paris.
La France industrielle. Paris.
Moniteur officiel du commerce et de l'industrie. Paris.
Les Nouvelles économiques. Paris.
Revue française de l'énergie. Paris.
La Semaine économique et financière. Paris.
La Tribune économique et financière. Paris.
L'Usine nouvelle. Paris.
La Vie française. Paris.

Public Opinion Polls

Institut français d'opinion publique. *Bulletin d'information.* No. 6 (December 16, 1944); 10 pp.

    Inquiry. July, 1954.

(See also, under Federal Republic of Germany: Public Opinion Polls, the publications of the Institut für Demoskopie.)

B. Federal Republic of Germany

Dailies and Weeklies

Allgemeine Zeitung. Mainz.
Bonner Rundschau. Bonn.
Christ und Welt. Stuttgart.
Deutsche Saar-Zeitung. Bad Kreuznach.
Deutsche Zeitung und Wirtschafts-Zeitung. Stuttgart.
Frankfurter Allgemeine Zeitung. Frankfurt.
Frankfurter Neue Presse. Frankfurt.
Frankfurter Rundschau. Frankfurt.
Hamburger Allgemeine Zeitung, later *Hamburger Anzeiger.* Hamburg.
Hamburger Echo. Hamburg.
Handelsblatt. Düsseldorf.
Hannoversche Allgemeine Zeitung. Hannover.
Industriekurier. Düsseldorf.
Kölnische Rundschau. Cologne.
Münchner Merkur. Munich.
Neue Ruhr-Zeitung. Essen.
Die Neue Zeitung. Berlin.
Neuer Vorwärts. Hannover.
Rheinischer Merkur. Koblenz.
Rhein-Neckar Zeitung. Heidelberg.
Die Rheinpfalz. Ludwigshafen.
Stuttgarter Zeitung. Stuttgart.

Süddeutsche Zeitung. Munich.
Der Tagesspiegel. Berlin.
Trierischer Volksfreund. Trier.
Die Welt. Hamburg.
Wirtschaftszeitung-Stuttgart. Stuttgart.
Die Zeit. Hamburg.

Political and Economic Periodicals [3]

Aussenpolitik. Stuttgart.
Bonner Hefte. Bonn.
Deutsche Studentenzeitung. Bonn.
Dokumente. Offenburg/Baden.
Europa-Archiv. Frankfurt.
Neues Abendland. Munich.
Der Spiegel. Hamburg.
Der Volkswirt. Hamburg.

Organs of the Political Parties

Deutschland-Union-Dienst. Bonn (D.U.D.).
Freie Demokratische Korrespondenz. Bonn (F.D.K.).
S.P.D.-Presse-Dienst.
Union-Dienst der C.D.U./C.S.U. (U.D.).

Political Opinion Polls

Emnid-Institute of Bielefeld. *Vor Volksabstimmung und Wahlen im Saarland,* 1955; 72 pp.
Institut für Demoskopie of Allensbach. "Die Franzosen über die Saar," "Die Saarabstimmung," "Bericht über Behinderung einer Bevölkerungsumfrage," "Franzosen und Deutsche über die Saar." *Jahrbuch der Oeffentlichen Meinung 1947–1955.* 1956; 412 pp.

C. Saar

Dailies and Periodicals

Allgemeine Zeitung. Saarbrücken. Organ of the D.S.P., later S.P.D./Saar. First no., August 10, 1955.
La Chronique sarroise: Bulletin bilingue d'information des Français en Sarre, édité par le service d'information de la Mission diplomatique française en Sarre, Saarbrücken: March, 1952–July, 1955.
Deutsche Saar. Saarbrücken. Organ of the D.P.S./Saar. First no., July 28, 1955.
Freie Saarpresse. Illegal paper of the S.P.D./Saar. Fortnightly, March, 1953–Summer, 1955.
Die Neue Saar. Saarbrücken. Until December 24, 1948, sub-titled *Wochenzeitung des M.R.S.,* and after that, *Wochenschrift für Politik, Kultur und Unterhaltung.* Weekly. First no., July 14, 1946.
Neue Saarbrücker Zeitung. Saarbrücken. After September, 1946, became *Saarbrücker Zeitung.* Independent. First no., August 27, 1945.

---

[3] *Cf.,* also, Studies: articles, pp. 377 *et seq.*

Die Neue Zeit. Saarbrücken. Organ of the K.P./Saar. First no., June 22, 1946.

Neueste Nachrichten. Organ of the C.D.U./Saar. First no., July 26, 1955.

Das Saarland. Saarbrücken. Organ of the D.P.S. First no., August 1, 1947. From May 23, 1949 to September 30, 1949, the *Saarland Abend-post.*

Saarländische Volkszeitung. Saarbrücken. Organ of the C.V.P./Saar. First no., June 22, 1946.

Volksstimme. Saarbrücken. Organ of the S.P.S./Saar. First no., June 22, 1946.

Professional Journals

Die Arbeit. Organ of the Syndicat unitaire [Einheitsgewerkschaft]. First no., July 31, 1946.

Gewerkschaftliche Rundschau. Saarbrücken. Organ of the Syndicats chrétiens in the Saar. First no., January, 1948.

Der Öffentliche Dienst. Saarbrücken. Organ of the Syndicat chrétien des services publics in the Saar. First published by the *Gewerkschaftliche Rundschau,* then independently.

Saar-Bergbau. Saarbrücken. Organ of the Syndicat unitaire des mineurs. First published by *Die Arbeit,* later independently until the end of 1952; until 1954, appeared as mimeographed pamphlets, some of them entitled *Gewerkschaftliche Informationen;* after 1954, became the *Bergarbeiterzeitung* (an unauthorized journal).

Der Saar-Eisenbahner. Saarbrücken. Organ of the Syndicat chrétiens des cheminots. First published by the *Gewerkschaftliche Rundschau,* later independently.

Saar-Handel. Saarbrücken. Organ of the Landesverband des saarländischen Einzelhandels.

Saarhandwerker mit Bau-Markt. Saarbrücken. Organ of the Arbeitsgemein-schaft des saarländischen Handwerks and of the Chambre des métiers sarrois. First no., January 20, 1949.

Saarländische Rechts- und Steuerzeitschrift. Saarbrücken. First no., October, 1948.

Die Saar-Wirtschaft. Saarbrücken. First no., December, 1948.

Public Opinion Polls

(See under Federal Republic of Germany.)

D. United Kingdom [4]

The Economist. London.
The Manchester Guardian.
New Statesman and Nation. London.
The Times. London.

E. United States

The Chicago Tribune.
The Christian Science Monitor. Boston.

---

[4] *Cf.,* Studies: articles, *infra.*

International Free Trade Union News. New York: American Federation of
Labor.
The New York Times.

II. *STUDIES*

1. Studies Relating to Particular Problems

Deutsch, Karl W. "Mass Communications and the Loss of Freedom in
National Decision Making: A Possible Research Approach to Interstate
Conflicts." *Journal of Conflict Resolution,* Vol. I, No. 2 (June, 1957);
pp. 200–212.

Duroselle, Jean-Baptiste. *De l'utilisation des sondages d'opinion en histoire
et en sciences politiques.* Brussels: Institut universitaire d'Information
sociale et économique, 1957; 66 pp.

Ehrmann, Henry W. *Organized Business in France.* Princeton: Princeton
University, 1957; 514 pp.

Furniss, Edgar S., Jr. *Memorandum on Interstate Conflicts.* New York:
Carnegie Endowment for International Peace, December, 1955. Mimeographed; 31 pp.

Gerbet, Pierre. "La genèse du Plan Schuman, des origines à la déclaration
du 9 mai 1950," *Revue française de science politique,* July–September,
1956; pp. 525–553.

Girard, Alain and Stoetzel, Jean. "L'opinion publique et la C.E.D.," *La
querelle de la C.E.D.* Cahiers de la Fondation nationale des sciences
politiques, No. 80. Published under the direction of Raymond Aron
and Daniel Lerner. Paris: A. Colin, 1956; pp. 127–155.

Lavau, Georges. "Note sur un 'pressure group' français: la Confédération
générale des petites et moyennes entreprises," *Revue française de science
politique,* April–June, 1955; pp. 370–383.
"Political Pressures by Interest Groups in France," *Interest Groups on
Four Continents,* ed. Henry W. Ehrmann. Pittsburgh: University of
Pittsburgh Press, 1958; pp. 60–95.

Meynaud, Jean. "Contribution à l'analyse des groupes d'intérêt dans la vie
politique française," *Revue de l'Institut de sociologie Solvay,* Nos. 2–3,
1956; pp. 225–256.
"L'intervention des groupes d'intérêt dans la politique économique,"
Revue économique et sociale, October, 1956; pp. 256–277.
"Essai d'analyse de l'influence des groupes d'intérêt," *Revue économique,*
March, 1957; pp. 177–220.
"Les groupes d'intérêt et l'administration en France," *Revue française de
science politique,* July–September, 1957; pp. 573–593.
Les groupes de pression en France. Cahiers de la Fondation nationale
des sciences politiques, No. 95. Paris: A. Colin, 1958; 371 pp.

Siegler, Heinrich. *Deutschlands Weg 1945–1955.* Schriftenreihe des Diplo-
matischen Kuriers. Cologne: Verlag Georg Koenig, 1955; 215 pp.

Vernant, Jacques. "L'économie française devant la C.E.D.," *La querelle de
la C.E.D.* Cahiers de la Fondation nationale des sciences politiques,
No. 80. Published under the direction of Raymond Aron and Daniel
Lerner. Paris: A. Colin, 1956; pp. 109–123.

Vocke, Klaus. "Politische Gefahren der Theorien über Deutschlands Rechts-
    lage," *Europa-Archiv,* October 5, 1957; pp. 10199–10215.
Wright, Quincy. *Memorandum on Interstate Conflicts.* New York:
    Carnegie Endowment for International Peace, December, 1955. Mimeo-
    graphed; 20 pp.

2. GENERAL STUDIES ON THE SAAR

Monographs

Altmeyer, Klaus, Szliska, Jakob, Veauthier, Werner, and Weiant, Peter.
    Das Saarland. Saarbrücken: Die Mitte, 1948; 811 pp.
Bellot, Josef. *Hundert Jahre politisches Leben an der Saar unter preussischer
    Herrschaft, 1815–1918.* Rheinisches Archiv, No. 45. Bonn: L.
    Röhrscheid, 1954; 251 pp.
Capot-Rey, Robert. *La région industrielle sarroise: territoire de la Sarre et
    bassin houiller de la Moselle, étude géographique.* Paris: Berger-
    Levrault, 1934; 637 pp., maps, illustrations.
Cowan, Laing Gray. *France and the Saar, 1680–1948.* New York:
    Columbia University Press, 1950; 247 pp.
Frisch, Sepp. *Die Saar blieb deutsch, ein Rückblick, 1680–1955.* Leoni am
    Starnberger See: Druffel Verlag, 1956; 200 pp.
Hellwig, Fritz. *Die Saar zwischen Ost und West. Die wirtschaftliche
    Verflechtung des Saarindustriebezirks mit seinen Nachbargebieten.*
    Bonn: L. Röhrscheid Verlag, 1954; 219 pp.
Hirsch, Helmut. *Die Saar in Versailles, die Saarfrage auf der Friedenskon-
    ferenz von 1919.* Rheinisches Archiv, No. 42. Bonn: L. Röhrscheid
    Verlag, 1952; 71 pp.
    *Die Saar von Genf; die Saarfrage während des Völkerbundregimes von
    1920–1935.* Rheinisches Archiv, No. 46. Bonn: L. Röhrscheid Verlag,
    1954; 96 pp.
Kloevekorn, Fritz. *Das Saargebiet, seine Struktur, seine Probleme.* Pub-
    lished with the co-operation of public officials and scholars in the Saar.
    Saarbrücken: Gebr. Hofer, 1929; 584 pp.
Limberg, A. von (pseudonym). *Geschichte des Saarlandes.* Saarlouis:
    Felten-Verlag, 1948; 343 pp.
Sante, Georg Wilhelm. *Die Saarfrage.* In association with Hans Bongard,
    Matthias Braun, Oskar Hammelsbeck. Saarbrücken: Saarbrücker
    Druckerei und Verlag, 1931; 104 pp.
Straus, Emile. *Die gesellschaftliche Gliederung des Saargebietes, eine sozio-
    graphische Beschreibung.* Thesis, Frankfurt, 1935. Würzburg:
    Triltsch, 1935; 179 pp.
Vidal de la Blache, Paul and Gallois, L. *Le bassin de la Sarre, clauses du
    traité de Versailles; étude historique et économique.* Paris: A. Colin,
    1919; 54 pp.
200 Jahre Bergbau an der Saar, 1754–1954. Bielefeld: G. Schuster, 1955;
    368 pp., appendices.

Articles

Champier, Laurent. "La Sarre, essai d'interprétation géopolitique," "Les
    principaux types de paysages humains en Sarre," *Arbeiten aus dem
    Geographischen Institut,* Vol. I. Saarbrücken: Universität des Saar-
    landes, Philosophische Fakultät, 1956; pp. 3–74, 75–80.

Goriély, Georges. *Etude sociologique sur la Sarre.* Typed, unpublished.

Hellwig, Fritz. "Die geschichtlichen Bezjchungen zwischen der saarländischen und lottringrischen Eisenindustrie," *Westmärkische abhandlungen zu. Landes und Volksforschung,* Vol. IV, 1940.

Mourin, Maxime. "Le Saint-Siège et la Sarre," *Politique étrangère,* July–August, 1956; pp. 411–426.

3. STUDIES ON THE SAAR CONFLICT, 1945–1955

Altmeyer, Klaus and Sinnwell, Erich. *Der 23. Oktober 1955; die Volksbefragung an der Saar in Wort und Bild.* Saarlouis: Hausen-Verlag, 1955; 54 pp.

Aubert, Jean-Philippe. *La question sarroise de 1945 à 1950.* Paper presented for a degree, Faculty of Arts. Lausanne: 1956. Typed; 59 pp.

Bosch, Werner. *Die Saarfrage, eine wirtschaftliche Analyse.* Mainz Universität, Forschungsinstitut für Wirtschaftspolitik, Veröffentlichungen Vol. 4. Heidelberg: Quelle und Meyer, 1954; 174 pp.

Buchleitner, Hans Peter. *Etappen auf dem Wege zum Saarland, 1945–1947.* Saarbrücken: 1954. Mimeographed; 105 pp.

Byrnes, James Francis. *Speaking Frankly.* New York: Harper, 1947; 324 pp.

Calvet, Jacques. *Essai sur la politique française en Sarre.* Paper prepared for the *diplômé* of the Institut d'études politiques. Paris: 1951. Typed; 127 pp.

Chardonnet, Jean. *La Sarre.* Paris: Ed. du Chêne, 1945; 32 pp.

Clay, Lucius DuBignon. *Decision in Germany.* Garden City, N.Y.: Doubleday, 1950; 522 pp.

Coquet, Lucien. *La thèse française: Sarre-Ruhr-Rhénanie.* Paris: privately printed, 1946; 6 pp.

Debray, Jean-Claude. *Le nouveau statut des échanges franco-sarrois et les perspectives qu'il offre.* N.p. or d.; 16 pp.

Dircks-Dilly, Jacques. *La Sarre et son destin.* Paris: Ed. du Vieux Colombier, 1956; 267 pp., maps.

Dischler, Ludwig. *Das Saarland 1945–1957.* Forschungsstelle für Völkerrecht und ausländisches öffentliches Recht der Universität Hamburg, Veröffentlichungen, Nos. 24–25, 30. Hamburg: 1956–1957. Mimeographed; 3 vols.

Forschungsstelle für Völkerrecht und ausländisches öffentliches Recht der Universität Hamburg. *Frankreich und das Saarland, 1945–1951.* 2nd enlarged ed. Hamburg: 1952. Mimeographed; 2 vols.

Gesetzgebung und Abkommen des Saarlandes. Hamburg: Nölke Verlag, 1954; 360 pp.

Hagmann, Hans Joachim. *Die saarländischen Landtagswahlen vom 30. November 1952.* Cologne: Deutsche Glocke, 1953; 240 pp.

Held, Robert. *The Political Geography of the Saarland.* Worcester, Mass.; 1949. Thesis, typed.

Hummel, Raimar. *Die Menschenrechte und die Erklärung der allgemeinen Menschenrechte der U.N. vom 10. Dezember 1948 im Recht des Saarlandes.* Saarbrücken: 1955. Thesis, University of the Saar. Mimeographed; 219 pp.

Hütten, Mokre, Wiebringhaus. *Europäisierung der Saar und Völkerrecht.* Saarbrücken: 1954; 32 pp.

Ingrain, Robert. *Une clef de notre securité à l'Est: la Sarre; renseignements généraux, impressions d'occupation.* Orléans: La Dépêche du Loiret, 1948; 14 pp.

Kaps, Paul H. *Rheinland-Pfalz und Frankreichs Saarpolitik nach 1945.* Kaiserslautern: Verlag Heinz Rohr, 1955; 88 pp.

Kitzinger, U. W. *The Economics of the Saar Question.* Oxford: Nuffield College, 1958. Mimeographed; 160 pp.

Kratz, Georg. *Mittelrhein-Saar.* Schriftenreihe der Hochschule Speyer, No. 7. Stuttgart: Kohlhammer-Verlag, 1954; 82 pp.

Kreutz, Ludwig. *Die Saarwirtschaft heute.* A survey of economic conditions in the Saar at the beginning of 1948 with an index of addresses. Saarbrücken: Industrie-Verlag, 1948; 286 pp.

Leonhardt, L. *Wo steht die Saarwirtschaft? Zeitgemässe Betrachtungen zum künftigen Schicksal der Saar.* Saarlouis: Felten Verlag, 1946; 35 pp.

Lottig, Hans. *Bibliographie zur Saarfrage 1945–1954.* Forschungsstelle für Völkerrecht und ausländisches öffentliches Recht der Universität Hamburg, Veröffentlichungen, No. 19. Hamburg: 1954. Mimeographed; 21 pp.

Martin, Klaus. *Die Errichtung der französisch-saarländischen Währungsunion im Jahre 1947 und die sich daraus ergebenden Massnahmen des französischen Staates hinsichtlich des Kreditwesens im Saarland.* Saarbrücken: Bock und Seip, 1955. Thesis; 129 pp., appendices.

Muller, François. *L'économie sarroise, ses problèmes, ses industries de base, sa position dans la CECA.* Paris: 1956. Thesis, Paris, Faculty of Law. Mimeographed; 406 pp.

Müller, Robert. *Le rattachement économique de la Sarre à la France.* Paris: Ed. scientifiques Riber, 1950. Mimeographed; 303 pp.

"Le problème sarrois," *Chronique de politique étrangère,* No. 5, 1956; pp. 601–736.

Reichel, Hans. *Wirtschaftliches und kulturelles Handbuch des Saarlandes.* Saarbrücken: Verlag Hans Reichel, 1955; 376 pp.

Roy, Francis. *Le mineur sarrois.* Thesis, Paris, Faculty of Law, 1951. Paris: Berger-Levrault, 1954; 212 pp.

Russell, Frank Marion. *The Saar, Battleground and Pawn.* Stanford: Stanford University Press, 1951; 204 pp.

"Die Saar—Grenzland und Brücke," *Internationales Jahrbuch der Politik.* Edited by Friedrich August Freiherr von der Heydte. Munich: Isar Verlag, March, 1956; 274 pp.

Schlachter, Frédéric. *Saarwirtschaft am Wendepunkt.* Saarbrücken: 1948; 48 pp.

Schmidt, Robert. *Saarpolitik 1945–1957.* Typed, unpublished; 3 vols.

Schneider, Werner. *Die Preisentwicklung der Saarkohle in den Jahren 1920–1950 und die Auswirkung der Kohlenpreise auf die Wettbewerbsfähigkeit der saarländischen Industrie.* Saarbrücken: 1951. Thesis, typed.

Thaden, Herbert. *Der industrielle Wiederaufbau an der Saar.* Heidelberg: 1948. Thesis, typed; 223 pp.

Welles, Sumner. *The Time for Decision.* New York: Harper, 1944; 431 pp.

Where are We Heading? New York: Harper, 1946; 397 pp.

Weymar, Paul. *Konrad Adenauer: die autorisierte Biographie.* Munich: Kindler Verlag, 1955; 782 pp.

4. ARTICLES ON THE SAAR CONFLICT, 1944–1955

Altmeyer, Klaus. "Kleines Kapitel saarländischer Nachkriegsgeschichte. Die alliierte Nachkriegspolitik zur raumpolitischen Gestaltung der Gebiete um Saar-Mosel, Pfalz," *Die Arbeitskammer,* April, 1947; pp. 112–118.

"Die Volksbefragung an der Saar vom 23. Oktober 1955," *Europa-Archiv,* Heft 11 (August 5, 1956); pp. 9049–9060.

Andlauer, Joseph, General. "Le rôle militaire de la Sarre," *Le Fait du jour,* No. 41 (March 25, 1947); pp. 8–12.

André-Fribourg, G. "La Sarre et la France," *Le Fait du jour,* No. 7 (May 21, 1946).

"Les Etats-Unis et la Sarre, 1919–1946," *Le Fait du jour,* No. 19 (September 17, 1946); pp. 1–26.

"L'arrivée des douaniers français," *Le Fait du jour,* No. 34 (December 31, 1946); pp. 22–25.

"L'Université," *Le Fait du jour,* No. 43 (April 8, 1947); p. 11.

"Le quatrième Reich passe à l'offensive," *Le Fait du jour,* No. 47 (May, 1947).

"D'un plebiscite à l'autre, 1935–1947," *Le Fait du jour,* No. 52 (1947); pp. 1–26.

Antoine, Anik. "Essai sur l'administration en Sarre," *Revue administrative,* May–June, 1952; pp. 309–318.

"L'aspect économique et financier du rattachement de la Sarre à la France," *Perspectives,* October 25, 1947.

Becker, Richard. "Das Saarproblem," *Aussenpolitik,* No. 4 (July, 1951), pp 284–290.

Bellenand, Claude. "Trait d'union entre la France et l'Allemagne, la Sarre est jalouse de son autonomie," *Politique internationale,* March, 1950; pp. 280–285.

Best, Rolf. "Der Gedanke des Rechtsstaates und seine Verwirklichung im Saarland," *Saarländische Rechtszeitschrift,* 1949; pp. 65 *et seq.*

Blind, Adolf. "Die Saarwirtschaft, Ende 1953," *Saarwirtschaft,* December 20, 1953; pp. 3–9.

Blun, G. "La Sarre devant l'inconnu," *L'Economie,* September 22, 1955; pp. 6–7.

Chardonnet, Jean. "Le rattachement de la Sarre, conséquences économiques," *Agence France-Presse: information et documentation,* December 13, 1947; pp. 3–5.

Chevallier, Louis. "La Sarre, épreuve de l'Europe," *Etudes,* June, 1952; pp. 363–370.

"Cinq ans de coopération franco-sarroise, résultat et perspectives," *L'Economie,* supplement to No. 278 (October 7, 1950); 8 pp.

Conrad, Kurt. "Wie sollte die Saarlösung aussehen," *Bonner Hefte,* No. 12 (June, 1954); pp. 12–17.

David, Pierre. "Réflexions sur les élections sarroises," *Terre humaine,* February, 1953.

Debré, Michel. "Politique française à l'égard de la Sarre, 1945–1950," *France-illustration,* No. 270 (December 15, 1950); pp. 667–668.

"La Sarre et l'union européenne," *L'Economie,* special number (1952).

"Le problème de la Sarre," *Saint-Cyr,* special number (April, 1953); pp. 38–40.

"La Sarre, étiage de notre faiblesse," *Le Rassemblement,* No. 6 (March, 1955); pp. 7–8.

Dehousse, Fernand. "Mission en Sarre," *Bulletin de la Société belge d'études et d'expansion,* March–April, 1956.

Delmas, Claude. "La Sarre et l'Allemagne—Situation et perspectives," *Féderation,* May, 1950; pp. 245–249.

Dircks-Dilly, Jacques. "Intérêt économique de l'union douanière franco-sarroise," *Moniteur officiel du commerce extérieur,* April 5, 1951; p. 838.

"Dix années de politique sarroise," *L'Economie,* October 20, 1955; pp. 4–6.

Donnadieu, James. "La France et la Sarre," *Revue de défense nationale,* February, 1946; pp. 162–181.

"La France et la Sarre," *Hommes et mondes,* February, 1947; pp. 339–355.

"L'économie sarroise," *Productions françaises,* May, 1948; pp. 6–67.

"En Sarre, allons-nous faire enfin une politique réaliste?" *Perspectives,* October 29, 1955; pp. 1–3.

Fay, Sidney B. "The Saar Problem—France and Germany in Conflict," *Current History,* Vol. XVIII, No. 105 (May, 1950); pp. 257–262.

Frenay, Henri. "La Sarre et l'Europe, choisir une politique," *Fédération,* May, 1950; pp. 250–253.

Friedländer, E. "The Saar Deadlock—An Interim Solution?" *The Spectator,* August 29, 1952; pp. 257–258.

"Le futur régime économique de la Sarre et ses répercussions sur l'économie française," *L'Usine nouvelle,* No. 11 (March 17, 1955); pp. 82–83.

Grandval, Gilbert. "Si la France veut," *Saint-Cyr,* special number (April, 1953); p. 34.

"Réalités sarroises," *Revue de défense nationale,* March, 1954; pp. 263–267.

Gyssling, Walter. "Dans la Sarre aussi il faut choisir une politique," *L'Année politique et économique,* November–December, 1951; pp. 374–381.

Hellwig, Fritz. "Saarwirtschaft zwischen Ost und West," *Bonner Hefte,* No. 9 (May, 1954); pp. 19–22.

Héraud, Guy. "Le statut politique de la Sarre dans le cadre du rattachement économique à la France," *Revue générale de droit international public,* Nos. 1–2 (1948); pp. 186–209.

Herly, Robert. "Le fait du jour en Sarre," *Le Fait du jour,* No. 21 (October 1, 1946).

Hirsch, Helmut. "Amerikas diplomatische Behandlung des Saarproblems," *Jahrbuch für internationales Recht,* No. 1 (1956); pp. 69–85.

Hoffmann, Johannes. "L'avenir de la Sarre," *Saint-Cyr,* special number (April, 1953); p. 34.

Jaeger, Jules Albert. "Remarques sur la Sarre," *Hommes et mondes,* October, 1952; pp. 255–264.

Javrier, L. P. "Les ressources énergétiques de la Sarre dans l'économie franco-sarroise," *Revue française de l'énergie,* March, April, May, 1951; pp. 187–193, 221–230, 251–255.

Laurent, Pierre. "La Sarre, une pierre neuve dans un édifice nouveau," *France-illustration,* special number, No. 270 (December 15, 1950).

"L'union franco-sarroise d'après les conventions conclues entre la France et la Sarre de 1948 à 1950," *Journal du droit international,* January–March, 1952; pp. 380–433.

"L'évolution de l'union franco-sarroise depuis 1950," *Journal du droit international,* July September, 1955; pp. 522–579, appendix, p. 718.

Lavergne, Bernard. "La Sarre, tombeau de l'idée européenne," *L'Année politique et économique,* November–December, 1952; pp. 431–436.

Le Mallem, Th. "Brève histoire de la Sarre," *Saint-Cyr,* special number (April, 1953); pp. 38–40.

Lesort, Gonzague. "Der Begriff der Souveränität und die französisch-saarländische Union in den Verträgen vom 20. Mai 1953," *Saarländische Rechts- und Steuerzeitschrift,* 1953; pp. 57–60.

Lomuller, L. "Le territoire de la Sarre," *Revue politique et parlementaire,* No. 51 (December, 1949); pp. 387–397.

Löwenthal, Richard. "Zankapfel oder Bindeglied, Notizen von einer Reise ins Saargebiet," *Der Monat,* No. 44 (May, 1952); pp. 145–154.

Lütkens, Gerhard. "Das Saargebiet und der Europarat," *Das sozialpolitische Jahrhundert,* 1949; pp. 296–297.

Mangin, Robert. "Il faut européaniser la Sarre," *Monde nouveau,* No. 64 (1952); pp. 31–43.

Massenon, Léo. "L'affaire sarroise," *Ecrits de Paris,* March, 1950.

Menzel, Eberhard. "Die Saarfrage," *Europa-Archiv,* No. 17, September 5, 1951; pp. 4259–4275.

"Die Diskussion über die gegenwärtige Rechsstellung des Saarlandes," *Europa-Archiv,* No. 11, June 5, 1954; pp. 6599–6616.

Merle, Marcel. "L'accord franco-allemand du 23 octobre sur le statut de la Sarre," *Annuaire français de droit international,* 1955; pp. 128–133.

Ollenhauer, Erich. "German Social Democrats Views on the Saar Question," *Socialist International Information,* December 6, 1952; pp. 1–4.

Perger, Gottfried. "Wer ist Gilbert Grandval ?" *Bonner Hefte,* No. 12 (June, 1954); pp. 7–8.

Plaisant, Marcel. "Le destin de la Sarre," *Revue des Deux-Mondes,* October 1, 1950; pp. 421–433.

"La politique sarroise de la France, le territoire de la Sarre," *Chronique de politique étrangère,* No. 6 (November, 1951); pp. 707–721.

Prittie, Terence. "France, Germany, and the Saar," *The Nation,* Vol. 170 (March 18, 1950); pp. 248–250.

"The Saar, Key to European Planning," *The Listener,* April 22, 1954; pp. 679–681.

"Les rapports franco-sarrois après les Conventions de mai 1953," *L'Economie,* supplement to No. 399 (May 28, 1953); 8 pp.

"Le rattachement éventuel de la Sarre à la France," *Cahiers du monde nouveau,* August–September, 1946.

Rehbein, Hans. "Die Wirtschaft des Saargebietes," *Europa-Archiv,* August, 1947; pp. 799–810.

Revire, Jean. "En Sarre, le provisoire n'a que trop duré," *Le Fait du jour,* No. 31 (December 10, 1946); pp. 21–22.

"Psychologie politique sarroise," *Le Fait du jour,* No. 32 (December 17, 1946); pp. 14–16.

"Pour une politique psychologique en Sarre," *Le Fait du jour,* No. 33 (December 24, 1946); pp. 19–20.

"La Sarre, la France et l'Europe," *Le Monde français,* No. 54 (March, 1950); pp. 355–364.

"La Sarre et la France, données psychologiques," *Fédération,* No. 64 (May, 1950); pp. 238–244.

"La Sarre et l'Europe," *Le Monde français,* November, 1950; pp. 179–186.

"Le problème de la Sarre," *La Revue des Deux-Mondes,* April 15, 1952; pp. 580–609.

Rothfels, Hans. "The Saar Problem in 1950," *American Perspective,* Vol. IV, No. 3 (Summer, 1950).

Ruland, Franz. "Die französisch-saarländische Wirtschaftsunion," *Saar-Wirtschaft,* December 15, 1951; pp. 1–3.

"La Sarre après les élections," *L'Economie,* supplement to No. 377 (December 11, 1952); 8 pp.

"La Sarre se plaint de la concurrence lorraine," *L'Entreprise,* No. 28 (May 15, 1954); pp. 19–21.

"La Sarre sera-t-elle un pont ou une pomme de discorde ? " *Bulletin d'information du Comité français d'échanges avec l'Allemagne nouvelle,* No. 4 (December 1, 1949).

Scheuner, Ulrich. "Die Rechtslage der Saarbergwerke," *Deutsches Verwaltungsblatt,* Heft 5 (1956); pp. 145–150.

Schneider, Heinrich. "Die Diskussion über die gegenwärtige Rechtsstellung des Saarlandes, eine Stellungnahme zu den Ausführungen von Prof. Dr. Eberhard Menzel," *Europa-Archiv,* No. 12, November 5, 1954; pp. 7003–7018.

Senf, Paul. "L'économie sarroise," *Documents,* February, 1955; pp. 261–273.

"Le statut actuel de la Sarre : La position française, celles des Etats-Unis et de la Grande-Bretagne," *Perspectives,* January 28, 1950; pp. 1–8.

"Le statut de la Sarre," *L'Economie,* March 18, 1954; pp. 7–8.

Strohm, Gustav. "Eine Lösung der Saarfrage in Sicht ? " *Der Volkswirt,* No. 37 (1949); pp. 8–9.

Süsterhenn, Adolf. "Europa und die Saar," *Bundesländerdienst,* November 3, 1953; pp. 2–7.

Taylor, A. J. P. "France, Germany, and the Saar," *International Journal,* Winter, 1952–1953; pp. 27–31.

Thilenius, R. "Das Saarschiff an der Wendemarke," *Aussenpolitik,* October, 1955; pp. 617–627.

Ungeheuer, Josef. "Nichts Neues an der Saar ? " *Bonner Hefte,* No. 14 (July, 1954); pp. 15–17.

Vansittart, Lord. "The Lesson of the Saar," *The National and English Review,* Vol. 134 (1950); pp. 182–185.

Verdier, Abel. I. "La légitimité des revendications françaises," II. "Comment intégrer la Sarre dans la vie économique française," *Le Monde,* May 7–8, 1946.

Vignes, Daniel. "Le referendum sarrois," *Annuaire français de droit international,* 1955; pp. 134–139.

Walz, Karl. "Wirkliche Freiheit gesucht," *Bonner Hefte,* No. 12 (June 12, 1954); pp. 4–6.

Weiant, P. "Die Saar im europäischen Wirtschaftsraum," *Mitteilungen der Industrie- und Handelskammer,* No. 9 (1951); pp. 307–315.

Wiebringhaus, Hans. " Zur völkerrechtlichen Stellung Deutschlands und des Saarlandes: Einige grundsätzliche Bemerkungen," *Saarländische Rechts- und Steuerzeitschrift*, Heft 4/5 (1953); pp. 53–57.
" Die derzeitige rechtliche Stellung des Saarlandes unter besonderer Berücksichtigung des 1. und 2. Teils des Berichtes von van der Goes van Naters," *Saarländische Rechts- und Steuerzeitschrift*, Heft 6 (1953); pp. 97–101.
" Die Entwicklung der Vertragsverhältnisse zwischen der Saar und Frankreich," *Archiv des Völkerrechts*, No. 4 (March 3, 1954); pp. 323–333.
" Die Auswirkungen der Abkommen über europäische Organisationen auf die Verfassung des Saarlandes," *Saarländische Rechts- und Steuerzeitschrift*, Heft 1 (1955); pp. 3–6.
Wiskemann, Elizabeth. " Bone of Contention," *New Statesman and Nation*, May 10, 1952; pp. 544–545.
" The Saar Problem," *World Review*, July, 1952; pp. 19–23.
" The Saar Moves Toward Germany," *Foreign Affairs*, Vol. XXXIV, No. 1 (January, 1956); pp. 287–296.
Zimmer, Peter. " Sozialismus, Demokratie, Weltanschauung, Referat auf der Morgenfeier der S.P.S. am 2. Dezember 1950," *Unsere Welt*, Heft 1 (January, 1951).

5. Studies Published in " La Documentation Française "

Notes documentaires et Etudes (later *Notes et Etudes documentaires*). No. 326, " La Sarre et la sécurité française." June 15, 1946; 18 pp.
No. 506, " Le statut de la Sarre depuis le traité de Versailles." January 8, 1947; 19 pp.
No. 1.300, " La situation en Sarre au lendemain de la signature des accords franco-sarrois du 3 mars 1950." March 22, 1950; 12 pp.

Articles et Documents. No. 783, " Le problème sarrois." December 15, 1946.

No. 827, " La France et la Sarre." January 28, 1947.
No. 862, " La France et l'Allemagne." March 4, 1947.
No. 903, " La Sarre et le rattachement économique." April 14, 1947.
No. 1.100, " Les élections dans la Sarre." October 28, 1947.

No. 1.171, " La Sarre." January 7, 1948.
No. 1.211, " La Sarre." February 16, 1948.
No. 1.237, " La Sarre." March 13, 1948.
No. 1.248, " La France et la Sarre." March 29, 1948.
No. 1.270, " La Sarre." April 28, 1948.
No. 1.278, " La Sarre." March 10, 1948.
No. 1.340, " La Sarre." August 4, 1948.
No. 1.384, " La Sarre." October 11, 1948.
No. 1.407, " La Sarre." November 20, 1948.
No. 1.419, " La France et la Sarre." December 11, 1948.

No. 1.433, " La Sarre et l'Union européenne." January 4, 1949.
No. 1.437, " L'accord culturel franco-sarrois." January 8, 1949.
No. 1.445, " La Sarre et la France." January 18, 1949.

No. 1.498, "La Sarre." March 21, 1949.
No. 1.522, "La Sarre." April 18, 1949.
No. 1.562, "La France et la Sarre." June 3, 1949.
No. 1.579, "La Sarre et l'Europe." June 23, 1949.
No. 1.593, "La Sarre et la France." July 9, 1949.
No. 1.601, "La Sarre." July 19, 1949.
No. 1.619, "La Sarre et le Conseil de l'Europe." August 9, 1949.
No. 1.634, "La Sarre." August 26, 1949.
No. 1.654, "La France et la Sarre." September 19, 1949.
No. 1.663, "La Sarre." September 29, 1949.
No. 1.673, "La Sarre." October 11, 1949.
No. 1.684, "La Sarre." October 24, 1949.
No. 1.696, "La Sarre." November 7, 1949.
No. 1.720, "La Sarre." December 5, 1949.
No. 1.731, "La Sarre." December 17, 1949.

No. 1.744, "L'avenir de la Sarre." January 2, 1950.
No. 1.750, "Sarre." January 9, 1950.
No. 1.770, "Sarre." February 1, 1950.
No. 1.783, "Sarre." February 16, 1950.
No. 1.795, "La Sarre et les rapports franco-allemands." March 2, 1950.
No. 1.811, "Sarre." March 21, 1950.
No. 1.823, "La Sarre et l'Europe." April 4, 1950.
No. 1.824, "Bonn et les Conventions franco-sarroises." April 5, 1950.
No. 1.826, "Sarre." April 7, 1950.
No. 1.834, "La Sarre et la République fédérale allemande." April 17, 1950.
No. 1.850, "Sarre." May 5, 1950.
No. 1.856, "La Sarre, la France et l'Allemagne." May 12, 1950.
No. 1.870, "La France et la Sarre." May 29, 1950.
No. 1.888, "Politique sarroise et Plan Schuman." June 19, 1950.
No. 1.921, "La mission européenne de la Sarre: un exposé du Dr. Heinz Braun." July 27, 1950.
No. 1.949, "L'accord triple France-Allemagne-Sarre." August 29, 1950.
No. 1.980, "La Sarre et l'Europe." October 4, 1950.
No. 1.990, "Impressions de la Sarre." October 16, 1950.
No. 2.030, "Une déclaration du président Hoffmann." December 1, 1950.

No. 2.058, "La Sarre et le Plan Schuman. Le troisième anniversaire de la Constitution sarroise." January 4, 1951.
No. 2.087, "Sarre." February 13, 1951.
No. 2.119, "Radio-sarrebruck." March 31, 1951.
No. 2.135, "La Sarre et l'Europe." April 23, 1951.
No. 2.147, "La politique de la Sarre: déclaration du président Johannes Hoffmann." May 9, 1951.
No. 2.184, "La Sarre et le rattachement économique à la France. L'économie de la Sarre après 1935." July 2, 1951.
No. 2.193, "La Sarre et l'Europe: un discours du ministre sarrois de l'Economie." July 16, 1951.
No. 2.277, "Mission européenne de la Sarre." November 12, 1951.

No. 2.299, " Semaine européenne dans le Pays de la Sarre." December 12, 1951.

No. 2.331, " La Sarre et Bonn." January 29, 1952.
No. 2.346, " Sarre." February 19, 1952.
No. 2.366, " L'européanisation de la Sarre." March 18, 1952.
No. 2.415, " Les gens de la Sarre." May 27, 1952.
No. 2.427, " La Sarre et l'armée européenne." June 14, 1952.
No. 2.435, " La vie culturelle dans la Sarre." June 25, 1952.
No. 2.454, " La politique sociale de la Sarre." July 23, 1952.
No. 2.474, " La main-d'oeuvre en Sarre et le rattachement économique." August 22, 1952.
No. 2.492, " Sarre." September 16, 1952.
No. 2.526, " Un Institut européen de l'Université de la Sarre." November 4, 1952.

No. 2.568, " La Sarre et l'idée européenne." January 3, 1953.
No. 2.651, " L'Université de Sarrebruck." May 2, 1953.
No. 2.726, " Internationale socialiste et politique sarroise. L'Institut d'interprètes de l'Université de la Sarre." August 22, 1953.

No. 0.30, " Sarre." March 13, 1954.
No. 0.48, " L'' européanisation ' de la Sarre : déclaration de M. van Naters." April 24, 1954.
No. 0.61, " Opinions sur le problème sarrois." June 1, 1954.
No. 0.143, " Que pensent les Sarrois de l'accord franco-allemand du 23 octobre ? " December 11, 1954.

No. 0.157, " La Sarre entre la France et l'Allemagne." January 18, 1955.
No. 0.240, " Régime des capitaux en Sarre." August 4, 1955.
No. 0.244, " L'ouverture de la campagne électorale en Sarre." August 13, 1955.
No. 0.253, " La question sarroise." September 6, 1955.
No. 0.273, " Avant le referendum sarrois." October 22, 1955.
No. 0.274, " Le referendum sarrois." October 25, 1955.
No. 0.275, " Après le referendum sarrois." October 27, 1955.
No. 0.298, " Les élections à la Diète sarroise." December 22, 1955.

INDEX

A

Acheson, Dean, 110, 301n, 302, 305n
Adenauer, Konrad, 55, 65, 66–67, 68, 70, 72, 77–78, 81–82, 89–92, 96–98, 99, 105, 106n, 110–112, 113–116, 118–121, 122–124, 127, 132, 133, 134–135, 139, 140, 144, 145, 146, 147, 149, 150, 152–154, 157, 158, 160, 163n, 164, 166, 170–173, 175, 178, 179–180, 181n, 183, 184, 189, 190, 193, 195, 197, 200–201, 202n, 206, 209–210, 212, 213, 214–215, 216n, 217, 218, 221, 226, 239–240, 244, 246, 247, 248, 272, 273n, 284, 286, 295, 298, 303–304, 306, 308, 309, 314, 316, 319, 320
Administrative Commission for the Saar Territory, 28
Alliances, regrouping of, 28, 60, 168, 173, 224, 303
Allied Control Council, 5
Allied High Commission in Germany, 97
  High Commissioners, 100, 139, 303–304
  French, see François-Poncet.
Allied Military Tribunal (Saarbrücken), 9n
Allies, 5, 6, 16, 20, 21, 24, 27, 28, 35, 41, 51, 57, 60n, 65, 72, 97, 117, 121, 124, 140, 167, 211n, 225, 244, 255, 301, 310, 312
  agreements with France (1948), 41
  declarations, 67, 107, 113
    see also Potsdam, conference and agreements.
  relations with Germany, 99
  relations with the U.S.S.R., 4, 18, 27–28, 39–40, 60, 71, 129, 223, 300, 305
    see also Alliances, regrouping of.
  See also United Kingdom; United States.
Alsace, 19, 139
  Canal, 202n
  sporting circles in, 49n
    See also Economic Commission for Lorraine, Alsace and the Saar.
Altmeier, Peter, 52, 53, 55, 111n, 153, 159, 180, 194n, 220, 239, 240, 246, 247–248, 316
Altschuler, Georges, 132n
Andlauer, Joseph, 7n
Arbeitsgemeinschaft der Arbeitgeber-Organisationen des Saarlandes, 256
Arbeitskammer, 258
Arend, Louis, 23n, 258
Arnold, Karl, 51, 220
Association des amis de la Sarre, 7n
Association française de la Sarre, 7–8, 11, 15, 219

B

Babouin, Robert, 61, 230
Baden-Baden (meeting at, January, 1955), 180
Banks,
  French, 19n, 32n
    Banque de France, 31n
    Banque nationale pour le commerce et l'industrie, 32n
  German, 32n, 172
  Saar, 47, 242n, 256, 257
    Crédit sarrois, 32n
    Deutsche Bank, 66
    Landeszentralbank Saar, 32n
    re-discount, 31n
    Roechling, 32n
Bardoux, Jacques, 7, 77n
Bäsel, Friedrich, 14n
Basic Law of the Federal Republic of Germany, see Constitution.
Bayern Partei, 78n, 279
Beamtenbund, 269n
Becker, Carl, 101n
Becker, Richard, 51, 66, 79, 85, 89, 102, 106n, 120n, 144n, 176, 221, 222
Belgium, 26
Bérard, Armand, 99, 163n
Berlin
  blockade, 39, 54, 272, 297
  Conference (January–February, 1954), 153
  Protocol, 41n
  uprisings, 130
Bernkastel (meeting at, November, 1949), 65n
Bevin, Ernest, 17, 27n, 64, 303
Bidault, Georges, 6, 9, 16–17, 22, 27, 28, 33n, 40, 131, 132, 135, 139, 145, 149, 153, 157, 163n, 166, 209, 210–211, 217, 226, 227, 300, 301
  Plan, 16, 22, 27
Birkenfeld, 28n, 253
Blanc, Thomas, 7n
Blankenhorn, Herbert, 66, 80, 99, 145, 159, 163, 176, 180n, 215, 248
Bliesbecken, 254
Blind, Adolf, 48, 161, 197
Bloc Sarrois des classes moyennes, see Saarländischer Mittelstandsblock.
Bloch, Pierre, 24
Blücher, Franz, 186n
Blum, Léon, 24n, 225
Boch-Galhau, Luitwin von, 254
Bodens, Wilhelm, 247
Bonn Conventions, 131–132, 133, 145, 153n
Bornewasser, Mgr., see Trier, Bishops of.
Bourbon-Busset, Jacques de, 44n, 124, 216

385

25

Date Due

AUG 7 '67			
	PRINTED	IN U. S. A.	